CW00342140

THE EURASIAN STEPPE

About the Author

Warwick Ball is a Near Eastern archaeologist and author who spent over twenty years carrying out excavations, architectural studies and monumental restoration throughout the Middle East and adjacent regions. Over the past fifty years he has lived, worked and travelled in most countries between Europe and China covered by this book, in particular in remote parts of Inner Asia. He has excavated in Iran, Libya, Ethiopia, Afghanistan (where he was Acting Director of the British Institute of Afghan Studies), Jordan, and Iraq (where he was Director of Excavations with the British School of Archaeology in Iraq). For five years he was founder editor and Editor-in-Chief of *Afghanistan*, the journal of the American Institute of Afghanistan Studies published by Edinburgh University Press. He has written widely on the history and archaeology of the region, including *Syria: An Architectural and Historical Guide* (3rd edition 2006) and *The Monuments of Afghanistan. History, Archaeology, Architecture* (2008). His book *Rome in the East: The Transformation of an Empire* was winner of the James Henry Breasted History Prize and was Choice Outstanding Academic Book in 2000, and in 2016 it was revised for a second edition. In 2019 two major academic books, *The Archaeology of Afghanistan* (Edinburgh University Press) and a revised edition of the *Archaeological Gazetteer of Afghanistan*, were published. The University of St Andrews confirmed in 2020 that it would be offering the honorary degree of Doctor of Letters on the author in recognition of his work in Near Eastern archaeology. Born in Australia, he now lives in the Scottish Borders.

THE EURASIAN STEPPE

People, Movement, Ideas

Warwick Ball

EDINBURGH
University Press

Edinburgh University Press is one of the leading university presses in the UK. We publish academic books and journals in our selected subject areas across the humanities and social sciences, combining cutting-edge scholarship with high editorial and production values to produce academic works of lasting importance. For more information visit our website: edinburghuniversitypress.com

© Warwick Ball, 2021

Edinburgh University Press Ltd
The Tun – Holyrood Road
12 (2f) Jackson's Entry
Edinburgh EH8 8PJ

Typeset in 11/13 Adobe Garamond by
Cheshire Typesetting Ltd, Cuddington, Cheshire,
and printed and bound in Malta by Melita Press

A CIP record for this book is available from the British Library

ISBN 978 1 4744 8804 4 (hardback)
ISBN 978 1 4744 8806 8 (paperback)
ISBN 978 1 4744 8807 5 (webready PDF)
ISBN 978 1 4744 8805 1 (epub)

The right of Warwick Ball to be identified as author of this work has been asserted in accordance with the Copyright, Designs and Patents Act 1988 and the Copyright and Related Rights Regulations 2003 (SI No. 2498).

Published with the support of the University of Edinburgh Scholarly Publishing Initiatives Fund.

Contents

Figures

Maps

Note on Transliteration

In general, diacritical marks have been avoided for the sake of simplicity, and familiar rather than more technically correct forms are used throughout.

With the multiplicity of written and spoken languages that this book covers, not to mention the languages in which studies of the many subjects are written, it is impossible to achieve consistency. Whenever necessary, an explanation is given in a footnote.

For L. W. Harrow

who first published me

Introduction

One phenomenon, which unites the history of the Middle East, Europe, South and East Asia is the role of nomadic peoples from the Eurasian steppe in the affairs of the sedentary peoples in the surrounding countries.
– Reuven Amitai and Michal Biran, 2005[1]

The importance of the Eurasian steppe has long been recognised, with the work edited by Reuven Amitai and Michal Biran quoted above just one of many such works that can now be cited. It was reiterated in 2019 by Michael Bonner, who notes that 'without an emphasis on the unity of Eurasia, the history of the world will appear to be random and perhaps even unintelligible'.[2] Bonner further emphasised the steppe's importance to Iran in 2020, a view anticipated by scholars such as Daniel Potts in 2014, Willem Vogelsang in 1992 and others.[3] The importance of the steppe for Chinese history has been recognised for even longer, notably by Owen Lattimore in 1940 in his groundbreaking *Inner Asian Frontiers of China*, and since by equally seminal works by Thomas Barfield in 1989 and Nicola Di Cosmo in 2002,[4] as well as many others that are referenced here throughout.

However, the impact of the steppe on Europe has received less attention, particularly in those works that focus mainly on western Europe. Such works tend to emphasise more the importance of the Mediterranean and to a lesser extent the Near East in the development of Europe. The huge impact of the Mediterranean and the Near East is not in doubt (on the contrary, I have emphasised their importance elsewhere),[5] but the Eurasian steppe is at least as important for the development and history of Europe – even western Europe – as it has been for China and the other centres of human endeavour on the peripheries of the steppe. This premise is the focus of the current work: that the history, languages, ideas, art forms, peoples, nations and identities of the steppe have shaped almost every aspect of the life of Europe.

The essential unity of the steppe, together with the fundamental effect it has had on Europe throughout history, questions the very idea of 'Europe' as a separate geographical, cultural and historical construct. The Urals,

Europe's conventional eastern boundary,[*] has in practice never been a cultural barrier, and archaeology demonstrates the Urals to have been a cultural unifying factor, not a barrier.[6] Herodotus (IV.45) regarded the boundary between Europe and Asia to be entirely random and wondered 'why three names [Asia, Europe, Africa] . . . should ever have been given to a tract of land which is in reality one'. Herodian, in the third century AD, put the dividing line between East and West at the Taurus Mountains. According to Metternich 'Asia begins at the Landstrasse', just east of Vienna's city walls,[7] reiterated in an account of the Avar conquest by Walter Pohl, who writes: 'Arguably, after 568 central Asia extended to the Vienna Woods.'[8] The Eurovision Song Contest (which can hardly be taken as authoritative) includes countries unquestionably beyond the borders of Europe, such as Israel and Azerbaijan. In questioning the conventional definitions of Europe and of East and West, Vladimir Petrovich Vasiliev in the 1840s pointed out that Moscow is east of Jerusalem and that Perm is on the same longitude as the mouth of the Indus.[9] Peter Rietbergen points out that the geographical centre of Europe is a few kilometres north of Vilnius,[10] but near the small village of Dilove in southern Ukraine an Austro-Hungarian monument of the 1890s marks the centre of Europe.[11]

In the steppe questions of centres and boundaries become largely meaningless, only directions[†] – and those directions have usually been of east–west movements. Since long before recorded history it has been the scene of movements of peoples who met few natural obstacles. Laurent Olivier concluded his 2010 discussion of Celtic art with the words: 'There now opens before us a vast continent long obscured, stretching from the British Isles in the Atlantic to the Steppes of the Urals and on to ancient China, a continent wherein lies other origins of European civilisation that have long lain hidden in the shadows of the Roman conquest'.[12] This volume traces those origins.

In the process, my aim has been, hopefully, to attempt a synthesis and consensus of the various topics, even though many of the subjects, such as the Khazars or the question of Indo-European languages, are controversial, and the study of others still in their infancy – and all are in a state of flux. This applies especially to the archaeology, where new discoveries constantly question the old ones and new technologies enable connections and conclusions to be made that were unthinkable to a previous generation. The subjects I discuss therefore are necessarily selective, as my purpose

---

[*] In Russia itself, on the one hand the Urals are emphasised as the division of Europe and Asia and roads across them have their token 'Europe/Asia' monuments. But on the other hand, in conversation, when 'Europe' or 'European countries' are mentioned, it is clear that Russia is *not* meant.

[†] 'In Russia there are no roads, only directions', usually attributed to Napoleon but probably of unknown provenance.

throughout is to focus on those subjects that shaped Europe, even at the cost of glossing over the effect on other regions such as the Middle East, South Asia or China (except where it was relevant to the effect on Europe).

In the following account it has not always been possible to preserve strict chronological and thematic order. There is an overall chronological narrative, but where an important topic becomes relevant, such as the question of Indo-European languages or the role of the steppe in the idea of the female warrior or the impact of the steppe on art, that topic is explored at that point. Hence, the archaeological account of Chapters 2 and 4 is interrupted by discussions of language in Chapter 3, Amazons in Chapter 5 and art in Chapter 6. The archaeological thread is not taken up again until Chapter 7 when discussing Hun origins.

Chapters 7, 8 and 9 cover the 'Migrations Period' at the end of antiquity with the entry of various steppe groups into Europe, but not in full chronological order and with many overlaps. The Huns are the subject of Chapter 7 and peoples from Inner Asia who now form European nations, such as the Finns, Bulgarians and Hungarians, the subject of Chapter 9. The Turks are discussed in Chapter 8, but most of the later – mainly Islamic – history of the Turks is omitted apart from occasional references, partly because it lies out of the present scope and partly because it is too large a subject (and I have discussed it elsewhere).[13] However, aspects of Turk history are included in Chapter 5, on women in steppe-derived societies, as well as in Chapter 10, on the Khazars, and part of Chapter 12, when the Timurids are briefly discussed. Other Turk-related groups, such as Bulgars and Cumans/Qipchak, are further discussed in Chapter 9.

The final three chapters, 11, 12 and 13, discuss the last great steppe eruption on Europe and its legacy: the Mongol invasions (Chapter 11), and the establishment and effect of Mongol states in Europe (Chapter 12), and in the legacy of the steppe in Russia (Chapter 13).

Before jumping in with both feet (and doubtless shooting oneself in at least one of them) much should be written on definitions. Names and terms such as nomad, pastoralist, migration, invasion, boundary, animal style, language, nationalism, state, Hun, Turk, Tatar, Amazon, Jew, Silk Road and many more have been questioned and should be defined. Some I have attempted, albeit perhaps superficially, others I have sidestepped, others ignored – otherwise this book would either be much longer or would never have been finished.

In covering much of the history of Eurasia for the past five thousand years or so I am not so much displaying my learning as revealing my ignorance. A huge amount has been omitted and much else has been glossed over. There will doubtless be something in this book, therefore, that will annoy just about everyone. But omissions have been hard decisions of necessity rather than choice: even in an ideal world, it is impossible to include everything or to even begin to take on board the vast amount of literature on so many of the topics covered here. Many a 'must read' work I have been forced reluctantly to put aside; the bibliography will give an idea of those I have not.* But in the years that I have spent shaping this volume, I did at least have the privilege of travelling to most of the places that I discuss. This has provided me with a sense of place and history that no amount of reading can replace.

* * *

The present book draws from an earlier work, *The Gates of Asia: The Eurasian Steppe and the Limits of Europe*. Although published in 2015 it is now out of print and unavailable. In the face of this, together with the huge amount of new material appearing on the Eurasian steppe and increasing interest in the subject, it was decided to revisit the earlier book. Although that forms the basis of the present work, there are substantial differences. It has been expanded from ten to thirteen chapters to incorporate new research as well as my own changing views. New chapters on the idea of the female warrior (Chapter 5), the emergence of the Turks (Chapter 8) and Russian identity (Chapter 13) have been added, and the Bibliography massively expanded. A former chapter on the Silk Road has been greatly abridged and relegated to just a section in Chapter 1, as I have covered the subject elsewhere.[14] It is, in other words, a new book rather than a new edition.

For the present volume I would like to thank Edinburgh University Press's anonymous reviewers who were kind enough to look at some of the drafts and offer comment. Wendy Ball drew the maps and offered welcome comment on many sections. Christoph Baumer, Eberhard Sauer and Elizabeth Willcox have kindly provided photos. Otherwise, all photos are my own. The late David Morgan was kind to examine preliminary drafts of my chapters on the Mongols and show me some (then) pre-publication papers he had written. I have also benefited from discussions with Nina Lobanov-Rostovsky on many matters concerning Russia and Russian art, mainly relating to the later chapters. The eagle eyes of the copy-editor Michael Ayton has saved me from many a howler, and Susan Tricklebank has supplied the index, without which the book would be of limited use. I owe a particular thanks to Leonard Harrow, who commissioned and edited the original book on which this is based. As always it has been a pleasure to work with Nicola Ramsey, Eddie Clark and their

---

* In this context, the later – and more important – stage of research was undertaken during the 2020 lockdown without access to specialist libraries. For example, I was only able to obtain a digital copy of the book edited by Nikolay Kradin, Dmitri Bondarenko and Thomas Barfield in 2003 (*Nomadic Pathways in Social Evolution*. Moscow: Russian Academy of Sciences, Center for Civilizational and Regional Studies) the day before delivery of this manuscript.

colleagues at Edinburgh University Press. To all I owe both thanks and apologies: thanks for their comments and suggestions, and apologies for advice I ignored – and for mistakes that have crept in since.

In writing a book on just a small part of the current work, Walter Pohl wrote that 'The historian of the Avars should not only gain a mastery over the Latin and Greek sources with all their nuances but must in addition deal in critical fashion with Iranian, Armenian, Syriac, Arabic, and Chinese texts, should be at home with Slavic, Hungarian, Turkic, and Mongolic linguistics and onomastics, be competent to interpret with caution the published and, to the greatest degree possible, unpublished findings of archaeologists, master the approaches and models of social anthropology, and, lastly, offer new insights into old problems discussed by colleagues in his own field'.[15] To these should be added (especially) Russian and the other main European languages, as well as probably Finnish, Sogdian, Khotanese Saka, perhaps Bactrian, Georgian, a few ancient Anatolian languages and a reasonable grasp of Indo-European linguistics together with a few other languages I have probably omitted. In addition to the disciplines of linguistics, philology and epigraphy, one must be reasonably competent in art history, archaeology, anthropology, botany, climatology, genetics, palaeontology and astrophysics (well, perhaps not the last).

Needless to say, even a fraction of this is not possible. In the early seventies the long late lamented Tony McNicoll once gave the soundest possible advice to a young researcher just embarking upon an archaeological career: 'Stick your neck right out, the bastards can only chop it off!'* Advice I have stuck to ever since.

---

* A. W. McNicoll (1942–85) in 1972, at that time archaeologist at large, then Director of the British Institute of Afghan Studies and the excavations at Kandahar; he went on to a lectureship at the University of Sydney, from where he directed the excavations at Pella in Jordan until his untimely death.

CHAPTER 1

THE NATURE OF THE STEPPE
Some Geographical Observations

A wide boundless plain encircled by a chain of low hills lay stretched before the travellers' eyes. Huddling together and peeping out from behind one another, these hills melted together into rising ground, which stretched right to the very horizon and disappeared into the lilac distance; one drives on and on and cannot discern where it begins or where it ends . . . The sun had already peeped out from beyond the town behind them, and quietly, without fuss, set to its accustomed task. . . . soon the whole wide steppe flung off the twilight of early morning, and was smiling and sparkling with dew. The cut rye, the coarse steppe grass, the milkwort, the wild hemp, all withered from the sultry heat, turned brown and half dead, now washed by the dew and caressed by the sun, revived, to fade again . . . In the grass crickets, locusts and grasshoppers kept up their churring, monotonous music. But a little time passed, the dew evaporated, the air grew stagnant, and the disillusioned steppe began to wear its jaded July aspect. The grass drooped, everything living was hushed. The sun-baked hills, brownish-green and lilac in the distance, with their quiet shadowy tones, the plain with the misty distance and, arched above them, the sky, which seems terribly deep and transparent in the steppes, where there are no woods or high hills, seemed now endless, petrified with dreariness . . . The music in the grass was hushed, the petrels had flown away, the partridges were out of sight, rooks hovered idly over the withered grass; they were all alike and made the steppe even more monotonous.
– Anton Chekhov, *The Steppe*[1]

A lack of physical obstacles characterising the steppe in many ways underlies much of European history for the past few thousand years; 'an army on horseback could march from a castle on the Baltic to a fort on the Black Sea without meeting a physical obstacle greater than a fast-flowing river or a wide forest', as Anne Applebaum observed.[2] Chekhov captures the essential but opposing natures of the steppe, both its relentless oppressiveness and its sublime beauty. The longest of his stories, *The Steppe* is partly autobiographical: Chekhov spent all his life on its northern fringes avoiding the steppe and its provincial towns that he so loathed, but was born on its southern fringes in Taganrog and returned to die on its southern fringes in Yalta.[3]

To some extent the steppe can be compared more to a sea than to land: the only boundaries to the seas are the shores around its edges. Similarly, the steppe's only boundaries are the geographic features that mark its edges: forest, desert or mountain range. Like the seas, the steppe has been subject to the constant movement of peoples who are eventually 'beached up' in the lands on its rim. Hence, 'in the conflict of hostile nations, the victor and the vanquished have alternately drove and been driven, from the confines of China to those of Germany' in the words of Edward Gibbon when writing of the steppe. Michael Khodarkovsky takes the metaphor further when he compares the caravan cities to sea ports, the caravans themselves to ships, and the nomadic raiders to pirates.[4]

The steppe

The steppe – roughly equivalent to 'prairie' in North America,[5] 'pampas' in South America, 'savannah' in Africa (although none is an exact equivalent) – is a belt of temperate climate grasslands between four and seven hundred kilometres wide that stretches from Hungary to eastern Siberia – a distance of some 7,000 kilometres (Figures 1.1–1.4; Map 1.1).[6] Originally they were uncultivated open, undulating plains; now, around 70 per cent of all food comes from such grasslands worldwide (Figure 1.5), although not all attempts at cultivation are successful (Krushchev's failed 'virgin lands' campaign in Kazakhstan in the 1950s being a notable example). Michael Frachetti emphasises the very limited suitability of the steppe for agriculture without artificial means, so that it is best suited for pasture,[7] much like the Scottish moors. This is emphasised by Jainhua Yang and Huiqiu Shao, who state that 'the steppe is a low-energy ecological environment in which one square kilometer can feed only 6–7 cattle. A pasture will be run out within 2–25 years, while the recovery of a pasture takes approximately 50 years', forcing many into continuous migration.[8] It has few natural barriers: the Urals (Figures 1.6, 1.7), often regarded as the natural boundary between Europe and Asia, is nowhere more than a low range of hills (although it does mark one notable natural change: to the west, with few exceptions the great rivers flow from north to south; to the east they are south to north).

To the north the steppe is bounded by the forest belt and to the south much of it is bounded by a combination of inland seas (the Black and Caspian Seas), mountain ranges and deserts. The transition is gradual in both cases, particularly in the south where the transition to desert is also widely fluctuating. The mountain boundaries are part of a more or less continuous Asian 'mountain belt' that comprises (from west to east) the Alburz in Iran (although this bounds the Caspian rather than the steppe), the Kopet-Dagh in Turkmenistan, the Hindu Kush in Afghanistan, and the massive Himalaya-Tienshan complex that blocks the Indian Subcontinent from Inner Asia.

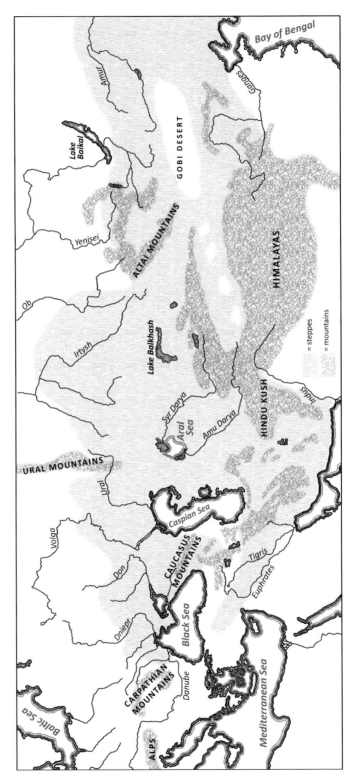

Map 1.1 *The steppe belt across Eurasia*

Figure 1.1 *The steppe at Salbyk in the Republic of Khakasia in Siberia. Note at least seven* kurgans *in the distance, a characteristic of steppe history throughout*

Although the steppe is characterised by open grassland and plains, it would be a mistake to confine discussions of steppe peoples solely to those areas, and 'steppe' is used loosely here. Mountain ranges formed a part of the steppe: the Urals, for example, have already been noted, but the Altai-Sayan complex also included a steppe environment that saw the initial development of steppe societies (and will figure largely in ensuing discussions).[9] Some of the most characteristic – indeed, definitive – remains of 'steppe people' have been discovered in high mountain regions, such as the Pazyryk burials in an alpine pasture in the Altai, or the even higher burials on the Ukok plateau at a height of 2,500 metres. Defining such regions as 'steppe' makes about as much sense as calling the Swiss Alps steppe. But the Altai has been described as a steppe cultural 'hub' that connects Mongolia, the China North Zone, the Kazakh steppe, Xinjiang, Tuva and the Minusinsk Basin, so is crucial to our study (Figures 1.8, 1.9).[10] Moreover, access to raw materials in the mountains both within and bounding the steppe defined much of steppe material culture. We also include to some extent regions as diverse as the desert oases of Xinjiang, the Anatolian and Iranian plateaux, and the plains of southern Afghanistan and north-western Indian subcontinent in our survey. There is also an inner Asian steppe 'micro-enclave' projecting into the sea: Crimea – effectively almost an island, connected only by the eight-kilometre Perekop Isthmus to the mainland and even narrower Arbat Isthmus. Although it is geographically outside the scope of

Figure 1.2 *The western steppe in Moldova, showing the black earth that characterises much of the earth in southern Russia, Ukraine and adjacent regions*

Figure 1.3 *High pastures at Pazyryk in the Altai, Siberia. Although not technically 'steppe', horses were one of the keys to steppe history throughout and Pazyryk one of the key sites*

Figure 1.4 *Preserved natural steppe grassland between Elista and Rostov-on-Don in southern Russia*

Figure 1.5 *The cultivated steppe between Elista and Rostov-on-Don in southern Russia*

Figure 1.6 *The Ural Mountains, between Kazan and Omsk, rarely more than the low range of hills seen here, the traditional boundary between Europe and Asia*

Figure 1.7 Evropa-Aziya: *a monument marking the 'border' between Europe and Asia in the Urals between Verkhoturye and Perm*

the inner Asian steppe, its extraordinary combination of steppe grassland and mountains is almost a microcosm of inner Asian geography – and was a key to much of the movement of steppe people throughout history (Figure 1.10).

Equally, an integral part of any discussion of the steppe is the vast forest belt to the north (Figure 1.11). Often the same cultural groups would bestride – or at least interact with – both zones, and trade with, and foraging in the forest by, steppe groups is also part of the story* – indeed, as

---

* Still a part of the Russian psyche today, as can be observed in the northern parts of both European and Siberian Russia, especially in the autumn: at weekends, the roads outside any city leading into the forest are lined with cars as the occupants forage for berries, fungi and other products, as well as with roadside stalls where the forest bounty is on sale. Foraging in the countryside was also an aristocratic pastime, a recurrent theme that comes across in nineteenth century Russian novels.

with the mountain and desert regions, it is essential to blur the bounda-ries.[11] But it is the grasslands of the steppe belt that remains the key to the movement of peoples, ideas and goods across Eurasia.

While recognising the vast distances, the transcontinental connections and the migration of populations across the steppe, it is essential to recog-nise the essential local and cyclical nature of the pastoral nomad as well. Most migrations were simply from summer to winter pastures, not over vast areas and not constantly on the move. Therefore, limited agriculture could be practised in the summer months, despite the marginal nature of the steppe. Michael Frachetti writes:

> I characterize the Eurasian steppe not as a vast highway of grass but as a mosaic of regionally differentiable eco-social spheres or landscapes. I present the geog-raphy of Eurasia as a jigsaw puzzle of discrete regional environmental contexts differentiated by major and minor rivers, mountain ranges, and diverse cli-matic and ecological micro-niches. I also characterize the cultural geography of the Eurasian steppe as complex and varied, with societies of different scales interacting to generate a dynamic rise and fall of political and economic arenas through time . . .[12]

Although 'temperate' (in terms of location between the equator and the poles), the immense continental land mass makes the climate extreme with harsh winters and hot summers, especially in the eastern parts when temperatures can fluctuate by as much as eighty degrees.[*] While seasonal migrations were naturally north and south, the more extreme conditions of the eastern steppes might explain why longer-term mass migrations in most of its history have been largely east to west.[13]

A major factor that affected movement in Eurasia is the existence of so many of the world's great rivers that flow across the steppe. West of the Urals the main ones are, from west to east, the Danube or Donau, the Prut, the Dniester, Dnieper, Donets, Don[†] and Volga. East of the Urals the main rivers are the Irtysh-Tobol-Ob system, the Yenisei and its tributaries, the Lena-Aldan system, and the Amur (Figures 1.12–1.17).

---

[*] The American Communist John Scott (1973), for example, who came as a volunteer welder to the gigantic new industrial complex at Magnitogorsk in the southern Urals in the 1930s, describes workers freezing to death on the scaffolding in winter temperatures of minus 40 centigrade, with temperatures correspondingly high in the summer. I personally have experienced huge fluctuations even from one day to the next in Siberia, from 37° to 15° in the space of one July day in Omsk, for example.

[†] The existence of so many river names in south-eastern Europe based on the root *don* or equivalent is thought to derive from the ancient Iranian root word *danu-* meaning 'river', although Danube/Donau is Celtic. The Volga is thought to derive from the Baltic language group. See Mallory 1989: 79–85. Presumably the River Don in Scotland and the Don in Yorkshire, as well as perhaps the Dee in Wales and the Tyne in Newcastle, come from the same root.

Figure 1.8 *A steppe–mountain combination: the Altai Mountains near Kuray in south Siberia, dominated by the peak of Mt Belukha, the mystical 'Shambala' of Nicholas Roerich*

Figure 1.9 *Upland pastures in the Altai in south Siberia*

Figure 1.10 *A 'steppe enclave' in central Crimea. Although Crimea is almost an island in the Black Sea, it exhibits classic steppe characteristics and is central to much of steppe history*

Figure 1.11 *A typical part of the Siberian forest belt near Yeniseisk*

Far from acting as barriers, they have invariably facilitated movement. Immensely wide though many of them are, they could always be crossed, either by boat in the summer or on foot in winter.* The great rivers of European Russia, for example, were famously the route of the Vikings from Scandinavia to the Black and Caspian Seas, a system of river movement that ultimately resulted in the foundation of the Russian state itself. Less well-known is the route between Elizabethan England and Safavid Persia in the sixteenth century, when the shortest route was via the Arctic. This was because the more obvious route, via the Middle East, was made problematic due to enmity between the Ottoman and Safavid Empires. English traders therefore would sail around the west and north coasts of Norway into the Arctic Circle to the White Sea, reaching Russia at the mouth of the Dvina near Arkhangelsk; just upstream there was actually an English colony at Kholmogory. Travel was then upstream on the Dvina to a comparatively short land crossing to the headwaters of the Volga north of Nizhni Novgorod. From there it was a straightforward journey down the Volga to the Caspian Sea, thence across the Sea to Persia.

The rivers not only facilitated north–south movements, but were also used for west–east movement. For example, in the early Russian penetration of Siberia, the earliest settlements were far to the north of most modern population centres, in the colder north rather than the more obvious warmer south: Perm, Verkhoturye, Tobolsk, Tomsk, Yeniseisk and others. This was because the Siberian rivers and their main tributaries converge further to the north: hence, the easiest route was to travel downstream on one river to its convergence with a tributary, then upstream on the tributary. This enabled shorter land crossings between the rivers, making it possible to zigzag across Siberia – 'tacking' as it were – making maximum use of river transport. It was only with the construction of the Trans-Siberian Railway in the late nineteenth century that the demographic centres of Russian colonisation moved further south; the later foundations such as Yekaterinburg, Novosibirsk and Krasnoyarsk are now the largest cities in Siberia. Today, rivers still occupy a particular place in the Russian mind and heart: the Volga, for example, remains 'Mother Volga'.

---

* I recall, on first witnessing the immense breadth of the Volga at Kazan, commenting to a colleague who lived across on the other side how difficult communication must be with just one bridge and no other for a hundred kilometres or so up- or downstream. His immediate response was that 'in winter we just drive across'.

Figure 1.12 *The Dniester River at Belgorod, near where it enters the Black Sea, overlooked by the fortress of Ak-kerman*

Figure 1.13 *The upper Volga at Plyos in northern Russia*

Figure 1.14*. The middle Volga at Saratov*

Figure 1.15 *The upper Yenisei River at Kyzyl, capital of the Republic of Tuva in the Altai*

Figure 1.16 *The lower Yenisei at Yeniseisk in Siberia*

Figure 1.17 *The Amur River at Khabarovsk in eastern Siberia*

The way of the nomad

Throughout the following pages, nomadism remains a constant theme, a characteristic of the steppe that contributed more than anything else to the great movements of peoples across it. But is nomadism just a transitory state: one that begins and ends with sedentarism? A transitional phase from hunter-gathering, through animal husbandry to nomadic pastoralism to inevitable sedentarism? Originally nomadic people such as the Bulgars and Magyars and Turks now form sedentary states, while those archetypal nomads, the Scythians, formed sedentary states on the fringes of the Eurasian steppe. On the other hand, a nomadic people who created one of the largest states in history, the Mongols, remain a predominantly nomadic society today (at least until very recently), while the people who dominate the steppe today, the Russians, come from a largely sedentary background with little history of nomadism (the association by some Russians in recent history with a perceived Scythian past notwithstanding: discussed in Chapter 13). As we shall see in the following pages, permanent settlement pre-dated nomadic pastoralism in most cases on the steppe, and transitions between hunter-gathering, nomadic and sedentary societies were complex, occurred at different times, were not universal and were not necessarily one way.*

Nomadism might appear at first to be irrelevant to the sophisticated sedentary societies of history: with few exceptions, most modern nations trace their origins to and subsequent evolution from a perceived ancient sedentary 'great civilisation'. Man's 'primeval state' of hunter-gathering societies only exists today in some cultures, such as the few that survive in Africa and Australasia. Hunter-gathering, therefore, is perceived as a developmental state – or rather the lack of it. Of course, it is no longer deemed correct to consider such modern societies as 'primitive';[14] anthropologists now view, for example, the culture of the Australian Aborigines as advanced, it having developed to the fullest capacity that their environment allows. Paradoxically, nomadic pastoralism (the slightly developed form of hunter-gathering) has existed right throughout and alongside some of the most sophisticated civilisations in history, down to our own day. Rather than evidence for a lack of development, nomadic pastoralism has competed with urbanism and the most advanced forms of sedentary societies on an equal footing throughout history. Indeed, it might even be

---

* Interestingly, Felipe Fernández-Armesto in 2000 defines all such societies as 'civilisations' in an impressive work perhaps pointedly entitled *Civilizations*, in marked contrast to Kenneth Clark's equally impressive title of the same name, but in the singular, from a previous generation in 1969. Even a historian of the stature of Fernand Braudel, in a similarly titled work in 1987, used the more cautious plural (but prefaced it with an essay on changing vocabulary).

Figure 1.18 *Nomads on the move in northern Afghanistan (photo courtesy of Elizabeth Willcox)*

viewed as more developed, as it has achieved more of an equilibrium with the environment around it, something many sedentary societies have yet to achieve (perhaps now more than ever). The main difference between nomadic and sedentary societies is not one of development or sophistication, but in material remains, the former leaving fewer traces in either the written or the archaeological records. The history of nomadic pastoralism is very much a history of Eurasia, a history of the movement of peoples, of armies and languages that have fundamentally affected every part of the continent.[15]

There are roughly three main forms of nomadic societies today. There are the full nomads, those who are continually on the move, such as some Bedouin and Touareg tribes or the variously labelled travelling communities throughout Europe. These can include traditional groups such as the Roma or circus and showground people. Such groups usually only move in small numbers, often just single families. Then there are the migratory nomads, those who migrate in the spring and autumn between summer and winter pastures, living in semi-permanent camps in summer and winter. These traditionally comprise whole tribes or even entire nations, such as Qashqai and Bakhtiari of Iran or the Kuchi Pashtuns of Afghanistan (Figure 1.18). This form of nomadism is more characteristic of the steppe nomads of the past examined here. Finally, there are the semi-nomads or transhumants, those who are nomads in the summer taking their flocks to pasture, but return to permanent villages in the winter. This mostly just involves one section of a community, usually the men, but can involve entire families. Transhumance is still a way of life in many parts of the world, such as in south-eastern Europe.

Perhaps one might now define a fourth category, the transient nomad. In an increasingly global economy there are now more and more transient workers such as Central Asians at the building sites of Moscow and St Petersburg or North Africans in agricultural work in Spain and France. In such modern cases, nomadism is usually just a transitory phase from one sedentary situation to another, such as with the Turks who uprooted from rural communities in Anatolian villages to partake of the German economic miracle and now form permanent urban groups in German cities. The transition from Panjabi villager to Birmingham urbanite, or Egyptian *fellahin* to menial workers throughout the urban Arab Middle East, is the same process (although unlike the Turks and Panjabis cited here, the Egyptian manual workers usually return to their villages). It is a mistake to characterise this as a particularly modern form of nomadism, as such movement has always existed: ancient Greek cities had their communities of *metics*, essentially guest-workers, for example.

Not included in this category is the refugee, often nomadic by almost every definition. But we are only discussing nomadism as a selected way of life here, even if it is enforced by economic necessity (as indeed much of sedentary life is). Mass refugees that characterise much of 'nomadism' today, becoming a major international political issue, are usually assumed to be a modern phenomenon. This is by no means true. The various Germanic tribes who came into the Roman Empire at the end of antiquity were refugees fleeing the Huns, and the many Central Asian Turkish tribes who entered Anatolia in the thirteenth century were refugees fleeing the Mongols.

The terms 'nomad', 'semi-nomad', 'transhumant', 'pastoralist' and 'nomadic pastoralist' are all terms used throughout this and the following chapters and in studies related to them, all terms that are difficult to define.[16] There is no neat definition, therefore, and we find frequent overlaps and combinations. All definitions are often questioned, and rightly so, but they still have value here so long as one recognises their limitations.

Leaving aside our possible fourth category above (where the Turkish *Gastarbeiten* arguably contributed substantially to the German 'economic miracle'), nomadic communities can make just as great an economic contribution as the sedentary communities do. By grazing their herds in areas of marginal agriculture, they make maximum use of available land and revitalise the soil. The produce of the marginal lands can also be major import items for their sedentary neighbours: namely milk and other dairy produce, but also many other animal products such as wool, felt and hides as well as rugs and other textiles. Nomad handicrafts can be imported and even imitated in urban workshops: recent studies of steppe metalwork, for example, have shown this pattern (discussed more in Chapter 6). Nomads have also been major traders and middlemen, often just as responsible for major trade items over long distances as more formalised trade networks and systems. This can even extend into such areas as money-lending, as some of the Pashtun Kuchi groups between Afghanistan and Pakistan have been known to do in recent times. There was never – or at least rarely – such a society on the steppe as the 'pure nomad'; at all times they existed in symbiosis with the sedentary populations.

Waves, hordes and movement

One must caution against the terms 'hordes', 'invasions' and 'waves', frequently used to describe steppe movements.[17] Such terms give a false impression of violent and sudden movements that were as often as not gradual, usually taking place over several generations, with assimilation and accommodation on the way, even though the end result might be long-term change. It is rare that a single definable culture or people emerges on the steppe, despite the tribal and national names that litter the history pages; such names were usually just that of a prominent group that incorporated many other tribes. Even such a sharply defined group as the Mongols incorporated Naimans, Tatars, Oirats, Karaits, Turks – and ultimately Armenians, Georgians, Iranians, Russians, Chinese and others. 'The cultures that ethnographers study are not pure, pristine entities developing in a vacuum', as Philip Kohl emphasises. 'Rather, they are almost always hybrids, fissioning or coalescing, assimilating or modifying the customs of the neighbouring peoples with whom they constantly interact.'[18]

A few further notes of caution must also be exercised. While it is true that it is important to emphasise processes of assimilation and accommodation in the movements – the 'marauding hordes' of popular imagination were the exception rather than the rule – one must at the same time guard against the pendulum swinging too far in the other direction. Steppe nomads were neither more nor less peace-loving than any other group. Through the harshness and vagaries of life of their environment, violence was often a natural adjunct to life on the steppe – and their incursions out of it. This is discussed further in later chapters.

They were rarely, too, mass movements that inundated the sedentary populations by numbers. In the 'barbarian' invasions of Europe, for example, numbers involved were tiny in proportion to the overall sedentary populations of Italy, France and Spain.[19] The Ostrogoths, for example, could not have numbered more than two per cent of the population of Italy. Even such a cataclysmic event as the Mongol invasion and occupation of Iran and the Near East – lasting over a century – has left little trace in the ethnic or linguistic record.* The 'mass movements' across the Eurasian steppes would hardly have displaced elites, let alone whole populations. Nomadism is undoubtedly crucial to the history of Inner Eurasia and the cultures on its rim, but it can often be overstated. To characterise the Ottoman or Timurid states, for example, as nomadic makes about as much sense as characterising the Achaemenid state as such because of the background of the nomadic Iranians, or the Umayyad because of a Bedouin background.

These wide open spaces have been the scene mainly of east–west movements: early Indo-European speakers, Scythians, Huns, Avars, Turks, Mongols, and others. This has been suggested to have been climatically motivated: because of the warmer temperatures of the western end of Eurasia created by the Gulf Stream, the west was more attractive to pastoralists, creating what has been termed the 'steppe gradient'.[20] Virtually the only time when it saw a west–east movement was the Russian expansion into Siberia in modern history, when it was calculated that by 1914 the Russian Empire had been expanding eastwards at the rate of fifty-five square miles per day over the previous four centuries.[21] Otherwise, whenever there was a west–east movement out of Europe it went elsewhere: Alexander or the Romans through the Near East (although these were never mass movements), for example, or the Atlantic seaboard nations via the sea lanes. This one-way movement out of Asia emphasises how little 'Europe' exists as a geographical construct: Europe is very much at the end of the larger land mass.

Two early developments are fundamental to the history of the steppe people: the invention of the composite bow and the emergence of horse riding. Bows may have been used as long as 20,000 years ago if the small flint projectile points found in Palaeolithic contexts are interpreted as arrowheads. The oldest plain wooden bows found in Germany and Denmark are between 8,000 and 12,000 years old. But it was the invention of the composite re-curved bow in Inner Asia, probably in the second millennium BC, that gave the steppe nomads their military advantage. These bows were strengthened with horn, bone or sinew to provide greater tension and their re-curve provided greater velocity (Figure 1.19).[22]

The earliest evidence for the domestication of the horse emerges after about 4800 BC, the horse having been bred from the wild Przhevalsky horse native to the steppe, somewhat later than the domestication of sheep, goat, cattle, camel and other beasts of burden. Although horses were domesticated, evidence that they were ridden is later, perhaps 4000 BC, and it was

---

* Contrary to the massive legacy in Russia, discussed further in Chapters 12 and 13. There remains only a very small pocket descended from the Mongols in central Afghanistan, the Hazaras, and even these have lost their Mongolian language and are Persian speakers.

the ability to ride the tough steppe horse that probably enabled the transition to full nomadism. The horse was highly mobile, it was hugely resilient, it could travel longer distances and faster than cattle, it required less fodder, it could forage for grass with its hooves under up to 50 centimetres of snow in conditions where cattle would otherwise starve. The development of the single-piece bronze bit in about 1200 BC allowed for further control and mobility. Horses thus became the most prestigious of animals, and it comes as no surprise to learn that the steppe nomads developed a horse cult: the royal burials of the Scythian period would include horse burials, along with all their trappings. The combination of the composite bow and the domesticated horse gave rise to a society that was to characterise the peoples of the steppe for all subsequent periods: the mounted archers. Control over both the horse and the bow allowed the archer to fire volleys with phenomenal rapidity while at full

Figure 1.19 Bronze sculpture of a Scythian horseman by Leonid Pozen (1889–90) in the Russia Museum, St Petersburg, showing the characteristic re-curved bow of the steppe and the backward 'Parthian shot'

Figure 1.20 The second-century AD bronze so-called 'Flying Horse of Gansu' in the Gansu Provincial Museum in Lanzhou, presumably modelled on the Ferghana horses, much coveted by Han China

gallop, both to the front and rear: the famed 'Parthian shot' (Figures 1.19, 1.20). By the last centuries BC huge bands of mounted archers from the steppe had become among the most formidable warriors in the ancient world, heralding the age of the first steppe empires.[23]

Dominoes and boundaries

The steppe environment is very limited, with severe restrictions for both stock-breeding and pastoralism. However, occasional fertile years can result in a sudden and enormous increase in animals which, by the following years when conditions revert to normal, can with equal suddenness simply not be supported by the steppe. There is consequent over-population and hence urgent need for more pasture – and hence, outward movement, often with cataclysmic result. 'Nomads were always in the process of movement and fusion. Therefore, it is very hard to determine the limits of their area of inhabitance in terms of archaeological culture in both geographic and chronological terms.'[24]

Life on the steppe is at once both bounteous and fragile. On one level, a simplified view of the pastoral nomad might appear to be one of equilibrium with both the environment and history. Various nomad groups subsisted since time immemorial by grazing their great herds over the almost limitless grasslands, hunting the wildlife and moving on seasonally with their families, household effects, tents and livestock in a rotation of migratory movements between pastures. For winter quarters steppe nomads would often move to sheltered areas, particularly forests. For this reason forests would often assume sacred status.* Such a pattern might not vary much for many generations.

An idyllic picture – but in reality a very fragile balance. Whenever this cycle was upset the entire balance between different nomad groups would be disrupted.[25] One group would be forced beyond its traditional area to conflict with the next. This in turn would disrupt the next group, occasionally resulting in the weaker group being absorbed and large-scale steppe confederations coming into being: what Thomas Barfield describes as 'imperial confederacies' or 'shadow empires'.[26] Either way it would set in motion a chain reaction throughout the steppe. Tadieusz Sulimirski compared it to the effect of billiard balls knocking against each other.[27] Such a 'billiard ball' or 'domino' effect is often dismissed by many historians and anthropologists with more complex and convoluted theories in constant searches for original ideas.[28] But the pattern did occur. This 'knock-on' pattern of tribal movements across Eurasia was understood as early as the fifth century BC in the account of the steppe by Aristeas of Proconnesus recorded by Herodotus.[29] The Germanic 'invasions' were set in motion by the Huns on their heels, and Peter Golden (citing Priscus) writes how they in turn were pursued by the Oghurs and Onoghurs, sent westward by the Sabirs, who in turn had been evicted by the Avars.[30] Often the original

---

* The sacred Ötökän Forest of the Turks is a good example. See Chapter 8. See also Golden 2011: 14–15.

cause would be unknown (the Hun invasions of the Near East through the Caucasian passes in 395, for example, were thought by contemporaries to have been caused by a famine in the steppe),[31] but the effects would be felt right across the Eurasian land mass, sometimes generations after the original event that prompted it. The spark that initially ignites a movement might be a drying up of pastures, a change in climate, over-population, a war by a neighbouring tribe or a political event far removed from the event that sets it in motion; the causes are many (there can even be none), and are usually unknown. Nomadic ('barbaric' in the sources) invasions of the Roman Empire, as well as of Russia, Iran, India and China at different times throughout history, have often been the result of this pattern.

Owen Lattimore long ago made the important distinction between 'Frontiers' and 'Boundaries'.[32] From the viewpoint of a great power, a physical 'frontier' is perceived as a line between civilisation and barbarism (the Islamic concept of the *dar al-salam* or 'realm of peace' versus the *dar al-harb* or 'realm of chaos'; the traditional conflict between Muslim and non-Muslim is a good example). Lattimore was discussing the Chinese Empire in this case (the Great Wall), but the principle applies equally to the Roman, British Indian or early Arab empires (the Roman *limes*, the Durand Line forming the frontier with Afghanistan, and the system of *rabats* or religious border forts). But equally, frontiers represent the limits of the growth of an empire. Buffer states, while mainly an artificial creation by strong empires, are at the same time a material result of the creation of boundaries (Figures 1.21–1.23).

From the viewpoint of the 'barbarian', boundaries are a barrier to natural expansion, and therefore constraining and limiting. They also cut across traditional patterns of movement, of pasturing, migration and trade patterns. It then becomes a vicious circle: the 'barbarian' is forced by these barriers to be aggressive: to raid, to break the barrier – in other words is forced into the mould of being 'barbaric'. The ensuing alienation of peoples beyond such boundaries culminates in the barriers being broken: an invasion by the 'barbarians' in other words which brings about the end of the barrier builders. The Roman Empire had its Germanic invasions, the Caliphate its Turkish invasions, the Chinese Empire its invasions from beyond the wall.

Lattimore argued that the first 'barbarian' invasions into China in the first millennium BC (Chou period) were not steppe nomads from beyond the Wall, the 'advance parties' of the later nomads such as the Mongols, but were of peoples probably ethnically similar to the Chinese and indigenous to within the Wall ('Wall' used here anachronistically) who were displaced by the advance and expansion of the Chou Chinese. Similarly, the Xiongnu and other later 'barbarian' nations north of the Wall may originally have been a people from *within* China who were pushed out to the fringes, the steppes, by the Chinese in much the same way that the indigenous Celts of

Figure 1.21 *End of the Ming Great Wall at Jiayuguan in Gansu; in the background are the Qilian – formerly Richtofen – Ranges*

Figure 1.22 *A Han-period beacon tower at Kizilgaha, Xinjiang*

Britain were pushed to the fringes by incoming Saxons and others (Lattimore actually uses the term 'Celtification' here).[33] Later studies confirm that the Northern Zone of China was culturally unified by nomadic groups on either side of what later became the Great Wall during the Warring States period. After the construction of the Great Wall the nomads migrated northwards, while those who remained south became increasingly Sinacised, both eventually becoming two distinct separate cultures.[34]

Barriers, by their very nature, are massively confrontational. Their immutability is exclusive: they exclude those beyond from sedentary civilisation – and, more important, from grazing and farming lands, as well as markets. They therefore create the very situation they attempt to avoid: in attempting to exclude the nomad, barriers paradoxically simply draw them in, creating conflict. In this sense barriers such as the Great Wall or the Roman *limes* are the real forerunner of modern imposed borders and lines of defence. Hence, Lattimore writes with relation to that greatest barrier of antiquity:

> No linear Frontier between China and Inner Asia could be permanently held and kept clean and clear by either the pastoral society of the steppe or the agricultural society of China. In practice, the front on which met the two major orders of society, and the numerous minor, satellite societies that oscillated between them, always broadened into a series of zones of impact and recoil, conquest and counter conquest, assertion and compromise.[35]

Thus, the very existence of boundaries – Great Walls, *limes*, *rabats*, or for that matter the Iron Curtain or the Berlin Wall – often contain the seeds of their own ultimate failure. Chinese history is *consistently* one of nomad nations overrunning both the Wall and China itself, from the nomads who propped up the Tang to the Manchus who saw out the end of the Chinese Empire.

Nomads and conquest

Throughout history, nomad societies have paradoxically often been militarily superior to the more sophisticated – and supposedly more powerful – sedentary nations, even great empires with their massive standing armies. China, Persia, parts of India, Rome, all at different times have been overthrown – or at least threatened – by ostensibly less developed nomadic groups. 'Only in individual, very rare cases has a nomadic state emerged without conquering and subjugating a sedentary population.'[36] The Great Wall is the ultimate visible manifestation of this paradox: though it was built supposedly to defend China against the steppe nomad, China more than most sedentary cultures has been periodically ruled by 'barbarian' groups from beyond the Wall.

This apparent paradox is perfectly plausible. In steppe society all adult males are 'soldiers' and no distinction is made between civilian and military. It is notable that there is no indigenous word for 'soldier' in the Turco-Mongolian languages: such a word is simply deemed unnecessary.[37] Nomads were, virtually by definition, all professional soldiers, in contrast to settled communities who generally had to rely on drafted armies with only a professional core: resilience is inherent to the nomadic lifestyle. A successful army is created by rigorous military training: the better the training, the better the soldier. This has been true from the first professional armies of antiquity (the Persian Immortals, the Macedonian phalanxes, the Roman legions, all of whom created empires) to the professional armies of today. With nomads, however, military training is a part of everyday lifestyle from birth. Children, girls as well as boys, learn to ride as soon as walk, simply because it is as essential to their lifestyle as walking. The extremely harsh life of the steppe into which nomads are born automatically makes them resilient – a toughening that puts the most rigorous military training into the pale. It is a life of forced marches, often through adverse conditions and extremes of weather. This is no occasional weekend training in a temporary camp by present-day reservists: a life in a camp was their permanent lifestyle.

This kept the nomads' effects to a minimum of basic necessities. Hence, the nomad could travel lightly and rapidly: the extraordinary mobility of nomad armies was natural for them as their way of life. This was reinforced by the animal which underpinned the steppe economy: the extraordinarily tough steppe pony, capable of travelling far greater distances than other breeds of horse, of enduring greater extremes, of foraging for fodder where no other horse could. The steppe produced vastly more horses than were needed for purely domestic purposes, and they regenerated naturally in huge numbers, without the necessity for artificial breeding. According to ethnographic observations, the average nomad family of the steppe in the eighteenth century required a minimum of twenty horses (as well as fifty sheep and six cattle) simply to survive, and many families had considerably more – the ratio of horse to man, woman or child in other words was at least four to one.[38]

Indeed, animals were a major factor in the military success of the steppe nomad, both directly as a means of transport and indirectly as a source of food (and is manifest in their art: Chapter 6). The question of whether a meat diet tends to more aggressiveness than a vegetarian one can be left to the dietician, but the meat diet of the steppe nomad did give them one great advantage over their sedentary opponents: all their food was on the hoof, either the horses they rode or the flocks and herds they drove. Less carnivorous armies were more dependent upon cereals for their diet; hence vast cumbersome logistics are required simply to supply the quantities of grain required to feed an army on the march, not to mention the need to demobilise and return from campaign to gather in the harvest.

Animals played another major factor in steppe prowess, for the natural activity of the steppe nomad was hunting, enforced simply to stay alive. Hunting is the nearest activity to warfare. It involved the use of the bow and accurate shooting, often at full gallop, and a hunt would involve all members of a tribe, including women: all nomads in other words were 'soldiers' and precision organisation and manoeuvring an everyday matter. Furthermore, the very lifestyle of the nomad was dependent upon strong charismatic leadership – 'captains' – in whom the members of the tribe could trust implicitly: this was simply the only way that the tribe could operate and survive. Without boundaries and fixed establishments, such as those that a sedentary state would have, nomadic societies had to place far more emphasis on social structure, cohesion and strictly enforced chains of command, hence their generally far greater military power. It was a ready-made army of which most commanders of more conventional forces could only dream. Furthermore, since women had to lead the same lifestyle, sharing with men the skills necessary for survival, they could be soldiers too – a 'fully mobilized society'.[39] Sexual inequality and seclusion of women would not only have been unthinkable on the steppe, it would have been impossible for practical purposes. Indeed, the steppe nomads were the origin of the Amazon legends – and graves of warrior women have been unearthed in the region (see Chapter 5).

The steppe and trade

Probably the most pervasive image associated with the geography of Eurasia is that of the Silk Road. It has become one of the best-known facts of the geography and history of Eurasia generally: for many, if they have heard of nothing else about Inner Asia, have heard of the Silk Road. There is hardly a book, exhibition or conference on any aspect of Central or Inner Asia that does not make reference throughout to the Silk Road (or Route) – indeed, it is often incorporated into their very titles – and its use as a metaphor for ancient trade has been adopted and expanded into many other areas: politics, tourism and academia.

Despite such a vast and ever-increasing literature on the Silk Road, there have been doubts. In 1940 Owen Lattimore refuted the generally held assumption that Xinjiang was deliberately opened up by the Chinese to export silk – a 'Silk Road' in other words – and suggests natural pop-ulation expansion. Lattimore fairly convincingly demolishes the myths of the Silk Road, remarking on the Western obsession with it. More recently, Nicola Di Cosmo outlines the Han expansion into Central Asia as 'primarily a strategic move within the wider context of the political and military confrontation between Han and Hsiung-nu' rather than as conforming to a Silk Road theory.[40]

In a general article in 1998, the essential meaningless of the term 'Silk Road' was debated, concluding with the words, 'the greatest value of the Silk Road to geography is as a lesson – and a very important one at that – in how quickly and how thoroughly a myth can become enshrined as unquestioned fact'.[41] This was claimed, perhaps rightly, as an over-statement by Daniel Waugh in 2010,[42] albeit based only on that article and not on its re-working into a more academic discussion on Roman eastern trade in 2000.[43] The question of its meaningless was repeated in 2008, concluding in how the image had become 'both band wagon and gravy train'.[44] These words were taken up by Khodadad Rezakhani in 2011, essentially re-asserting this claim and adding further to the argument that the Silk Road was 'The Road That Never Was' (the title of his paper).[45] The Silk Road was separately questioned as 'A Romantic Deception' by Hugh Pope.[46] Partly as an answer to Pope, Susan Whitfield, a formidable scholar of Inner Asian history, posed her own question in her paper 'Was There a Silk Road?', cautiously reasserting its validity in scholarship but admitting that the term might eventually become obsolete. In acknowl-edgement of the growing debate, however, Whitfield opens her 2020 book, *Silk Roads*, with the words 'There was no "Silk Road"'.[47] Valerie Hansen, in an impressively researched book, has debunked many of the myths of the Silk Road,[48] and Ursula Brosseder cautions against 'the eye- and mind-catching concept of the Silk Roads'.[49] Now, scholars at least need to argue the case in order to justify the use of the term,[50] hedging the term with 'so-called' or placing Silk Road in quotation marks.[51] The question of the Silk Road therefore is not so much what it was or was not, but *why* a myth became fact.

In listing the main commodities and inventions most commonly asso-ciated with the Silk Road – printing, paper, gunpowder, the compass and religions for example – it is the very movement of these that actually dis-proves the existence of a route rather than the other way round. The screw propeller and the crankshaft, for example, took between five and twelve centuries to travel, the Persian windmill six centuries. Printing, between the world's oldest extant printed book, the Diamond Sutra of 868, and the Gutenberg Bible of 1450 is a gap of nearly six centuries; paper, at some twelve centuries, took double the time; the magnetic compass took eleven centuries; the wheelbarrow, crossbow and cast iron between five and twelve centuries; and gunpowder some four centuries.[52] Buddhism took between five and eight centuries to reach China, being first recorded in the Han court in the first century BC but confined to foreign quarters in Chinese cities until the late first century AD and reaching the Tarim in the mid-second century, implying an east to west spread across China rather than arriving overland from Central Asia.[53] Yet it has been stated confidently that 'With the opening of the Silk Road Buddhism rapidly spread across East Central Asia'.[54] Christianity was hardly quicker if the doubtful sixth-century Nestorian stele in Xian is evidence. At this rate the average rate of travel on the Silk Road works out at the astonishing speed of something between *twelve and eighteen inches per hour*, which is about half the average speed of a snail.[55]

In sum, there is no ancient source that mentions such a road, route or network spanning Eurasia, and very little archaeological evidence. In the face of such singular lack of support the term has been broadened and a new term coined: the oxymoron 'Maritime Silk Road'.[56] It is true that there is ample evidence for a complex trade network in the western Indian Ocean, although this too has been overstated and again silk was not the main commodity traded.[57] More important, the broader the term 'Silk Road' becomes, the more meaningless it becomes.

The origin of 'Silk Road' as a term is relatively recent and has been well summarised elsewhere[58] when in 1877 the German geographer Baron von Richthofen coined the term. Since then, the term has not only gained credence but has caught both the popular and the academic imagination with enthusiasm. Any number of vague tracks through most countries between the Mediterranean and China are confidently pointed out as the 'Silk Road', not only by tourist guides but by government agencies,

Figure 1.23 *A pathway signposted as the 'Silk Road' at the medieval Armenian remains of Ani in eastern Turkey*

Figure 1.24 *Russia and China on the Silk Road: exhibition at the National Museum of China, 2016*

the media, university departments and a vast number of publications, both popular and specialist (Figure 1.23). The Silk Road is even extended back in time to prove the existence of other routes and movements. It is now accepted that there is a 'prehistory' of the Silk Road based upon the development of wheeled transport in the Urals.[59] At the Lower Palaeolithic Denisov Cave in the Altai Mountains of southern Siberia (Figure 2.1) where early hominin remains dating back some forty thousand years have been discovered, it is described officially in the on-site information as evidence that the Silk Road passed through there in Palaeolithic times.[60] A series of specialist academic publications entitled the 'UNESCO Silk Roads Project', for example, represents only one of many such usages now in vogue in academia, where the existence of the 'Great Silk Road' is cited as 'indisputable'. There are Silk Road Studies at the highest academic levels in major universities. The School of Oriental and African Studies at the University of London, for example, offers an 'Art and Archaeology of the Silk Road' course. The British Library offers an online Silk Road Gallery and presented a major exhibition in 2004 entitled 'The Silk Road. Trade, Travel, War and Faith', which prompted a number of Silk Road books.[61] There is now a rash of 'Silk Road' conferences, projects, exhibitions, institutions and publications of every description, many at the highest academic level, where the term has even expanded to encompass all world history to the present.[62]

Once the assumption of the 'Silk Road' has been made, it soon becomes an unquestioned fact. One archaeological study, for example, states that 'With the opening of the Silk Road Buddhism rapidly spread across East Central Asia', and 'We have seen how Europeans and Chinese came to discover . . . each other . . . in the first centuries BC'.[63] Thereafter the 'Silk Road' litters the work as a central unquestioned fact around which the history and geography revolves. A work on pre-European world systems actually states that 'the Romans called [it] the Silk Road' when we know that the Romans had no such concept.[64] The examples cited here are just a tiny fraction of similar statements that litter scholarly studies.

So why has the Silk Road become so engraved? Could it just be wishful thinking? The myth stems partly from late nineteenth-century obsession with mapping, exploring, plotting and creating routes. It was the age of great railway projects, the Ordnance Survey, the Survey of India and similar grand schemes for connecting the world. Hence, recognising ancient routes where none existed. But nineteenth-century geography was always tempered with romanticism. Flecker's 'Golden Road to Samarkand' is one such image, and the history of nineteenth-century exploration became heavily romanticised and mythologised, from Rider Haggard to Rudyard Kipling. Once the image was created it snowballed into images of something mystical, fabulous and alternative. The 1960s and 1970s, with its hippy route to the East and love of exotica, was a quixotic descendant of the image. The image of the Silk Road has become useful to politicians in pursuing an international and cosmopolitan image; it has become useful to scholars in pursuing much needed research funds. In particular, it has become one of the biggest selling points of a worldwide tourist industry as most countries in Asia, from Turkey through to China, have hastened to 'join' the Silk Road, and overnight their ancient remains and architectural splendours have been re-labelled 'Silk Road' cities to attract increasing tourist numbers.

The fall of the Iron Curtain in 1989 prompted further Silk Road obsession. The newly independent former Soviet states of Central Asia, unlike Georgia or Armenia or Lithuania, had no history of nationhood: the nineteenth-century Emirate of Bukhara or the various Turkmen Khanates were no forerunners of Uzbekistan or Turkmenistan, let alone Tajikistan or the even more amorphous Kazakhstan. There were also no freedom struggles precipitating their independence: the Central Asian States had no Gandhi or Bolivar or Ben Bella but independence happened almost overnight. This led to a search for a historical identity, something in the past to provide a positive but uniquely Central Asian image. The Silk Road was seized upon. It had all the right ingredients: internationalism, glamour, exoticism, luxuries, a joining together of peoples, free trade, the movement of ideas, a veritable ancient 'United Nations', a time when Central Asia was the hub of a vast international network – all positive images in a post-Soviet, post-Communist world. So heady was the Silk Road myth in replacing the former Communist ideology that Russians too lined up to join the bandwagon (Figure 1.24). Slotted in at the end of conclusions or tacked on to a sub-heading to so many post-Soviet works on almost any aspect of the history, geography or archaeology of Eurasia will be a token reference to 'the Great Silk Road', almost as if compulsory reference to it has replaced the compulsory Marxist slant of an earlier generation.

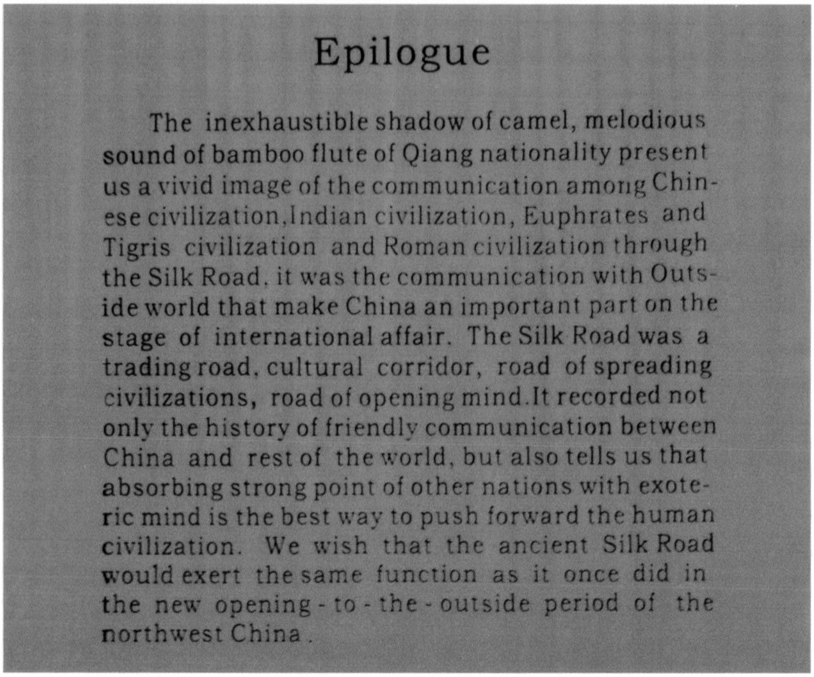

Epilogue

The inexhaustible shadow of camel, melodious sound of bamboo flute of Qiang nationality present us a vivid image of the communication among Chinese civilization,Indian civilization, Euphrates and Tigris civilization and Roman civilization through the Silk Road, it was the communication with Outside world that make China an important part on the stage of international affair. The Silk Road was a trading road, cultural corridor, road of spreading civilizations, road of opening mind.It recorded not only the history of friendly communication between China and rest of the world, but also tells us that absorbing strong point of other nations with exoteric mind is the best way to push forward the human civilization. We wish that the ancient Silk Road would exert the same function as it once did in the new opening - to - the - outside period of the northwest China .

Figure 1.25 *Caption in the Gansu Provincial Museum, Lanzhou, 2016*

The image of the Silk Road gathered further strength from changes in post-Maoist China. In China's opening up to the West, its commercial revolution and massive export drive, its westernisation and neo-nationalism, the Silk Road is the perfect image (Figure 1.25). An image, moreover, that is perceived as China's very own, a time when ancient China supposedly initiated a worldwide trade network, when Chinese ideas and inventions travelled westwards to revolutionise the globe. Nothing is more *Chinese* than silk: a Chinese invention and a Chinese route. In contemporary China the Silk Road is now both an image and metaphor as strong – and as Chinese – as the Great Wall.[65]

The modern Silk Road industry received further support from an unexpected quarter: Turkey. The collapse of the Soviet Union opened up an entirely new hinterland for Turkey right across Asia that spoke languages close to Turkish. Turkey was the first western country to exploit the new commercial possibilities: a new Turkish world. More important, the Turks, up until then still facing their Europe and the Ottoman legacy, were re-awakened to the huge past of the Turkish-speaking peoples in Central Asia and beyond, and the Silk Road was seen as a part of this Turkish history. The Silk Road now forms a regular and familiar part of the advertising industry throughout Turkish speaking lands – *Ipekyol* or *Büyük Ipekyol* – from Turkey through to Kyrgyzstan, from fashion brands to Turkish-sponsored engineering projects and conferences (Figure 1.26).

Hence, the 'Silk Road' has become more than image: it has become a major industry in a way that Von Richthofen could never have conceived. Its 're-opening' has been formally announced on several occasions even by heads of state. The formal opening of the Iran–Turkmenistan rail link at the border town of Sarakhs in Iran on 13 May 1996, for example, attended by eight regional heads of state, was billed as a formal 're-opening' of the Silk Road for the first time since antiquity.[66] The rail link between Iran and Armenia was announced as 'the Silk Road on Rails'.[67] A Turkish plan in 1998 to establish a communications network throughout Europe and Asia was signed in Baku as a 'Silk Road agreement'. A treaty in 2004 between twenty-three Asian nations to establish a highway network between Asia and Europe was formally described as a 'new Silk Road'.[68] Chinese plans in 2008 to build a road from its Pacific coast through Central Asia to Europe was launched as 're-building the Silk Road' and its planned trans-Eurasian rail network hailed as the same.[69] The re-opening of a Himalayan pass between China and India was lauded as 're-opening the Silk Road'.[70] The Chinese built road into Tibet is proclaimed as 'The Famed Silk Road'.[71]

Figure 1.26 *Magazine in Gaziantep, Turkey, announcing a Silk Road Forum in 2012*

The Silk Road has now become far more than a mere route: it is part of the ether. A 27,000-kilometre-long fibre-optic cable linking twenty countries was announced as the opening of a 'Silk Road telecom link'; there is a Silk Road radio station in Uzbekistan in co-operation with UNESCO and UNDP, and a Silk Road online game.[72] Notoriously, there was a 'Silk Road' online drug market-place. The Silk Road has even taken to the skies – there is a 'Silk Way' Airline in Azerbaijan[73] – and beyond into space with the Chinese space programme being described as 'the Silk Road to the Cosmos'.[74] As well as the sea, the ether, prehistory, all of history, all of Asia, into Africa and outer space – the meaning of the Silk Road has expanded to include so much that as a term it has become essentially meaningless.

Despite the many notes of caution cited above, modern academic studies have become almost obsessed with the idea. Virtually all discussion of ancient trade with the East revolves around it, with the 'Silk Road' being cited as the glib explanation for questions of ancient trade, geography and international relations. Nowadays there seem to be few references to the history or geography of the Inner Asian countries without some reference to it. The Silk Road has spread into academia as a potent image that provides a source of much-needed funding. There are now Silk Road departments in universities, chairs of Silk Road Studies, any number of Silk Road academic conferences, projects, journals and publications throughout the world. A cursory glance at the Edinburgh University online catalogue reveals nineteen entries bearing the title 'Silk Road' or 'Route'; the British Library 245 entries and 141 actual titles; the School of Oriental and African Studies library 186 entries with 58 titles and five 'Silk Road' journals.

What, if anything, can one make of the Silk Road? That there was movement throughout Eurasia is not in doubt. But there was never any such 'road' or even a route in the organisational sense; there was no free movement of goods between China and the West until the Mongol Empire in the middle ages, silk was by no means the main commodity in the trade with the East, and there is not a single ancient historical record of such a road. Of course, there was trade in the ancient world, but it makes as much sense to label, for example, the trade in ivory from West Africa to the Mediterranean the 'Silk Road': true, silk did not figure, but neither did it figure on the 'Silk Road' – and the ancient West African trade routes were more organised and systematic than any Eurasian overland ones were.

That the Silk Road had become incontrovertible fact even among historians fits uncomfortably in an academic environment. As a theme for tourism there is little harm: it is no less true than the idyllic romanticised pictures of empty palm-fringed beaches and faultless hotels that litter brochures. Most of the tourist industry is, after all, about selling an idea. As an invented history and identity for newly emerging nations it is as good as any and a far better symbol than nationalist or extremist ideas that can sadly characterise emerging identities. But as a glib answer to the historical complexities of Eurasia, to the movements of cultures, ideas and goods, it has no sound value. Worse, such glib answers stifle scholarly enquiry.

Language and people

More will be discussed about language in Chapter 3. For the moment it is just necessary to observe that the Inner Eurasian land mass has usually been dominated by three main linguistic patterns – mostly identifiable with ethnic groups – throughout history. From earliest history until late antiquity – roughly 5000 BC to the late first millennium AD – the Indo-European languages were dominant. Proto-Indo-European was the first, from which most of the present-day languages of Europe, Iran and the Indian Subcontinent are descended. One of the earliest sub-branches of this language group, Iranian,* soon emerged to dominate the steppe and its adjacent regions: various Cimmerian, Scythian, Sarmatian and Alan tribes, not to mention the Medes, Persians and Parthians who eventually controlled much of the Near East, all belonged to this group.

By late antiquity a gradual ethnic displacement on the steppe and the forest belt occurs with the emergence of Ural-Altaic groups, at first Finno-Ugrians, Huns, Avars and related groups, but then of various Turk-speaking groups.[75] The Turks were seemingly irresistible – and not necessarily by force of arms – for Turk-related languages soon displaced or absorbed not only many of the earlier Iranian groups, but also many of the earlier Iranian language groups, leaving only pockets of Finns, Estonians, Hungarians and Mongols on the fringes. The list of these various Turk tribes, nationalities and dynasties is almost endless: Tuoba, Oghuz, Bulgars, Khazars, Uighurs, Kirghiz, Qipchak, Cumans, Karakhanids, Ghaznavids, Seljuks, Mamluks, Tatars, Mughals, Ottomans – the names become a roll-call of Eurasian history, and they have left an indelible imprint from China through to Europe.

The third group to dominate the inner regions of Eurasia – although they never really displaced the Turks – was another Indo-European group who began to rise to prominence at about the same time that we see the arrival of the Turks. These were various Slavic groups. Slavic-speaking countries have comprised approximately half the European land mass for the past thousand years.[76] As the Turks came from the east, the Slavs came from the west, and Poles, Czechs, Ukrainians, Slovaks, Moravians and Russians have been a major factor in Europe since that time, but, with the Russian expansion into Siberia in modern history, expanded to the easternmost reaches of the Eurasian continent.[†] Of course, the above observations are gross over-simplifications of complex and controversial language movements. But they serve to emphasise that Iranians, Turks and Slavs represent a history of Europe as much as of Asia.

---

* The term 'Iranian' has a broad linguistic as well as a modern political meaning, and the two must be differentiated. An Iranian from a linguistic point of view means, of course, an Iranian, but also a Pashtun, a Baluch, a Tajik, an Ossetian, a Kurd, and – in more ancient times – a Scythian, Soghdian, Alan, Khwarazmian, and many other related groups. To differentiate the two meanings some scholars now use 'Iranic' for the languages.

† It is significant that the major academic publisher Brill of Leiden has a single category for 'Slavic and Eurasian Studies'.

CHAPTER 2

THE BEGINNINGS OF EURASIA
Permanence, Movement and Prehistory

This territory [north-central Eurasia] 'knew' both great highs and great lows, glory and decline, technological inventions and adoptions, social consolidations and disintegrations. Perhaps the most important consequence of its development was that this area organically evolved into large networks of Eurasian interactions.
– Ludmila Koryakova and Andrej Epimakhov[1]

The archaeologists Ludmila Koryakova and Andrej Epimakhov open the concluding chapter of their seminal overview of the Bronze Age in the Urals and western Siberia with the above words emphasising the importance of the region for the wider land mass: a single 'Eurasia' already by the Bronze Age.

The term 'Eurasia' seems self-explanatory (Europe-Asia: Europe *and/ with* Asia),* yet as a word it was coined surprisingly recently. It does not appear in the 1994 *Oxford English Dictionary* although 'Eurasia' was a fictional super-state in George Orwell's classic 1949 novel of a dystopian future, *Nineteen Eighty-four*. The word 'Eurasian' does,† however, appear in that edition of the *OED*, meaning someone of mixed European and Asian parentage, more specifically a term used in British India for one of mixed British and Indian parentage.[2]

Works concerning Eurasia are commonly used in the context of Inner Eurasia – effectively Inner Asia. 'Eurasia' usually includes Central Asia, rarely the Far East, South Asia, the Middle East or Europe.[3] Usually the term relates to movements westwards out of Asia: peoples, ideas, language. One has an impression of inner Eurasian history being somehow blank, with wave after wave of 'folk' appearing mysteriously but periodically out of Mongolia – a 'Mongolian generator of peoples'[4] or 'Asia's storehouse of people'[5] – to burst upon the sedentary fringes eventually to be swallowed up and disappear, leaving the steppe a void once more until the next 'wave' appears over the horizon. In fact the long cultural development and prehistory of inner Eurasia is just as venerable – and just as important – as any

---

* 'Asiarope' would never have worked.
† The loaded term 'Eurasianism' is explored in Chapter 13.

Figure 2.1 *The Lower Palaeolithic cave of Denisov in the Urals*

of the other more traditional regions of human development elsewhere. On the fringes of inner Eurasia, recent discoveries of human remains dating back some 1.8 million years at Dmanisi in Georgia have rewritten the story of human – or at least hominin – movements out of Africa. At the Lower Palaeolithic Denisov Cave in the Altai Mountains (Figure 2.1) remains of a different species of hominin – 'Denisovans' – dating back some forty thousand years have been discovered. Traces of hunter-gatherer communities in the form of temporary camp sites, and tools made from flint, bone, ivory and antler, have been recorded throughout, as well as a vigorous art, such as the Upper Palaeolithic cave paintings at Shulgan-tash (Kapova) in the southern Urals fourteen to sixteen thousand years old (Figure 2.2).

With the end of the last Ice Age there was a rise in temperatures between nine and twelve thousand years ago. In the Near East this coincided with the first domestication of plants and the beginnings of agriculture. In the steppe, stone tools became smaller and more refined, the bow and arrow more widespread – arrowheads are a significant portion of the archaeological assemblage – eventually to develop into the short but deadly re-curved composite bow (Figure 1.19) of the steppe warrior that could fire arrows with greater force and more rapidity than the conventional bow.

Communities, while still hunter-gathering, seem to have become smaller and more mobile, marking the beginning of pastoral nomadism. The process culminated some six thousand years ago with an expansion of

Figure 2.2 *Reproductions of Upper Palaeolithic cave paintings at Shulgan-tash in the southern Urals (photography of the originals is prohibited, but reproductions have been made in the cave itself)*

the grasslands, mainly to the north (perhaps as a result of climate change) and the beginning of the domestication of animals and stockbreeding, much of it introduced from the Near East. Communities became partly sedentary, as the increase in grasslands supported limited agriculture. In addition, domesticated herds could be controlled more, and the arrival of pottery-making techniques allowed for greater cooking and storage capabilities. There is increasing evidence for wide-ranging contacts, both throughout the steppe zone and southwards with the more sedentary cultures. The Bronze Age at the end of the fourth millennium BC sees the beginning of wheeled transport on the steppe, allowing greater mobility and migrations of whole tribes with their possessions over vast distances.[6] The period between about five and two thousand BC, therefore, experienced the appearance of increasing movement across the steppe. But at the same time it saw the parallel development of permanent settlements.[7]

Permanence in a nomadic environment

The image of movement and nomadism was a characteristic of the Eurasian steppe in the past, and movements from the steppe into, and influences on, Europe is the theme of this book. But it is not characterised solely by movement. Henri-Paul Francfort cautions against an overemphasis on the movement of peoples in prehistoric Eurasia: 'Focussing systematically on mainly human migration as an explanation for the parallel design that appear in widely dispersed archaeological sites leads, we think, to assuming too many migrations from too many places to too many other places',[8] anticipated by Michael Frachetti who views the steppe as a 'jigsaw puzzle' of 'a more nuanced process of emergence and metamorphosis of Eurasian populations in locally durable contexts'.[9]

The steppe, therefore, had important prehistoric sedentary cultures. In a case study of the Koksu Valley in Semirechye, surveys showed that settlements as well as burials and petroglyphs existed side by side throughout the Bronze and Iron Ages in clusters of eight hundred metres or less, through to the medieval period – a continuity from about 2500 BC to AD 1000.[10] It is important to emphasise that both settlement and nomadism – and gradations in between – were permanent characteristics of the steppe.

Such sedentary cultures were the fifth–fourth millennium Chalcolithic Cucuteni-Tripolye Culture of the south-western steppe and the Balkans, the late fourth millennium Maikop Culture of the Kuban Steppe north of the Caucasus, the third–second millennium 'Country of Towns' of the Urals, the slightly later Andronovo Culture of western Siberia, and the middle and late Bronze Age 'Bactro-Margiana Cultural Complex' of Central Asia (albeit more marginal to the steppe). Many of these cultures exhibit considerable sophistication comparable to the better-known early civilisations of the Near East. The Chalcolithic and Bronze Age archaeology of the steppe can present a confusing picture of a multiplicity of archaeological 'cultures' in different places at different times (usually named either after the site where they were first identified or a common distinctive feature, such as grave types). Such cultures usually have many 'subcultures' with even more confusing names, and while exhibiting the distinctive cultural traits that define such a culture, they at the same time exhibit many overlaps with those that existed before, after and contemporaneously. Dates are often controversial, there are many inconsistencies and the field is in a constant state of flux with new studies emerging which it is almost impossible to keep abreast of. The following account, therefore, probably suffers from over-simplifications that would make a specialist shudder, and is not entirely in chronological order, but is an attempt at an overall picture of the steppe and its different cultures/peoples before they emerged into history.

The Cucuteni-Tripolye 'mega-sites'

The Chalcolithic Cucuteni-Tripolye Culture, roughly 4500 to 3600 BC (although elements have been recognised earlier and continued later), covered a large area north-west of the Black Sea extending across northern

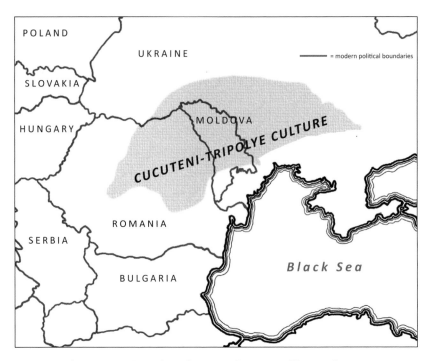

Map 2.1 *The Cucuteni-Tripolye culture in Ukraine, Moldova and Romania*

Romania and Moldova (where the culture is known as 'Cucuteni') and south-western Ukraine (where it is known as 'Tripolye' or 'Tryplillia': Map 2.1).[11] Although these included small farming communities and small-to-medium settlements (identified by artefacts common to the culture), the settlements were generally larger, more numerous and older than the earliest city-states of Mesopotamia, with approximately five thousand sites now identified. Some cover up to four hundred hectares in two, three or even five concentric rings of houses with populations estimated as high as thirty thousand. The site of Tollyansky between the Bug and Dnieper Rivers, for example, was three and a half by one and a half kilometres in area with an estimated population of ten thousand; some sites had up to three thousand houses. Settlements were usually carefully planned from the beginning, usually on a circular system with radiating lanes, open spaces and work areas, and did not grow organically from natural expansion of population. Houses were often two-storey and twenty to thirty metres in length. The largest excavated – at Nebelivka in Ukraine – measured sixty metres long by twenty metres wide, presumably for communal use, although the purpose of this giant building remains uncertain. Farming was practised, and copper was imported in the form of ingots probably from Thrace, where traces of extensive copper mining have been recorded in the Chalcolithic period. Such a trade in itself suggests sophisticated organisation, perhaps even a state system. The ingots were

Figure 2.3 *The highly distinctive Cucuteni-Tripolye ceramics in the National Museum, Chişinau. Note also the Scythian bronze cauldrons in the background*

re-worked and made into axes, adzes, chisels and other tools, weapons and ornaments. Art comprised simple clay figurines, mainly female, as well as some quite sophisticated stone sculptures and highly distinctive polychrome pottery (Figures 2.3, 2.4).

For reasons not fully understood, this extraordinary Chalcolithic culture that has been described as a 'flourishing Balkano-Ukrainian proto-civilisation'[12] came to an end. It appears that the sites were simply abandoned peacefully rather than ended suddenly by violence, such as invasion (although there is some suggestion of movement into the area from the steppe to the east). There is evidence of burning, but this has been explained as ritual immolation rather than sacking. Climate change has been suggested as a possible cause. There may have been some disruption on the steppe caused by the migration westwards of the Srubnaya and Yamnaya (discussed below), in turn perhaps caused by the same postulated climate change. Such a 'chain reaction' was in any case to become a feature of the movement of peoples over the steppe. The archaeological remains that followed in the early Bronze Age in the area appear much inferior and seem to owe little to the Tripolye, although the Bronze Age Maikop Culture in the Kuban steppe (below) might have received some stimulus, and there is some evidence for an eastward movement of Cucuteni-Tripolye.

These admittedly spectacular Chalcolithic remains probably received some stimulus at least from the earlier Neolithic cultures of Anatolia.

Figure 2.4 *Terracotta Tripolye female figurines at the site museum of Orheiul Vechi in Moldova (left) and the Iasi Museum in Romania (right)*

At first sight these settlements might appear to question the origins of civilisation in Mesopotamia. But archaeologists are careful to emphasise that they were just large settlements, 'megasites', and not cities in the (admittedly later) Mesopotamian sense. There is little evidence of complexity, monumental architecture, social stratification or specialisation; hence, the Tripolye sites are described as 'gigantic settlements' rather than true urban centres and did not develop further. Size certainly remained a feature of the steppe: the much later Iron Age Cherlomes (proto-Slav) fort of Belskoye of the in the first millennium, for example, located in the Vorksla Valley in Ukraine, was a staggering 4,400 hectares, or seventeen square miles.[13] As with Cucuteni-Tripolye, the simple explanation for such giganticism on the steppe was that mere space was never an issue.

Further east of the Cucuteni-Tripolye in the steppe proper of Ukraine and southern Russia the fifth millennium sees the expansion of the Neolithic Sredni Stog Culture. Mainly cattle herders and

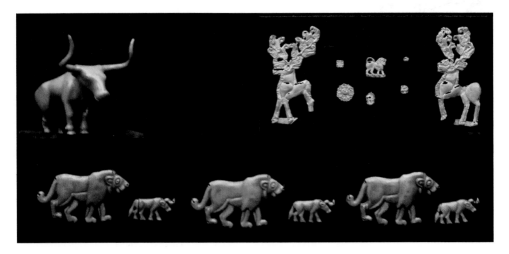

Figure 2.5 *Objects from the Maikop Treasure in the Adygea National Museum in Russia (not to the same scale)*

agriculturalists, they might also have been among the first horse riders of the steppe. There is also some evidence of a western movement of the Sredni Stog after about 4000 BC towards central Europe, marking a western movement of steppe peoples – or at least their culture – that was to characterise the steppe in subsequent millennia and bring a fundamental change to the older Neolithic cultures of Europe.

Maikop: treasures, wheels and burials of the north Caucasus

The Maikop Culture of the north Caucasus and Kuban steppe, roughly 3700 to 3000 BC, exhibits some characteristics of a settled population.[14] However, it is known almost solely from its *kurgans* or tumulus burials, which are mainly associated with nomads, about a hundred and fifty of which have been discovered (Map 2.2). The culture is named after the immensely rich royal burial of Maikop first excavated in 1897. It is characterised by highly intricate decorated gold, silver and bronze objects found first at Maikop and subsequently at numerous other burials covering roughly the area of the Kuban River watershed of southern Russia centred on Adygea (Figure 2.5).[15] On the one hand the sophistication of these objects suggests a sedentary population with the necessary tools, equipment and specialised craftsmen. But on the other hand they are found almost solely in the stone-lined burial pits that characterise the Maikop

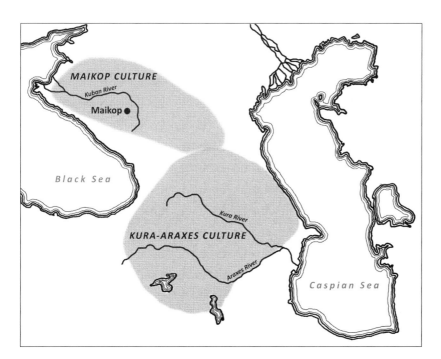

Map 2.2 *The Maikop and Kura-Araxes cultures of the Caucasus*

culture, as well as other nomadic cultures. It has been suggested that these objects were never meant for everyday use, but were made solely for burials.

Only about thirty Maikop settlements have been recorded. Although not many have been excavated, they are generally surrounded by a wall made of stone in the mountain areas, or a ditch in the steppe. Dwellings are very small pisé structures comprising just a single room. Some of the graves contained disassembled wagons, among the earliest known, albeit solid wheeled carts and not the spoked chariots found later at Sintashta (discussed below).* The Maikop culture therefore seems to have been one of semi-nomadic cattle breeders, practising some agriculture.

A feature of the Bronze Age culture along the northern foothills of the Caucasus and the eastern shores of the Black Sea are the still little understood megalithic 'dolmen' graves, of which many thousand have been mapped (although many have been destroyed). At Kyzinka, some forty kilometres east of Maikop, for example, is a group of some six hundred dolmen tombs which have been related to the Maikop culture (although this is still uncertain). Roughly cubical chambers are made of six stone slabs, each up to two metres square, with the front pierced by a circular hole to allow burials, stopped by a mushroom-shaped stone plug (Figure 2.6). The contents of one at Tsarskaya has been radiocarbon-dated to 3300–3000 BC, but others might be later. Another, displayed in the Adygea National Museum, was decorated with paintings depicting horsemen and a bow with quiver;[16] it was originally covered with a mound, making it a dolmen chambered kurgan.†

Contacts of the Maikop Culture were very widespread, both with the Tripolye Culture to the west and the Uruk Culture of Mesopotamia, where there was trade. Turquoise, lapis and carnelian objects found in the burials also suggest trade further east as well. The contacts with Mesopotamia assume significance in view of the later movement of the Kuro-Araxes Cultures out of the Caucasus into the Near East.

Across the Caucasus and beyond: the Kuro-Araxes expansion

A major cultural movement that probably included some form of migration has been discerned in the archaeological record of the 'Kuro-Araxes' or 'Early Transcaucasian' Culture of the late fourth/early third millennium (Map 2.2). Located south of the Caucasus, it probably grew

---

* Stuart Piggott (1992: 35–6), in tracing the remarkable consistency in cart gauges from the prehistoric steppe to the modern era, views such early wagons as the origin of the modern standard railway gauge of 4 feet 8½ inches, or 1.43 metres, as set by George Stephenson in 1825 on the world's first railway in Yorkshire, and remaining standard since.

† They appear to belong to an entirely separate tradition to the dolmen tombs and megaliths of Vera Island, discussed below.

Figure 2.6 *Bronze Age funerary remains at Gelendzhik on the Black Sea coast of Russia*

out of the earlier Maikop Culture to the north. The period saw the spread of distinctive pottery styles and other related material from the Caucasus into the Near East as far as north-western Iran and Palestine (where the pottery is known as 'Khirbet Kerak Ware'). These 'peoples of the hills' and their culture probably represent a dispersion rather than an invasion; they have been tentatively identified with the Hurrians in ancient Near Eastern records. Often, the pattern on the Eurasian steppe in this early period has been recognised as a series of responses to fragile but interrelated connections covering much of the known world. Hence, it is suggested that the Kuro-Araxes expansion southwards was a response to the earlier 'Uruk expansion' northwards from southern Mesopotamia into Anatolia, while the Kuro-Araxes cultures to the south of the Caucasus were in turn a response to the earlier Maikop cultures to the north of the Caucasus, themselves stimulated by the even earlier expansion of the fifth-millennium Cucuteni-Tripolye culture of southern Ukraine.[17]

Movement from the Caucasus has also been interpreted by similarities between the Maikop Culture and the later Hattian Culture of the third millennium BC in Anatolia. This is particularly apparent with the burial methods at Alaca Höyük and the spectacular 'royal standards' discovered there. It is argued, therefore, that the Hattian culture was the result of – or at least influenced by – migrations from the Maikop region

some time about 2200 BC (although this must remain speculative).[18] The
Hattians were the immediate antecedents (in cultural terms at least) of
the Hittites, one of the best-known civilisations – and empires – of the
Ancient Near East.[19] Since the Hittite language is the oldest identified
Indo-European language it has been further suggested that the people
of the Maikop Culture spoke an Indo-European language, bringing the
language with them to Anatolia from its origins deeper in Russia. Both
the argument and the links are fairly tenuous and controversial (the little
that is known of the Hattian language is that it almost certainly was *not*
Indo-European; the 'Indo-European question' is explored further in the
next chapter).

Another movement of peoples from the steppe into the sedentary
Near East has been recognised in the Mitanni Empire of the Near East
of the mid-second millennium BC. The Mitanni was one of the major
powers of the Near East at the time, maintaining the balance of power
between the Hittites to the north, the Egyptians to the south and the
Assyrians to the east. It was dominated by an Iranian elite, presumed
from the Eurasian steppe, who are known from written documents in the
Mitanni texts to have worshipped such well-known Indo-Iranian divin-
ities as Indra, Mitra and Varuna. Mitanni documents also include fragments of a horse training manual written in an Iranian language, again
suggestive of steppe origins. They might possibly have been a branch of
the same group, or part of the same movement, that may have dominated
Mycenae in around 1600 BC.[20]

In the nationalist politics that emerged after the collapse of the Soviet
Union, Maikop and the Kuro-Araxes expansion took new turns. Maikop
itself became the capital of a new republic within the Russian Federation:
the Republic of Adygea, an ethnic Circassian state the majority of whose
people practise Islam. But the region of the northern Caucasus is also home
to many groups of ethnic Turks. Bizarrely, this has led one archaeologist
from the region, an ethnic Turk, to claim anachronistically that because
of possible links with the Hattians of Anatolia, the people of the Maikop
culture must have been Turkish speakers. Furthermore, due to an old,
but long since convincingly disproven, theory that the ancient Sumerian
language – and the world's first writing system – of fourth-millennium
Mesopotamia was related to Turkish,* it was claimed that the spread of
Kuro-Araxes pottery into the ancient Near East represented a movement of
'Maikop Turks'. This supposedly led to 'Caucasian-Turks' bequeathing to
posterity the world's first written language, Sumerian, a branch of Turkish
(indeed, specifically the Karachai-Balkar dialect of Turkish spoken in the

---

* Although the theory is no longer subscribed to by most people in Turkey itself, remnants
of it still survive in names such as the Sümer Bank or the 'Sumerian' surname Akurgal.

north Caucasus). A farrago of nonsense of course, but just one of many examples that will recur in this book of how even such a benign discipline as archaeology (inter-disciplinary scholarly feuds notwithstanding) can be subverted by politics and nationalism.[21]

An island sanctuary: the megaliths of Vera Island

Still not fully understood in terms of how (or whether) they fit into the overall picture of the steppe cultures are the recently investigated Eneolithic megalithic chambered tombs on Vera Island in Lake Turgoyak in the southern Urals, to the south-west of Chelyabinsk. From the mid-fourth and into the third millennium BC, the island contained two elaborate tombs and an unfinished third, together with several standing stones (dolmens) and a settlement site. The tombs included crudely carved animal megaliths: bovine, feline (or lupine) and ram. Despite the existence of the settlement, surrounding cultures were still primarily hunter-gathering, so this might have been for just temporary or cultic purposes, as the entire island with its unique monuments is interpreted as religious (indeed, a long abandoned Old Believer monastery was built on the island in the nineteenth century). Comparisons were drawn with megalithic structures of Europe, the Mediterranean and Near East, but any direct links are unproven, although long-distance communications are postulated. No links are suggested to the North Caucasus–Black Sea megalithic structures, although these are much closer. The relationship to the slightly later Yamnaya Culture is unclear, although that period was one of 'unprecedented exchange'.[22] The excavators speculated that the builders might have been Finno-Ugrians, as their original homeland was probably in the south Urals, but associating prehistoric remains with language groups is always problematic. No link can be made to the later Finno-Ugrian remains in the White Sea (discussed in Chapter 9). Only further investigations will solve some of the problems of this intriguing site.[23]

Yamnaya and Afanasievo Cultures: the first Indo-Europeans?

Developing from the earlier Neolithic Sredni Stog Culture, the 'Pit-grave' or Yamnaya Culture of the Pontic steppe – stretching roughly from the Dniester to the Urals – emerged in roughly 3300–2500 BC (Map 2.3). They were among the first steppe people to use wheeled transport – wagons – on a large scale. There is also some of the earliest evidence for tents, suggesting mobile dwellings or covered wagons such as characterised later steppe nomads (Figure 2.7).[24] There was also extensive copper working, and even some evidence for early iron forging by the late Yamnaya period. The culture is known almost solely from burials, with very few settlements: hence, the people were probably among the first nomadic

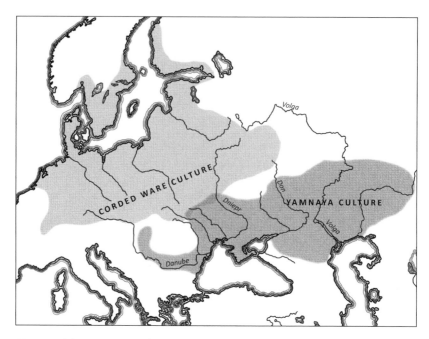

Map 2.3 *The Yamnaya and Corded Ware cultures*

Figure 2.7 *Conjectural reconstruction of a tented wagon in the Museum of Inner Mongolia in Hohhot, such as was used by many nomadic societies*

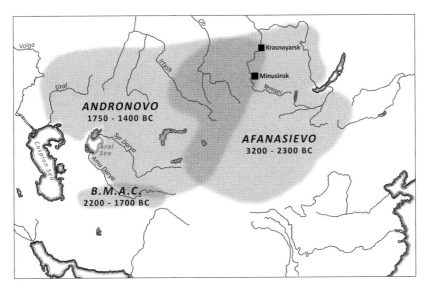

Map 2.4 *The Afanasievo and Andronovo cultures of Siberia*

pastoralists. The culture has been associated with Indo-European origins, and a Yamnaya/Indo-European migration after about 3000 BC is then postulated into eastern Europe (discussed in the next chapter). First and foremost, as E. E. Kuzmina notes, 'it furthered the unprecedented expansion of exchange'.[25]

Closely connected to, and overlapping chronologically (but slightly later) with, Yamnaya was the Afanasievo Culture of the Minusinsk Basin in southern Siberia, a mixed hunting and fishing culture with localised pastoralism.[26] Many have viewed both as simply variants of a single culture stretching from the Dnieper to the Yenisei roughly between 3400 and 2400 BC (Map 2.4, Figure 2.8). The Afanasievo is further characterised by sophisticated metalworking, with large quantities of bronze and other objects recovered from burials. This anticipates the upsurge in fine bronze, gold and other metal objects that is such a feature of the later Scythian burials in the same region. This, and that the bodies recovered from the burials exhibiting Europoid characteristics (confirmed by DNA), suggests that both the Yamnaya and Afanasievo were 'proto-Scythians'

Figure 2.8 *An Afanasievo pot in the National Museum of Khakasia in Abakan*

who later covered much the same area. Together with linguistic and material evidence (see Chapter 3), this has led to the suggestion that the Yamnaya-Afanasievo 'people' were possibly the proto-Indo-Europeans before they separated further into different cultures, with the Afanasievo breaking off from the Yamnaya and migrating eastwards to eventually become the Indo-European Tokharian speakers of western China.[27]

Newcomers from the east? The mysterious Okunev of south Siberia

Figure 2.9 Okunev stone heads in the Abakan (left) and Minusinsk (right) museums

Intrusive into the Afanasievo culture in the Minusinsk region and extending into Tuva and north-eastern Mongolia was the Bronze Age Okunev Culture of the late third and early second millennium BC, characterised by richly decorated anthropomorphic stone sculptures (Figures 2.9 and 6.33–6.35; discussed further in Chapter 6).[28] Although the art displays some of the characteristics of both earlier Afanasievo and later Scythian art, the burials themselves were of Mongoloid newcomers, the first of a people that would eventually displace the Europoids of the region. It has been suggested that their arrival might have displaced one group of the Afanasievo, resulting in them migrating to western China where they became the Tokharians speaking an Indo-European language. It is further suggested that the Okunev 'people' were the ancestors of the Kyrgyz, who emerged in the Minusinsk basin in the sixth century AD before they migrated south to their present homelands, but this is impossible to substantiate.

A country of towns and chariots

A large area in the southern Urals, roughly between Magnitogorsk and Orenburg, has been dubbed the Bronze Age 'Country of Towns' because of the large number of proto-urban, planned, fortified settlements excavated there (Map 2.5).[29] Dating from about 2100 to 1700 BC, it is roughly contemporary with, and connected to, the 'Catacomb' and 'Abashevo' cultures on the steppe to the west of the Urals and the 'Andronovo' culture to the east (discussed below). The two key sites are Arkaim (Figure 2.10) and

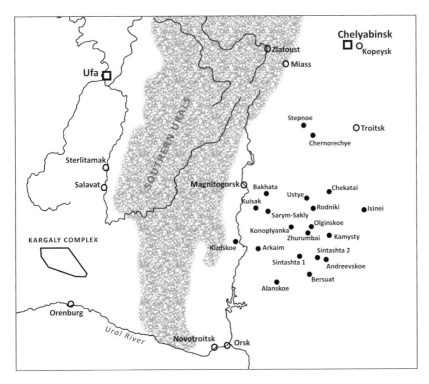

Map 2.5 *The 'Country of Towns' and the Kargaly complex in the southern Urals (adapted from Kohl 2007)*

Figure 2.10 *Model of the Arkaim settlement at the site museum of Arkaim*

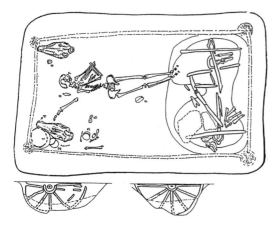

Figure 2.11 *Chariot burial at Krivoe Ozero in the Country of Towns (after Kuzmina 2008: Fig. 11.1)*

Figure 2.12 *Petroglyph of a chariot and animals at Chuya in the Altai*

Sintashta; hence, it is often referred to as the 'Sintashta Culture'. Settlements are typically circular or oval with planned radial streets, usually situated on river bluffs. Construction is mainly of timber and pisé, fortified with timber ramparts. Extensive ancient copper mining has been discovered in the region: mining and metal working is presumed to have been the main industry and the reason why it developed so extensively along urban lines. Horse rearing was important, as were animal sacrifices: some 77 per cent of burials had evidence of animal sacrifice, especially of horses. Burials containing the remains of horse-drawn chariots with spoked wheels are recorded throughout (Figure 2.11), evidence for the earliest recorded chariots in the world. The earlier wagon burials (with solid wooden wheels) of Maikop and Yamnaya suggests that this was the culmination of a long steppe development of wheeled vehicles. Later steppe societies were to develop large covered wagons for transporting entire communities over long distances (Figure 2.7). The homogeneity of both settlements and economy in the Country of Towns suggests a structured society and unified community organised over a wide area. The presence of fortified settlements, chariots and the large amount of weaponry found in the graves suggest that warfare was a significant factor. The image of the chariot became a major image in the rock art across Eurasia (Figure 2.12). Over one hundred petroglyphs depicting horse-drawn chariots have been recorded in the Koksu Valley of Semirechye alone, evidence of the importance of its development and rapid spread.[30] Indeed, the Chinese pictogram for chariot 车 was adapted from the petroglyph images.[31]

The settlements are on average twenty to thirty kilometres apart. A preponderance of cattle bones in the excavated sites suggests that rather than stock-breeding, cattle was given in exchange for metal, as pasture is limited. Only limited evidence exists for cultivation. The huge evidence for metalworking suggests that an overwhelmingly important part of the workforce – perhaps the majority – were specialised metallurgists. Throughout the Bronze Age the Urals was one of the major metallurgical centres in Inner Eurasia, and traces of metalworking have been recorded in almost every house in the Sintashta settlements. Tin was obtained from sources in eastern Kazakhstan.[32] Funerary feasts were important: animal remains in just one burial would have provided an estimated 2,700 kilos of meat, enough to feed three thousand people.[33] An analysis of the funerary rituals shows close similarities to those described in the Rig Veda and Avesta, suggesting that the Country of Towns might have been the original homeland of the Indo-Aryans and perhaps of proto-Zoroastrianism. Ludmila Koryakova and Andrej Epimakhov sum up this important culture:

> The specific attributes of the Sintashta archaeological complex can be characterized by the following: (1) systemic character of site localizations; (2) highly organized settlements with elaborated fortifications and sectional architectural planning; (3) complex burial sites with a high concentration of the remains of sophisticated ritual practice comprised of several variations in the association between human bodies and animals; and (4) the significant presence of metal objects, weaponry, wheeled transport of rather advanced construction for that time, and an eclectic set of ceramics.[34]

Succeeding the Sintashta was the second-millennium Srubnaya Culture,[35] of which the most important region is the vast Kargaly mining complex covering an area of some five hundred square kilometres north of Orenburg (Map 2.5). Extensive mines have been mapped, some extending for several kilometres. The most characteristic site investigated was that of Gorny, which contained hundreds of objects associated with metallurgy. As with the Sintashta, metals were exchanged for cattle and horses: the cattle bones found represent about twenty thousand cattle. The metal that was worked in the Kargaly area was traded over a wide area, with Kargaly metal being found as far west as the Don. Radiocarbon analyses have produced dates of about 3000 BC for the earliest mines, and mining continued into the early first millennium (indeed, the region is still a mining centre today). In assessing the part played by the southern Urals and the development of connections across the steppe, E. E. Kuzmina writes:

> it is clear that, within a short period of time, a new culture spread throughout the Steppe from the Don to Central Kazakhstan, characterized by advanced metallurgy and the emergence of chariot warfare. Its center was situated in the Southern Urals, where fortified fortresses have been discovered. V. V. Otroshchenko believes that the origin of this new culture came out of

the necessity to protect the area of the copper mines, the metallurgists them-selves, and their products. This opinion seems convincing to me.[36]

The beginning of the nomad cultures

Andronovo, Seima-Turbino and forest–steppe symbiosis

The Andronovo Culture[37] might have grown out of, or at least have been related to, the Sintashta and Srubnaya. Andronovo is the name of the village in the Minusinsk Basin near where a burial was first excavated in 1914 that gave its name to the culture (Map 2.4). It spread across a vast area, from the Volga-Urals to the Minusinsk Basin and southwards to the Tienshan and as far as northern Afghanistan,[38] roughly between 1750 and 1400 BC (although the beginnings have more recently been re-dated slightly earlier).[39] The Andronovo was fairly homogeneous, but with numerous variations – subcultures – within it. It is characterised by livestock breed-ing (mainly cattle) with semi-permanent settlements in semi-subterranean houses. There is evidence for extensive metal working, with a high tin content producing harder bronzes: it is estimated that between thirty and fifty thousand tons of copper ore were mined at the Kenkazgan mine in central Kazakhstan alone, for example. Similarities apparent from the funerary remains with later Zoroastrian rituals, namely a special fire and dog ceremonial, suggest an element of proto-Zoroastrianism. A unique discovery of an extraordinary mass sacrifice of at least fifty dogs in about 1750 BC on the middle Volga, where they were skinned, roasted and eaten, has been interpreted as a possible male coming-of-age ceremony relating to such dog rituals.[40] The Andronovo culture is generally agreed to be Indo-Iranian, perhaps proto-Scythian.[41]

There is a later spread of the culture northwards into the steppe-forest belt. Consequent contact with the proto-Ugric Seima-Turbino Cultures of the forest is suggested by the similarities of the later Finno-Ugric deities, Numi-Torum and Mir-Susne-Hum, with the Indo-Aryan Varuna and Mitra cults.[42] Late Andronovo material spread to Semirechye and into western Xinjiang where it has been found in cemeteries in the Pamirs.[43] Kuzmina has associated this with the spread of Indo-European speakers, perhaps forced into continuous migration because of the limited resources of the steppe.[44]

The Andronovo sees the development of sophisticated cattle breed-ing. Both dairy and beef cattle breeds have been recognised in the skeletal remains, as well as three different horse breeds. The limited environmental resources of the steppe meant that herds had to be constantly moved, rotated radially around a settlement (regeneration of the steppe takes about fifty years). Over a period of twenty-five years or so the steppe would become over-grazed, requiring a community to move on. Hence, settlements tended to have a lifespan of just twenty-five to fifty years. It was the actual increase in the development of technology and other refinements generally that led to semi-nomadism. Better management of food production resulted in increasing herds and populations, in turn resulting in increasing pressure on available land, in turn leading to segments of the population having to be on the move. In other words, pastoral nomadism was a result of the expansion of sedentarism, not the other way round. Hence, there is a general pattern in steppe cultures of an initial development of permanent settlement, leading to settlement rotation, leading to pastoralism, then leading to full nomadism by the twelfth to ninth centuries BC.[45]

The Seima-Turbino was a semi-mobile culture of fishing and hunting communities that spread from the Altai through to Finland in the forest-steppe zone. It was also characterised by sophisticated tin-bronze working – indeed, it is in the Seima-Turbino that bronze knives with elaborate animal head pommels first appeared (discussed in Chapter 6). Dates have swung from the late third millennium to the eighth century BC, with recent radiocarbon dates now favouring earlier dates, probably beginning about 1900 BC. The beginnings probably just pre-dated the Andronovo, but existed largely alongside and contemporary with it.[46]

The Oxus Civilisation

The (clumsily named) 'Bactro-Margiana Cultural Complex' or BMAC of the late Bronze Age in Central Asia had connections with the civilisations of Mesopotamia, Elam and the Indus Valley, as well as the newly discovered one of Jiroft in south-eastern Iran. Although, unlike Mesopotamia or the Indus, Bactro-Margiana did not have any writing system that has so far been discovered, it is now recognised as a centre of early civilisation in its own right, on a par with the better-known ones: part of a broader 'Oxus Civilisation'.[47] However, although heavily influenced by the cultures of the steppe, it lay outside the area of the steppe itself, so is mainly outside the present discussion where we are concerned more with the implications that the steppe cultures had for Europe.

The dance of the steppe: movement over vast areas

Despite the presence of permanent settlements comparable to the great sedentary centres of the Near East, movement has nonetheless been a characteristic of the Eurasian steppe as far back as these earliest periods, 'one of the principal means in later prehistory for the establishment of inter-regional connections and the diffusion of technologies', as Philip Kohl emphasises.[48] This movement was for the reasons outlined in Chapter 1: the fragility of life on the steppe could, with few exceptions, only support

limited permanent settlements with small populations. As soon as populations began to increase, they had to keep on the move so as to maximise
the use of available grazing lands.

Archaeologists have recognised evidence for cultural connections and
a complex exchange network for commodities and metal-working technology stretching from the Carpathians and Balkans across the Ukraine
and southern Russia to the Black Sea region and the southern Urals as
early as the Neolithic and Chalcolithic periods in the sixth and fifth millennia. From there metal technology spread to the Yenisei in Siberia and
into Shang northern China, where it influenced the emergence of early
Chinese bronze working.[49] This at least represents some form of west–east
movement, specifically of metallurgy. A north-eastwards movement of
metalworking technology from the Pontic Steppes to the Urals is discern-
ible in the fifth–fourth millennia BC,[50] and the Seima-Turbino Culture
represents an east–west movement, from the Altai to Europe in the Bronze
Age. At that time the whole area was sparsely populated with vast areas
that were essentially empty, hence a natural region for migration. The
diffusion of wheeled vehicle technology across Europe, the Eurasian steppe
and the Near East in the Early Bronze period is further evidence of early
movement in the area.[51]

The Bronze Age of the steppe has been characterised as a 'world system'.[52]
While we can recognise its interconnections, such a claim is perhaps an
overstatement. It was characterised by permanent and semi-permanent
settlement, technological activity, increasing social complexity, and some
eastward movement of technology. While the various cultures described
above were distinctive, continuous threads throughout link them together
in various evolutionary chains: the development and spread of wheeled
vehicles, for example, or the trade in metals or the evolution throughout
the steppe of certain types of bronze tools and weapons. The Sintashta
Culture in the second millennium was probably the high point. A general
climate warming by the second half of the second millennium BC resulted
in an increase in both human and animal population, followed by an
arid phase between about 1100 and 700 BC. This resulted in the drying of
pastures, followed by disintegration and collapse of the sedentary cultures
forcing a western movement of nomads. Koriakova and Epimakhov conclude that 'One can say that this time (1000–800 BC) was probably the
most dramatic moment in the prehistory of Eurasia. It set in motion a
chain of recurrent westward migrations that continually disrupted the cultural sequences in Central Eurasia.'[53] Ultimately, this resulted in a general
disruption of the steppe in the latter half of the first millennium BC when
Scythians, Yuezhi, Xiongnu and others impacted against the more settled
areas on the rim: Europe, Iran, China.

In reconsidering the Seima-Turbino culture, Michael Frachetti sounds
a cautionary note that can apply to the Bronze Age in general. He ques-

tions the idea that the widespread distribution of similar artefacts across the steppe was necessarily due to the migration of specific groups/cultures, such as the Seima-Turbino, Andronovo and so forth. Rather, it was due to a complex interaction and exchange system by different groups:

> The model presented in this study suggests that culture groups of the steppe are creations of archaeologists, and although these are useful as heuristic guides for classifying data, they can obscure the flexible continuities of pastoralist landscapes through time ... Cultural identity was not necessarily imported through the acculturated pockets of long-distance immigrants but was transferred through the networks of interaction shaped by strategic variations.[54]

David Anthony, however, writes that, by the late Bronze Age,

> between about 1900 and 1800 BCE, for the first time in history a chain of broadly similar cultures extended from the edges of China to the frontiers of Europe. Innovations and raw materials began to move across the continent. The steppe world was not just a conduit, it also became an innovating center, particularly in bronze metallurgy and chariot warfare. The chariot driving Shang kings of China and the Mycenaean princes of Greece, contemporaries at opposite ends of the ancient world at about 1500 BCE, shared a common technological debt to the LBA [Late Bronze Age] herders of the Eurasian steppes.[55]

As the two opinions above show, the picture of the development of the steppe and its cultures is constantly changing as new discoveries occur, new ideas formulate and new controversies arise. Nowhere is this more so than in the origin and spread of the Indo-European languages.

CHAPTER 3

INDO-EUROPE
Prehistory and Language

If there was an Indo-European language, it follows there was a people who spoke it: not a people in the sense of a nation, for they may never have formed a political unity; and not a people in any racial sense, for they may have been as genetically mixed as any modern population defined by language. If our language is a descendant of theirs, that does not make them 'our ancestors', any more than the ancient Romans are the ancestors of the French, the Romanians, and the Brazilians. The Indo-Europeans were a people in the sense of a linguistic community.
– M. L. West[1]

Nearly all European languages belong to a single linguistic group: Indo-European. The exceptions are Finnish, Saami and Estonian as well as (more distantly), Hungarian (Finno-Altaic-Ugrian), Turkish (Altaic),* Maltese (Semitic, albeit with considerable Italian, Spanish and English borrowing) and Basque (no known language group). With the exception of Basque, all these non-Indo-European languages are incomers. But so too are the Indo-European languages themselves. This has so completely eradicated all traces of pre-Indo-European languages in Europe with a near-linguicidal thoroughness apart from the occasional geographical name that glimmers through that Indo-European has become 'us' as Europeans. This, of course, took an extreme form with the Nazis, but even rationally the search for Indo-European roots – linguistic and geographical – has occupied more academic energies than similar questions of the common origin of other language groups.[†]

That the spread of a language goes hand in hand with the spread of a people – indeed, the one is the result of the other – is so well attested by history that it hardly needs reiterating: the spread of Spanish into Central

---

* Not conventionally viewed as a 'European' language. But apart from the Turkish province of Thrace, there is the large number of Turkish speakers – mainly Tatars – in Russia and Ukraine, now the second-largest language in Russia after Russian itself.
† Lamberg-Karlovsky (2002: 75), in comparing Indo-European studies to Altaic or Dravidian studies, writes that 'The fact that these language families are of far less interest to the archaeologist may have a great deal to do with the fact that it is primarily speakers of Indo-European in search of their own roots who have addressed this problem'.

and South America by the conquistadores and settlers is an obvious example. Migration, therefore, can explain the spread of a new language. But mass movement of peoples, and with them their language, was rarer than is often thought. The spread of English to Australia by English-speaking settlers with a coast-to-coast thoroughness, for example, is the exception rather than the rule: it is usually comparatively small elites who bring a language, eventually to transform the language of a much more populous subject people, that is the norm. The linguistic transformation of Anatolia by incoming Turk elites is a good example, or the Indo-European speakers of Pannonia by the incoming Uralic-speaking Magyars. But even such an elite/subject population model can work in reverse: the linguistic transformation by the subject Slavs of their incoming Bulgar Turk overlords, for example, or a similar 'Slavicisation' of the incoming Germanic-speaking Vikings into medieval Rus, or the equally Germanic Norman invaders in Normandy transformed into French speakers (just as the originally Germanic Franks became Romance speakers). Roman elites left their linguistic trace in western Europe as the Romance languages – but hardly a trace of Latin (or Greek, the language of the Eastern Roman Empire) survives in the Near Eastern provinces of the Empire.

Might such completely opposite linguistic transformations – elite to subject versus subject to elite – find an explanation in the influence of women? Could it be that migrating elites who linguistically transformed their subjects, such as Turk speakers in Anatolia or Hungarian in Pannonia, brought their womenfolk with them, so that their descendants continued speaking their (quite literal) mother tongue? And conversely, could it be that those elites who adopted the subject peoples' language, such as the Bulgars in Bulgaria or the Vikings in Rus, had not brought their womenfolk with them so were forced to marry locally, hence their descendants speaking *their* mother tongue? Such issues are broader than can be answered here and probably impossible to substantiate, but in any study of language one must never underestimate the power of the mother tongue (and even the reconstructed proto-Indo-European language is referred to by philologists as a 'mother tongue').

The spread of peoples and languages, therefore, is an immensely complex process, and the original location of a language – a 'homeland' – and its association with a 'people' equally complex, with no glib explanations.

Philosopher's stone or can of worms: the search for the Indo-Europeans

For many years, both the 'Holy Grail' and the massive pitfall of steppe prehistory has been the search for an Indo-European homeland. This has been described as 'an intellectual minefield strewn with the corpses of learned reputations, or worse, the still twitching maimed' by Stuart Piggott, while David Anthony has written: 'fierce disagreements have continued about almost every aspects of Indo-European Studies'.[2] It has long been recognised that most of the world's languages can be grouped together into broad interconnected 'families': Semitic, Indo-European, Ural-Altaic, Sino-Tibetan, Polynesian, Bantu and others. At a lecture in 1786 to the Asiatic Society of Bengal, the philologist Sir William Jones – at that time Chief Justice of India – was the first to articulate the theory that the ancient languages of India and Europe were not only connected but must have had a common origin. The implications are enormous: it suggests that peoples as diverse and widely separated as Bengalis at one end of the old world and Irish at the other were, at some point in their ancestry, linguistically a single people. And not just linguistic; poetic connections too have been recognised. Even the names of 'Ireland/Eire' and 'Iran' go back to the same root: Vedic Sanscrit *Aryaman*, Avestan Persian *Airyaman*, Gaulish *Ariomanus* and Irish *Eremón* (the legendary first king of Ireland – from Irish *aire* meaning 'noble chief') from the proto-Indo-European *Aryo-men*; the Sanscrit and Avestan *aryá* means 'trusty, honourable, worth' – hence 'Aryan', all variants probably deriving from the proto-Indo-European reconstructed word *$h_4erós$ meaning 'tribe' (an asterisk in front of a word is a convention that denotes a reconstructed form). The same root *Arya* has been related to the *Ala* or *Ali* prefix in the Alazones, a western Scythian tribe,[3] as well as the city of Herat, Greek Areia and ancient Persian Haraiva, and its river, Hari, in western Afghanistan. The search for that common origin – both the place and the time – has absorbed the attentions of many philologists and archaeologists ever since.[4]

In modern times, as well as the term 'Aryan' having been perverted by the Nazis (not to mention by Aryan supremacists in both the USA and Russia),[5] the Shah of Iran took the title *Aryamehr*, 'Light of the Aryans', and the national airline of Afghanistan is 'Aryana'. The name 'Erin' and variant 'Arian' is a popular forename for both sexes, usually (but not always) of Irish connection, and 'Aryana' is a popular girl's name internationally.[*]

On the one hand it argues against the concept of Europe and Asia as separate cultural – or at least linguistic – entities. This is implied in the term that was coined for this common group of languages: 'Indo-European'. On the other, it opened up another can of worms – who was there first, was it 'us' or 'them'? – and behind the search one catches the occasional glimpse of that age-old struggle for cultural and racial – or at least linguistic – supremacy. Hence, the Indo-European

---

[*] Although its apparent variant, Arianna, is not connected, but is a Spanish form of the Greek Ariadne.

question has absorbed huge amounts of academic energies, debate and controversy. The question is, therefore, a heavily loaded one, subject on the one hand to some of the most magnificent scholarly detective work of the past century or so, and on the other to extravagant claims, political jockeying and myth-making.

For example, it has been claimed that 'the question of where the Indo-European languages originate is an important question, as it deals with the place of origin of an essential part of *us*' [emphasis added].[6] But such a claim does not include the millions of African Americans, Latin Americans or Africans who for the past hundred years or more have been speakers of an Indo-European language as a first language – English, Spanish, French, Dutch – but are not perceived as 'us'. There is a theoretical proto-Indo-European *language*, but there are no proto-*Indo-Europeans*. Furthermore, almost no present speakers of an Indo-European language apart from Russians would feel 'at home' or even the remotest affinity with the postulated homeland. The above example is perhaps an unfair one, and the author quoted almost certainly by no means implies such exclusivity or inclusivity, and 'homeland' is a solely theoretical construct, but it does demonstrate the pitfalls trodden by even the most authoritative investigators.

Sir William Jones was not the first to observe such connections. As far back as the 1580s a Florentine merchant, Filippo Sassetti, voiced similar observations when resident in Goa, and there were others who also anticipated Jones.[7] Doubtless the connections were recognised even in ancient times. It was claimed, for example, that the first-century AD Anatolian philosopher Apollonius of Tyana, who supposedly travelled to India, knew Indian languages and Persian as well as Greek; this is suggestive of some awareness of linguistic connections. Even Herodotus speculated on common linguistic origins, admittedly between Greek and Egyptian, which in itself has spawned a huge amount of modern wild goose chasing.[8] Linguistic connections between ancient Greek and Old Persian would doubtless not have been lost on diplomatic entourages of both sides in the Graeco-Persian wars as they struggled to interpret the subtleties of each others' negotiations.

Histories in prehistory

The whole question of Indo-European origins is too large a subject to examine in detail here. Very broadly, it concerns two main methods of approach, philology and archaeology, with much overlap (and argument) between the two. Philologists have started with known Indo-European languages and, by tracing their development in reverse, as it were, have partially reconstructed a theoretical proto-Indo-European language: a 'mother language' or 'proto-Indo-European' that is at the root of all.* The routes in arriving at the roots are not always direct, but make considerable use of cognates.[9] A good example is the Indo-European root word for 'oak', *doru-*. This might have no resemblance to the Latin for oak, *quercus*, but is cognate with the Latin *durum* meaning 'hard' and is used now to describe varieties of hard wheat such as *durum triticum* used for making pasta. It resurfaces as the cognate English word 'durable', but also completes the circle with English 'tree', the Persian *darakht* meaning 'tree' and the modern Gaelic *darach* meaning 'oak'. Archaeologists, on the other hand, have used as their starting point ancient cultures that are known from their written records to have spoken an Indo-European language (the ancient Hittite, Avestan Persian and Vedic Indian cultures, for example) and then, by tracing their material culture backwards, have arrived at an older material culture from which the later ones might have evolved. The conclusions do not always agree, and the Indo-European 'homeland' has bounced around from the Baltic, central Europe and the southern Russian steppes to Anatolia, Central Asia, western Siberia and northern India as a result (Map 3.1).[10]

Since Jones' observations, philologists have by and large reconstructed the connections between the various languages, with fairly convincing 'family trees' that demonstrate the roots and divergences. Within the broad Indo-European group various sub-groups have been identified: Celtic, Germanic, Slavic, Iranian, Indo-Aryan, and so forth. Very broadly, they have been separated into two major groups which philologists have termed *centum* and *satem*, based upon the root word for 'hundred' common to the two groups: English 'century', for example, in the one group, modern Persian *sad*, 'hundred', in the other. The two groups very loosely, although not consistently, follow a west–east pattern. The *centum* group includes most western Indo-European languages, such as the Romantic, Germanic and Celtic languages, but also an ancient eastern anomaly, Tokharian. The *satem* group is found mostly further east and includes the Anatolian, Indo-Aryan, Iranian and Armenian languages, but also Albanian, Slavic and Baltic.

The earliest Indo-European written language was Hittite, which emerged in early second millennium BC Anatolia, and belongs to the *satem* group. Various elements of Hittite material culture – pottery styles, architectural techniques, some burial rites, for example – are convincingly traced back in archaeology to roots in Anatolian prehistory. This has led

---

* It must be emphasised that 'proto-Indo-European' is no more than a theoretical tool that is used to explain linguistic connections, and cannot be regarded as an extinct language in the same way that, say, Sumerian or Hittite are, even though some reconstructions (Anthony 2007: 14, 31) have been confirmed by later discoveries of ancient inscriptions of extinct languages.

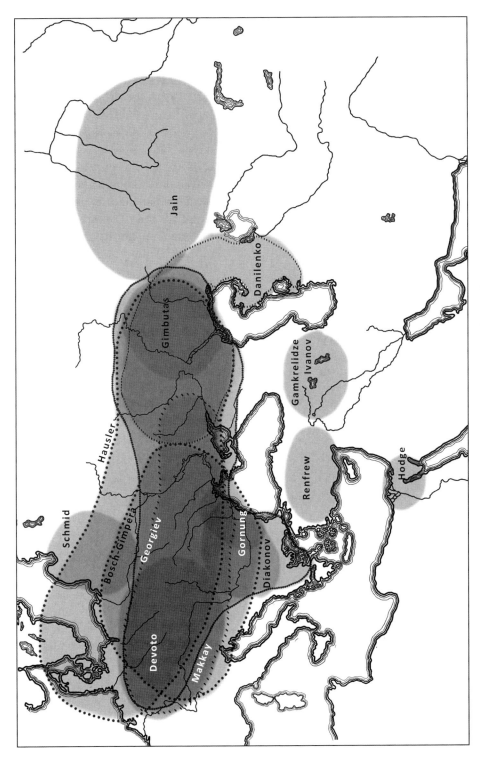

Map 3.1 *The Indo-European homeland problem according to different authorities (after Mallory 1989)*

some archaeologists to propose that the origin of the Indo-European languages was in the Neolithic cultures of Anatolia, notably Çatal Höyük and related sites, and that the languages followed the spread of related material cultures out of Anatolia. The prehistorian Colin Renfrew has led the way in this argument, and another archaeologist, Barry Cunliffe, has traced a continuous cultural dissemination throughout Europe from Anatolia as a result.[11]

Renfrew's Anatolian thesis has been supported by using 'language-tree divergence' software.[12] However, the theory has not gained general acceptance among philologists, whose arguments, based on linguistic reconstructions, usually reach quite different conclusions (although the spread of agricultural technology out of Anatolia and into Europe remains convincing). Common words in the component Indo-European languages have been traced back to reconstruct a proto-Indo-European 'world picture'. This has enabled both a time and a place to be broadly proposed. To give some very general examples, most Indo-European languages contain common root words for agriculture, which places the time for the spread to *after* the domestication of plants and animals, attested archaeologically to be before about 7500 BC in most parts of the old world. In particular words relating to the domestication of sheep such as 'wool', 'felt' and (cognate with 'felt') 'beat', 'roll' and 'press' are indicative, for although sheep were domesticated for their meat, it was not until after 4000 BC that they were domesticated for their wool.[13] Words relating to iron-working, however, have been demonstrated to be non-Indo-European: loan words, hence demonstrating that the Indo-European dispersion took place *before* the Iron Age in the first millennium BC. Further study of loan words indicates when the proto-Indo-Europeans came into contact with other language groups – Altaic (in Siberia), Migrelo-Kartvelian (in the Caucasus), or Semitic (in the Near East), for example – and so roughly maps the trajectory. In particular, loan words in proto-Indo-European from the Finno-Ugric group from the northern forest belt reinforce a northern origin. Without going into the details, the date for the dispersal of the proto-Indo-Europeans has in this way been placed linguistically to about 4500 to 2500 BC, with most opinion favouring the earlier dates.[14]

Movement can also be traced by detecting a substratum of an earlier language, usually surviving in names of geographical features such as rivers and mountains, which tend to remain when different peoples – and their languages – arrive. To take a comparatively recent example that can be checked by written records, large parts of southern Russia and Ukraine, now predominantly Russian- and Ukrainian-speaking, preserve Turkish geographical names indicating a previous population speaking a Turk-related language: the River (and Crimean War battlefield) Alma, for example, or Mount Demerdzhi National Park, both in Crimea (the former the Turkish for 'apple', the latter the Turkish for 'iron-worker').* Or the survival of names such as St Louis and New Orleans in parts of otherwise English-speaking North America suggesting an earlier French occupation, while names such as Nantucket or Massachusetts indicate an even earlier native American population. Place-names scattered right across Europe and into Anatolia cognate with 'Celt' indicate a far wider spread of Celtic peoples in antiquity than their present location suggests. 'Celt' is cognate with 'Gaul' and 'Gallic', hence Gaul itself (all of ancient France, as well as 'Cisalpine Gaul' in northern Italy), but also 'Galatia' in Anatolia, two 'Galicias' in Ukraine and Portugal, and 'Gaelic' in Scotland. In the often strange way that consonants shift, 'g' and 'w' can interchange (as 'William' and 'Guillaume' or 'war' and 'guerre' do between English and French). Hence, 'Wallachia', 'Wales' and 'Walloon'. Loan words can also indicate the trajectory: for example, words of Polynesian origin in English such as 'hula', 'taboo', 'ukulele' or (most recently) 'wiki', suggest that English speakers once came into contact with the South Seas. Of course, we know all of these recent examples simply from well-documented history without the need for complex linguistic juggling. But it does demonstrate how 'history' can be reconstructed simply from linguistics for times and places where no historical sources exist and be projected back into prehistory.

So much for the approximate date and trajectory. The homeland calls for even more delicate linguistic footwork, much of it based upon the evidence of flora and fauna. Linguistic reconstructions have shown, for example, a common vocabulary deriving from the words for beech, oak, fir and other trees; other words have been traced back to common roots relating to wolf, bear, otter, beaver, hare and – interestingly – salmon (or perhaps trout), cold water fish (and correspondingly, the word for tuna, a warm water fish, has been demonstrated to be borrowed into Indo-European languages). Absent have been common Indo-European words for city, olive, wine, ass or oil. For the sake of brevity a hugely complicated[†] – and still controversial – argument is vastly over-simplified here and much other evidence (the evidence of the wheel, for example) omitted,[15] but such linguistic reconstructions indicate a northern temperate origin, probably in the steppe rather than the forest belt (but this is disputed). The main point is that it argues against any Mediterranean or Near Eastern origin, otherwise so often the answer to many 'origin' questions. The general consensus has located this Indo-European 'homeland' very broadly in the region west of the Urals in Russia. This region corresponds in the archaeological record with the Bronze Age Yamnaya culture west of

---

* The existence, on the other hand, of Greek place names, such as Sevastopol or Simferopol or Odessa, does not indicate former Greek populations, even though they are archaeologically attested; these are modern revivals, and are discussed further in Chapter 13.
† But huge fun.

the Urals, roughly contemporary with and connected to the Afanasievo of the third–early second millennia BC. The Afanasievo has been suggested to be the origin of the spread of Indo-European language into China, the Tokharians (discussed below). The Yamnaya in turn has been associated with the contemporary but slightly later 'Corded Ware' pottery culture in northern Europe, suggesting a spread from one to the other (Map 2.3). The Yamnaya Culture therefore has been identified with the much sought-after Indo-European 'homeland', and recent DNA evidence has confirmed a prehistoric 'massive migration' into western Europe:[16] an 'out of Yamnaya' scenario that might be compared to the original 'out of Africa' scenario for the spread of Homo Sapiens. The 'Corded Ware people' are cited as evidence for the bringers of new languages.

But some studies of the relationship of Corded Ware with indigenous pottery styles question the 'massive migration' theory and suggest a more complex scenario, where the language 'was not enforced through invasion or mass migrations but through well-established routes of communication that facilitated the movement of people', and that 'we need not expect the arrival of large numbers of people to explain the introduction of Proto-Indo-European'.[17] Even the Yamnaya is conceded by the original investigators to be only the 'best known proxy', and the 'exact source could have been another, yet unsampled, group of people'.[18] DNA sampling is still in its infancy, and Patrick Geary cautioned against over-dependence on DNA, emphasising that it is 'no silver bullet' and 'requires critical analysis and interpretation as well as improved methodologies no less than any other approach to the past'. In particular, glib explanations as to questions of historical identities can be 'misguided and even dangerous'.[19] Probably the best one can say is that prehistoric Europe was 'multi-layered' including indigenous and both Near Eastern and steppe elements.[20]

The 'Country of Towns' east of the Urals discussed in Chapter 2 (Map 2.5) was a development of the Yamnaya-Afanasievo culture as we have noted. This, as well as similarities with ancient Iranian and Indian cultures, has led to the suggestion that the area was the homeland of the Indo-Aryan language group, one of the first languages to break away from the proto-Indo-European. This in turn has led to the two key sites there, Sintashta and Arkaim, being consciously promoted as an 'Aryan homeland' and has turned the area into a rather dubious pilgrimage centre for new-age Aryan supremacists.[21] It has been suggested that the development of the spoked wheel chariot, of which the earliest examples have been found at Sintashta (Figure 2.12), together with the domestication of the horse on the Eurasian steppe might have been responsible for the spread of Indo-European 'peoples' over such a wide area in antiquity. The suggestion remains controversial. However, that the 'Sintashta people' were the original Indo-Aryans can be postulated but is no more proven than that the 'Yamnaya-Afanasievo people' were the original proto-Indo-Europeans:

without written records we can never know what language a people *spoke*, however convincing the hypotheses. Perhaps it is best to locate the original homeland simply in 'Eurostan', as M. L. West tactfully wrote.[22]

The devil in the divine: is there a common Indo-European identity?

Can one speak of an Indo-European common heritage, other than linguistic? There are common threads that run through the poetry, world view, mythology and religion of most Indo-European-speaking peoples. Common poetic elements have been recognised in 'Hittite, Luwian, Lycian, Lydian, Sidetic, Phrygian, Gaulish, Celtiberian, Welsh and Tokharian' verse, for example, and many other examples in poetry and poesy in the other Indo-European languages have been analysed as well.[23] Common religious elements have been recognised in Old Slavic, Russian, Vedic, Mitanni and Iranian religions.[24] There is a common wolfish* and werewolf association in Indo-European foundation myths, from Hittite references and burial rites to the foundation of Rome and ancient Irish and Icelandic mythologies, probably originating in Avestan sources.[25] One recalls too the story of Mowgli in Rudyard Kipling.

There are probably more common links through mythology and religion. Gods have winged footwear in Hittite, Greek (Hermes) and Nordic (Loki) mythologies, for example, and do not eat food in Greek, Nordic and Indian myths. Divine twins occur as the Vedic Asvíns, the Greek Dioskouroi, Latin Castor and Pollux, possibly Anglo-Saxon Hengist and Horsa, and variant forms in Celtic and Baltic myth.[26] Vedic myth is full of bovine imagery, also found in Greek myth, such as the legend of Zeus and Europa or the legend of Io changed into a cow by Hera. It also occurs in Zoroastrian, Latvian and Russian myth. Such imagery probably has its origin in the importance of cattle to the livelihood of the early Indo-European pastoralists. In Old German mythology all mankind is descended from Mannus (hence our word 'man'), the son of Tuisto (cognate with 'twin') in turn born of the earth. Similarly Manu is the mythical ancestor in Sanscrit, from the root *mánu*, again meaning 'man'. There is a common belief, found throughout European mythology as well as in Bronze Age Anatolia, that all births were attended by a supernatural female who predetermined the life of the child (one recalls the wicked fairy at Princess Aurora's birth in the Sleeping Beauty legend). The imagery of spinning or weaving (weaving one's fate) is a common one in such legends. At death, Greek, Indian and Zoroastrian beliefs speak of crossing water,

---

* Note, however, that similar wolfish origin legends also occur in Altaic peoples, most particularly the Turks, discussed in Chapter 8.

all of which have a dog guarding the entry into the after-world, as does Nordic mythology as well. The discovery of the late Bronze Age mass dog sacrifice mentioned in the previous chapter might also relate to such dog symbolism.[27] The Vedic Sanskrit *vánasah* (from the proto-Indo-European *vénos*) meaning 'loveliness' finds its way into Latin as Venus. The Vedic god *priyā Diváh* (the proto-Indo-European *priyā* meaning 'dear', 'loved', or 'own'), the 'beloved daughter of Dyaus' the sky god (see below), surfaces as the Norse goddess Frigg/Freya (hence our Friday) and Old Czech Prije. The Vedic Indian pastoral god Pūsan was associated with goats, has a bushy beard and keen sight, roams the countryside, protects cattle and is a guardian of the roads; the Greek god Pan has goat's legs, a bushy beard and keen sight, roams the mountainsides, views the flocks and is found on rocky tracks. Pūsan/Pan is probably cognate with the proto-Indo-European word 'to guard, watch over'. The English fairy is the Persian *pari*, Armenian *parik*, all the same supernatural being.[28]

More ubiquitous – unsurprisingly – is the king of the gods himself and cognates. This goes back to the proto-Indo-European root *diw/dyu*, meaning 'bright sky' or 'light of day' or 'celestial one'. 'From this come Vedic *devá-*, Avestan *daēva-*, Old Phrygian *devos*, Oscan *deívā*, Messapic *deiva*, *dīva* 'goddess', Venetic *deivos* 'gods', Latin *deus*, proto-Germanic *tīwaz*, Old Irish *día*, Old Church Slavonic *Diēvas*, Latvian *Dievs*.'[29] And of course Greek *theos* and Zeus, the equivalent of the Vedic Dyáus (compare Hittite *sius*). In Greek mythology Zeus was the supreme god, unlike the cognate Vedic Dyáus, who was just a celestial or sky god, but from the Greek *theos/zeos* we get a whole range of related English words such as theocracy, theology, theophoric, theosophy, and so forth.[30] The root *dāu* has also been recognised as an Indo-European loan word in Assyrian inscriptions referring to the toponym *Kindāu*, suggested as a reference to one of the gods in the Median pantheon.[31] Even the Roman equivalent of Greek Zeus, Jupiter, which at first sight appears unconnected, is a Latinisation of *dyeu-pater*. There is an even wider range of vocabulary derived from the Latin *deus*, such as deify, deity, divine, divinity (compare Old Persian *daeva*), but also devil, diabolic and so forth, as well as *Tues*day and German *teufel*. The related proto-Indo-European word is *di/dei* meaning 'to give off light', hence our English word 'day'.[32]

Of course, winged gods, divine twins and supernatural midwives might well occur in Mayan, Polynesian and Bantu mythologies too, and it is as well to guard against seizing upon connections where none might exist. But the linguistic connections at least are sound, and some underlying characteristics must surely have followed. J. P. Mallory finishes his seminal work on Indo-European linguistics and origins with:

> the most secure legacy of the Indo-Europeans is surely to be found in the language spoken by over two billion people in the world. It is irrelevant

whether we regard ourselves as Europeans, Asians, Africans, or Americans, we cannot escape this legacy if we speak an Indo-European language. We cannot ask questions of where, when, who or how, or answer them without our most basic pronouns, we cannot count, refer to the basic parts of our bodies, describe our environment, the heavens, basic animals or relatives, or express our most fundamental actions, without making frequent recourse to an inherited system of speech that our linguistic ancestors shared 6,000 years ago.[33]

There are few neat fits, and it is important to emphasise that we are dealing above all with an *absence* of most of the evidence, not a presence, and new discoveries throw up fresh trails – and further anomalies. 'In short, there is no easy way to locating the Indo-European homeland; there is no certain solution' as the authors of one of the latest major studies of the problems conclude.[34] The following are two examples of the pitfalls into which the study of Indo-European archaeology can stumble.

The great Tokharian trek

The first concerns one such anomaly that has caused particular obfuscation. Archaeologists excavating in the oases of Turfan and Kucha in northern Xinjiang in China at the beginning of the twentieth century discovered manuscripts dating between the sixth and eighth centuries AD written in an extinct language (Figure 3.1). The language was named 'Tokharian' by modern philologists after an ancient Greek account of a tribe, the Tokharoi, who entered northern Afghanistan in about the first century BC (although there is little evidence that this tribe necessarily spoke the language now attributed to them). The name also occurs in some of the Central Asian texts, confirming the Tokharians as ancient inhabitants of Xinjiang. The name survives as the modern province of 'Takhār' in north-eastern Afghanistan, itself deriving from the 'Takhāristān' of the medieval Arab geographers, corresponding roughly to ancient Bactria.

The language, written in a variation of the Aramaic script, was deciphered. The manuscripts were found to consist mainly of Buddhist texts translated from the Sanskrit, as well as treatises on magic, medicine, and even occasional business transactions. It was furthermore found to be an Indo-European language. This in itself occasioned no surprises, as other languages in the east belong to the same group, such as Scythian or Persian or Sanskrit. But closer analysis revealed a more astonishing element. Tokharian was not, after all, a satem language related to Persian or Sanskrit or the other Indo-Iranian languages of the east as one would expect, but was a centum language related to the ancient European languages, and it was claimed by some that Tokharian 'is closely related to the ancient forms of Celtic'.[35] This view is now, of course, modified, but the resemblances are nonetheless astounding.

Figure 3.1 *The site of Subashi in the Kucha Oasis in Xinjiang, where documents of Tokharian A were discovered*

Chinese sources suggest that the Tokharians – they refer to them as the Yuezhi, although the identification is not conclusive – were originally from Gansu to the east of Dunhuang, and that they migrated to Xinjiang sometime after about 800 BC. But the centum – 'Celtic?' – element in their language gave rise to a theory that there must have been a migration across some three thousand miles of the Eurasian steppe to the western borders of China by an early Indo-European tribe – quite separate and distinct from those tribes who eventually evolved into the Iranians and Indians – from eastern Europe sometime after 1400 BC, from where they further migrated to Xinjiang. The wanderings of the Tokharians/Yuezhi did not stop in Xinjiang, for after the first century BC they migrated further west in response to pressure from Xiongnu/Hun movement further east and entered Afghanistan. There, in the first few centuries AD, a Tokharian elite founded the Kushan Empire of Afghanistan and India, one of the great empires of antiquity (hence the survival of their name Takhār in the area of Afghanistan they first entered). It is suggested that the name 'Kushan' derives from the *Guishuang*, the name in the Chinese sources of one of the five tribes of the Yuezhi. As if this is not confusing enough, a further obfuscation occurs with the written language of the Kushan rulers. This was not Tokharian but Bactrian, an ancient Iranian satem language related to Sogdian and Parthian, written at first in the Greek script and then later in Kharoshthi, an Indian script (albeit deriving from the Aramaic script).

No element of Tokharian has been detected in the Bactrian inscriptions and the language of the Kushan rulers remains unknown.[36]

A more extreme view, proposed by W. B. Henning in 1968, is that the Yuezhi of China were originally the Guti – identified as Indo-European on no evidence – recorded in Mesopotamian texts invading Mesopotamia in about 2200 BC from the north-east, bringing about the end of the Akkadian Empire. Then, having done so, they trekked east to China – then presumably turning around and trekking west again to found the Kushan Empire. The theory is dismissed by C. C. Lamberg-Karlovsky, who rightly points out that 'there is not a shred of archaeological evidence for a migration from Mesopotamia to China, nor is there a parallel in the realm of the Yuë-chih for a Mesopotamian-Gutian material culture'.[37]

Theories relating to these Indo-European-speaking groups in western China have been given a considerable shake-up following studies of the much-publicised mummies of Xinjiang.[38] These mummies bear a physiological resemblance to northern European physical types, leading to some exaggerated claims that 'the Europid [*sic*] features and strapping physiques . . . clearly testify to their Western origins'.[39] There is even the astonishing suggestion that the mummies represent 'Celts' from the Cucuteni-Tripolye culture in Moldova and Ukraine (where there is no evidence that they were Celts) who trekked to China via the Luristan Bronzes and Bactria (where they discovered orgies).[40] Analyses of the fabrics associated with them have shown similarities with prehistoric groups in northern Europe, such as the Hallstatt Culture of Switzerland, associated with the early Celts. At first sight this might appear to fit neatly with the theories of hypothetical European trekkers – the 'proto-Tokharians' – of 1400 BC or thereabouts. But it raises almost as many questions as it answers. To begin with, radiocarbon dates suggest that some at least of the mummies might date back to 2500 or even 3000 BC, far earlier than the supposed great trek and earlier than the emergence of the Indo-European language of Tokharian. The dates vary enormously, but excavations between 2002 and 2005 by Chinese archaeologists identified a 'Xiaohe Culture' dating from about 2500 to 1700 BC where most of the mummies were found (and dated). The culture shows some similarities with the Bronze Age cultures of south Siberia, from where people might have migrated, and this is supported by DNA.[41] In this context it crucial to emphasise that the mummies are solely accidental, mummification as the result of desiccation in the dry – and often saline – conditions of Xinjiang, and not a process enacted by a specific culture (unlike mummies in the Egyptian sense, a deliberate act by a unique culture to preserve the corpse). It must also be remembered that textile comparisons were only be made with Europe because of the abundance of evidence and textile studies there; similar comparisons with the textiles of ancient China or Vietnam, for example, where we have less evidence (at least available to Western scholarship), might show up as many (or less or more) similarities.

A suggestion of Indo-Iranian language groups in the steppe north of China led to an assumption that 'European'-looking faces on some of the art, as well as the mummies, must be Indo-European speakers.[42] As recently as 2019 the mummies are simply 'presumed' to be Indo-European speakers, a result of an equally assumed (and equally fallacious) 'Silk Road of the Bronze Age'.[43] The appearances can also be exaggerated: such physical types also exist in the native populations of Siberia. To some extent the evidence of the mummies begs the question of the origin of the 'European' physical type, which might well have been Siberia rather than Europe: the DNA of the Afanasievo Culture in the Minusinsk Basin indicates the Europoid type in Siberia as far back as the fourth millennium BC, and recent DNA analyses of the mummies show mixed physical make-up, both Europoid and Asian, the mix probably originating in south Siberia.[44] Most of all, it is a grave mistake to equate language with physical types. There is not a scrap of evidence that the mummies spoke a European language, their 'European' appearance and the occurrence of Tokharian (not found with the mummies) notwithstanding. All one can say for certain is that the mummies are very ancient, that they for all intents and purposes appear to be indigenous, and that there is at present no firm evidence that the Tokharians came from anywhere beyond Gansu.

Westward-ho: hard-wired to win

Another example of how culturally loaded this Holy Grail can become occurs in a work that follows Renfrew's view of the origins of the Indo-European languages in Anatolia.[45] In a search for the origins of a distinct 'European' identity, it begins with the premise that 'Europe came to dominate the world during the course of the second millennium AD' and so poses the question 'Why was it, then, that Europe above all other regions managed to achieve such dominance?' In searching for an answer the author suggests, 'What made Europe so influential was the restlessness of its people: it was almost as though they were hard-wired to be mobile', and further: 'What we can reasonably say of Old Europe is that people were always on the move.'[46] Such mobility – if it existed – in Europe between 6000 and 5000 BC is offered as an explanation for why Europe came to rule the world in the second millennium AD, something inconceivable seven thousand years later, let alone that it ignores the fact that many other peoples – steppe nomads, Arabs, many others – were at least as (and usually more) mobile than Old Europeans. The author then argues that the Indo-European peoples were responsible for a perceived 'full Neolithic package'[47] crossing Europe at 'lightning speed' between 7000 and 5000 BC ('lightning'?), after 'The movement began with . . . boatloads of farmers from Asia Minor' who 'fanned out westwards'[48] across Europe, 'hard-wired to be mobile', as if it were some preconceived precision military operation arranged by the Neolithic High Command directing field operations from the headquarters in Çatal Höyük, 'almost as if there were a competition to move on and see what lay beyond . . . driven by a pioneering ethic embedded in the psyche'.[49] Already by the time it had reached Greece this originally Near Eastern Neolithic culture is referred to as 'now distinctly European' in character because of its 'pioneering ethic embedded in the psyche . . . that would have become socially embedded', 'a competition to move on and see what lay beyond':[50]

> And so . . . it can be fairly said . . . the very foundations of European society were established. . . . there was also an inbuilt ethic of pioneering that drove the early farmers inexorably forwards . . . an innate desire to explore the unknown, drawn on westwards by a curiosity to discover the wonder of the setting sun . . . we are dealing with real people with aspirations and hopes . . . it has become clear that many of the significant advances seen in Europe resulted from indigenous energies and inventiveness.[51]

In linking the Neolithic culture with the Indo-European language group – as well as a whole package of emotive attributes – the argument is essentially circular: the Neolithic was the bringer of Indo-European languages into Europe; the Indo-European languages originated in the Neolithic of Anatolia; therefore the Indo-Europeans brought the Neolithic Revolution. It is also inherently contradictory: on the one hand the inventiveness came from the Near East, on the other hand it was due to indigenous superior 'European' energies and inventiveness. One almost senses a post-Maastricht European Union spirit being transposed onto prehistory when the author further writes that 'There is a feeling of energy, of vigour and of a real enthusiasm for innovation and change [in the Europe of the third and second millennia BC]. It is almost as if . . . communities embrace a pan-European spirit . . . for the excitement of the new.'[52] In the author's subsequent book on Eurasia, it is wisely prefaced that 'there will be an absence of any reference to speculations about language'.[53]

Some movement into Europe from Anatolia and the Near East has been confirmed by DNA, but it was hardly a massive migration 'fanning out' to alter subsequent European demography, let alone a key to European superiority. The spread of Neolithic farming technology from Anatolia and the Near East has been confirmed by archaeology: small though such a movement of people might have been, their influence was considerable (albeit not linguistic), and as with the 'out of Yamnaya' thesis the movement out of Anatolia was neither a 'massive migration' nor a 'Neolithic invasion'.[54]

The Anatolian origins of the Indo-European languages have been convincingly refuted by the philologists.[55] However, the theories of the spread of Neolithic technology from Anatolia into Europe remain valid: archaeology has convincingly demonstrated a movement of farming techniques from Anatolia into south-eastern Europe from about 6200 BC, as well as north-eastwards from the Balkans into the Pontic steppe: it was no 'Indo-European' movement (their language is unknown, although there is some slight suggestion it might have been Afro-Asiatic).[56]

* * *

Questions such as who the Tokharians were in particular and who the Indo-Europeans were in general serve to demonstrate just how complex 'our' origins are: European, Asian or in between. They serve also to demonstrate just how complex defining 'us' or any other people can be: the language we speak, the way we look, or the culture we practise. Essentially, it is largely as irrelevant as Hermann Hesse's 'glass bead game'. Above all, it shows how irrelevant such questions can be when trying to place peoples and cultures into neat pigeon-holes: any people are a product of complexity, anomaly and cross-fertilisation.

Archaeologists are correct to emphasise the pitfalls in attempting to trace the movement of Indo-European languages and a fallacy in assuming an Indo-European 'identity'.[*] It is important to emphasise above all that the question concerns the movement of *languages*, and not necessarily that of material cultures and even less of peoples, and widely different peoples can share a common culture and even common language. A study of skeletal remains of early first-millennium Saka communities in the lower Oxus, for example, revealed two distinct physical types, Europoid and Mongoloid, but both sharing an identical material culture.[57] To put it another way, place a native of Bengal next to a native of Iceland, and they are self-evidently different people, despite a common linguistic origin. Or take, for example, the fundamental influence of English upon the languages of the Indian Subcontinent, yet the number of descendants of actual British settlers there is very small. Languages move huge distances, peoples less so, despite history implying so-called 'waves' of invaders at different times, and modern DNA tests usually show up surprising conservatism in populations.

The question has been further distorted in modern times by one linguistic term, Aryan, being hijacked for political ends. While Nazi theories of cultural and racial superiority might be an extreme example, much milder – and even scholarly – fallacies have arisen from the cardinal mistake of attempting to equate the proto-Indo-European language with

---

[*] Although describing it as a 'deadly sin' – see Anthony 2006 – is perhaps going too far in the opposite direction: material culture *can* be related to a language (like people speak a like language) and migration *can* explain culture change.

a specific people. Even identifying it with an archaeological culture, such as the Yamnaya, is problematic. From there it has become a short step to attributing specific characteristics to an invented 'Indo-European people', and hence an 'Indo-European invasion' or series of invasions that reinvigorated the lands they penetrated, where archaeology confirms the arrival of new peoples, if not quite an 'invasion', from western Europe at about 3000 BC to India over a millennium later. In other words the language became a people, the people an invasion, the successful invasion victories, the victories superiority, and the Indo-Europeans 'us': an 'Indo-European supremacy'.

While such notions are admittedly no longer popular, elements of them (stripped of the idea of superiority) still survive in some scholarly literature and have prompted equally reactionary responses. On the one hand, an Indian response has viewed the theory of the Indo-Iranian invasion of the Indian Subcontinent as essentially retrospective neo-colonial, and re-interprets the linguistic evidence as having originated in India.[58] On the other, an 'eco-feminist' school interprets the invasions as essentially aggressive, destructive and masculine, that brought an end to prehistoric arcadias based upon matriarchies that worshipped mother-goddesses.[59] Politics and ideologies are never far from linguistics or archaeology.

The search for a common Indo-European 'homeland' must, therefore, be a purely theoretical one; turning it into a search for some cultural, ethnic or racial origins risks it deteriorating into a search for the philosopher's stone. Or to put it another way, the origins of the different Indo-European-speaking peoples of today are as varied, diverse and individual as the lands in which they dwell.

What the whole complex question of Indo-European origins does demonstrate is just how little barriers between Europe and Asia have been since the beginning. The origins, dispersal and break-up of the Indo-European-speaking peoples above all are a manifestation of the nature of the Eurasian steppe belt which produced it: a region of restlessness, of endless fluctuation, of the mixing and movement of peoples. The latter half of the second millennium AD has seen Indo-European-speaking peoples migrate westwards in vast droves to populate all of North and South America with Spanish, Portuguese, English and French speakers, just as their ancestors came westwards from the steppe to change the linguistic face of Europe, leaving only pockets of Basque or Maltese as the only speakers of languages outside the Indo-European family. This outward movement from Europe amounted to some 44 million people between 1821 and 1914 alone according to some estimates, a movement without parallel in history.[60]

In a stimulating and cautionary essay by C. C. Lamberg-Karlovsky that prompted equally stimulating responses from a range of prominent archaeologists and philologists in the pages of *Current Anthropology*, the author concludes:

> Passages from the Avesta and the Rigveda are quoted by various researchers to support the Indo-Iranian identity of both, but these passages are sufficiently general as to permit the Plains Indians an Indo-Iranian identity. Ethnicity is permeable and multidimensional, and the 'ethnic indicators' employed by Kuzmina can be used to identify the Arab, the Turk, and the Iranian, three completely distinctive ethnic and linguistic groups. Ethnicity and language are not so easily linked with an archaeological signature . . . In the context of a renewed fashion of relating archaeology, culture, and language it is well to remember that neither sherds nor genes are destined to speak specific languages, nor does a given language require a specific ceramic type or genetic structure.[61]

Such cautionary notes provide a balance and perspective, and rightly so. But at the same time too much caution risks sitting on the fence: scholars such as Renfrew, Cunliffe and others cited here are equally right to stick their necks out, as without such bold views discussion would stultify and not proceed. It is equally right to be wrong.

CHAPTER 4

HISTORY AND MYTH
Cimmerians, Scythians and Sarmatians; Gog, Magog and Excalibur

The barbarian host attack on swift horses:
strong in horses and strong in far-flung arrows
laying waste the neighbouring lands far and wide.
Some men flee: and, with their fields unguarded,
their undefended wealth is plundered,
the scant wealth of the country, herds
and creaking carts, whatever a poor farmer has.
Some, hands tied, are driven off as captives,
looking back in vain at their farms and homes.
some die wretchedly pierced by barbed arrows,
since there's a touch of venom on the flying steel.
They destroy what they can't carry, or lead away,
and enemy flames burn the innocent houses.
Even at peace, they tremble on the edge of war,
and no man ploughs the soil with curving blade.
This place sees the enemy, or fears him unseen:
the earth lies idle, abandoned to harsh neglect.
– Ovid, *Tristia* III. X, 41–78

Ovid was exiled by Augustus to the remote Greek colony of Tomis on the western shores of the Black Sea. His poem *Tristia* is an expression of the revulsion he felt towards his backwater surroundings, as well as his homesickness for Rome. It is also a first-hand account of a Scythian raid, one of the best accounts of the Scythians since Herodotus, and perhaps the greatest evocation of the contrast between the ways of the steppe and the city. Ovid was never allowed to return to Rome, dying in Tomis in AD 17. Delacroix's painting *Ovid Among the Scythians* in the National Gallery in London was inspired by this story, as was the Australian novelist David Malouf's *An Imaginary Life*, a fictionalised account of Ovid's exile and his encounter with the Scythians.[1] It also partly inspired Berlioz's composition *Tristia* (although the title is the only resemblance of the music, based more on *Hamlet* than Ovid's lament). By the time of Ovid's exile the Scythians were well known to the Romans and Greeks, especially through the contact made with them by Greek colonies on the Black Sea. This chapter will examine the effects of this contact. But before that the origins of the Scythians, their spread across the Eurasia and the establishment of Scythian kingdoms east and west is explored. The overall theme of violence in Ovid's lament is one that recurs in the contact between steppe nomad and sedentary settlement.

In the early first millennium BC the Eurasian steppe is broadly designated as 'Scythian', characterised by similar styles of arms, horse harnesses and 'animal style' of art as were common to steppe culture from Romania through to Siberia and the Northern Zone of China. It would be a mistake, however, to consider these peoples and their culture as 'Scythian' in too great an ethnic sense. The Scythians were mainly a nomadic elite ruling settled – and nomadic – populations, with whom the cultural contacts went both ways. In Book IV, Herodotus in the fifth century BC emphasises the great diversity among the various 'Scythian' tribes, with differences in customs, lifestyles and traditions. These range from completely sedentary societies with permanent settlements to total nomadic lifestyles. To some extent, the term 'Scythian' was a general blanket term used by the sources to refer to all of the nomadic groups on the Eurasian steppes; the term may have included Sarmatians, Huns and other groups of similar nomadic groups, and ultimately would end up almost as ethnically meaningless as 'Hun', 'Frank', 'African' or 'Indian'.* As well as in the Classical sources, the Scythians appear in Assyrian and biblical sources as the *Ashkenaz*, in Iranian and Indian sources as the *Saka*, in Arabic as the *Saqlāb*, and in Chinese as the *Sai*. The Classical and Iranian sources also differentiated the *Sacaraucae*, meaning 'Royal Scythians', identified with the *Sai Wang* of the Chinese sources, which means the same thing. Arabic *Saqlāb* can also mean 'Slav', from which it might have derived. Other variants are Scythes, Skuthes and Skuza, as well as perhaps Sugda, Sogdia and Sagittarius. 'Goth' (German 'Gott') is also possibly cognate with 'Scythian', probably just meaning 'the people' like many another ethnym.[2]

The last chapter described how Indo-European languages emerged. By the time of the historic periods, it was Indo-European-speaking groups who predominated in the Eurasian steppe, broadly designated Scythian. Although leaving no great cities or civilisations, the Scythians were one of history's more successful people. They established themselves across much

---

* As late as the tenth century Byzantine sources occasionally still referred to the Bulgarians contemptuously as 'Scythians'. See Obolensky 1971: 159. 'Franks' or *Farangi* has remained a popular name used by Arabs to refer to all Europeans ever since the Crusades. 'Africa' was originally just a southern Mediterranean province of the Roman Empire, but expanded as a designation for all the indigenous peoples of the continent regardless of ethnicity. 'Indians' is still the term used to describe the indigenous populations of North and South America, as well as India itself (where the official name is Bharat), and in the past was also used to describe Ethiopians and other Africans. Today the term 'African' is a blanket term to describe the peoples of the entire continent south of the Sahara (rarely north), peoples who are more ethnically, linguistically and culturally diverse than Europeans.

of Eurasia, they founded kingdoms throughout, and they left a legacy in art that has lasted until modern times. Theirs is a complex story. In the account that follows it is not always possible to follow a strictly chronological order, as different groups in different regions at different times are described.

The Scythian homeland

Karasuk origins

Towards the end of the Bronze Age after about 1400 BC a new culture evolved from the former Andronovo in south Siberia. This was the Karasuk (Map 4.1, Figure 4.1), named after a cemetery site where it was first identified in the 1920s on the Karasuk River near the village of Batieni in Khakasia.[3] It has been recorded mainly in the Minusinsk Basin and the Altai-Sayan Mountains, where so many of the early Inner Eurasian cultures

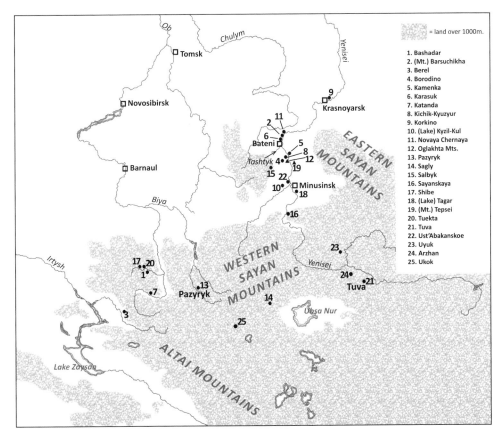

Map 4.1 *The main Scythian-related archaeological sites of south Siberia (adapted from Piotrovsky et al. 1978)*

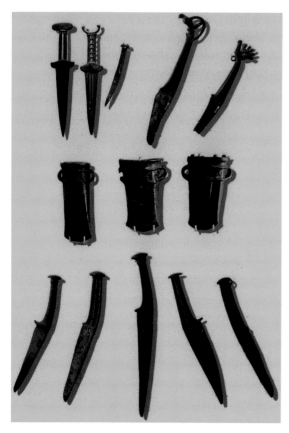

Figure 4.1 *A selection of Karasuk bronze weapons in the Minusinsk Museum*

formed and flourished. The dates are generally thirteenth to eighth centuries BC. Round about 1000 BC a slightly moister and warmer climate in south Siberia resulted in an increase in grazing lands, causing a transition to full pastoral nomadism and increased mobility. Mastery of metal working in the Minusinsk Basin also gave the nomads increasing ability in steppe warfare. This resulted in the emergence of the first steppe incursions into western Central Asia, the Near East and eastern Europe over the course of the first millennium BC.

Some settlements have been identified but with only small and very thin cultural layers; the Karasuk is known almost solely from burials, with over two thousand excavated, implying seasonal moves. Large numbers of animal bones are recorded, 50 per cent of which are ibex, the remainder cattle, horse and goat. Overall this is evidence for animal husbandry, but hunting and some agriculture were also practised. Huge numbers of bronzes have been recovered, especially knives (Figure 4.1). These are typically curved, single-edged knives with ring, 'mushroom' or animal head pommels, designed for hunting rather than warfare. DNA analyses of skeletal remains from Karasuk burials have confirmed the people of this culture to have been Europoid, implying a smooth evolution from the Andronovo rather than the arrival of new peoples, with an equally smooth transition into the succeeding Tagar Culture. However, an examination of Scythian skeletal remains in the lower Oxus, for example, revealed both Europoid and Mongoloid physical types within the same cultural assemblage.[4] There are cultural connections with the bronze cultures of China's Northern Zone, which was influenced by the Karasuk.

The oldest material so far discovered to be identified as 'Scythian' (and probably fully nomadic) was found in the spectacular Arzhan 1 burial mound in the Tuva Republic in Siberia, dating to the late ninth/early eighth century BC. Here, archaeologists in the 1970s discovered a royal

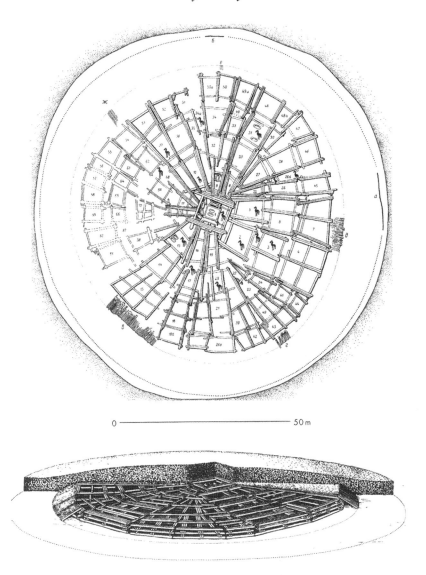

Figure 4.2 *Plan and part-reconstruction of Arzhan 1 Kurgan in Tuva (after Gryaznov)*

burial within an immense wooden structure covered by an earthen mound. The objects recovered, as well as those from the slightly later Arzhan 2 mound nearby in the 1990s, are among the most spectacular to have been discovered in Siberia. The discoveries are made all the more important for being by scientific excavation rather than chance finds or unprovenanced looting. The objects from both burials are in the 'animal style' of art characteristic of Scythian culture (Chapter 6), and the excavations at Arzhan have left the Scythian nature of the occupants and builders in little doubt (Figures 4.2–4.4; see also Figures 6.5, 6.8, 6.20 and 6.24).[5]

Figure 4.3 *The excavated Arzhan 2 Kurgan. Note the place of main burial off centre to the left*

Figure 4.4 *Reconstruction of the Arzhan 2 burial in the National Museum of Tuva in Kyzyl*

North of Tuva in the Minusinsk Basin and the neighbouring republic of Khakasia are the largest concentrations of Scythian burial mounds so far found (Figure 4.9; see also Figure 1.1). Since this is the same region as the Karasuk and the earlier Andronovo, this region is a likely candidate for a 'Scythian homeland' with a continuity of development that goes back into the Bronze Age and perhaps earlier. In other words, the appearance of Scythian culture in this region cannot be viewed as something that appeared from elsewhere, but is indigenous. The region is geographically well defined, the watershed of the upper Yenisei River bounded by the Sayan Mountains to the east and the Kuznetsk Alatau Mountains to the west which merge into the Altai (Figures 1.8, 1.15).

Tagar monumental kurgans

The region also boasts massive Scythian stone remains. These are the immense 'royal kurgans' of the Tagar Culture (Map 4.1). The distinctive Tagar, which developed out of the Karasuk, was confined mainly to the Minusinsk Basin of southern Krasnoyarsk Province, but elements are found as far north as Tomsk. It is named after the excavations that first identified it on Lake Tagar and is characterised by vast numbers of burials. It covers most of the Iron Age of the first millennium BC, and is identified with the Scythians. The culture is generally interpreted as nomadic, but the existence of some sickles found in excavations implies agriculture, hence settlement, albeit limited.[6]

The region has one of the largest concentration of archaeological sites in Asia, almost entirely of kurgans – some thirty thousand have been recorded – prompting one early investigator to describe the entire area as 'a gigantic cemetery'.[7] Their kurgans are – unusually – square in plan, formed by a stone foundation with upright megaliths marking the entrance and corners. This distinctive shape is in contrast to the circular stone foundations surrounding the slightly earlier Arzhan kurgans further south in Tuva, as well as the later Scythian kurgans of the western steppe. The Tagar kurgans were then covered to form earth pyramids. The massive Salbyk Kurgan, for example, in the so-called 'Valley of Kings' in Khakasia, was originally covered by an earth pyramid that probably stood twelve metres or more high. Barsuchiy Log in the same area was not much smaller (Figures 4.5–4.8). These two examples have been fully excavated, but the sense of their original height can still be seen in the vast number of similar-sized kurgans in the region. The 'Cyclopean' foundations of Salbyk incorporated massive megaliths up to fifty tons in weight from quarries between twenty and seventy kilometres distant.[8] Today, extensive necropolises comprising hundreds or even thousands of mounds with their distinctive square stone foundation walls and upright corner megaliths are a familiar feature of the landscape of Khakasia. The largest concentration is in the Kazanovka Archaeological Reserve, the largest such reserve in Russia, containing kurgans, settlements, petroglyphs, standing stones and other monuments from the Bronze Age to the Middle Ages; those of the Tagar culture predominate (Figure 4.9; see also 6.35).[9]

Figure 4.5 *Entrance to the excavated Tagar giant 'royal kurgan' of Salbyk in the Minusinsk Basin*

Figure 4.6 *Model of the Salbyk Kurgan in the Minusinsk Museum*

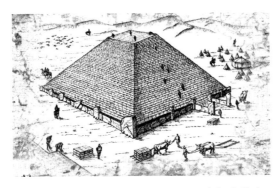

Figure 4.7 *Theoretical reconstruction of the Salbyk Kurgan (from information on site)*

Figure 4.8 *The excavated Tagar kurgan of Barsuchiy Log in the Minusinsk Basin. Note the standing stones on the far side marking the entrance*

Figure 4.9 *Tagar kurgans in the Kazanovka Archaeological Reserve in the Republic of Khakasia*

The frozen tombs

Closely related to the Tagar is the Pazyryk Culture, also identified as Scythian, in the Altai Mountains.[10] This was named after the spectacular discoveries of frozen Scythian tombs high up in the Altai between 1929 and 1949 (Figures 4.10–4.14; see also Figure 1.3). They are now dated fifth to third centuries BC, rather than the earlier dates first proposed. The burials are different from the kurgans of the steppe, consisting of burial chambers built of logs and then covered by low mounds of stones (Figure 4.12). It was these stone mounds that allowed for the almost perfect state of preservation of the contents, for water was able to trickle down and freeze and so preserve the tomb in ice. Hence, as well as preserved cadavers, the tombs contained preserved objects of otherwise perishable material, such as wood, bone, leather and textiles, including carpets and felts that are among the oldest in the world. One of the most impressive objects was a complete four-wheeled wooden carriage (probably a funerary carriage as its construction is too flimsy to withstand heavy usage, let alone the mountains of the Altai: Figure 4.13).

Similar discoveries of burials frozen in ice were made in the 1990s on the Ukok Plateau, high up in the Altai at a height of 2,500 metres. This included the famous female burial in a hollow log (the so-called 'Ice Princess') and all her elaborate clothing and other paraphernalia such as her distinctive high conical felt hat, which probably identifies her as a shaman (Figures 4.15–4.18). The distinctive pointed felt caps of associated burials appear similar to the *Saka tigraxauda* or 'pointed cap Scythians' depicted on the Persepolis and Bisitun reliefs (Figure 4.21). The Ukok finds were divided between the National Museum of the Altai Republic in Gorno-Altaisk and the Museum of the Institute of Archaeology in Akademgorodok outside Novosibirsk. The latter included the 'Ice Princess' herself, which then became the subject of a tug-of-war in the post-Soviet nationalist politics of the region, with the Altaians attributing several natural disasters to her removal from their territory and claiming her as national property. She has since been transferred to Gorno-Altaisk: as in so many cases that recur in this narrative, politics as well as treasures are never far below the surface in archaeology.

A similar Pazyryk Culture burial was at the massive Tuekta kurgan lower down in the Altai (Figure 4.19) that included horse trappings and decorations in the distinctive 'fantastic beast' style of steppe art. This included a unique wooden boss that has been compared to a bronze shield found in the River Thames.[11] In the same area a series of small, stone-slab-lined burials excavated at Chultukov Log (Figure 4.20) included a female wearing a necklace of Egyptian faience beads.[12]

Figure 4.10 *The excavated Pazyryk burial mounds in the Altai, scene of the most spectacular frozen tomb discoveries*

Figure 4.11 *One of the burial mounds at Pazyryk, still with fragments of the log tomb chamber surrounding the excavated remains*

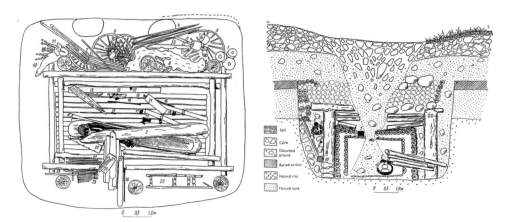

Figure 4.12 *Plan and section of Kurgan 5 at Pazyryk with the disassembled chariot (after Gryaznov)*

Figure 4.13 *Reconstructed replica of the Pazyryk chariot in the National Museum of Altai in Gorno-Altaisk*

Figure 4.14 *One of the wicker shields from Pazyryk in the Hermitage*

Figure 4.15 *Reconstruction of the Ukok male (left) and female (right) burials in the National Museum of Altai in Gorno-Altaisk. Note the deer depicted on the wooden coffin*

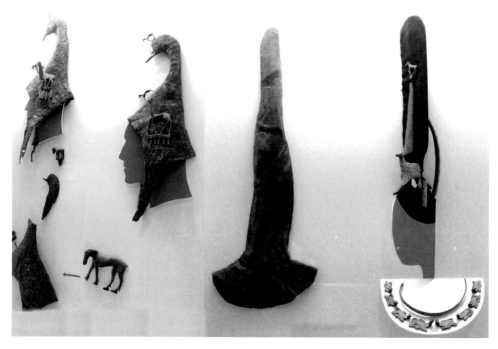

Figure 4.16 *Headdresses from the Ukok burials in the Akademgorodok Museum*

Figure 4.17 *Felt horse trappings from the*
Ukok burials in the Akademgorodok Museum

Figure 4.18 *Reconstruction of the 'Ice Princess' in the Akademgorodok Museum*

Figure 4.19 *The excavated kurgan of Tuekta in the Altai*

Figure 4.20 *Stone burial chamber at Chultukov Log in the Altai*

To the western steppe

Sometime in the early first millennium BC Scythian tribes moved from their homeland in Inner Asia, travelling northwards around the Caspian Sea, so that by the seventh century much of Inner Eurasia from the Black Sea through to Mongolia became populated by Scythian-related nomads. By the second half of the first millennium BC the Scythians formed a recognisable culture that stretched across Eurasia from the Yenisei to the Danube (Map 4.2). Although it would be a cardinal mistake to view this as a structured whole – a form of 'proto-empire' – it was nonetheless the largest single cultural unit that had hitherto occurred on the steppe, or indeed anywhere else. Its homogeneity is confirmed in both historical records and archaeological discoveries. Herodotus, for example, recorded specific Scythian cultural characteristics in the Black Sea steppe, such as horse sacrifice at funerals or the inhalation of hemp seed under miniature tents supported by a wooden framework; such practices were graphically confirmed in modern times by archaeological discoveries of evidence of the same practices in the Altai thousands of miles away (and evidence from art and archaeology also indicates widespread use of opium, ephedra and other narcotics among the steppe nomads).[13] The same discoveries revealed objects, such as textiles and other items, drawn from places as far apart as China, Egypt and Persia. The tenth-century Arab traveller to Russia, Ibn Fadlan, describes the burial of a pagan Ghuzz Turk chief with all possessions and including horse sacrifices that is almost identical to the Scythian burials described by Herodotus.[14] As Gibbon observed when writing of the Scythians long before such discoveries were made, 'the banks of the Borysthenes, of the Volga, or of the Selinga, will indifferently present the same uniform spectacle of similar and native manners'.[15] After the third century BC, Classical Greek art would be added to the mix to form the Scythians' own distinct but unified artistic styles that can be

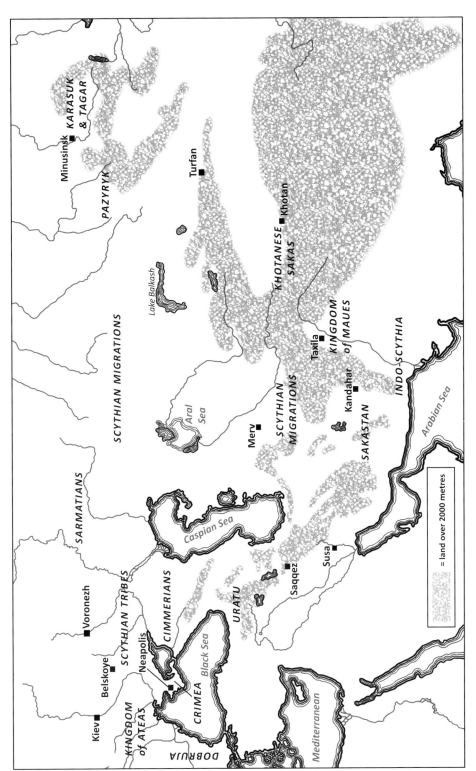

Map 4.2 The Scythian world

found across this vast region and beyond. But while recognising its unified cultural characteristics, at the same time it would be a mistake to ignore distinctive differences among the different communities.

Although originally nomadic, Scythian groups later founded important kingdoms as far apart as Dobruja (Dobrogea) on the Romanian Black Sea coast, Sind in South Asia and Khotan in China. The first of these might have been at Ziwiye in north-western Iran in the early seventh century BC. A later movement of the probably related Sarmatians from the Urals had resulted in further displacement of Scythian tribes in the steppes. This led to the eventual foundation of the Scythian kingdom in the Crimea in the late fourth/early third century BC. Other groups migrated to Sistan in the Irano-Afghan borderlands and to north-western India and western China, where they also successfully founded kingdoms. Some authorities even recognise some of the great empires of antiquity, such as Achaemenid Persia or the Kushans of Central Asia and India, to be ultimately of Scythian descent,[16] which might be overstating the evidence. These Asiatic kingdoms will be briefly examined before we turn to those in Europe.

Another nomad movement out of Central Asia that did form a kingdom – indeed, an empire – was that of a group related to the Sakas. This was the third movement of Iranian tribes from Central Asia: the Parthians. Like the Medes and the Persians before them, the Parthians were initially little more than a tribal confederation, until in about 238 BC they seized control of the trans-Caspian territories of the Seleucid Empire under the founder of their dynasty, Arsaces. Building up a power base in what is now Turkmenistan and Khurasan, ruling first from Nisa (near Ashkhabad) and then from Hecatompylos (near Damghan), by the middle of the second century the Parthians invaded Seleucid territory. By about 141 BC the Parthian king Mithridates I ruled an empire almost as large as the former Achaemenid one. The subsequent history of the Parthians, however, is beyond the scope of this book.[17]

From Kurdistan to India and China: the Scythian kingdoms in the East (Map 4.2)

Kurdistan

A possible early 'Scythian kingdom' in Kurdistan and Azerbaijan around the modern town of Saqqez in north-western Iran might be the earliest of the kingdoms. The Scythians had probably entered north-western Iran through the Caucasus gates, a regular route for invaders. Whether it was a kingdom in the full sense is disputed. The name of 'Saqqez' itself might derive from 'Scythian', or *Saka* in Persian. The Scythian identity is based almost solely on the seventh-century BC site of Ziwiye near Saqqez, where a spectacular 'royal burial' was discovered in the 1940s. Both the treasure

associated with the burial and the nature of the funeral appears to have
been that of a Scythian chief, and the Scythian influence on the art is not
in doubt: a crouched animal (variously interpreted as a tiger or a deer)
on a gold pectoral, for example, can be compared to an almost identical
motif of an eighth–sixth-century bronze crouched tiger from China in the
British Museum.[18] It has been identified as the grave of King Bartatua,
known from Assyrian inscriptions through his marriage to the daughter of
King Essarhaddon of Assyria. Bartatua died in 645 BC, which fits with the
date of the treasure. The kingdom, such as it was, was eventually absorbed
into the Median kingdom. However, the nature of the discovery – much
of the treasure was looted before excavations were carried out – has left
many questions about the Ziwiye finds, and even its Scythian identity is
doubted.[19]

From Sakastan to Indo-Scythia

Various Saka groups were well-known to the Achaemenids in the sixth
and fifth centuries, where they are depicted on the Persepolis reliefs
(Figure 4.21), but the main groups known to them were those on their
north-eastern borders in Central Asia. It was through this porous and
very open border – one authority has appropriately dubbed it 'the Herat
gap'[20] – that Scythian tribes moved southwards sometime in the second
century BC, probably taking advantage of a weakening of Parthian rule in
the area. They settled in the Iran-Afghan borderlands known as Sistan –
originally 'Sakastan', deriving from *Saka*. As well as the name Sistan, the
Scythian name survives there in the 'Ishak-zai' tribe, also known as the
'Sak-zi', in modern Afghan Sistan.[21] Sistan was the homeland of the great
Parthian noble family, the Surens, which may have been Scythian in
origin.[*] Sistan – or Zabul further east in south-eastern Afghanistan – was
the homeland of the legendary Persian warrior Rustam, one of the great
heroes of the epic *Shahnameh* or *Book of Kings* compiled by Firdausi in
the eleventh century. The 'Rustam cycle' in the *Shahnameh*, part of which
was popularised in English by Matthew Arnold's epic poem *Sohrab and
Rustum*, is generally recognised to be Sistani in origin, although whether it
is Parthian or Scythian is disputed.[22]

From Sistan the Saka conquered much of southern Afghanistan.
However, the Scythian period in southern Afghanistan is a very shadowy
one in the archaeological record, with most of the evidence only gleaned
from numismatic studies. The fortress city of Kandahar in southern
Afghanistan, one of the few places where a substantial Saka presence has

---

[*] According to Armenian historical tradition, St Gregory the Illuminator, the evangeliser
of Armenia, was a member of the Suren noble house: see Marshall 1970: 155.

Figure 4.21 '*Pointed cap Scythians' depicted at Persepolis*

been recorded, might have formed a base for further Saka incursions into South Asia in the first century BC. There they formed a kingdom in the region of Sind in the southern Indus, known in Hellenistic sources as 'Indo-Scythi' and in Indian sources as *Saka-dvipa*, 'land of the Scythians'. Indo-Scythia lasted into the first century AD, although the chronology is very imprecise. They became patrons of Buddhism, leaving their mark on a number of Buddhist monastery complexes in the region. They may also have left their mark in the characteristic Saka Central Asian style of dress consisting of baggy trousers and long shirt, still worn in Afghanistan and Pakistan today (Figure 4.24). From Sind there seem to have been further Saka migrations into the south of India, where it has been suggested that the present-day Todas of the Nilgiri Hills are descendants of a group of Saka invaders. The identification is based upon archaeological, historical, linguistic and ethnographic evidence.[23]

From China through the Karakoram Passes

A west–east movement of tribes into the north-western borderland of China has been detected in the late fourth century BC. They are assumed to have been Indo-Iranian speakers because of the characteristic 'fantastic beasts' motif in their art derived from Pazyryk, suggested to have been Scythian tribes displaced by Alexander of Macedon's incursion into Central Asia.[24] Be that as it may, the linguistic anomaly of the Indo-European-speaking Tokharians in the northern oasis towns of Xinjiang was discussed in the last chapter. They were known in the Chinese sources as the Yuezhi, but the same sources also refer to another Indo-European group in the southern oasis towns, known as the *Sai*, who settled mainly in Kashgar, Yarkand and Khotan in the second century BC, identified with the Sakas of Persian sources. As well as Scythian Inner Asian, their material culture shows influences from India. The Sai/Sakas remained an important group of city-states south of the Taklamakan Desert over the following five

Figure 4.22 *The Buddhist stupa of Rawak in the Taklamakan Desert, part of the ancient kingdom of Khotan*

centuries or so, at times semi-independent and at other times coming under the sway of neighbouring kingdoms.

Khotan (modern Chinese Hetien, ancient Yutian) was the main Sai/Saka centre. Records of a written language were discovered there at the end of the nineteenth century, now known as Khotanese Saka.[25] These are the only records of the written Scythian language ever recovered (although some signs on a silver bowl from the late fourth-century BC Issyk burial in Kazakhstan – site of the so-called 'Issyk Golden Man' – have been interpreted as a possible Saka writing system).[26] Saka Khotan was an important buffer kingdom of the Han Empire between the second century BC and the second century AD. This was not only because of its strategic value in the western borderlands, but also because of the jade found in the foothills of the Kunlun mountains to the south, where there are extensive traces of jade working, greatly prized by the Chinese. The heyday of the kingdom of Khotan was after the third century AD when it became one of the most important kingdoms of Xinjiang. The capital seems to have been the site of Yotkan, within the modern Khotan oasis. It is an area of extensive low mounds where Aurel Stein excavated many important objects, particularly terracottas with Irano-Classical motifs, but there were no buildings of any note.[27] More extensive remains of the Khotan kingdom are preserved in the desert to the north (Figure 4.22).

Groups of Saka from Xinjiang migrated through the Karakorum passes into Kashmir and the north-western Indian subcontinent, probably in

Figure 4.23 *Petroglyph in the Indus gorge between Chilas and Thalpan left by passing Scythians*

the late second century BC, leaving their mark in a series of petroglyphs in the gorges of the upper Indus (Figure 4.23).[28] Here they founded another kingdom based at Taxila, not far from Rawalpindi (Figure 4.24). Its first king, known from his coinage, was Maues who ruled in about 80 BC. The subsequent Scythian kingdom of the upper Indus and Hindu Kush region is known mainly from its coinage and the occasional mention in Indian sources. It was distinct from the near-contemporary Scythian kingdom of the lower Indus in Sind reviewed above, and the two are often confused. The northern Scythian kingdom probably only lasted into the early first century AD when the coinage stops after the last king, Azes II. Both kingdoms were probably absorbed by the Indo-Parthian kingdom that ruled in north-western India.[29]

Figure 4.24 *The excavated Saka-Parthian-period remains at the Sirkap area of Taxila*

As in Sistan, the Scythians of the northern Indus region have left their mark in place names in the region, such as 'Sajawand' or 'Sakawand' in eastern Afghanistan near Gardez. Significantly, this is near Mir Zakah, the site of the greatest coin hoard ever found anywhere in the world, first of some eleven thousand coins in 1947 and then an astonishing further two tons of coins in the 1990s. A significant portion of these are Saka.[30] They have also left a linguistic mark on the Wakhi language, the language spoken by a small minority found mainly in the Wakhan Corridor high up in the Pamir Mountains of north-eastern Afghanistan as well as in neighbouring districts in Tajikistan, China and Pakistan. Since these were the passes through which the Saka presumably entered north-western India, the Wakhis are probably a remnant Scythian group, and their language the only place now in the world where this once widely spoken language has survived.[31]

The western steppe

The above account of Scythian origins and the emergence of Scythian states in the east has taken us down to the early centuries AD. In order to discuss their encounters with western cultures – in particular the Greeks – and the eventual relationship of steppe nomads with Rome, it is necessary to return to when steppe nomads first enter Near Eastern and Classical sources in the first millennium BC, when archaeology indicates an east–west movement of proto-Scythian nomads, probably in the tenth century BC.[32]

The Gomer, the Ashkenaz and Gog and Magog

In the beginning of the first millennium BC the northern Black Sea steppe region was inhabited by Cimmerians, whom the Scythians eventually displaced. Cimmerian remains have been identified at Chernogorovka in Ukraine and associated with the so-called 'Novocherkassk Hoard' in Russia.[33] The Cimmerians had an early Scythian form of culture and their language probably belonged to the Iranian group, and they were not 'a people in whom modern erudition has too fondly traced the ancestors of the Cymry, or ancient Britons', as Edward Bulwer Lytton wryly remarked in the nineteenth century.[34] Indeed, some suggest that the Cimmerians were Scythians merely under a different name; they might be distantly derived from the Karasuk culture of the Minusinsk Basin (or at least have been bearers of their culture),[35] which has been identified as 'proto-Scythian'. Cimmerians first appear in Assyrian sources in the late eighth century BC and in biblical sources, where they are known as the *Gomer*. From their bases on the Pontic and Kuban steppes they penetrated the Caucasus, from where they made a number of devastating raids over the course of the seventh century BC. Much of Anatolia was devastated as the Cimmerians raided in turn the kingdoms of Urartu, Phrygia and Lydia. The king of Phrygia himself, Midas II, committed suicide after the Cimmerian attack on his capital of Gordion. Other Cimmerian raids extended as far as Assyria and Palestine. However, devastating though these raids may have been, they were never more than raids; there were no concerted efforts at conquest nor attempts at carving out a Cimmerian kingdom in Anatolia, and there was little long-term impact. In the end, the Cimmerians seem to disappear into history as suddenly as they appeared.

The Cimmerians were probably absorbed by the related Scythian tribes who came after. The Scythians, raiding Assyria in the 670s BC, probably came through the Caucasus. They certainly left a trail of destruction there when they destroyed the Urartian city of Teishubani in the sixth century, modern Karmir Blur on the outskirts of Yerevan. Their destruction accidentally preserved much of the city and many of its contents, which now form probably the best collection of Urartian artefacts so far recovered (divided between Yerevan and the Hermitage). The collection includes large numbers of Scythian arrows. As a result of these raids, the Scythians entered biblical tradition as the *Ashkenaz*, and biblical references to Gog and Magog (mainly in *Ezekiel* and *Revelations*), mythical raiders from the north, are probably references to both the Cimmerians and the Scythians.

First Scythian settlements in the western steppe

There was a second movement of Scythians from the east into the southern Russian/Ukrainian steppe in the seventh century BC, and a definite Scythian identity emerges there by the fifth. After the sixth century the evidence of the burials indicates a steady migration of Scythians from the Kuban to the north Pontic steppe. A Scythian-dominated state emerged by the end of the sixth century. Their material culture was more than just kurgans and their grave contents, for the seventh- to third-century BC proto-Slav site of Belskoye on the Vorskla River in Ukraine indicates a high degree of sedentarisation. Belskoye consists of a city surrounded by ramparts still standing up to ten metres high for a thirty-six kilometre circuit, enclosing an area of some 4,400 hectares, or seventeen square miles. As well as permanent dwellings, the city included well-defined industrial areas and was protected by two forts with their own ramparts. The industrial areas included a bronze smelting furnace; Belskoye is thought to be one of the largest metallurgical centres of the later first millennium in the region. It might be identified with the ancient city of Gelonus mentioned by Herodotus. Over two thousand kurgans have been located in the vicinity. Another urban Scythian site has been identified at Kamenskoye on the

Dnieper River opposite Nikopol. It covers an area of some twelve square kilometres and included potteries and permanent dwellings.[36]

Such examples of massive urban settlement in a nomadic environment seem hardly surprising. The evidence of the Tripolye Culture demonstrates a tradition of sedentarism thousands of years old, and this remained a permanent feature among the indigenous people of the western steppe. The 'Scythian' nature of such settlements has been disputed: they have also been interpreted as proto-Slav. They probably in any case only represented a Scythian incoming elite ruling over indigenous sedentary populations. Scythian and Scythian-related objects have been found further west in eastern Europe where it is known in the archaeological record as the Vekerzuk culture of the sixth–fifth centuries BC. Some objects are even found as far west as Slovenia and Silesia, which suggests possible Scythian raids or at least trade. The lavish gold hoard and other objects found in the complete burial of a Scythian chief at Vettersfelde (now Witaszkowo) in Brandenburg have even led some to suggest that there might have been a Scythian state in Germany, perhaps formed by Scythians fleeing Darius' advance into south-eastern Europe.[37] However, 'the role played by the Scythians in the history of central and eastern Europe should not be exaggerated', as Karl Jettmar cautions.[38]

From the sixth century BC the Scythians appear increasingly in mainstream written history through substantial contacts with two major ancient civilisations at the fringes of their domain: the rising empire of Persia which they encountered in Central Asia to their south, and the Greek colonies on the Black Sea to their west. Various Scythian groups were well-known to the Achaemenids of Persia in the sixth and fifth centuries and are depicted on royal reliefs (Figure 4.21). Their relationship with the Achaemenid Empire was a complex one: its founder, Cyrus the Great, was killed while on campaign against the Scythian-related Massagetae in Central Asia in 530 BC. Darius made an ill-fated campaign against the Scythians in the Balkans to the west of the Black Sea, a campaign that brought the Persians into Europe for the first time. The relationship, however, was by no means one-way. There were many artistic stimuli that went both ways between Persian and Scythian, and much of early Persian history has been interpreted in terms of its relationship with the Scythians.[39] Warlike tribes on the fringes of great empires were always valuable recruiting grounds, and tribal enemies could also become valuable allies: the relationship is a familiar one, from that between Romans and Germans in ancient history to that between the British and Pathans more recently. Hence, Scythians were also recruited as major units in the Persian army. But this does not concern us here so much as their relationship with the Greeks.

Contact and conflict: the Greek states of the Black Sea

Cicero describes the Greek colonies on the Black Sea as 'the hem of Greece sewn on to the fields of the Barbarians'.[40] The relationship between Greek and Scythian was a complex one. The initial impetus for Greek settlement in the region came about in the early first millennium BC by a combination of over-population in the homelands in Asia Minor and the lure of trade in metals and fishing in the Black Sea. The latter was a particularly strong motivation with the rich fishing waters at the mouths of the great rivers that come into the Black Sea. Hence, the earliest colonies (mainly from Miletus in Asia Minor), such as Tyras, Olbia and Berezan, were fishing colonies on river estuaries at the western end of the Black Sea. Chersonesus, a colony at the southern tip of the Crimean peninsula, in contrast had little fishing but, being the shortest crossing point across the Black Sea from Anatolia, was founded probably as a stepping-stone along the Crimean shore to the rich fishing grounds of Kerch at the eastern end of Crimea.[41]

Panticapaeum (the name has been interpreted as meaning 'fish way') was founded by Milesian colonists in the early sixth century BC overlooking the Cimmerian Bosporus (the modern Straits of Kerch). This initiated a spate of colonisation around the eastern end of Crimea: Tyritaca, Nymphaeum, Cytacaeum, Cimmericum, Theodosia, Parthenicum and Myrmecaeum, which by the mid-sixth century formed a Greek – or at least Hellenised – enclave that was eventually to form the Bosporan kingdom (Map 4.3). Tanaïs, far to the north-east where the Don enters the Sea of Azov, was founded as a sub-colony by the Bosporan Greeks in the early third century BC. Thus, there emerged two groups of Greek colonies at the western and eastern ends of the northern Black Sea coast.

Olbia became the centre of the Greek the colonies in the western Black Sea, and archaeology bears witness to its prosperity in the sixth century BC. As well as fishing, Olbia had a good anchorage and was the terminus of trade with the interior. Fishing therefore was soon supplemented by trade, particularly with the establishment of the Scythian hegemony on the steppe in the sixth century. The Scythians had learnt of the advantages of good trade relations with the Greek world. A Scythian unit of archers served Athens as a mercenary 'police force' in the late fifth–early fourth century BC, becoming a popular motif on vase painting.[42] The Black Sea colonies were independent *poleis* along the Greek model from the beginning, but in 438 BC there was a coup in Panticapaeum by Spartocos, from a Hellenised native family of Panticapaeum, beginning the hegemony of the Spartocid dynasty. Between 344 and 310 BC the Spartocids conquered Theodosia in the west and territories to the east (with the aid of twenty thousand Scythian infantry mercenaries and ten thousand Scythian

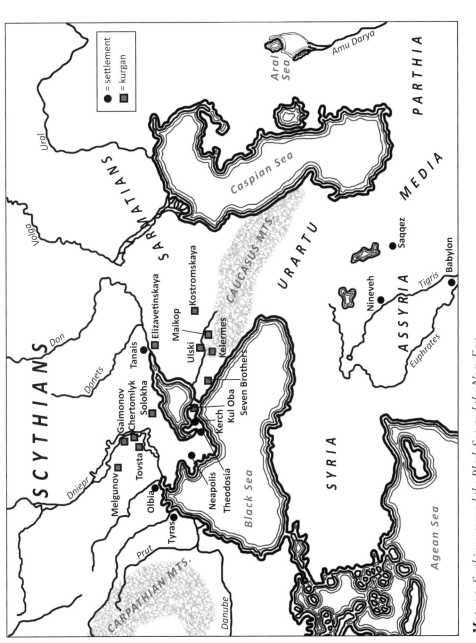

Map 4.3 *Scythians around the Black Sea and the Near East*

cavalry, constituting 90 per cent of his forces), unifying the Greek colonies and forming the Bosporan Kingdom.[43]

In the third and second centuries BC there was a weakening of the Bosporan Kingdom, corresponding to a rise of the Scythian kingdom in the interior of Crimea and the arrival of Sarmatian groups in south Russia. This eventually resulted in the downfall of the Spartocid family, as the Greek cities were forced to look for outside protection. The nearest power was the neo-Persian Kingdom of Pontus, based in northern Anatolia, ruled by King Mithridates VI. However, in wishing to avoid one master, the Scythians, the Greeks merely invited another: Mithridates incorporated the Bosporan kingdom in 107 BC and established garrisons in the other northern Black Sea Greek cities, including Chersonesus and Olbia. He defeated the Scythians, but soon entered friendly relations with them and even established a marital alliance.

The Scythian cultural impact on the Greeks in the Bosphoran Kingdom was particularly high. Scythians had already settled in the region before the arrival of the Greeks, but there appears to have been little conflict. The Greeks were more interested in colonising the coastal fringe, while the Scythians remained largely inland. There was, in any case, an abundance of land. Many of the 'Greek' settlements would furthermore have included an increasing number of Scythians. The contact, therefore, was both intimate and largely peaceful.

Local cults were brought to the capital of Panticapaeum, and the resultant Bosporan religion was a result of the interaction between Greek settlers and local Scythian traditions. Greek burials were increasingly in Scythian style kurgans. By the first centuries AD a Graeco-Scythian syncretic culture and religion emerged. This was the cult of Celestial Aphrodite (Aphrodite Ourania) and the anonymous 'Most High God' (Theos Hypsistos). Both cults were linked to dynastic power. Aphrodite Ourania was the common cult throughout, and is probably derived from – or at least identified with – the Scythian cult of Argimpasa. The Theos Hypsistos cult was centred more in Tanaïs than Panticapaeum.[44] It was considered sympathetic to Judaism, and while there were some Jewish connections, the evidence is inconclusive. The region certainly retained Judaic elements: the same region later saw the rise of the medieval Jewish Khazar Khanate, and the Crimea became a centre for Karaite Judaism. There is also some evidence that some form of Iranian-style fire worship was practised: a seventh-century fire temple, for example, at the Krasnoye Znamya Kurgan in the north Caucasus has been likened to 'Median fire temples'.[45] It is suggested that such temples and practices were brought back from Scythian raids in the Middle East.

By the end of the Greek kingdom of Bosporus in the fourth century, this and the other Greek colonies around the Black Sea had become almost completely 'Scythianised'. Although Greek names were still preserved – with a desperation, one senses, at maintaining some form of Greek identity – and some Greek was still spoken, the material culture had become virtually indistinguishable from that around it.

The Black Sea Scythian kingdoms[46]

Scythians groups had migrated around the Black Sea and into south-eastern Europe by the sixth century. These were the Scythian tribes against whom Darius I of Persia campaigned so unsuccessfully in the late sixth century. The arrival of the Sarmatians in the fourth century and their displacement of Scythian power on the southern steppe resulted in the foundation in the late fourth/early third century BC of several Scythian kingdoms. This might have been in response to Greek colonisation and the consolidation of the eastern city-states into the Bosporan kingdom. A Scythian state on the southern Ukrainian steppe to the west of the Black Sea emerged in the late fifth–early fourth century BC when the tribes were united by King Ateas. He struck coins and campaigned in Thrace and Macedon, but he was killed (at the age of ninety) by Phillip II of Macedon in 339, after which the kingdom collapsed.

In the third and second centuries BC the Sarmatians crossed the Don and penetrated as far as the Kuban, forcing the Scythians there to retreat to Crimea and put pressure on the Greek cities, which were thus put on the defensive and made more unstable. The period corresponded to weakness in the Aegean, with Athens long in decline and its successor Rhodes also declining. Rome by then was rising as the new power in the eastern Mediterranean, but it had no interests at this time in the Black Sea. With the retreat of Scythian tribes from the Kuban to the Black Sea area, two small 'Neo-Scythian' states were founded. One was situated in Dobruja, on the right bank of the Danube, probably founded by those Scythians left in the region after the defeat of King Ateas. This lasted from the end of the third to the beginning of the first century. One of its kings, Skylos or Skylas, was noted by Herodotus as one of the rare Scythian rulers who 'went Greek'. Skylas would enter the Greek city of Olbia on a regular basis and discard both his Scythian dress and customs, following Greek ways. When this was discovered by his warriors he was immediately put to death. Skylas' gold signet ring was actually found in the Danube delta in modern times, probably at the very site of his execution.[47]

The other Scythian kingdom was founded in central Crimea under King Skiluros at the end of the third century. The core comprised the southern foothills and the steppe country of central Crimea, but at its greatest height it extended as far as the lower Dnieper and the lower Bug. The capital was Neapolis Scythica (modern Kermenchik on the outskirts of Simferopol). It was fortified in the first century BC with strong ramparts

Figure 4.25 *Part of the reconstructed ramparts of Neapolis Scythica on the outskirts of Simferopol in Crimea*

(part of which has been reconstructed: Figure 4.25) and had paved streets and Greek-style public buildings adorned with wall paintings. The earth wall and ditch across the Crimean peninsula marking the boundary of the Bosporan kingdom might date from this time (Figure 4.26), the first such instance of 'walling off the barbarian', which will be encountered again later (Chapter 10). Other Scythian towns in the Crimea were established at Chabum and Palacum according to the sources, and archaeology has identified three more, with at least a further fifty smaller settlements. After the end of the second century AD archaeological evidence shows that the Scythians had almost abandoned their nomadic lifestyle and established a network of small, fortified towns and agricultural settlements. Only the elite maintained the former Scythian nomadic lifestyle.[48]

The second century BC seems to have been the height of the Crimean Scythian kingdom. King Skiluros annexed much of the lands belonging to the Greek city-state of Chersonesus, and expanded his kingdom through-out north-western Crimea at the expense of the Greeks, with Kerkinitis and Kalos Limen (modern Yevpatoria and Chernomorske) captured. Even Olbia on the western shore of the Black Sea became subject, and Skiluros struck his own coins there. There is also some suggestion that the Scythians established a fleet. The Scythian kingdom maintained its independence from both the Pontic kingdom under Mithridates and the Romans, despite a defeat at the hands of the former. In the first century

Figure 4.26 *The Bosporan Wall across Crimea separating the Greek Bosporan kingdom on the coast from the Scythian kingdom inland*

AD a war was fought against the Bosporan Kingdom, which was only saved from defeat by Roman military intervention. But despite the success of Roman arms in the Crimea, the Scythian kingdom managed to maintain its independence, only declining after the third century with the Gothic invasions. By the fourth century, '[t]he distinctive nature of the 1,000 year history of the Scythian culture in the Crimea'[49] had disappeared.

Sarmatian warriors

The Scythians were succeeded on the south-western steppe by the Sarmatians, a people related to the Scythians. They might initially have just been a sub-group in the Bronze Age Andronovo culture of Siberia, but diverged in the early first millennium when the tribes moved westwards.[50] However, Soviet era archaeologists viewed the whole area from the lower Syr-Darya to the southern Urals as a Sarmatian 'single economic and cultural zone' in the fourth–third century BC.[51] Herodotus describes the Sarmatians (or Sauromatians in its earlier form) as descended from the union of Scythians and Amazons. Many female Sarmatian burials contain weapons, evidence of the high status enjoyed by their womenfolk, in common with other steppe people (discussed in Chapter 5). The Sarmatians migrated to the southern Urals region, becoming distinct from the Scythians by the fifth or fourth century BC. Their migration from south Siberia may have been the result of disruption on the steppe caused by the rise of the Xiongnu in Mongolia (Chapter 7). The spectacular gold treasure from the burial at Filippovka in the Orenburg region (now in the National Museum of Bashkortostan in Ufa) dates from this time (Figures 6.3, 6.6 and 6.13).[52] Like the Scythians they spoke an Iranian-related language, but there were many cultural differences. The Sarmatians were pastoralists rather than semi-nomadic herders like the Scythians, and less inclined to permanent settlements. The Sarmatians buried their chiefs in kurgans with rich burial offerings, with similar gold, metalwork and art styles to the Scythians'. Their weapons and armaments, however, were distinct. The image is conveyed of more warlike men (and women), with the Sarmatians favouring heavily armoured cavalry with scale armour and the long sword as opposed to the Scythians' lightly armed horsemen and short sword. The curved hunting knife that characterised the Scythian and earlier Siberian cultures gave way to the straight dagger for stabbing as the knife of choice.[53]

An arid phase in the mid-first millennium BC might have caused the Sarmatians to move from the southern Urals.[54] From the fourth century BC they began to move into the Black Sea region, displacing the Scythians in the late third century on the steppe. By the third century BC a branch of the Sarmatians had established themselves in the area stretching from the Kuban to the Dnieper in the south Russian-Ukrainian steppe. This Sarmatian branch seems to have been united under strong leadership, and they are known in western sources as the 'Royal Sarmatians' when in the first century AD they may have established a 'kingdom' described cautiously as a 'transitory, unstable early-state formation' that minted coins in the name of a 'king' Farzoi.[55] In the first century AD, Sarmatian tribes started crossing the Danube into the Roman Empire, hence into mainstream western history. They are known under different tribal names by the Roman historians. The main ones are the Iazyges, the Roxolani, the Aorsi and the Alani, who entered Roman territory in different migrations. The latter in particular were to have a major impact, with Alan sub-tribes spreading southwards into the Caucasus and westwards from Poland to the Black Sea and central Europe. The ancestors of the Alans (who might have been a non-Sarmatian tribe) might have been the Wusun, an inner Asian nomadic group on the north-western borderlands of China, mentioned in Chinese sources as early as the first century BC.[56]

The impact on the Roman military was so important that it has been described as a 'Sarmatisation' of the Roman army. Their heavy cavalry armour (in turn influenced by the Parthians, who, it must be noted, were of Central Asian origin before they came to Iran),[57] consisting of small iron or copper plates sewn onto leather, together with the lance and long broad sword was adopted by the Roman army and is depicted on Trajan's

Figure 4.27 *The cavalry barracks at the Roman fort at Chesters on Hadrian's Wall, where Sarmatian cavalry auxiliaries were posted*

column in Rome. From the time of Marcus Aurelius in the second century Sarmatian cavalry auxiliary units were posted to the remote frontiers of the empire. Evidence of the Sarmatians has been found – mainly in archaeology – from frontiers as wide apart as Poland and Georgia to Portugal and Northumberland. Both Hadrian and Marcus Aurelius had to fight several wars against Iazygian and Roxolani tribes in Dacia (present-day Romania), and conflict continued intermittently throughout the third and fourth centuries. On occasion the tribes would fight each other, as one or the other would side with the Romans.

As a result of the peace that Marcus Aurelius established with the Sarmatians, eight thousand Sarmatian cavalry auxiliaries had to be provided for the Roman army, most of them stationed in Britain. A detachment of Sarmatians was posted on Hadrian's Wall at the fort of Chesters (Figure 4.27),[58] and such Sarmatian cavalry units within the late Roman army, it has been suggested, might have been one of the sources of the Arthurian legends.* Indeed, the town of Bremetennacum, modern Ribchester in Lancashire, became effectively a Sarmatian settlement that was still in

---

* Sarmatian mercenary units on Hadrian's Wall form the basis of the 2004 Jerry Bruckheimer film *King Arthur*, although with the appearance of Guinevere from darkest Scotland fighting in a leatherette bikini alongside the knights, the film somewhat departs from both history and Arthurian legend.

existence as late as the fifth century AD, and is depicted on a funerary stele.[59] The Sarmatian warrior worship of a sword fixed in the ground has been suggested as furnishing the origin of the Excalibur legend. This appears to have been a long steppe warrior tradition: Ibn Rusta in the tenth century, for example, describes how the Viking Rus ruler – whom he calls by the steppe title of Khagan or *khāqān* – would plant a naked sword in the earth pointing towards his newborn son.[60]

The Alans were the last to move into western Europe, after having established hegemony over the other Sarmatian tribes by the middle of the second century. They also penetrated southwards into Armenia and even into Iran in several devastating raids, following the well-trodden paths of the Scythians centuries before. Close on the heels of the Alans in the fourth century came the Goths, who in turn were pursued by the Huns.[61] Although these two latter invasions split the Sarmatians into two groups, thereby bringing an end to their history as a distinct unit, both Huns and Goths incorporated Alan units into their armies, as indeed did Rome – a good warrior never had to want for an employer. In the third century a Goth confederation spread from the Baltic to Crimea. Their defeat by the Huns in the fourth century sent them westwards into the Roman Empire, eventually forming a kingdom under Theodoric the Great in Italy. A remnant group, isolated from the main nation, fled into the mountains of Crimea and formed a Gothic kingdom. This Gothic kingdom of Crimea came under Byzantine rule in the sixth century, and Byzantine history records the revolt of the Prince-Bishop John of Gothia against the Khazars in the eighth century. The independence of the Crimean kingdom of Gothia was eventually brought to an end by the Tatars in 1475. But as late as the sixteenth century the Habsburg ambassador to the Ottoman court, Ogier de Busbecq, records the language of the Crimean Goths, still extant in his day, noting its differences with German.[62] Gothic was still recorded as a spoken language in Crimea as late as the seventeenth century, when Goths finally disappear from history (apart from Nazi plans to revive 'Gotland' in occupied Crimea in the 1940s – and as a fashion statement among the youth of early twenty-first-century Europe).

The invasion of the Huns in the fifth century (see Chapter 7) swept the Alans before them. Some joined the Huns in their wars, but other Alan units are recorded joining the Vandals and Suevi in their invasion of Gaul and Spain before settling in Lusitania (modern Portugal). Some groups of Alans even accompanied the Vandals in their invasion of North Africa. Indeed, the Vandal kings included *Rex Vandalorum et Alanorum* in their titles until the end of the Vandal kingdom in North Africa in 533. The Vandals had migrated from Slovakia to Tunisia via Spain and Morocco, some four thousand kilometres; the Alans who accompanied them had started from the Don, a distance of some five thousand kilometres.[63]

Groups of Alans were still recorded in southern France until well into the seventh century, and they survived as isolated communities on the fringes of central Europe for a surprisingly long period, long after Huns, Avars and even the Romans had disappeared. Alan mercenaries fought in Byzantine armies against the Seljuks in the twelfth century. The name 'Serb' is of non-Slavonic origin, and is thought to initially refer to a Sarmatian tribe. According to John of Marinolli, ambassador of Pope Benedict XII to the Yuan court in 1342–6, there were even Alan (Ossetian) units in the Mongol army in China numbering up to thirty thousand.[64] They are recorded as a distinct people in Crimea as late as the seventeenth century.[65] A region of the north Caucasus was still known as 'Alania' into the late Middle Ages. They survive today as the Ossetians in the same region, their direct descendants, still speaking an Iranian language.[66] Although the origin of the Ossetian language in Sarmatian is not in doubt, genetic studies have demonstrated that the ancestors of the Ossetians were indistinguishable from neighbouring non-Ossetian Caucasian populations by the fifth–sixth centuries.[67]

The Scythian and Sarmatian legacy

The Goths and various other eastern Germanic tribes were heavily Sarmatianised. Indeed, many of their armies incorporated large numbers of Sarmatians, as already noted. Hence, the emergence of the medieval institution of the heavily armed, equestrian knightly aristocracy is derived from the steppe tradition rather than that of the Romans. This is probably a Sarmatian legacy (and we have already observed how the Sarmatians influenced the late Roman army).[68] Polish aristocracy have traditionally seen themselves as descendants of Sarmatian chiefs. This was viewed as little more than a tradition without historical basis, as the Slavic origin of the Poles is not in doubt. However, archaeological discoveries of Sarmatian insignia – the so-called 'tamga' signs – from chiefly burials, depicted on grave stelae, belt buckles, bronze mirrors and other items of ornament, have shown a close resemblance to Polish aristocratic coats of arms (officially abolished in 1920) after the eleventh century – centuries before the archaeological discoveries (Figure 4.28). The Sarmatian tamga signs in turn derive from the earlier Iranian identity marks – *nishan* signs – that are found throughout western Eurasia as far back as the first millennium BC.[69]

While the Scythians and Sarmatians, unlike other peoples of Eurasian steppe origin such as the Finns, Estonians, Hungarians and Bulgarians, have left behind no modern European nation, they are in the end one of the more successful. Although the Scythians are remembered mainly as nomads, they founded kingdoms as far apart as Romania, Crimea, Iran, Afghanistan, Pakistan, India and China, many long lasting. No other

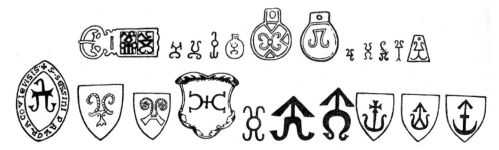

Figure 4.28 *Sarmatian tamga signs (above) compared to Polish coats of arms (after Sulimirski 1963)*

people until the modern period have founded so many and such wide-spread states. Scythian soldiers policed ancient Athens, and it will be seen in later chapters how Scythian identity resurfaced in that of modern Russia. The Sarmatians, although not as widespread, have left their mark – literally in the case of Poland – from the Urals and Caucasus to the Balkans, from Britain to Portugal, to the sword of Excalibur.

But probably the greatest legacy of the ancient steppe people was in two areas that still resonate today. One was the legend of the Amazons and the idea of the female warrior; the other was in the vigorous art styles that they practised. Both are the subjects of the next two chapters.

CHAPTER 5

AMAZONS
Women of the Steppe and the Idea of the Female Warrior

Fifteen days journey from the city of Samarcand, in the direction of China, there is a land inhabited by Amazons, and to this day they continue the custom of having no men with them, except at one time of the year; when they are permitted, by their leaders, to go with their daughters to the nearest settlements, and have communication with men, each taking the one who pleases her most, with whom they live, and eat, and drink, after which they return to their own land. If they bring forth daughters afterwards, they keep them; but they send the sons to their fathers. These women are subject to Timour Beg; they used to be under the emperor of Cathay, and they are Christians of the Greek Church. They are of the lineage of the Amazons who were at Troy, when it was destroyed by the Greeks.
– Ruy Gonzales de Clavijo[1]

One of the most potent images originating in the steppe is that of the female warrior: the Amazon. Whether viewed as the ideal of power, beauty and desire, or the idea of a woman taking over male roles and excelling at them, the image of the female archer on horseback at full gallop or commanding armies is a potent one: history can never resist a warrior queen. Since ancient times, Semiramis, Boadicea and Joan of Arc have been favourite heroines, and the idea of a warrior woman is still a perennial theme in popular culture. Invariably beautiful, warlike yet nubile, and usually tragic, they are written about by both contemporary and later writers with a lasciviousness equal only to these writers' disregard for truth. The idea captured the imagination of the ancient Greeks; the image persisted into the Middle Ages as late as the fifteenth century and is as alive today as it ever was. In fact de Clavijo's description above is lifted almost verbatim from Herodotus, so he would not have heard it from informants during his sojourn at Samarkand. However, it does contain a grain of truth: the fact that he locates them to the east of Samarkand, rather than in Anatolia or the Pontic steppe of the classical accounts, does at least suggest reports reaching him of the high status of women among the steppe nomads east of Samarkand, and so the same steppe nomadic origin of the classical Amazons myths two thousand years before.[2]

Greeks bearing myths

The origin of the Amazons lies in ancient Greek myth. They are first mentioned by Homer, who describes them as 'equal to men' in their fight with Bellerophon. Such a description implies admiration. Since the Bellerophon stories occur before the Trojan Wars, centuries before Homer's own time, the myth is presumably Bronze Age in origin. Amazons were encountered by Jason and his Argonauts, another Bronze Age legend, on the southern shores of the Black Sea in Anatolia. But Herodotus and others locate the 'historic' Amazons on the shores of the Sea of Azov and other ancient writers to the east of the Don – in other words, at the edge of the known world – and most associate them in some way or another with the Scythians. They are variously described as either a tribe of Scythians or as a separate tribe who mated seasonally with the Scythian men before sending them away; male offspring would either be sent to the fathers or simply dispatched, with female children retained and brought up to fight. Herodotus also relates how the women of Scythia revolted against their men-folk while they were away for years raiding Media, and mated with the slaves left behind.[3] This has left indirect traces in both the archaeological and historical record, as Scythians invaded Media in the seventh century BC and established a kingdom there (reviewed in the previous chapter).

The term 'Amazon' is suggested as deriving from *a-mazos/a-mastos* or *a-mazoon* ('breastless'; cf. the word 'mastectomy'), referring to the removal of one breast – or occasionally both – either by cauterisation before puberty or mastectomy after it according to myth. This arose from the misconception that breasts impeded use of the bow. In fact the breast is no impediment to firing a bow; more likely it was an attempt at 'de-feminisation' in the popular Greek imagination, to make the Amazons appear less feminine. This is almost the equivalent of emasculation, which creates eunuchs, to make men less masculine. However, most Greek depictions of Amazons show them fully endowed (Figure 5.1).[4] An alternative derivation is from *maza*, which means barley bread or gruel (cognate with 'maize'), suggesting their diet. Modern philological studies have shown no convincing argument for the derivation of their name, either from Greek or non-Greek languages, despite numerous attempts. Suffice to say that the origin of the name is unknown.[5]

One theory is that the Amazons are largely inventions of the very male-dominated Greek mind, as the 'other' representing the exact antithesis of male domination. Hence, Amazons are a frequent motif in Greek art, often in the 'Amazonomachies' of Greek (male) warriors battling with Amazons (with Amazons on the losing side).[6] They have also been associated with some of the great heroes of Greek legend, either as protagonists or in a more amorous role (or both), emphasising their ambivalence in

Figure 5.1 *Modern and ancient images of the Amazon. Modern bronze representation in the National Museum of Chuvashia, Cheboksari (left) and a Hellenistic marble statue in the Pergamon Museum, Berlin (right)*

the Greek mind. As well as Bellerophon's heroic battle, Achilles fought Amazons, killing their queen Penthesilea but then killing his friend Thersites for accusing him of being in love with her. Other heroic dalliances with Amazon queens involved Theseus and Heracles. The former fathered a daughter, Hippolyte, by the Amazon queen, the latter had to seize the Amazon queen's girdle as one of his twelve labours. Another legend associates Heracles with the Scythian snake-goddess (Figure 5.2), with the Amazons descended from the union. They are even associated with real historical personages: Tomyris, the 'Amazon' warrior queen of the Massagetae (a Scythian tribe), supposedly defeated and killed Cyrus the Great in battle as vengeance for the death of her son; Alexander of Macedon supposedly received a proposal of marriage from the Amazon

Figure 5.2 Greek representation of the Scythian serpent goddess from Panticapaeum in the Kerch Museum, Crimea

queen of Scythia during his Central Asian campaign (which he rejected, having other fish to fry). But even as amorous roles in Greek myth, Amazons are no different from the losing side on Amazonomachies: as women, they must be dominated, they still represent the alien, the enemy, the 'other'. Hence, Amazons are no more real than the giants or centaurs, but are the enemy 'others' also frequently depicted in Greek battle art as imaginary beings to be overcome and defeated as well: 'dead giant, dead Amazon, dead Persian, dying Gaul', as Caroline Vout succinctly observes of the Roman versions of a 200 BC Acropolis group.[7]

According to Aristaeus of Proconnesus (recorded by Herodotus), as early as the seventh century BC men and women among the Issedones had equal authority. The Issedones were a steppe people related to the Scythians, although their location is disputed, from anywhere between southern Ukraine and Siberia.[8] The second-century AD writer Polyaenus gives an account of the third-century BC Sarmatian queen Amage, who mounted a coup against her husband and waged war against the Scythians.[9] According to Byzantine sources, the Sabir tribes of the Urals in the fifth century were ruled by a 'Queen Boa' commanding some twenty thousand soldiers. But for all they figure so highly in Greek writing, Greek art and the Greek imagination generally, nobody had ever actually *seen* an Amazon, merely imagined them. The Greeks after all were perfectly familiar with the Scythians – there was even a contingent of Scythian archers in Athens[10] – and if any were female they would surely have raised eyebrows and left their mark in history. Most of the evidence for steppe warrior women rests on weapons found in female Sarmatian graves. The Romans were even more familiar with the Sarmatians than the Greeks were with Scythians, incorporating them into their own army, depicting them in illustrations such as on Trajan's column in Rome. From the invasions of late antiquity, when many Sarmatian tribes such as the Roxelani, Alans and others invaded the empire, numerous descriptions survive: there is not one single illustration or description that even hints that any of these warriors were women. They were, therefore, just an idea right from the beginning.[11]

Matriarchy in 'Old Europe'

Archaeology has revealed some possible origins of the Amazon myth. The main evidence comes from the Scythian and – especially – Sarmatian graves of the Iron Age. But before reviewing this, we should consider an older element that might be relevant. The suggestion that the Amazon myth was the memory of an earlier matriarchal society was first made in 1861 by J. J. Bachofen,[12] a theory further elaborated by the archaeologist and anthropologist Marija Gimbutas, one of the pioneers in the study of what she termed 'Old Europe': the prehistory of south-eastern Europe (extending to Malta in the west and western Anatolia in the east) before the invasion of the Indo-Europeans some time before 4000 BC. Referring to the pre-Indo-European Neolithic and Chalcolithic cultures of Europe as 'Great Civilizations',[13] Gimbutas interpreted them and the society of 'Old Europe' as essentially matriarchal, dominated by the worship of mother-goddesses, living at one with the environment where men were relegated to second place in society. This prehistoric arcadia was brought to an end with the Indo-European invasions that were essentially aggressive, destructive and masculine, ushering in male domination, conflict and wholesale devastation of the environment.[14]

Gimbutas was a major scholar who carried out pioneering work in both European prehistory and Indo-European philology, so her studies demand respect. Her 'eco-feminist' ideas have made her a cult figure in feminist circles in America. However, doubt has been cast on many of her 'Old Europe' theories by many archaeologists (and not just by male ones)[15] and much of her Goddess argument is essentially circular. Archaeological and linguistic studies now regard the Indo-European 'invasions' as unwarlike ('more like a franchising operation than an invasion', as David Anthony put it)[16] and the warrior myth largely a product of nineteenth-century romanticism and racial theory.[17] But might matriarchy/female warriors be distant folk memories of the period of migrations into the Balkans from the north in the first millennium, and then later Greek efforts to understand from where they came? And there is one aspect of the Indo-European spread that conquered: a near-total 'linguicide', extinguishing all pre-Indo-European languages with the exception of the sole pocket of Basque (Chapter 3).

Evidence from archaeology

Of course there is never smoke without fire, and archaeology can supply the fire – or at least a smoulder. There is some evidence for a change from societies with matriarchal elements in the Neolithic and Chalcolithic periods to more patriarchal societies in the Bronze Age on the steppe. But this was unlikely to have corresponded with the extreme view interpreted by Gimbutas of a sudden change from wholly matriarchal peaceful Neolithic societies brought about by incoming masculine Indo-European conquerors (although admittedly Gimbutas is discussing societies further west in 'Old Europe'). The changes were more likely to have been gradual within the same societies, brought about by a slow evolution from the pastoral and agricultural economies of the Neolithic to the stock-rearing and semi-nomadic economies in the Bronze Age on the steppe and the consequent increase in male labour. In extreme cases recorded in some of the Andronovo burials this took the form of the wife – or other symbolic female victim – being sacrificed at the husband's death and buried alongside to accompany him in the afterlife. Similar practices were still observed by Arab travellers in the Middle Ages on the Russian steppe in the middle Volga.[18] But the practice quickly disappeared on the steppe in the Bronze Age, probably due more to the increasing economic value of living, working widows rather than any particular moral considerations. And despite the patriarchy of steppe societies, women were always traditionally of higher status than their sedentary sisters. The old matriarchal systems to a large extent coexisted with the patriarchal; it was never one-sided. There is also evidence in some Bronze Age Yamnaya graves on the western steppe of occasional leadership roles for women.[19] Since the Yamnaya are now regarded as the proto-Indo-Europeans (Chapter 3), this somewhat contradicts the image of essentially masculine and aggressive Indo-Europeans.

Some evidence for female steppe warriors has been found in China. At the late thirteenth-century BC Shang royal capital at Anyang, the intact tomb of the 'warrior queen' Fu Hao was excavated in the 1970s. Fu Hao was a non-Chinese consort – assumed to be from the steppe – of the Shang king Wu Ding, and her exploits are recorded on Shang oracle bones as leading armies into battle. The grave goods of another tomb of a female at Baifu, north of Beijing, dating from the late eleventh–early tenth century BC, included a bronze helmet, numerous horse fittings and over sixty bronze weapons. A second female tomb at Baifu also contained similar grave goods, albeit not as rich. Both are assumed to be non-Chinese, presumably from the steppe.[20]

Excavations of Scythian and – more commonly – Sarmatian burial mounds in southern Russia and Ukraine have revealed the graves of women buried with weapons, usually bows and spears, but occasionally also with swords. This is not so surprising: the very harsh, rigorous life of the steppe nomad demanded a more equal role for women than in the sedentary life of the towns and villages, where women were usually relegated to more traditional roles. The ancient Greek male mind would view this with horror, as standing in stark contrast to their own womenfolk who were allowed no public life beyond the household.

Scythian culture was a very diverse one. Most Scythians were at least semi-nomadic pastoralists comprising many different tribes. There was a strong hierarchy dominated by a military elite who left behind the most spectacular of the tombs (Chapters 4 and 6). Scythian women traditionally had high status, and both Herodotus in the far west and the second–first-century BC Chinese historian Sima Qian in the far east note that Scythian women enjoyed equal status with the men.[21] On occasion, some might even be warriors, and be buried with their weapons. The burial of a rich woman at Kurgan 22 at Volnaya Ukraina included a sword, but armaments are generally more common in graves of ordinary women than the elite.[22] However, it must be emphasised that most female Scythian burials were characterised by jewellery rather than weapons.

Scythian art characteristically illustrated male warriors, but there is not a single depiction of a female warrior. Elite burials have a high percentage of violent injuries. Although the evidence for the sex of burials is uneven, whenever the skeletons of 'warrior burials' – burials with weapons – are analysed the overwhelming majority are of adult males. Burials of armed Scythians where the skeletons have been shown to be female have been recorded, but the evidence is slight.[23] On the other hand, one must guard against sexing a burial by indirect evidence alone: weapons = male, mirrors and jewellery = female does not necessarily follow. Even so, the overwhelming evidence points to Scythian society of the western steppe as being heavily militarised and male-dominated.

There is more evidence for armed women among Sarmatian burials. Although those with weapons were mainly male, 20 per cent of female burials also contained weapons. At the excavations of the Sarmatian cemetery of Pokrovka near the Russian–Kazakh border, for example, 94 per cent of male burials included weapons, but so too did 15 per cent of female (most of whom, interestingly, were teenage) – but 75 per cent of female burials contained domestic items. Many female burials included religious trappings, and evidence for priestesses in ancient steppe society has been found across Inner Eurasia (the 'Ukok Princess' being a famous example). Of high-status burials, 75 per cent were female.[24]

A complete set of horse harnesses was found in an early Iron Age female burial from Tasmola in central Kazakhstan. The female burials at Tasmola indicate the status of women as equal to that of men: 'Numerous harnesses and altars from women's tombs indicate that women played an important role in the production, life and even wars of the Tasmola culture.'[25] Almost all cult objects from Tasmola, including altars, were from the female burials, also implying a shamanistic role, a role also noted in the Altai frozen tombs (Chapter 4). Similar altars found in the lower Syr Darya region were also from female burials.[26]

Archaeologists rightly caution against sexing an ancient burial on the evidence of burial objects alone without skeletal or DNA evidence, but equally one should not jump to conclusions of Amazons simply because a female burial might contain weapons. A sword is just a sword, and might be as symbolic in male burials as in female, simply indicating status or caste (in India, for example, belonging to a warrior caste – *kshatriya* – is regardless of either sex or fighting prowess). Arrows, knives and horse trappings might be evidence of warriorhood, but is equally evidence for hunting, of which all members of a tribe would have partaken – and all women would ride as much as the men. Female skeletal evidence of death in battle might indicate warrior status, or merely that women were slaughtered in a raid. Women in a tribe would in any case need forms of self-defence in the event of an unexpected raid by a rival tribe when their men-folk were off on a hunting party – or raiding some other tribe's women and cattle (and a word relating to 'cattle raiding' is among the small number of reconstructed words in proto-Indo-European).[27] Some of the women – younger, stronger, more aggressive (and those in the Pokrovka burials cited above, one recalls, were mainly teenage) – might have received special training for this.

Evidence from ethnology

The more active role of women on the steppe receives considerable support from ethnic studies. Mongol women, for example, actively participate in traditional male sports and activities such as the hunt* as well as – at least until recently – warfare, and partake in decision making on all levels. Gender roles among modern Kazakh nomads were observed to be male-dominated, albeit with a high level of egalitarianism.[28]

A noted example is the life of Qutlun, the daughter of Qaidu Khan, the fourteenth-century ruler of the Chaghatai Khanate in Central Asia and a descendant of Genghis Khan. Qutlun was a warrior who accompanied her father on campaign and fought in battle. She insisted that she would only marry a man who could beat her in single combat; none did, so she remained unmarried until gossip eventually forced her into marriage.

---

* The acclaimed 2016 documentary film *The Eagle Huntress*, the story of a thirteen-year-old girl both participating in the hunt and competing in the Mongolian eagle competition, has been cited in support of this, but in fact is evidence of the opposite: the entire point of the film is that she is unique.

Marco Polo, to whom she was known as Aijaruc (Mongolian for 'Bright Moon'), describes her as 'very beautiful, but also strong and brave . . . so tall and muscular, so stout and shapely withall, that she was almost like a giantess'.[29] Mamluk envoys to the Golden Horde in the fourteenth century expressed amazement at the equality of Mongol women.[30] Marco Polo, William of Rubruck and John of Plano Carpini all emphasise the high status of Mongol women and their place in decision making, as well as their proficiency in such 'manly' pursuits as horse-riding and archery. In the Mongol Empire women exerted powerful influence and were involved in decision making, often at the highest level, although their positions remained as wives and mothers of powerful men rather than executive positions in their own right.[31]

The early Bulgars of the steppe were said to have used armed women in the wars fought by the founder of the first Bulgarian Empire, Khan Krum, in the ninth century (discussed further in Chapter 9).[32] Ibn al-Faqih in the tenth century wrote of the pagan steppe Turks that both boys and girls, on reaching maturity, are presented with a bow and arrow and encouraged to fend for themselves. He further writes that the women fight with the men and even on occasion rape enemy men.[33] On the other hand, as regards another major steppe nation, the Avars, the very little evidence we have suggests that Avar women – even the elite – were very much subordinate.[34]

Ottoman women: a case study

Did the greater sexual equality of steppe people continue after sedenterisation? The position of women under the Ottomans – Christian as well as Muslim – makes an interesting case study. In a groundbreaking account of the position of women in eighteenth-century Europe, Margaret Hunt examines women in Ottoman society* and overturns many preconceived assumptions.[35] Western perceptions of the role of women under the Ottomans were determined above all by a West European fascination with the Ottoman imperial harem. This fascination was backed up by a huge eighteenth- and nineteenth-century West European vogue for lascivious 'orientalist' art depicting vaguely titillating harem scenes and other mild erotica, let alone an only slightly more serious (but equally misleading) fashion for operas ranging from Mozart's *Il Seraglio* to Rossini's *Italian Girl in Algiers* (and a huge number of others).

---

* Unusually – and refreshingly – Hunt takes a whole view of 'Europe', to include Russia and the Ottoman Empire, not the narrow view that so many historians take of including only western Europe.

Of course, sex is an endless source of fascination – and prejudice – for all societies, and not just in terms of Christian attitudes towards Muslims,* and polygamy was the main institution that appeared to set Ottoman marriage and women apart from Christian Europe. Ottoman women, however, enjoyed considerable rights. For example, they could initiate divorce proceeding (domestic violence, abuse of property rights, or a husband taking a second wife without permission were all valid grounds), and Islamic law enforced provision by the ex-husband for a divorced woman's financial support commensurate with the standard she had enjoyed while married. Few women elsewhere in Europe enjoyed such rights until the nineteenth century. It also awarded divorced women custody of the children: boys until the age of seven, girls until puberty.

Property laws for women in the Ottoman Empire were in advance of any in most European countries before the nineteenth century, so much so that even Christian women in the Ottoman Empire generally preferred the Muslim courts over their own Orthodox ones (usually run by the clergy) because of the fairer deal they would receive. For example, following the conquest of Cyprus in 1571 the number of women flocking to the Muslim courts was a matter of considerable concern to the Orthodox clergy. The Seljuks too accorded particular prominence to women in their courts.[36] Successful recourse to the law courts became standard practice for women of all classes – and religions – in Ottoman lands from the fifteenth century onwards, a practice entrenched in traditional Islamic law. Hunt cites, for example, that in the approximately 10,600 court cases between 1603 and 1627 in Kayseri in Anatolia, 17 per cent of the litigants were women, usually in cases involving property but also in those involving divorce and domestic violence.[37]

Indeed, women generally enjoyed superior property rights in Ottoman lands, both in terms of inheritance and independent control of assets. Many could become major investors, patrons and philanthropists in their own right. In the same statistics for Kayseri cited above, 40 per cent of all property cases were brought by women. Up to a third of all buyers of commercial property and investors in Aleppo in the mid-eighteenth century were women, and many women in general in the Ottoman Empire grew immensely wealthy in their own (as opposed to their husband's) right and became major property owners.

Women's relative financial independence frequently achieved physical form in the surprisingly large number of mosques, madrasas and charitable institutions that were endowed by women. This practice began as far back as the Seljuk period when many major architectural religious complexes

* In this context it is worth noting that perhaps the biggest source of prejudice of extreme Islamicists today towards 'Western' societies is the perceived sexual mores of its women.

in Anatolia were endowed by or dedicated to leading Seljuk women. The tradition of female endowments was continued by the Ottomans: of the six mosque complexes built in Istanbul by Süleyman the Magnificent's family, three – a half – were endowed by women of the royal house. Hafsa Sultan – Süleyman's mother – built a complex in Manisa comprising a mosque, madrasa, hospice, primary school, kitchen, hospital and bath-house, altogether employing a staff of a hundred, while Mihrimah – his daughter – built similar complexes both at Uskudar and at the Edirne Gate of Istanbul (both complexes designed by Sinan). Haseki Hürrem (Roxelana) – his wife – endowed mosque complexes in Istanbul, Edirne, Jerusalem, Mecca and Medina, the Jerusalem complex alone comprising a mosque, a fifty-five-room hospice, a bakery, kitchen, cellar, granary, woodshed, refectory, lavatories, inn and a stable. The Yeni Valide Mosque on the Golden Horn – the last of the great imperial mosque complexes in Istanbul and now one of the city's more visible landmarks – was begun by Safiye Sultan, the mother of Sultan Murad IV, and completed by Turhan Sultan and included a mosque, a bazaar, madrasa, fountain, library, mausoleum and caravanserai.[38]

Of course it would be a mistake to view the position of women under the Ottomans with rose-tinted spectacles, but it is equally important to recognise the misconceptions. The rights of women in Ottoman society to a large extent are grounded in traditional Islam. But they also derived from a separate Turkish tradition reaching further back into their Central Asian nomadic roots, a tradition that continued under the Ottomans. In Turkish Central Asia many great buildings were accordingly dedicated to or endowed by women. Samarkand's greatest mosque, the Bibi Khanum, comes to mind, as does the great funerary complex of the Shah-i Zindeh, which commemorates mainly women of the Timurid household, or the huge complex built by Queen Gawharshad at Herat. The Turks brought the tradition with them into Anatolia, and the conquest of India by a separate group of Turks, the Mughals, resulted in what is probably the most famous building in the world dedicated to a woman: the Taj Mahal.

The idea of the warrior woman

In a fascinating 1995 study, Marina Warner analyses the often uncomfortable fact that the female form has been used since antiquity to personify abstract ideas, from the images that personify ancient classical cities to the armed figures who personify modern ideas of liberty, victory, or even modern nations such as Great Britain: 'Why should Truth be a woman? or Nature? or Justice? or Liberty? Not, certainly, because women have been more free, just, truthful, nor even (though this one has a double edge) more natural', as one of the reviews states on the rear cover.[39] The image and idea of the warrior female bequeathed to us by Greek views of the steppe are perennial ones that have never left us. As early as the thirteenth century a French miniature depicts the women of Scythia – presumably Amazons – besieging a fortress,[40] and they were a popular motif in Greek art, as we have noted. The fourteenth-century fictional traveller Sir John Mandeville wrote 'and beside Sichem [Scythia] is the lande of Amazony, wherein dwell none but women', as well as a chapter 'On the Kingdome of Amazony'.[41] Armed women became a popular theme in Renaissance and Baroque paintings, either as Amazons themselves, such as Claude Deruet's seventeenth-century Amazon cycle in the New York Metropolitan Museum,[42] or portraits of queens (even Elizabeth I), who would routinely be depicted bearing arms (usually in the guise of Minerva).[43] A particular popular theme throughout was that of an armed Judith either beheading Holophernes (often depicted in grisly details) or lovingly cradling the result.[44] Even abstract ideas could be personified by armed women, such as the triumph of Wisdom over Ignorance,[45] or (in the nineteenth century) the personification of (military, masculine) victories on many a triumphal arch where winged victories were invariably female. Or the armed Liberty – bare-breasted (for no other reason than to remove all doubt as to her sex), despite her bearing a musket with fixed bayonet – leading the people in Eugène Delacroix's famous revolutionary painting in the Louvre.

Probably the greatest 'warrior woman' of the Middle Ages that has excited the imagination ever since was a teenager, Joan of Arc. To a certain extent the phenomenon of Joan of Arc was also the phenomenon of youth. Marina Warner explains twelve-to-fourteen-year-old hermits, prophets and holy men of the Middle Ages as part of her background,[46] and one recalls the so-called 'Children's Crusade' of 1220 supposedly preached and led by the twelve-year-old French peasant boy Stephen.[47] History has shown time and again that men will follow a youthful warrior with energy and charisma – Babur, for example, springs to mind, or Alexander of Macedon, but there are many others – with blind, almost unquestioning fanaticism. It is no coincidence that the rise of the cult of youth since the 1950s also saw the rise of the female warrior in popular culture reviewed below (all of whom, it goes without saying, are young).

Elsewhere, in recent history Soviet propaganda promoted Stalin as the 'father figure', with the citizen as his 'family', but what was lacking in order to make the 'trilogy' complete was a mother figure.[48] Stalin's own wife had committed suicide, but even if there had been a convenient wife or other mother figure, a US-style 'First Lady' cult would have been inappropriate in Russia. However, there was – and is – the ancient idea of 'Mother Russia', an idea stemming directly from the earth, from the steppe. Hans Günther takes a musical example:

Figure 5.3 *Soviet-era 'Mother/Amazon' figures at Yerevan, Tbilisi and Kiev*

The 1936 Soviet song ['Broad Is My Motherland'] is unquestionably about the gigantic body of the motherland, the blood of her rivers, and the hair of her fields and forests. In this song, as in many other phenomena of the 1930s culture, something new – the mother archetype – reaches beyond the bounds of the revolutionary epoch and finds expression.

And further: 'The young people, the earth mother, and the wise father – all of them together form the happy Great Family . . . The motherland sings, and bread abounds.'[49]

Hence, towering over the capital cities of many of the Soviet Bloc countries – Yerevan, Tbilisi, Minsk, Kiev, Budapest, Bishkek, Riga,* for example – are giant mother figures: 'Mother Armenia', 'Mother Georgia' and so forth, but in fact symbols of Mother Russia's domination. And those at Yerevan, Tbilisi and Kiev at least are Amazons: they wield swords (Figure 5.3). The greatest of all, of course, is the gigantic Stalingrad War Memorial at Volgograd, the largest free-standing statue in the world, an Amazon figure wielding a sword and facing the Volga (the 'blood of Mother Russia' – and one recalls that the Volga in Russia is 'Mother Volga'), defending Mother Russia against the invader – but in facing the Volga it is facing east, not west whence the Germans invaded but the direction from where the steppe hordes came (Figure 5.4).

Marina Warner draws attention to a modern fashion for masculinity in women: 'Current ideals of female beauty are leaner, tougher, and

---

* Those at Bishkek and Riga, while still gigantic, do not tower over the city but are comparatively modest. All from personal observation.

Figure 5.4 *The giant Amazon/Stalingrad victory monument at Volgograd*

stronger by contrast to the not so distant past';[50] and modern women wear trousers, unthinkable for one's grandmother's generation. Part of the current feminist empowerment of women – or the exact opposite? Over the past few years there has been a revival of the idea of the female archer in popular culture and cinema. Examples are in such films as *Prince Caspian, The Hunger Games, 300: The Rise of an Empire* and *The Hobbit: the Desolation of Smaug*. In all of these cases, publicity images have specifically depicted a female archer in the act of drawing the bow: Susan in *Prince Caspian*, Katniss in *Hunger Games*, Artemisia in *300* and Tauriel in *Hobbit*. The idea of the Amazon has become a popular and

Figure 5.5 *Amazons in the movies: films whose publicity images feature iconic female archers*

potent advertisement (Figure 5.5). In the case of *The Hobbit*, the archer-elf Tauriel is not in J. R. R. Tolkien's original story, but has been deliberately created by the film makers, presumably as a concession to modern demands. In both literature and on the screen, Philip Pullman's extraordinary creation of the northern witches in *His Dark Materials* is another incarnation of the Amazon idea: beautiful yet ferocious, passionate and desirable yet jealous, bare-armed and diaphanously clothed, armed with bow and arrows and riding cloud pine instead of horses, they are the very embodiment of the Amazon.

Figure 5.6 *Amazons as advertisement: gun advertisement on the side of a van in Vladivostok*

There is an increasing number other examples in cinema and video games of female action heroines: the Chinese swordswoman *Mulan* (both the 1998 Disney animated and the 2020 live action versions), the martial artist Jen Yu in *Crouching Tiger Hidden Dragon*, Batman's Catwoman, Xena the Warrior Princess, Lara Croft Tomb Raider, Buffy the Vampire Slayer, the 'real' Amazon *Wonder Woman* (in both television and cinematic versions), to give just some examples.[51] There are the far more ambivalent (and downplayed) chariot-riding Amazon archers (interestingly, all black Africans) in the arena in Ridley Scott's *Gladiator* (all slain by the gladiators).[52] There is even the image of (a Scottish) Guinevere in a leatherette bikini fighting with bow and arrow alongside the knights in the 2004 Jerry Bruckheimer film *King Arthur* – or the equally unrealistic one of a full-armour-clad Maid Marion leading a cavalry charge against a French invasion in the 2010 Ridley Scott film *Robin Hood*.

The imagery has progressed from archery and swords to firearms: the sadistic (but of course beautiful) female mass killer in the James Bond movie *Goldeneye*, for example; and gun advertisements – typically in the USA but increasingly elsewhere as well – routinely feature a scantily clad women brandishing or firing sophisticated weaponry (Figure 5.6).[53] All are latter-day Amazons, at once both bowing to feminist demands for greater female roles and at the same time pandering to male fantasies – as well as the fantasies of women, who like to see strong women dominating men? And all are just as fictional as the originals. To some extent, the idea of the Amazon has become part of the ammunition of feminism: women as well as men are to welcome an idea that seeks to place women on an equal footing to men. At the same time, the image of the weapon-wielding female in Figure 5.6 objectifies and diminishes women. And surely the desire to become a warrior – to kill and be killed – is not something that women as well as men should admire, but something they should abhor. Feminism with militarism? Whatever they were, the Amazons were, and remain, a potent symbol.

A 'lande of Amazony'?

In conclusion, it must be said that the Amazons, unlike Sarmatians or Scythians or other peoples of the southern Russian steppe, are mythical, with no hard evidence for their existence. But many myths are founded on some fact, however small, and it is possible to find some archaeological basis for the myth. And whether mythical or merely wishful thinking, the image of the female warrior is one of the most persistent themes in our – and many other – cultures (Figure 5.7). It finds its echo in, for example, the icon of Britannia (Figure 5.8), or the image used for a belligerent – or at least revolutionary – France by Delacroix, or the many statues of 'Mother Russia' wielding a sword seen throughout the former Soviet Union (Figures 5.3, 5.4). In a recent spate of books on the Amazons, the term 'Amazon' has been broadened to define virtually any dominant woman in ancient and recent history,[54] and *The Encyclopaedia of Amazons* includes any strong woman, both fictional and non-fictional, from Annie

Figure 5.7 *Amazons as décor: image in the lobby of the Hotel Don Plaza at Rostov-on-Don*

Figure 5.8 *Amazons as currency: a Swiss two franc coin and a British fifty pence coin*

Oakley to 'Zobeida the Whipper' in the definition.[55] Is this just wishful thinking, to make up for the paucity of hard evidence for troops of warrior women fighting in battles in antiquity?

There is one element in the Amazon myth that rings true where women are the equal to men in martial skills: archery. Hence the Greek myths of female mastectomy and the large numbers of bows and arrows found in Inner Asian female burials (which, it must be emphasised, would have been used more for hunting rather than for warfare). Hence too the recent equestrian 'steppe' sport originating in Hungary of shooting arrows at targets from horseback at full gallop, which has found particular popularity among women.[56] Another fighting skill where women are the equal of men, requiring skill rather than physical strength, is represented by the various Far Eastern forms of martial arts. But despite contemporary forms of mechanised and more remote warfare which can be fought as much by men as by women (Kurdistan's female battalions are a frequently cited example, but this is an exception rather than the rule),[57] warfare and violence generally has been overwhelmingly male throughout history.

What does it all add up to? It has to be said that nobody had actually *seen* an Amazon. Weapons in female burials might be as symbolic as weapons in male ones, and the occasional rare reports of female fighters are at best hearsay, at worst rumours. Even such famous historical fighting women as Zenobia of Palmyra or Joan of Arc only ever led armies rather than actually joining in the mêlée of fighting (roles in fact no different from male commanders', from Caesar to General Eisenhower).

Ultimately, the idea of the Amazon represents extremes of both male and female fantasy. On the one hand they were the worst male nightmare and very antithesis of femininity: breastless – hence sexless – androgynes who suppressed both their sexuality and their men-folk, killing males and taking over the male role. The ultimate antithesis of the existing Greek order in other words, where womenfolk were completely subservient to their men, hence located on the very fringes of the civilised world in Scythia. On the other hand they represented male fantasy: the ultimate embodiment of unfettered female sexuality, the dominatrix who chose her sexual partners at will without romantic attachment, demands or obligations – a narrow line between swords and shields and whips and leather. For women they represent achieving the ultimate equal footing with men: warfare (never mind that warfare can be viewed as a depravity). Perhaps it is for these reasons that Amazons have remained such a potent image since antiquity, when Sarmatians and Scythians have long since sunk to obscurity, while the Maikop and Karasuk cultures have never even left the academic libraries.

CHAPTER 6

THE ART OF THE STEPPE
From Animal Style to Art Nouveau

What has made Scythian art so distinctive is that the vast majority of surviving objects are of gold, and of a gold of beautiful quality and frequently of excellent craftsmanship.
– Esther Jacobsen[1]

Being nomadic for so much of their history, the Scythians have naturally left few material traces in terms of settlement: no great cities, temples, or palaces. There is one fixed abode, however, which even nomads cannot do without: their burials. These are known as *kurgans* in Russian (a Turkish loan word) or *mogila* in Ukrainian: underground burial chambers, often constructed of wood, covered by high mounds of earth, whose distinctive silhouettes are often the only relief on the otherwise flat Eurasian steppe (Figure 1.1). Kurgans can be monumental structures in the full sense of the word. Those in Khakasia in Siberia are often massive stone structures, such as the immense megalithic Salbyk Kurgan described in Chapter 4. Many kurgans enclose impressive wooden structures, among the largest and oldest wooden structures known, such as Besshatyr in Kazakhstan where the source of the logs was over two hundred kilometres away, or Arzhan 1 in Tuva where an astonishing six thousand tree trunks were used in the construction (the average log cabin uses just fifty logs). The huge Tolstaya Mogala in Ukraine was covered by some half a million cubic feet of topsoil. However, there was no depression surrounding it from where the topsoil might have been taken. Analysis showed that the topsoil comprised carefully layered pieces of turf taken from a location four kilometres away.[2] Clearly, the Scythians expended as much care and labour on their funerary monuments as many a settled culture did on its temples and palaces.

A related monument in Mongolia and adjacent regions are 'deer stone-*khirigsuur*' complexes: ritual sites of the late Bronze Age of about 1200–700 BC (although dates are disputed), consisting of often massive stone mounds surrounded by square or circular stone frames, occasionally connected by radiating arms. They are best described as ceremonial complexes, but their exact function is uncertain: ritual or funerary (although they are often not associated with burials). They are often associated with carved stone stelae three to four metres high, the so-called 'deer-stones'.[3]

But it is not the architecture for which these kurgans are renowned so much as their contents.[4] Many of the Scythian elite were buried with a vast array of treasures: gold vessels, weapons, felts, carpets and other textiles, as well as items of every-day use. Fabulous treasures from nomad tombs have been found not only in Ukraine and Russia, but also in Thrace, Bulgaria, Iran, Siberia, Kazakhstan, Kyrgyzstan, Mongolia and China. These objects form showpieces of the Hermitage in St Petersburg and have become familiar worldwide from international exhibitions show-casing Scythian gold.

Gold

Esther Jacobsen rightly emphasises the importance of gold in Scythian art in the quotation at the beginning of this chapter, further emphasising that more gold art has survived among the Scythians than from most other ancient cultures. This is partly because gold is immutable so can survive in perfect form, but the same is true of, for example, Persian or Syrian gold, which has not survived

Figure 6.1 Bronze deer in mid-movement: top from Ukok in the Institute of Archaeology Museum at Akademgorodok, bottom two in the Minusinsk Museum

in anywhere near the same quantity. This may be because of gold's intrinsic value, hence its being more prone to recycling and looting in antiquity. Its intrinsic value also perhaps makes it more prone to study, the fascination for gold being universal. But the same can be said of Scythian gold. The point that Jacobsen makes is that it *has* been plundered: in by far the majority of excavated kurgans the contents have been looted, usually in antiquity. What we see now of Scythian gold must, therefore, represent a tiny fraction of the amount of Scythian works of art and craftsmanship that originally existed: 'There is no doubt that the vast majority of what was originally made for the Scythians has been lost . . . and . . . object

Figure 6.2 *Replica of a Scythian gold cover for a* gorytus *from Kelermes in the Krasnodar Museum (original in the Hermitage)*

Figure 6.3 *Sarmatian wooden stag covered in gold leaf from Filippovka in the National Museum of Bashkortostan, Ufa*

types we now know only through one or two examples may have originally referred to a substantial number.'[5]

Herodotus recounts the foundation legends of the Scythians north of the Black Sea. These tell of four gold objects that fell to earth from heaven: a cup, a sword, a yoke and a plough. Accordingly, gold was, in effect, worshipped by the Scythians for its own sake rather than for its intrinsic value as an exchange commodity. This receives added support when we observe that even many wooden or bone objects were coated in gold leaf to simulate gold (Figure 6.3). Hence, the Scythian tribes would hold an annual gold festival.[6] This is confirmed by the quantities of gold found in Scythian tombs, evidence not so much of wealth – nomads would have little need of a cash economy – but of the sacred nature of gold (see e.g. Figures 6.2, 6.7, 6.11, 6.15, 6.21, 6.24 and 6.26). There is emphasis on gold bowls (Figure 6.16), representing heaven; swords too are given prominence, although it must be admitted that ploughs are generally conspicuous by their absence. But if gold was regarded for its own sake rather than its monetary value, the fact that so many 'royal tombs' were robbed so soon after burial seems to belie this: it is surely only worth robbing a royal tomb if the profit is high enough to justify the risks – unless they were robbed by the successor chief and the objects re-interred in the successor's tomb. Are many of the gold objects, therefore, simply recycled: effectively heirlooms, already many generations old at the time of deposition? It has in fact been recognised that objects in a Scythian burial assemblage often represent a wide variety of dates, styles and provenances, such as the Achaemenid sword in the Chertomlyk kurgan, already more than a century old when it was deposited.[7]

There is another reason why gold features so largely: it is the easiest of metals for a nomad to procure and handle. Gold is rare, found only in small quantities in specific localities that might be far distant from one's base. This, for example, is one reason gold was relatively rare among the ancient Persians: there are few natural deposits in Iran, and the Parthians were the only major ancient power which did not issue a gold coinage. For nomads, this is less of a problem; migrating vast distances is their way of life and they would have had access to sources of gold that might be many thousands of miles away – through inter-tribal exchange or raids across the steppes, if not directly.

Figure 6.4 *Leather cut-out decoration of a beast from Ukok in the Institute of Archaeology Museum at Akademgorodok*

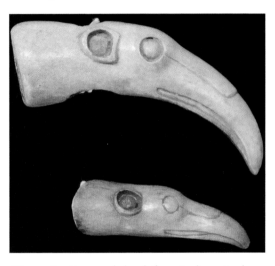

Figure 6.5 *Bone eagle heads from Arzhan 1 in the National Museum of Tuva, Kyzyl*

Figure 6.6 *Sarmatian gold limbs and head of a bear reconstructed from Filippovka in the National Museum of Bashkortostan, Ufa*

Figure 6.7 *Replica of a Scythian gold plaque of a feline from Kelermes in the Krasnodar Museum (original in the Hermitage)*

These sources, usually alluvial gold in mountain streams, are furthermore easy to tap by simple panning and similar methods, without the sophisticated mining for copper or iron that requires a sedentary population. The mountains on the fringes of the Scythian world, the Urals, the Caucasus and the Altai, are moreover all gold-bearing. Because of gold's intrinsic worth it is also easier to transport in the form of small objects of great value: nomads could not have their wealth tied up in permanent fixed structures, such as palaces, or bulky commodities; tribal wealth in the form of gold was easy to transport, usually on one's person in the form of ornament. In effect the tribal chief was the palace (or at least the state treasury). Their other form of transportable wealth was the hoof, and horses often figured as highly in Scythian burials as gold did.

Figure 6.8 *Bronze plaque in the form of a coiled beast from Arzhan 1, ninth to eighth century* BC, *National Museum of Tuva*

Most of all, gold is the easiest of metals to work. Copper and, especially, iron requires sophisticated processing techniques that were only possible in fixed, permanent settlements (such as the 'Country of Towns', Chapter 2). Gold requires none of this: it melts at much lower temperatures than copper or iron, so can be smelted in furnaces that would be easily available to a nomad. It can also be worked comparatively easily with fairly simple tools, all of which can easily be transported on a nomad's seasonal migration.

The nomad's way of life also involved long periods of leisure, usually in the winter months, and decorative objects are often the result of such leisure. Carved objects of wood and bone are a characteristic of the nomadic lifestyle everywhere and at all times. Such skills would easily be transferred to working gold into the wonderful objects, ornaments and works of art that so characterise Scythian culture. The subjects depicted on these objects were equally a part of their way of life: their myths, the world of the steppe about them and the animals they observed there. This gave rise to their most distinctive style: the 'animal style'.

The main elements of Scythian and Sarmatian art

The most distinctive feature of the art of the steppe was defined by Michael Rostovtzeff in 1929 as the 'animal style'.[8] The term has since been questioned;[9] nevertheless it is a recurrent motif and remains in common use, so is a convenient shorthand for the present purposes (so long as one remembers its limitations). Steppe animals, such as deer, are depicted in a very vigorous manner with exaggerated swept-back antlers, often dramatically depicted in mid-movement (Figures 6.1, 6.2 and 6.3). Indeed, Karl Jettmar defines the animal style as essentially one of movement and power (Figure 6.4):

> The number of motifs is skilfully limited, and these in turn are reduced to bare essentials. Apparently the idea is to evoke tension, the potential ability to move rather than movement itself. The animals' bodies remind us of springs; their joints are accentuated; everything expressive of greed and power is emphasized – the jaws of the felid, the tusks of the boar, the antlers of the stag.[10]

Esther Jacobsen further observes that

> a distinctive aspect of Scythian art [is] its ability to capture the distinguishing aspect of a living creature, the essence, as it were, of the animal or human. In the early period, that is the seventh and sixth centuries, that essential vitality almost always resulted in an animal that is peculiarly 'centred,' seemingly focused on its own intrinsic vitality and fate. That concentrated vitality depended on the very stylization characterizing the archaic style.[11]

As well as deer and other steppe and forest animals, eagles, boars, leopards and other felines feature, as well as mythical birds and animals such as griffins, often depicted in minute detail (Figures 6.5–6.7). A recurrent motif is one of animals with their backs in a pronounced curve, sometimes even forming a circle. This often gives the impression of the animal in motion, caught, as it were, in full gallop. The motif has also been interpreted as the paws tied together, as if for sacrifice.[*] It is certainly one of the most powerful images of Scythian art, and a gold breastplate in the form of a feline curved around to form a complete circle is one of the most powerful objects in the Peter the Great collection in the Hermitage. Although known to have come from Siberia broadly, this collection is unprovenanced. But following the discovery of a near-identical breastplate at Arzhan 1, the motif is now thought to have originated in south Siberia (Figure 6.8). It was dated securely to the early Iron Age in the ninth–eighth century BC, and might be compared to a coiled tiger–dragon hybrid bronze from China of the same date. Although characteristic of the Tagar culture, the 'coiled feline' motif became a feature of some of the later art of Mongolia and Xinjiang, as well as the lower Syr Darya region of Kazakhstan. Coiled wolves are also common, found in contexts as far apart as fifth-century BC north-west China and sixth-century BC Crimea.[12] Rebecca O'Sullivan and Peter Hommel relate these to a broader 'curled predator' motif that is found throughout the steppe and in China (Figure 6.9).[13]

Another motif is mythical and non-mythical creatures in exaggerated twisted positions. Also characteristic are the hugely exaggerated horns and antlers, usually on deer and ibex, but also goats and mythical creatures. The origin of these can be traced to such images depicted on Bronze Age petroglyphs (e.g. Figure 2.12, although petroglyphs are notoriously difficult to date).[14] The motif is found throughout the steppe from Ukraine through to Mongolia, with elements spreading into Chinese art: a particularly fine gold example of a fantastic beast was found at the Nalingaotu cemetery in Shaansi, now in the Xian Museum (Figure 6.10); similar examples are found in Xinjiang and elsewhere.[15] In a discussion of the mythical creatures that typify steppe art, O'Sullivan and Hommel view such 'fantastic beasts[†] . . . as a result of established worldviews, rather than the artistic domestication of monstrous creatures' (Figures 6.10–6.13).[16]

A related theme is animals in combat, recurrent throughout the steppe. It has been suggested that this originated in Assyrian art, becoming prominent, for example, in the art of Persepolis.[17] The Persepolis animal combat motif had a particularly long afterlife, recurring in art as far apart in time

---

[*] Or asleep: most animals, especially felines, curl round almost into a complete circle when sleeping.

[†] In their chapter entitled 'Fantastic Beasts and Where to Find Them', a nod to the 2016 David Yates/J. K. Rowling film of the same title.

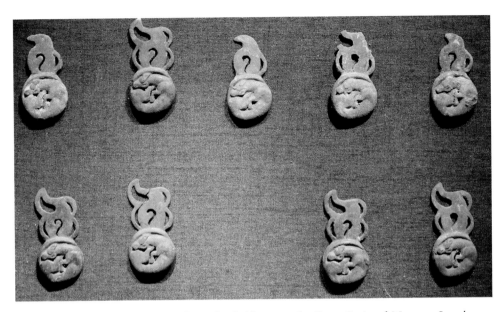

Figure 6.9 *Bronze plaques in the form of coiled beasts in the Gansu Regional Museum, Lanzhou*

and space as a fourth-century BC Hecatomnid sarcophagus in Caria, an eleventh-century Seljuk mosque in Diyarbakır and a thirteenth-century Armenian monastery at Gladzor.[18]

Combat scenes also characterise the 'belt plaques' – the so-called 'Ordos Bronzes' – of the proto-Xiongnu and Xiongnu (Chapter 7) in the second century BC to first century AD, although other animal scenes are also common (Figure 6.15).[19] They are found mainly in Mongolia, the trans-Baikal region of Siberia and northern China, although similar bronze belt buckles depicting fantastic beasts are found as far west as Georgia in the first century BC to third century AD.[20] The origin lies in the animal styles of the steppe, such as the wooden and textile objects from Pazyryk, although it is also argued that the style developed independently from the bronze styles of the northern zone of China.[21]

Articles of Scythian art generally fall into four very broad categories: vessels, horse trappings, personal adornment and weapons. Vessels

Figure 6.10 *Late fourth century BC gold figure of a beast from Nalingatou in Shaanxi, now in the Xian Museum*

Figure 6.11 *Fantastic beasts in wood from Ukok in the National Museum of Altai in Gorno-Altaisk*

Figure 6.12 *Fantastic beast in felt from Ukok in the National Museum of Altai in Gorno-Altaisk*

Figure 6.13 *Fantastic beast in gold and wood: Sarmatian ladle from Filippovka in the National Museum of Bashkortostan, Ufa*

include bowls, jars, vases, cups, rhyta (drinking horns) and bottles, many made of gold or gold-plated silver. The emphasis on bowls recalls the legend recorded by Herodotus of a gold bowl falling from the sky, the bowl perhaps representing the sky itself (Figure 6.16). Many of these

Figure 6.14 *Fantastic beasts in gold: third-century* BC *crown from Aluchaideng, Inner Mongolia, in the Inner Mongolian Regional Museum, Hohhot*

Figure 6.15 *Combat scenes on Xiongnu bronze plaques from Ivolginsk in the Ulan Ude Museum*

depict the everyday life of the Scythian nomad in intimate detail. The most famous – and most often illustrated – are those from Gaymanova Mogila, Chertomlyk, Solokha and Kul Oba, all from the Pontic steppe.[22] Forming a separate category of vessel are the distinctive bronze pedestal cauldrons that are found in almost every nomadic context right across the Eurasian

Figure 6.16 *Gold vessel from Kelermes in the Krasnodar Museum*

Figure 6.17 *Bronze cauldron in the Novocherkassk Museum*

steppe (Figures 6.17 and 6.18), still characteristic of Alan elite burials as late as the early medieval period (and the word relating to 'cauldron' is one of the small number of proto-Indo-European reconstructions,[23] testimony to its importance among steppe peoples). Whether they were for ritual (mainly funeral) or domestic use has long been debated: pottery imitations suggest ritual (as the form would not be practical as a pottery vessel), but their depiction on petroglyphs suggest possible domestic use.[24] The cauldrons show Chinese influence, mainly in the handles, and the style probably originated in the bronzes of the Shang Dynasty of the second millennium BC where they are known as *fu* cauldrons. The largest concentration is in the Guanzhong area of Gansu, dating from the Western Zhou period.[25] A macabre addition to the steppe corpus of vessels are drinking cups as war trophies made from the skulls of enemies. These were occasionally gilded, and were used mainly for ceremonial purposes.

Figure 6.18 Bronze cauldrons in the Minusinsk Museum

It is hardly surprising that horses came in for particular attention in steppe art, as horses are a mainstay of the life of the steppe nomad (and horse sacrifices figured hugely in Scythian funerary rites, with over four hundred sacrificed at Arzhan 1, for example, with almost as large numbers in later Scythian burials in the north Caucasus).[26] Horse trappings could be highly decorative: plaques, bits, cheek pieces, breastplates and other horse ornaments were ornately wrought or carved and often depicted animals: animal art for animals (Figures 6.19 and 6.21). The more rigid parts of harness, such as bits and cheek pieces, were of bronze, but also decorated and occasionally gilded. A wide variety of materials was used for horse decorations: as well as bronze and gold, decorated leather and wood (also occasionally gilded) were used, as well as patterned felts (Figures 4.17 and 6.12). Saddles, bridles and reins glittered with gold ornament in some of the horse decorations. A peculiarity of some of the horse burials in the Altai – notably Pazyryk – was false antlers placed on

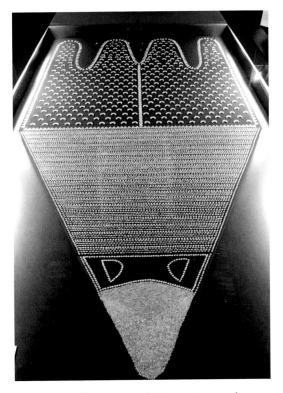

Figure 6.19 Sarmatian gold decoration on a horse blanket from Dachi on the Don, re-assembled in the Azov Museum

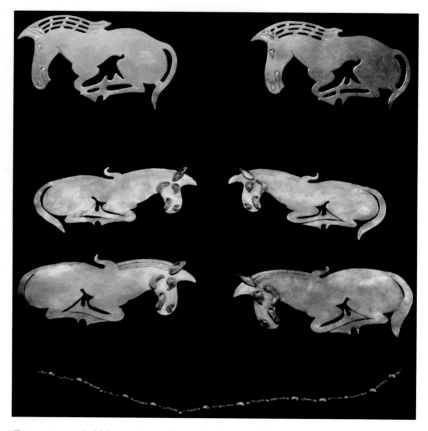

Figure 6.20 *Gold horse plaques from Arzhan 2 in the National Museum of Tuva, Kyzyl*

the heads (Figure 6.21). Deer had important totemic significance in the steppe: the so-called 'deer stones' of the second millennium were one of the sources of the animal style (see below), and deer motifs are one of the most recurrent themes in the animal style (Figures 6.1, 6.2 and 6.3).

Articles of personal adornment cover a wide variety, both jewellery and clothing. Of the former, of which large numbers have been found, many are gold. They include pectorals, torques, armbands and bracelets, diadems, belt plaques and buckles, rings, pendants, fibulae and other items of jewellery such as earrings and necklaces (Figures 6.22 and 6.23). Pectorals are particularly elaborate and often depict mythical scenes and everyday life, such as the magnificent one from Tolstaya Mogila.[27] Earrings were also often extremely elaborate and finely worked, often incorporating further pendants (and presumably rarely worn: it would take a stout ear indeed to bear such weight for any time). They were usually objects of female adornment, but could also be male (males would usually have just one earring, as opposed to two for females). Included in the general category of adornment were mirrors, usually silver and showing Chinese influence, and ornamental combs. Indeed, a comb is one of the most important objects of Scythian art: the famous Solokha gold comb in the Hermitage is one of the most magnificent works of gold craftsmanship in the collection.[28]

Gold also figures on clothing: large numbers of gold plaques, beads, sequins and other gold ornaments, sometimes numbering in the thousands, would be stitched onto a garment. This has enabled the form of the garment to be reconstructed when the textile itself has decayed. Thanks to the frozen tombs of the Altai, many of the actual garments themselves have survived virtually intact, such as those of the supposed female shaman from Ukok: leather boots, a woollen dress, silk blouse, sheepskin coat, and a distinctive high-pointed felt headdress (Figures 4.15 and 4.16). A similarly distinctive high-pointed headdress was found with the burial of the fourth-century BC 'Golden Man' at Issyk in Kazakhstan (although its sex

Figure 6.21 *Horse decoration in the form of false antlers from the Altai, as well as wooden horse trappings below, now in the Hermitage*

was never fully established: it might be female, as it bears comparisons to the Ukok female shaman).[29] High pointed headdresses seem to have been a feature of Scythian elites or even entire tribes. Achaemenid inscriptions refer to the *Saka tigraxauda* or 'pointed-hat Scythians' as a Scythian sub-group, and Scythians with pointed hats are depicted on the Bisitun and Persepolis reliefs (Figure 4.21) as well as the famous gold beaker from Kul-Oba in the Hermitage. The tradition survived into the Hellenistic period of the first century BC and is seen in royal sculptural portrayals as far apart as the Iranian-related mountain-top dynastic complex of Nemrut Dağ in Turkey

Figure 6.22 *Sarmatian gold belt plaques from Dachi, now in the Azov Museum*

Figure 6.23 Sarmatian earrings and necklace from Dachi, now in the Azov Museum

and the urban site of Dalverzin-tepa in Uzbekistan.

A more unusual medium of personal adornment is the human body itself, thanks again to the state of preservation in the frozen tombs. These are tattoos, notably from Pazyryk. They depict abstract designs, but also animal designs are popular, often of fantastic animals, and particularly of deer.

The most important objects in many of the elite tombs were weapons: bows, arrows, swords, knives, standards, finials, spears, axe heads, daggers, helmets, shields and generally the full range of armoury. This is hardly surprising: warfare – or at least hunting – was a way of life for the steppe nomads. These are found, as is to be expected, in male burials, but weaponry also occurs in female burials, particularly among the Sarmatians (Chapter 5). The most characteristic Scythian weapon is the *gorytus*, a combined bow and arrow case. They are depicted on the Persepolis reliefs, and many that are found around the Black Sea show clear evidence of Greek influence or even direct Greek workmanship specifically for Scythian clients. The gold-decorated cases are among the finest works of Scythian (and Greek) art, depicting Greek and Scythian mythological scenes as well as the everyday life of the nomad. Particularly fine examples are from Melitopolski and Chertomlyk in Ukraine, as well as Elizavetinskaya near Rostov-on-Don.[30] The oldest is probably that found in Arzhan 2 in Tuva (Figure 6.24). The gorytus had a

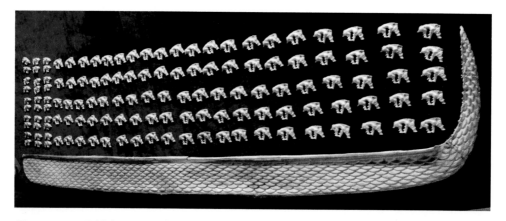

Figure 6.24 Gold decoration that adorned a gorytus *from Arzhan 2 in the National Museum of Tuva in Kyzyl*

surprisingly long life. It was still being used in Ottoman ceremony, if not for actual warfare, as late as the sixteenth century; a form of them was still used for hunting in Moldova until recently (Figure 6.25).[31]

Equally characteristic of Scythian armoury is the *akinakes* case, the distinctive scabbard for the Scythian short sword (Figure 6.26). These are also depicted at Perspeolis, and a particularly fine gold akinakes is a part of the Achaemenid period Oxus Treasure. Like the gorytus, the gold akinakes scabbards lend themselves to particularly elaborate decoration. Some of the finest examples are from Velikaya Bilozerka, Tolstaya, Kelermes, Solokha and Elizavetinskaya[32] in national collections in Ukraine and Russia. Sarmatian swords were longer than the short Scythian swords. Daggers and swords could also be very elaborate, with highly decorated gold hilts and sheaths (Figure 6.27).

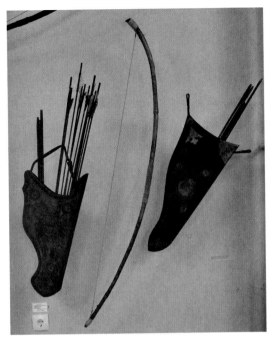

Figure 6.25 *Survival of the* gorytus: *a form of bow and arrow case still used comparatively recently in Moldova (in the National Museum in Chisinau)*

Knife decoration was part of a long tradition going back to the decorated in-curved, single-bladed bronze knives of the Karasuk period in

Figure 6.26 *Statues of Scythian warriors in Evpatoria Museum in Crimea. Note the characteristic Scythian sword, or* akinakes, *in the figure on the right*

Figure 6.27 *Sarmatian scabbard from Dachi in the Azov Museum*

south Siberia (Figure 4.1) which in turn influenced the Bronze Age cultures of China's Northern Zone.[33] Elaborately decorated bronze axes are also a part of the Karasuk tradition. The occasional finds in the western steppe of such in-curved knives, such as the Borodino Treasure, must be regarded as exceptions. In a survey of 395 bladed Scythian weapons from the forest-steppe belt of eastern Europe they were virtually conspicuous by their absence. Only twenty-seven single-bladed weapons are illustrated in the survey, few of them in-curved, and displaying little if any resemblance to the Karasuk types – indeed, a Thracian origin for the type is suggested.[34] Otherwise all were double-bladed straight swords and daggers: none had animal head pommels (although the animal style characterised other artefacts from the same contexts, including decoration on the gorytuses and even some of the hilts). Might the animal head pommels be characteristic of knives rather than daggers, hence an emphasis on hunting? This suggests that the society of the western steppe might have been dominated more by warfare than by hunting, an assertion, however, that is difficult to substantiate.

Shields were made of wood, but often with a gold boss and other gold decorations, and intact decorated shields made of wicker have been recovered from the Altai (Figure 4.14). Helmets were of bronze (Figure 6.28), but ceremonial helmets of gold have also been recovered, such as the magnificent gold helmet from Perederiyeva Mogila in the National Museum in Kiev depicting Scythian combat scenes.[35] Bronze helmets in late Shang/early Zhou Shanxi Province in China have been compared to a near-identical helmet from Kelermes.[36] A magnificent third-century BC gold headdress depicting crouching animals and with a cap topped by a gold eagle with a turquoise head was found in the Ordos in 1973 (Figure 6.14).[37]

A distinctive feature of the ceremonial armoury of the steppe are the standards or finials of bronze, gold or gilded wood. They can be purely geometric designs but are often in the form of animals, particularly ibex, and are often described in the literature simply as 'pole tops'. Many were just that, perhaps finials to tent poles (Figure 6.29), but many do not incorporate a socket for a pole, so might be standards of uncertain ceremonial purpose. A particularly spectacular series were discovered in the 1980s in the fifth- to fourth-century Sarmatian graves of Filippovka in the southern Urals, now in the Bashkortostan Archaeological Museum in Ufa. They consist of highly stylised deer with disproportionately large and elaborate antlers carved from wood and covered in gold leaf (Figure 6.3).[38]

Beyond the steppe, elements of the animal style found their way into the fourth- to third-century BC 'Colchian' treasure from Vani in Georgia.[39] It is also recognised in the spectacular first-century BC gold treasure of Tillya Tepe in northern Afghanistan.[40] A large gold circlet weighing sixteen kilos and depicting

Figure 6.28 *Scythian bronze helmet from Kelermes in the Krasnodar Museum*

animals in the steppe 'Sarmatian style' was found at Pattan on the Upper Indus, which was unfortunately broken into pieces before being recovered by the authorities.[41]

One cannot view steppe art in terms of a single style. Although recognisably interconnected, the art was, like the nomads themselves, constantly on the move and evolving. It was always absorbing elements from the cultures and civilisations around – Chinese, Persian, Anatolian and Greek are the main ones – and in turn contributing to them. Above all it must be emphasised that an article of steppe art was designed to be seen but not looked at. A belt buckle or a horse bit was nothing more than a belt buckle or a horse bit: nobody (except perhaps the wearer) would actually look at the individual pieces in the way that modern art historians do. But the whole – the entire decked-out man/woman/corpse/horse/wagon – was very much designed to be looked at, for show – and presumably on special occasions only when even the whole would be but a small part of a greater whole. Then one would no more notice the belt buckle than the cut of the hair, the horse bit than the breed of horse. A person adorned is the

Figure 6.29 *A Scythian bronze standard from Novocherkassk in the Azov Museum*

person, not the sequin; one admires the classic car, not the hub cap.

Origins of the 'animal style'

Just how, when and where this style emerged – or even if there is such a distinct style – is subject to considerable controversy. What is certain is that while it is probably correct to describe much of Scythian art as animal-style, the reverse is not true: the animal style is not exclusive to the Scythians.

The first excavations of Scythian kurgans and the fabulous works of art contained in them were made in the eighteenth century in the southern Russian steppes around the Black Sea. The period also saw a rediscovery of the ancient Greek colonies bordering the Black Sea. This, together with Russia's reassertion of a Classical identity (discussed in Chapter 13), led the excavators to interpret the most spectacular objects in the Scythian kurgans as works of Greek art. There is undoubted Greek influence in many of the finest objects and, indeed, undoubted Greek imports depicting Greek mythological scenes. But the main reason for their interpretation as Greek was a prejudice that actually dates from the ancient Greek view of the Scythians: they were barbarians. Simple nomads ('barbarians'), it was argued, would be incapable of creating such sophisticated works of art: only the specialised workshops of the Greek colonies – if not the cities in the Greek homelands – were capable of such achievement. It was therefore suggested that these objects must have been imports from the Greek world made specifically for the Scythian market ('not, on the whole, a happy marriage', as John Boardman remarks)[42] or, at most, made by Greek craftsmen working in the Scythian camps, either as captives or as travelling artisans.

The debate to some extent still continues, albeit modified and in reference to a much smaller corpus of material confined only to those of overt

Greek influence. While the series of sumptuous fourth- to third-century BC tumuli from the Bosporan kingdom, such as the spectacular tombs at Kul-Oba and Tsarski Kurgan (Figures 6.30 and 6.31), are essentially 'Scythian', many of those buried in them were Greek families. The style of the art in these tombs is Hellenic as well as Scythian and Anatolian, but of a specifically Bosporan style or 'school', neither quite Greek nor quite local. Otherwise, the main consensus now is that the vast majority of objects found in the kurgans elsewhere are the work of the Scythians themselves. This change in attitude is partly due to the recognition that even the most so-called 'primitive' peoples are capable of producing works of art of the highest standard: Yoruba bronzes, for example, or Palaeolithic cave paintings. More important has

Figure 6.30 Exterior of the Tsarski Kurgan near Kerch in Crimea

Figure 6.31 The interior of the Tsarski Kurgan

been the further discoveries that demonstrate the roots of Scythian art earlier in the Bronze and Iron Ages of Inner Asia.

Petroglyphs are possibly one of the origins of steppe art, for as far back as the Palaeolithic animals were depicted in caves (Figure 2.2). Throughout Eurasia most early cultures have left their mark in the petroglyphs incised, engraved or stippled onto rock surfaces. They are found everywhere, but probably the largest numbers occur in Inner Asia broadly. These range from individual markings pecked onto boulders by passing nomads to vast outdoor galleries of petroglyphic art numbering many thousands of individual images, such as at Tamgaly in Kazakhstan or Gobustan in Azerbaijan. Many are intricate works, and are almost invariably associated with nomads – or at least with people on the move generally, such as those on the ancient trade route of the upper Indus (Figure 4.23). Petroglyphs are notoriously difficult to date. The only partially reliable way is stylistic, by comparison with securely dated objects from close by. They cover virtually all periods from the palaeolithic to comparatively recent times, but most are thought to be from the Bronze and Iron Ages. They usually depict the nomadic life around them. Hence, there is a preponderance of hunting and animal scenes, themes that lie at the roots of the Scythian lifestyle. A large number occur in the Altai at Chuya and Kalbaktash, in the same region of the Pazyryk Culture depicting precisely such scenes (Figures 2.12 and 6.32). As well as the formulation of Scythian art, some have detected the beginnings of the Central Asian epic tradition in elements of the rock art of south Siberia, such as the *Manas* epic of the Kyrgyz and the *Shahnameh* of the Iranians.[43]

A discovery that has altered many of the views of the evolution of Inner Asian art has been that of the Bronze Age Okunev Culture of south Siberia in the late third and early second millennium BC.[44] This culture is characterised mainly by the extraordinary anthropomorphic stelae, gathered together in large numbers in the museums of Abakan and Minusinsk (Figures 2.9, 6.33 and 6.34). The style had a wide impact and has been recognised on rock engravings as far south as the upper Indus and Ladakh,[45] as well as the 'sun-head deities' depicted in the Bronze Age rock art of the Altai and north-west China (Figure 6.36).[46] The stelae are almost entirely anthropomorphic, unlike later Scythian styles. But it does demonstrate the emergence of a highly developed and distinctive tradition of art in the Scythian homelands. And while mainly anthropomorphic, the stelae also included animal scenes and abstract patterns that found their way into Scythian art.

What has altered the earlier Hellenocentric views of Scythian art more than anything else has been the discoveries and dissemination of an immensely rich metalworking tradition in the Minusinsk Basin of south Siberia in the late Bronze and Iron Ages. This is particularly associated with the Karasuk Culture, recognised as proto-Scythian. The bronze

Figure 6.32 *Petroglyph of a humanoid and a fantasy beast at Kalbaktash in the Altai*

metalwork is of outstanding quality. Much of it is associated with horse riding, either horse trappings or objects decorated with images of horses. A particular characteristic of Karasuk art is the highly distinctive decorated bronze in-curved, single bladed knives, where the hilt would end in an

Figure 6.33 *Okunev sculpture in the National Museum of Khakasia in Abakan*

Figure 6.34 *Okunev sculpture in the Minusinsk Museum*

Figure 6.35 *Okunev petroglyph at Kazanovka in Khakasia*

Figure 6.36 *Rock engraving of a 'sun-head deity' in the Biysk Museum in the Altai*

animal finial (Figure 4.1). These knives have been found over a very wide area, far beyond the immediate area of the Karasuk culture itself, even in areas that had their own bronze knife traditions. Clearly they were appreciated as objects for their own sake. The animal-hilted knives and related decorative artefacts have also been suggested as one of the origins of the animal style.[47]

Knives with distinctive animal head pommels appeared in the Seima-Turbino Culture between about 1900 and 1400, probably first appearing in the earlier part of that span.[48] Similar knives were found as far west as Belgorod-Dniestrovsky in Ukraine in the 'Borodino Treasure'.[49] This influenced the style of knives in China as early as the Shang period,[50] these knives being compared to Seima-Turbino. So distinctive were these knives that they were imitated in jade in China: being of jade they had no practical value, but were merely prized as ornaments.[51] Under the Shang and Western Zhao these animal pommels developed into more elaborate styles in Mongolia and China's Northern Zone, depicting mainly rams but also deer, horse, ox and goat, with the style spreading to other objects such as cheek pieces and swords. The Northern Zone styles in turn spread into the central plains of China.[52]

Also distinctive are the so-called 'deer-stones' of Mongolia, trans-Baikal and the Altai, often associated with the *khirigsuur* complexes. Large numbers of them were re-used in later Scythian burials, hence making their date and function uncertain. But their re-use also suggests some form of continued cultic veneration – indeed, many of the deer stones are still venerated today. They characteristically depict deer, as the name implies, with distinctive swept-back antlers, but human faces (suggested to be shamans), weapons and other animals also figure (Figures 6.37 and 6.38).[53] The swept-back antlers in particular anticipate the similar motif in the animal style of the steppe. They are often not associated with burials, which has led to the suggestion that they might be memorials or cenotaphs.[54] As objects they might have evolved out of the earlier third millennium BC anthropomorphic gravestones of the Okunev culture in the Minusinsk Basin.

An older anthropomorphic tradition in the western steppe is represented by the funeral stelae of the Yamnaya and related Usatovo Cultures of the late fourth–early third millennium (Figure 6.39: that from Chişinau is dated on its label to the fifth–fourth century BC).[55] A surprising parallel for these funerary stelae was discovered by accident at Hakkâri in eastern Turkey 1998 (Figure 6.40). These were thirteen stelae depicting human figures carved from local stone completely unlike any sculptures previously known in Turkey or adjacent regions. They were taken to the museum at Van, and subsequent excavations revealed a chamber tomb dated to the second millennium BC, but its association with the stelae is uncertain. The influence of the steppe is unmistakeable, but how it arrived remains unknown.[56]

Figure 6.37 *Deer stone at Tamchinsky in Buryatia*

Figure 6.38 *Image of warrior on a stele in the Altai related to the deer stones of Mongolia*

Such anthropomorphic stelae continued in steppe tradition: the grave markers of the first millennium AD Turk Empire are a similar concept, as are the later Polovtsi grave markers or *kamennye baby* of the southern Russian steppe, similar in inspiration if not exact style (Figure 6.41). These later became one of the inspirations for the Russian avant-garde, in particular the work of Natalia Goncharova.[57] Even today in the Altai the local population erect wooden 'stelae' that are either anthropomorphic or in the form of horse-heads or other totemic animals (Figure 6.42).

The discovery that probably did most to locate the origin of the animal style was the excavation of the huge Arzhan I kurgan in the Tuva Republic in the 1970s by Mikhail Gryaznov. The kurgan comprised a royal burial within an immense wooden structure covered by an earthen mound. Although it had been plundered, the bodies of the two richly caparisoned 'royal' couple were found, together with seventeen attendants and over four hundred horse sacrifices. Objects included bronze and gold horse trappings, weapons and other objects and, most important, a magnificent coiled bronze feline (Figure 6.8), almost identical to a gold version in the Siberian collection of Peter the Great in the Hermitage discussed above. This added weight to the suggestion that the 'animal style' might have originated in south Siberia, although influences from China, Persia

Figure 6.39 *Anthropomorphic stelae from the steppe: National Museum, Chişinau (left); Novocherkassk Museum, Russia (middle); Kerch Museum, Crimea (right)*

Figure 6.40 *Anthropomorphic stelae from Hakkâri in eastern Turkey, now in the Van Museum*

Figure 6.41 *Polovtsi* kamennye baby *grave markers of the southern steppe: Azov Museum (left), Novocherkassk Museum (right)*

and Urartu later entered. The suggestion was reinforced by the even more spectacular discoveries of the slightly later Arzhan 2 royal burial nearby in the 1990s by a Russian–German team. This consisted of a large circular enclosure in stone (now preserved) covered by an earth mound. Although this too was looted in antiquity, the main burial was off-centre so was missed by the looters (Figures 4.3, 6.21 and 6.24). It consisted of a log burial chamber that contained the 'royal' couple with many thousands of gold and other metal objects in a more mature animal style. These

Figure 6.42 *Modern animal and anthropomorphic wooden totems in the Altai*

included a magnificent gold torque on the male burial, a gold headdress with two outstanding gold pins – among the finest works of craftsmanship in Scythian art – on the female, a gold *gorytus*, and an ornamented gold dagger, and both were dressed in clothes that were sewn with many thousands of gold discs and miniature horse plaques (Figure 6.20). The Scythian reverence for gold and the animal style of the objects are not in doubt.[58]

Later survivals of steppe art

The art was as vigorous as the people who practised it. So vigorous were these distinctive steppe styles that they continued to evolve long after the Scythians themselves had disappeared. Indeed, distant echoes of the styles are still with us today.

A continuous development of the steppe animal style can be traced in subsequent cultures of the steppe. This has been found not only in the successor states of the eastern steppe – the Xianbei and the early Turk cultures – but in the art of the Avars, the Volga Bulgars, the Mongols and the later Golden Horde of the western steppe down to the fifteenth century, surviving in such works as the fantastic beasts depicted on some middle Islamic metalwork.[59] A fine tenth–fourteenth-century silver archer's wrist-brace from Volga Bulgaria, for example, is in an unmistakable steppe animal style.[60] A sixth- to seventh-century East Slav gilded silver plaque of a stylised horse from the Martinovsk treasure in Ukraine is a frequently cited example of later animal style (Figure 6.43).[61]

The animal style has also been discerned in 'ancient Germanic' art, such as the Witaszkowo (formerly Vettersfelde) gold hoard in Poland, as well as other Scythian-related objects in Slovenia and Silesia. Scythian objects are fairly common in what is known as the Vekerzug Culture in the Carpathian basin.[62] The style was recognised in early Celtic art of the first millennium BC in the 1930s by the 'founding father' of Celtic art history, Paul Jacobsthal, seen for example in the style named after the excavations at La Tène in Switzerland.[63] Mythical and backward-facing creatures are motifs common in the Iron Age art in both western Europe and northern China, as well as various forms of abstract design. The styles of tumulus burials, such as the sixth–fifth-century BC grave at Vix in France and others elsewhere in south-west Germany

Figure 6.43 *A sixth-century early Slav silver plaque from Martinovka (after Talbot Rice)*

and Slovenia have been compared to the Scythian kurgans of the Black Sea. Similar grave objects – wagons, chariots, weapons, horses, mirrors – occur in the burials of both regions. A particularly striking comparison has been made between a wooden boss from Tuekta in the Altai and a third–second-century BC bronze shield from Wandsworth in England.[64] Of course, none of this necessarily implies that the Scythians themselves spread so far west, but it does demonstrate the pervasive attraction of their art forms and subsequent spread and influence in Europe.[65]

The treasure found in 1683 in the grave in Belgium of the Merovingian King Childeric, who died in 482, has been described as 'Scythic'. Such styles (Style I) were also recognised among the treasures of a Merovingian queen, probably the mid-sixth-century Queen Arnegunde, whose tomb was discovered in the mid-twentieth century under St Denis.[66] Elements of the style appear in Irish and Celtic art and appear in the exquisite workmanship of some of the gold treasures that have been unearthed, as well as in manuscripts such as the *Book of Kells* and the *Lindisfarne Gospels*.[67] The sixth–seventh-century Anglo-Saxon ship burial of Sutton Hoo, whose treasure is one of the showpieces of the British Museum, also contained objects that have been traced to the animal style, perhaps via early Slavic art.[68] This received confirmation with the dramatic discovery in 2009 of the Anglo-Saxon 'Staffordshire hoard', where further influences from the steppe were recognised.[69]

A mix of Sarmatian and Germanic elements has been recognised in the third century AD and later art of Hungary. New arrivals from the steppe came into Europe with the Avars in the late sixth century, and some Avar art has been labelled 'neo-Scythian'.[70] Avar belt buckles in particular recall those of the earlier Xiongnu depicting combat scenes and fantastic beasts (particularly the griffin), and other elements of their art are in a steppe-related animal style. A crescent gold pectoral from an Avar royal burial at Kunbábony in Hungary resembles similar Rouran (proto-Avar) objects in inner Eurasia.[71] Many elements of Scythian art were carried on into the early medieval 'Migrations Period' in Europe, where its influence is acknowledged. Emma Bunker writes:

> Heroes or highwaymen, their greatest legacy is their art – lavishly wrought weapons, ornaments and horse trappings which reflect the life of a militant people on the move. The outstanding feature of this art is its concentration on animal (and bird) themes, currently described as the 'Animal Style', a quasi-international manner of decoration which flourished from China to Ireland during the Iron Age and, later, in the barbarian art of the Migrations period.[72]

The power of the animal style proved extremely durable. Elements resurfaced, for example, in Viking and Nordic art of the ninth–tenth centuries, where the style is recognised in the sinuously curving animals and abstract decorations both on artefacts and in architecture. The art is recognised as owing nothing to the Classical and Mediterranean styles, but as found solely in northern Europe and representing an 'unbroken line' from early Germanic and Migrations Period art.[73] Although these traces have been discerned, it must be emphasised that there are many missing links: there is no such thing as a smooth, continuous artistic tradition from Scythian to Medieval European art. Whether such influences in western Europe were the result of continuity from the steppe traditions or rediscovery through their burials cannot be proven.

Steppe animal style has been recognised in the old Russian art of the Kama region, as well as in medieval Bulgaria and elsewhere. In other words, the style simply never disappeared in the western steppe.[74] Elements were revived in a new movement in Europe in the late nineteenth and early twentieth centuries. This was the art nouveau, a style that was artificially created near the end of the nineteenth.[75] It was a deliberate attempt to move away from the Classicism that dominated the more imperial styles of eighteenth- and nineteenth-century Europe. The English art critic John Ruskin, for example, championed the rediscovery of the Middle Ages. This found its expression in William Morris and the Arts and Crafts movement in the mid-nineteenth century and the work of the Pre-Raphaelites, all cited as among the origins of art nouveau. There were numerous other threads, parallel movements and practitioners throughout Europe as well as in Russia (discussed further in Chapter 13), which culminated in one of the most innovative styles in European art at the end of the nineteenth century. It impacted not only upon art, but also on architecture, furniture, interior design, metalwork, graphic design, the art of the book, and virtually all aspects of visual expression.[76]

The sources of art nouveau were almost anything that was non-Classical (although some Classical elements recurred). Celtic and Viking art have long been recognised, as well as Japanese, Islamic and early medieval art generally. The 'Russian style' formulated in the nineteenth century, which itself incorporated Scythian and Tatar elements, was another source. The later nineteenth century saw a revival of interest in Celtic and Viking art, and this in turn incorporated elements of the Scythian animal style. But some art nouveau elements appear to have been drawn directly from Scythian art without Migration period or Viking intermediaries.[77]

Scythian art survived among the eastern Slavs, and elements of it continued virtually uninterrupted in the wood carvings and textiles of the Russian peasants into modern times. Tamara Talbot Rice writes: 'It was in this way that these designs were not only incorporated in the folk art of south Russia, but eventually played a part, if only a small one, in moulding the decorative traditions of western Europe.'[78] In 1887 the all-powerful Russian art critic Viktor Stasov published his volume of *Slavic and Eastern Ornament*, which provided further inspiration for the artists of the time.

Figure 6.44 *Abramtsevo interior, preserving traditional Russian folk art. Note the fantastic beast plaque*

Such designs were adopted by the 'World of Art' movement in the nineteenth century, a movement which sought to escape from the western Classical styles which had dominated modern Russian art and turn instead to folk roots. There was a conscious revival by the 'Abramtsevo Circle' outside Moscow in the 1870s which anticipated the Russian art nouveau, when many items of folk art were collected, such as the extraordinary decorated wooden distaffs which preserved ancient styles (Figures 6.44 and 6.45). The animal patterns that adorn the surfaces of early Russian churches and wooden architecture generally are, it has been suggested, also survivals of Scythian styles (Figures 6.46 and 6.47).[79]

It is notable that the art nouveau (or 'style moderne' as it was known in Russia) was especially popular in the areas of the former Russian Empire and eastern Europe. Prague, for example, was the home of one of the prime innovators of art nouveau, Alphonse Mucha, and St Petersburg, Moscow, Samara, Lviv and other cities – especially Riga – probably contain the most art nouveau buildings in the world.[80] 'In a wider perspective, with its organic motifs, botanical flourishes, and graphic references to the animal and vegetable world, the Style Moderne captured and symbolized the very ethos of the flowering of the [Russian] Silver Age.'[81] Fantastic beasts are still alive and well adorning Russian buildings in the twenty-first century (Figure 6.48).

Figure 6.45 *Wooden distaffs at Abramtsevo*

Figure 6.46 *Traditional wooden architecture in Tomsk*

Figure 6.47 *Traditional wooden architecture in Tomsk*

Figure 6.48 *Animal-style elements in twenty-first-century architecture in Rostov-on-Don, in the heart of ancient Scythia*

CHAPTER 7

TWILIGHT OF THE GODS
The Huns, Attila and the End of Antiquity

Even as, a thousand years ago, the Huns under King Attila made such a name for themselves as still resounds in fable and legend, so may the name of Germans resound through Chinese history a thousand years from now.
– Kaiser Wilhelm II in 1900[1]

Up until the first few centuries AD the peoples of the steppe who impacted upon Europe were dominated by groups speaking Indo-European languages, notably the Scythians. This was the same group of languages spoken by nearly all of Europe in antiquity: there was less linguistic diversity then than there is now. Inner Asia and Europe in antiquity was essentially a unit, linguistically speaking. From a little before the middle of the first millennium AD groups of people speaking entirely unrelated languages started coming to the fore on the Inner Asian steppe and entering Europe, where they still remain. These were people speaking various Uralic and Altaic languages. Although originating in the eastern limits of Inner Asia, far from imposing divisions in Eurasia they merged and mingled, adding to the linguistic and cultural diversity: Europe became an even more complex intertwining of both eastern and western cultures.

The first of these non-Indo-European speakers to arrive who may have spoken an Altaic language were the Huns.[2] Although their legacy in Europe has always been viewed as at best minimal, at worst negative (although these views have been reassessed), their advent marked both an end and a beginning. The Huns arrived at the time of the collapse of the old order in western Europe: the collapse of the Roman Empire in the West, a collapse to which the Huns contributed. It also marked the beginning of a new order: the emergence of Germanic western Europe and the beginning of nation states. But not just Germanic: the period also sees the arrival of new peoples from Asia who were to play a major part in the establishment of European nation states, such as Hungarians, Bulgarians and Turks soon after the Huns. Although the Hun invasion did not result in the establishment of a nation state in Europe, they formed the vanguard of peoples who did, 'ultimately shaping the modern ethnic geography of Europe'.[3]

The end of civilisation?

The End of Civilisation is the subtitle of a work published in 2005 questioning the then-current thinking that the fall of Rome was a largely peaceful transitional period to the emergence of Germanic Europe.[4] The question of whether the invasions of late antiquity were destructive or constructive remains a controversial one. Group after group of mainly Germanic invaders entered the Roman Empire: Franks, Burgundians, Sueves, Vandals, Goths. But many were themselves fleeing the even greater menace further east: the Huns. Who were these extraordinarily ruthless new people who seem to have appeared so unexpectedly on the borders of the Empire?

According to contemporary descriptions they appear to have been a Mongol-related group, so they presumably originated far off in the east: indeed, they have been referred to anachronistically as 'Mongol horsemen' and their appearance in Europe as the 'Tartar yoke', anticipating later views of the Mongols.[*] Although there is practically no evidence for the Hun language, the Huns probably spoke an Altaic language. The Altaic group includes Turkish, Mongol, Manchu, Tungus and other more obscure languages of the Siberian steppe and forest. It might also be distantly related to Finnish and Hungarian in the west and Korean and Japanese in the east, although this is controversial. Indeed, 'Altaic' may not even be a real group at all, the vast number of loan words between Turk, Mongol and Tungus simply giving the illusion of a group.[5] Further to the north was another language group, Uralic, mainly in the forest belt on either side of the Urals. After about 1500 BC there was a western movement of peoples speaking Uralic-related languages into north-western Europe, although a sub-group of Uralic speakers, known as Ugrians, remained in the Kama-Ural area. Ugrian-speaking groups later moved southwards into the steppe area and Altaic elements moved into north-western Siberia, merging with remnant Ugrian groups. These movements are examined more in the next chapters. For the moment, it can be noted that the Huns were probably a product of such an interplay of peoples and languages on the steppe. However, there is no consensus as to what language group Hunnic belonged to, although most indications suggest it might have been related to Turk[†] – many of

---

[*] Pirenne 1939: 26 and 29, where he also refers to them as the 'Yellow Peril', a term that would be unacceptable today, although still used in official circles in Australia as late as the 1960s to justify involvement in the Vietnam War.

[†] Analysis of the very few Xiongnu – presumed Hun (discussed below) – words that have survived in Chinese transcriptions shows this to be not so, where the Xiongnu language is unlikely even to have been Altaic. Evidence is extremely slim either way and the Chinese sources are vague and contradictory. The Xiongnu language might have been related to Kettish, a very obscure Siberian forest language that became extinct in the nineteenth century. See Golden 2006: 85 and 2011: 27.

the tribal names, for example, can be related to Turkish, although a few are Germanic and Iranian.

It was the alien nature of their features and physiognomy that ancient observers not only found repellent but also instilled instant terror. This, as well as their sheer relentlessness with a ferocity and thirst for destruction, led the contemporary world to consider them not quite human. Hence, Ammianus Marcellinus, in the fourth century, wrote:

> the Huns . . . are so monstrously ugly and misshapen that one might take them for beasts . . . they have no need of fire nor of savoury food, but eat the roots of wild plants and the half-raw flesh of any animal whatsoever . . . they are all without fixed abode, without hearth, without law, or settled mode of life.[6]

Even Gibbon, writing over a millennium later, wrote of the Huns as 'an ugly, and even deformed race'.[7] This has some element of truth (apart from racial prejudice), as skeletal remains have confirmed that many Huns artificially deformed their skulls in childhood. Other contemporary writers such as Eunapius believed that they were unleashed upon mankind as a punishment for their sins, anticipating later views of the Mongols. To some extent this is a result as much of their novelty as their savagery: although the Huns were not necessarily more destructive than the various Germanic tribes before them (or than the Romans themselves), the Romans already had centuries of shared experience with Germans: one *knew* the Germans. The Huns, on the other hand, were entirely alien: their appearance, their names, their customs, their language, their very smell, even their origins – indeed, we still know little more even today. And they were relentlessly destructive: such was the capture and destruction of the heavily fortified city of Naissus in 441, for example, that an envoy from Constantinople seven years later found the city still empty apart from the bones of those slain still so thick on ground that it was difficult to find a clear space to camp.[8] Their strangeness and savageness, plus the fact that they struck when both the Eastern and the Western Roman Empires had never been weaker, made contemporary observers elevate them to even greater savagery than they actually displayed. The image of the alien, barely human savage who appeared from nowhere remained to haunt the forests of eastern Europe: perhaps it is no coincidence that legends of werewolves, vampires and other such semi-humans originated in the same areas of south-eastern Europe in which the Huns first appeared.[9]

Of the original late-antique sources for the Huns, the most reliable is probably that of Priscus. He accompanied an embassy to Attila's court so was one of the few whose account is based upon first-hand knowledge. The other main ones are Ammianus Marcellinus, Eunapius and Procopius. Priscus' view is surprisingly moderate; indeed, he found traits to admire among them. Christopher Kelly, when writing about Attila, sounds a cautionary note when he writes that 'After all, it is always reassuring to think of our enemies as godless barbarians. It is troubling to learn that they might be more like us than we would ever care to admit',[10] and in general follows Priscus' more moderate view of Attila and his court. Indeed, Priscus describes how in Attila's camp he encountered a Greek who had 'gone native' after being captured in a Hun raid on the Danube but now preferred his present to his former life.[11]

Origins in the East

If western sources struggled to discover who the Huns were, they had equal difficulty in identifying their origins. In fact, Eunapius' account in the fourth century contains an element of truth when he writes that they originated in the Caucasus, as it was the Huns' invasions through the Caucasus passes that marked their first appearance in the west.[12] According to Ammianus Marcellinus, they came from the area north-east of the Sea of Azov, while other contemporary accounts linked them to the Parthians, the Royal Scythians and even to the Trojan Wars. Spurious links to the Trojan Wars and Scythians were probably little more than literary devices of late-antique authors demonstrating their knowledge of the Classics to cling to the learning of the Classical past. But links to the Parthians and Scythians, while also spurious, do at least link the Huns to Inner Asian origins. The term 'Scythian' was in any case often used as a lump-all term for the steppe nomads, just as later the same term was used by the Byzantines for the Bulgars. But to give such writers their due, the identification with the Scythians was, on the whole, an attempt to identify the Huns with people known from earlier literature. The only consensus was that 'they surpassed every extreme of ferocity', in the words of Ammianus Marcellinus.

The Huns were probably related to the *Xiongnu* (*Hsiung-nu*) of the Chinese sources, and their eruption into Europe a long-term consequence of the Chinese expansion into Inner Asia. The identification of the Xiongnu with the people known variously as Huns, Chionites and Hephthalites is subject to dispute. They are also identified with the *Hayatila*, *Hyaona*, *Hyon* of the Iranian sources and the *Hunas* of Indian sources, the cause of as much disruption in both Europe and India as they were in China.[13] The Xiongnu are first recorded in the Chinese sources as a 'barbarian' group in the late third century BC, roughly in the area of Mongolia. But they may originally have been located further south, pushed out by the unification of China under the Qin in the third century, a process of marginalising originally sedentary peoples by the aggressive policies of expansionist states reviewed in Chapter 1. Such policies can have the effect not only of creating confrontation – effectively 'barbarisation' – but also of forcing sedentary people into a nomadic lifestyle.

Chinese sources for the late Western Zhou to early Warring States period (404–221 BC) record the closely related Rong and Di people (often used interchangeably), mainly within the (anachronistic) Great Wall region, and the Hu people beyond in the steppe zone. The Di were non-Chinese who had invaded China in 628 BC and created the Dai state, which ended in 475 BC.[14] The Hu were a non-Chinese ethnic group of horse-riding archers north of the Great Wall, probably ancestors of the Xiongnu. Skeletal remains correspond to ancient north Chinese types, merging with north Asian/Mongoloid. The Zhao was the first state to build long walls to resist them, later extended under the Qin. Many Hu remains have been recorded in Ninxia and Inner Mongolia, with burials characterised by large numbers of horse sacrifices. Objects found in the burials derive from the Eurasian steppe to the north rather than those of the Rong and Di to the south. Animal plaques are a particularly charac-teristic artefact, and are found throughout the Chinese Northern Zone, the Ordos and the trans-Baikal region of Siberia. A magnificent gold headdress depicting crouching animals and with a skullcap topped by a gold eagle with a turquoise head found in the Ordos in 1973 is attributed to the Hu (Figure 6.15).[15] In the latter half of the first millennium BC the Hu spread into north-eastern China and, together with people south of the Wall who migrated northwards, formed the Xiongnu Confederation at the turn of the third century BC, the first of the united steppe powers.[16]

The Xiongnu may have been connected with the earlier Bronze Age Okunev culture further west in south Siberia which had disappeared at the end of the Bronze Age. The Okunev had a highly developed artistic tradition and the skeletal remains indicate a Mongoloid physiognomy. Whether or not they are related, the Xiongnu graves in the Baikal area confirm them to have been of Mongoloid type, as are the present Buryat population of the region. The Xiongnu therefore were probably a part of the broader Turco-Mongolian peoples, which included other related ancient groups known in the Chinese sources such as the Xianbei, the Jin, perhaps the Wusun, and later the Tangut and the Khitan.[17]

In the second century BC the Xiongnu united the steppe tribes to form a huge nomadic empire under the formidable warrior king Maodun, who defeated the Yuezhi of Gansu and turned their leader's skull into a drinking cup. The Yuezhi consequently migrated westwards (where their descendants eventually founded the Kushan Empire). The empire reached its height under Huhanye in the mid-first century BC. The term 'empire' here is probably a misnomer compared to the more organised and cen-trally ruled Chinese Empire – or indeed the other great sedentary empires of antiquity, such as the Persian or Roman. The Xiongnu was more a loose confederation of different steppe tribes on a vast scale under a Xiongnu elite, what Thomas Barfield has termed a 'shadow empire' (a term also appropriate for the later steppe formations, such as the Turk or Liao).[18]

Chinese imperial policy in the last few centuries BC – it amounted to an obsession – was aimed at evicting the Xiongnu from their borders by diplomatic and military means; the construction of the Great Wall was the most visible manifestation of this policy.

The Xiongnu wars came at huge cost to the Han: tens of thousands of Chinese dead and a hundred thousand horses lost in the 'victory' of 119 BC at a cost of seven hundred thousand *chin* of gold (one *chin* being 244 grams of gold, roughly $122,000 at today's rate, or £85,400,000), 80 per cent loss of men in the campaign of 104 BC, and only thirty thousand surviving out of an initial force of a hundred and eighty thousand a short time later. 'In bounty money alone the 119 BC campaign must have devoured half the treasury's [of the Han state] annual receipts.'[19] When subsidies resumed under the Later Han – much of it in the form of silk (92,400 metres per annum at its height) – it was equivalent to $130,000,000 per year in value, or 7 per cent of China's revenue.[20] Eventually, the Xiongnu were driven away from China and onto the immense Eurasian steppe belt towards the west. This resulted in the long-term displacement of other tribal groups who were already occupying the steppe belt. It was to have immense ramifications all over Eurasia.

After the death of Huhanye the empire split into warring factions, out of which the chief Zhizhi emerged as the ruler of the Northern Xiongnu. His 'empire', centred very roughly on modern Kazakhstan, seems to have been in a state of perpetual warfare with rival Xiongnu groups as well as with the Chinese. The Chinese eventually defeated the Northern Xiongnu in 35 BC when Zhizhi was killed, after which they became less of a problem for the Chinese. They presumably remained in the area as groups of nomadic tribes, however, as it was from this area that the Huns, the putative descendants of the Xiongnu, invaded both Europe as well as Iran and India after the fourth century AD.

There is no general consensus that the Huns grew out of the break-up of the Northern Xiongnu and their subsequent fragmentation and dispersal: scholarship is divided.[21] On the one hand Étienne de la Vaissière, for example, asserts that 'The Huns are beyond doubt the political and ethnic inheritors of the old Xiongnu empire'[22] on both linguistic grounds and the evidence of their distinctive cauldrons, while on the other hand Ursula Brosseder rejects the link between the two on much the same grounds,* but concludes wisely that 'We should think of the Huns as a social conglomerate rather than a monolithic group'.[23] Suffice it to say, the court remains out.

---

* The use of cauldrons found in archaeological contexts identified with both groups at either end of Eurasia is often cited as evidence that they are the same, but these distinctive cauldrons, in various shapes and forms, are a fairly universal feature of all early steppe nomads. See Chapter 6.

There are, for sure, many characteristics in common between the Xiongnu and the Huns: their physical description by both Chinese and Classical sources suggesting a Mongoloid origin; their reputation for ruthlessness and ferocity; elements of their military organisation; the nomadic lifestyle. It is suggestive, too, that later Hun negotiations with the Roman Empire repeated many elements of the earlier *Heqin* (*Ho-chin*) agreements between the Xiongnu and the Chinese. Attila's stipulation that the Huns had free access to border markets in his negotiations with Rome in 435, for example, or the frequent demands for Byzantine royal princesses as wives for Hun rulers (such as Attila's demand for an imperial bride from Theodosius) recall earlier demands that the Xiongnu made on the Chinese.[24] Such arrangements, however, were probably fairly standard ones between nomadic and sedentary states. There was a Gothic version of just such a treaty with Rome between 332 and 367, for example, with similar stipulations for border markets, the supply of auxiliary troops, and so forth.[25] Like the Xiongnu, the Huns also practised a form of sky worship in common with many other steppe nomads (inasmuch we know anything about Hun religion), and their consultation of oracle bones is also suggestive of Chinese links.* Comparisons of the mythologies of the Xiongnu and the Huns show important differences but also important similarities, common to many steppe peoples.[26]

To the Chinese, 'Xiongnu' meant to some extent simply 'those barbarians out there' rather than a specific ethnic unit, much the same as 'Hun' became in western sources: both terms rapidly became pejorative ones. The Xiongnu-Hun identity is largely academic as both were steppe tribal confederations that incorporated large bodies of non-Hun and non-Xiongnu tribes; even if totally distinct (which is unlikely), both would have incorporated elements of each other in any case. Even if it can be proved that the Xiongnu are the same as the Huns of the European sources, there is no way that they could be the 'same' people in the fifth century AD in Europe as those in second-century BC Mongolia: no people are the 'same' after seven centuries, even if they preserve the same name, especially over such distance: twenty-first-century Americans, for example, are not the 'same' as fourteenth-century Britons.

Whether or not the Xiongnu and the Huns are the same is unimportant. What is important is that the Chinese defeat of the Xiongnu resulted in a huge, long-term displacement of steppe nomads, a chain reaction that would have a knock-on effect right across Eurasia, 'the tide of emigration which impetuously rolled from the confines of China to those of

---

* Although the Chinese practices of heating bones and interpreting the resultant cracks, attributed as early as the Shang period in the second millennium BC, might have no connection to the Hun practice, which consisted of interpreting the bones of sacrificial animals after they had been scraped.

Germany' in the words of Gibbon.[27] The early Turks were another group caught up in these events. By the middle years of the fourth century AD the Huns had become an important – and menacing – nomad confederation on the northern borders of the Persian Empire at whose name both Rome and Iran had cause to shudder. It was to result in an avalanche of 'barbarian' tribes into Europe, not only of Huns but those driven before them as well: Franks, Burgundians, Sueves, Vandals and Goths. In recent years the idea of the Gothic nation fleeing across the Danube (in 376) to seek refuge in the Roman Empire from pursuing Huns, and the whole question of massed migrations, have been questioned by many historians. But Peter Heather argues that Ammianus' account of these events is substantially accurate: that this is exactly what happened.[28]

Xiongnu material remains

Excavations of sites identified with the Xiongnu to the east of Lake Baikal have revealed a surprisingly sophisticated sedentary culture. Large-scale excavations at the third–second-century BC site of Ivolginsk (or Nogolka) near Ulan Ude, for example, revealed a planned, densely settled urban area with houses laid out in rows dominated by a large building in the centre, the whole surrounded by ramparts, the largest Xiongnu site so far excavated (Figures 6.17 and 7.1). There was also extensive evidence for agriculture, animal husbandry and a high degree of metalworking and

Figure 7.1 *The ramparts and outer ditch of the Xiongnu site of Ivolginsk in Buryatia*

Figure 7.2 *A line of supposed Xiongnu fortification walls near Lake Baikal*

craftsmanship. It is dated by Chinese coins and other related Chinese artefacts between the end of the third and the early first century BC.[29] Grains of millet were found in the excavations as well as a ploughshare, but such agriculture as did exist was small and, it has been suggested, was carried out by Chinese prisoners or immigrants.[30] Other excavations at the rich Xiongnu graves at Noin Ula in Mongolia reinforce this view. Extensive – albeit flimsy – fortifications have also been recorded in the region to the north-west of Lake Baikal, comprising single lines of uncut stones circling the tops of hills (Figure 7.2) as well as at Merkit 'Castle' further south in Buryatia towards the Mongolian border (Figure 7.3).[31] Elsewhere, the Chinese-style Liling Palace near Abakan has been interpreted as the official residence of the Xiongnu administrator for the Minusinsk Basin.[32]

Some 216 graves were also excavated from Ivolginsk cemetery as well as the nearby cemetery at Derestuy. These, together with further Xiongnu burials excavated in the Ilmova Valley in Buryatia and elsewhere in Mongolia, reveal distinctive trapezoidal dromoses with multi-chambered tombs, dated to the first century BC and AD. The design owes more to north Chinese traditions than the steppe.[33] In the same region of Buryatia many graves have been recorded, and some excavated, consisting of square, multi-chambered stone construction tombs with a long tapering approach on one side (Figure 7.4).[34]

Figure 7.3 *Merkit Castle, a supposed Xiongnu fort in Buryatia*

Figure 7.4 *Excavated Xiongnu grave in Buryatia*

The Huns in Central Asia, Persia and India

Before turning to the Huns in Europe, one must first examine their conquests further east. Only by the overall picture is it possible to appreciate just how great a threat the Huns posed to the sedentary empires of antiquity: Chinese as well as Persian, Indian and Roman. In the latter part of the fourth century a succession of Hunnic tribes appeared in Bactria and established control over the Hindu Kush mountains at Sasanian expense.[35] Formerly these tribes were all lumped together under the general term of 'Hephthalites', but recent numismatic and historical studies have identified several distinct Hun groups: the Chionites, the Kidarites, the Alkhan, the Nezak and the Hephthalites proper, generally termed 'Iranian Huns'. To these one can possibly add a sixth Hunnic group known from early Islamic sources ruling south of the Hindu Kush from the seventh century, the Zunbils, who hung on until the ninth century (although they might have been Turk: accounts are unclear). Procopius makes the point that although the European Huns and the Central Asian Huns belonged to the same stock, those in Central Asia were more than mere nomadic raiders and possessed 'a lawful constitution', issued coins, established settlements and were generally more sedentary than their European cousins.[36] Much of the chronology and relationship between the various groups is controversial, and there is also confusion between some of them.

According to Greek sources it was the Chionites who first invaded Bactria in about AD 350, but it is unclear whether this group appears in the numismatic record. The Kidarites were the first of the Hunnic groups to issue coins in Bactria, emerging soon after the mid-fourth century (although dates are disputed). A king called Kidara, with his capital at Balkh, ruled north and south of the Hindu Kush between about 312 and 337. Alkhan Hun coins then appear from about AD 390 onwards south of the Hindu Kush. Probably at first subordinate to the Kidarites, the Alkhans replaced them after the mid-fifth century and extended their conquests into northern India. A separate group of Huns with distinct coinage, the Nezak Shahs, emerged south of the Hindu Kush from about 560 until becoming absorbed by a Turk kingdom there in about 748.

Of the various Hunnic groups, the Hephthalites have left the most record in the sources. Their wars of the first half of the fifth century with the Sasanians were the greatest the Sasanians ever fought, greater than Sasanian wars with the Romans. They came near to bringing the Sasanian Empire to its knees: indeed, the Sasanians were tributary to the Hephthalites for a while. In 457 Emperor Peroz overthrew his brother Hormizd III with the aid of the Hephthalites, but later perished in a war against them in 484. The Hephthalites absorbed the Alkhan Huns and established a major empire which extended from Central Asia to the Indus Valley.[37]

The Huns – 'Huna' in Indian sources – were at first resisted by the powerful Gupta emperor of India, Skandagupta, in 458. But after the death of Skandagupta his empire collapsed, partly as a result of Hun pressure. By the early sixth century the Huns under Toramana had established their own rule over much of northern and western India. This was consolidated by Toramana's son and successor Mihirakula, who has the reputation in Indian historical tradition of unmitigated cruelty – an eastern Attila. Hephthalite rule, however, did not last for long. King Yasovarman of Malwa led a confederacy to defeat the Huns in 528, forcing them to withdraw to Kashmir. In the mid-sixth century the Oxus empire of the Huns was overthrown by the Turks allied to the Sasanians.

The Hun/Hephthalite invasion of Afghanistan and north-western India has been described in Indian and Chinese sources as wreaking utter devastation, with cities and monasteries laid waste, many of them never to recover. This is regarded as the beginning of Buddhist decline in the region, and the Chinese pilgrim, Xuanzang, who travelled through there in the middle seventh century, writes of once-flourishing Buddhist centres reduced as a result of Hun destruction. The archaeological record does not entirely support this picture, with monasteries not only flourishing during this period but producing vigorous new sculptural styles of Gandharan art. Some at least of the Hephthalite princes appeared to have settled in the region and to have created a period of stability, becoming patrons of the local religion. After the collapse of the main Hephthalite kingdom, remnant Hephthalite petty states survived for a while longer in some places. It has been suggested that the warlike Rajput clans of later medieval western India are descended from these Huns. Tenth-century and later sources record descendants of the Hephthalites known as the Khalaj, speaking a language that was distinct from either Turkish or Persian. The Khalaj were still recorded as a distinct tribe in the fourteenth century, although by that time their language had become Turkised. By the sixteenth century the name had become Khalji or Ghalji, and is recorded in the context of Babur's campaigns into India. They are still known today in the same region of eastern Afghanistan as the Ghilzai according to some studies, although by now speaking only Pashtu in common with the surrounding Pashtun tribes – possibly the only known descendants of the Huns anywhere in the world.[38]

A Hun kingdom in Europe

By 370 the Huns had occupied the area to the north of the Black Sea roughly between the Don and the Dniester Rivers, subjugating the Alans in the process (Map 7.1).[39] This brought them up against the Ostrogoths to the west of the Dniester, whom they attacked. No reason

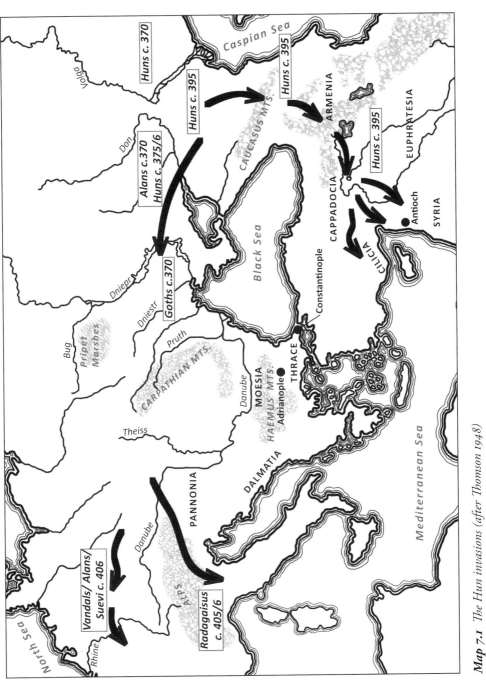

Map 7.1 The Hun invasions (after Thomson 1948)

Huns c. 370

Huns c. 395

Caspian Sea

Huns c. 395

ARMENIA

Volga

EUPHRATESIA

Alans c. 370
Huns c. 375/6

Huns c. 395

Don

CAUCASUS MTS.

Antioch

CAPPADOCIA

SYRIA

Goths c. 370

Dniepr

Black Sea

CILICIA

Dniestr

Bug

Pripet
Marshes

Pruth

Constantinople

CARPATHIAN MTS.

Danube

MOESIA

THRACE

Theiss

HAEMUS MTS.

Adrianople

DALMATIA

Mediterranean Sea

PANNONIA

Vandals/ Alans/
Suevi c. 406

Danube

ALPS

Radagaisus
c. 405/6

North Sea

Rhine

is given for their migration westwards from Inner Asia, although some contemporary observers speculated on the drying of pastures further to the east. There may be some truth in this – the arrival of such a large body of horsemen in the area would in any case have depleted the pastures even if a drought had not. In 370 the Huns broke through the Dniester defences sending the Ostrogoths towards the Roman frontier on the Danube. The Danube was a hardly more effective barrier than the Dniester, and the way to Constantinople lay open. On 9 August 378, the Roman army led by the Emperor Valens met the Goths in battle at Adrianople (modern Edirne) and was routed, the Emperor himself among the slain.

The Huns themselves crossed the Danube in the winter of 395 when the river froze, but more devastating was their attack on a new front. In the same year they broke through the Caucasian passes and entered the Near East. Over the following two years they raided throughout Armenia, Cappadocia and northern Syria until a peace was negotiated in 398. In the end it was only a reprieve, for ten years later the Huns raided across the Danube once again, led by Uldin, the first Hun whose name we learn in the western sources. With memories of how close Constantinople came to falling to the Goths still fresh, there was a massive strengthening of the Danube defences – particular attention being given to the fleet – and new walls were built by Theodosius for Constantinople. The Theodosian land walls, completed in 413, successfully defended the imperial city for another thousand years.

This sheer gratuitous savagery and destructiveness of the Huns in their first round of wars in the late fourth century took even the Romans by surprise, inured as they were by then to barbarian encounters. Previous invasions – mainly by the Goths and their vanguard – were unlike the Hun onslaught. For the Goths were themselves fleeing from the Huns, looking to the Roman Empire for protection rather than destruction, wanting to become Roman rather than overcome Rome. And once they were settled inside the frontiers the Romans found that they could, in the end, become productive agriculturists, loyal subjects and staunch allies. The Goths and the other Germanic groups even became Christian (albeit of the Arian heresy). The Huns, on the other hand, remained immune to conversion, despite a number of evangelical missions and despite such missions being received politely, albeit disinterestedly, by the Hun rulers themselves.* In the long run the Huns rarely sought anything beyond, at best, plunder and, at worst, destruction.

---

* In 533/4, 'Grod, the king of the Huns' in Crimea, together with his army, came to Constantinople to request conversion and was accordingly baptised, with Justinian himself acting as Grod's godfather according to Pseudo-Dionysius of Tel-Mahre. On returning to Crimea Grod had the Hunnic idols destroyed, which so angered his fellow

This is not to say that occasional alliances between Roman and Hun were not made: like any other 'barbarian', the Huns could also be a useful source of mercenaries. Even before Uldin crossed the Danube in 408 there seems to have been some alliance – or at least collaboration – with the Romans in driving off other invaders. In 437 the Roman general Aetius, for example, used Hun mercenaries to massacre the Burgundians of Gaul. This event was one of the inspirations of the Nibelung legend – and ultimately of Wagner's epic operatic cycle. The ensuing period of the early fifth century sees various factions in the increasingly unstable Roman Empire buying Hun support to play one side off against another. The result, unfortunately for the Romans, would simply draw more Huns into the Empire.

The existence of Hun tribes within the imperial borders became an issue when Rua, the Hun leader who succeeded Uldin, sent an ultimatum to Constantinople for the return of the tribes to Hun territory: Rua was trying to unite all Hun tribes under his own rule. For all their savagery, the Huns were certainly not wanting in either strategic planning or intelligence: the ultimatum had been timed perfectly when the Empire was distracted from its Danube frontier by wars against the Vandals in North Africa to the west and against the Persians to the east. Constantinople had little choice but to negotiate. However, Rua died suddenly in 434, to be succeeded by his two nephews Bleda and Attila.

The kingdom of Attila

The following year Constantinople concluded the treaty with the Huns that had been negotiated with Rua. The terms were harsh: as well as Hun trading rights re-affirmed, Hun fugitives were to be returned and an annual tribute of seven hundred pounds of gold was to be made. For all its harshness, the Huns seem to have kept their side of the bargain over the following years: depredations against the Roman Empire ceased and we hear little of Attila. It is assumed that Attila had turned his attentions eastwards and was consolidating his position during this time as some form of long-term strategy for a grand invasion of the Roman Empire. This involved having his brother Bleda murdered, subjugating the neighbouring tribes and building up a 'Hunnic Empire'. However, there is little evidence of this; having secured an agreement with the Empire he

Huns that Grod's brother had him killed and the remaining Christian Huns fled. See Pseudo-Dionysius 1996: 51–2. There was some proselytisation by Armenian missionaries of a doubtful Hun group in the Kuban at the same time. A remnant Hun group in the northern Caucasus in the tenth century adopted Christianity briefly, but renounced it shortly after (Obolensky 1971: 87–8).

may simply have been pasturing his flocks – albeit with raids against neighbouring tribes on the side – in the time-honoured manner of the steppe nomads.

For it was the Romans, not the Huns, who, in dishonouring the treaty, forced Attila to turn westwards. This was in response to a Roman raid across the Danube in 435 when the Bishop of Margus crossed the Danube to desecrate and rob the Hun royal graves. The Empire had, further-more, defaulted on the payments promised to the Huns. Hun retribution was swift and devastating and the Balkan provinces south of the Danube frontier reeled once more. The army of Theodosius II which was sent to oppose the Huns was slaughtered and the road to Constantinople lay open once again, leaving the Emperor with little choice but to request terms. Accordingly, a new peace treaty was negotiated in 443, re-affirming the former one. This time Attila could dictate his own terms: Hun fugitives* were not only to be returned but a bounty was to be paid in addition to immediate payment of arrears of tribute and an increase in the annual tribute to a thousand pounds of gold. The Romans had little option but to accede. Another treaty was made in 448.

But the Romans remained duplicitous. In 449 the Emperor Theodosius II sent an embassy led by Maximinus to the camp of Attila, accompanied by the historian Priscus, who recorded the story. They were also joined by a separate embassy from the Western Roman Empire led by Romulus, the grandfather of the future Emperor Romulus Augustus, the last Western emperor. Unbeknown to Maximinus, he was unwittingly a part of a plot that had been arranged by Chrysaphius, one of Theodosius II's senior court officials, to assassinate Attila. The plot was betrayed and Attila demanded Chrysaphius for punishment. This resulted in a new embassy and further negotiations, when Attila was bought off and a new treaty concluded in 450. However, later in the same year Theodosius II died unexpectedly, and his successor Marcian promptly annulled the treaty with the Huns.[40]

In 451 Attila withdrew from the Eastern Roman Empire and headed westwards. The Western Roman Empire's dealings with the Huns, under Valentinian II and his general Aetius, had been equally duplicitous. Attila's ostensible reason was to attack Rome's ally the Visigoths. There ensued complex negotiations, which involved – among other things – Attila being granted the Roman title of *magister militum*, or commander-in-chief, like Gothic chiefs before him. The Western Roman army by then comprised mainly Goths and Alans. The same year Attila invaded Gaul and sacked Metz, and city after city fell to the onslaught. Orleans was relieved by

---

* It is not known who such fugitives were: it seems unlikely that they would be Huns fleeing their own people, but presumably non-Hun indigenous groups – perhaps Scythians? – in eastern Europe fleeing Hun rule.

Aetius with his army of Goths and Alans – a case of fighting fire with fire. The Huns on their side also included Ostrogoths and Gepids. The ensuing Battle of the Catalaunian Fields – 'a conflict . . . such as could not be paralleled either in the present or in past ages', in the words of Cassiodorius* – near Châlons-sur-Marne, however, was inconclusive.

Despite its inconclusive result, the Battle of the Catalaunian Fields has been regarded as 'one of the decisive battles of the world', a triumph of West over East, of European civilisation over Asiatic barbarism, of saving infant European Christendom from paganism, and other emotive epithets. Hyun Jin Kim rightly dismisses the racial and religious hyperbole that often characterises such accounts. He further points out that even a Hun victory in Europe would not have meant the end of Christianity as the Huns, in common with most steppe empires such as the Mongols, had a policy of religious toleration.[41] Attila in fact was almost defeated by Aetius – dubbed 'the last of the Romans' by Gibbon[42] – but Aetius was politically astute enough not to press his advantage. The Huns were, after all, former allies, and a balance of power was required to be maintained among the barbarians, without any side gaining the uppermost. The Romans did not want the Goths to become too powerful any more than they wanted the Huns to be. In the last days of the empire in the west, difficult decisions had to be made, so Attila was allowed a reprieve.

Attila, however, did not thank the Romans, and the following year he invaded Italy. His sack and destruction of Aquileia brought about one indirect effect on medieval Europe: the survivors fled to the more easily defensible marshy grounds and islands at the mouth of the Po. (The event forms the opening scene of Verdi's opera *Attila*.) From these marshes, Venice was born. Verona and other cities in northern Italy also fell and Milan surrendered. A delegation led by Pope Leo I eventually persuaded Attila to turn back from Rome – probably more due to an outbreak of plague in the Hun army than Attila being swayed by Leo's piousness. Emperor Marcian in the meantime sent an army to attack the Huns in their homeland. Attila accordingly retreated, albeit vowing war against the Eastern Roman Empire following this latest Roman abrogation of the treaty. However, Attila himself died the following year in 453 from a surfeit of wives. 'After a decade of mayhem stretching from Constantinople to Paris, Attila the Hun died from the after-effects of one too many wedding nights', as Peter Heather remarks.[43]

After Attila's death the Hun confederation – it was never really an 'empire' – soon fell apart. We still read of groups of Hun warriors

---

* Quoted in Gibbon 1901, III: 464 – and anticipating Cervantes' famous words 'the greatest occasion that past or future ones can hope to see' on the Battle of Lepanto in 1571.

throughout the latter half of the fifth century, either as isolated raiding parties or as mercenary units in one or the other of the Roman armies, although the label 'Hun' was becoming increasingly meaningless. Bede even records Huns accompanying the Saxon invasions of England in the sixth century.[44] But there was no further united front. The collapse of Hun power on the steppe inevitably created a vacuum, for round about this time we begin to hear of new nomad nations forming on the eastern European steppe: Avars and Bulgars.

The Avars, Bulgars and others will be reviewed in the next chapters. For the moment, many of the Huns were incorporated into the later Bulgar state, and in the sixth century groups of Huns are recorded as forming mercenary units in various other armies – some groups are even recorded as settled and leading peaceful lives in parts of eastern Europe. Huns are recorded as late as the tenth century in parts of central Europe, but by then the term probably had as little ethnic meaning as Winston Churchill's references to 'Huns' in the twentieth.* In the late seventh and into the eighth century a Hun 'kingdom' – or at least communities – is recorded in that great watershed of beached-up odds and ends of people from earliest antiquity, the Caucasus. They were subjects of the emerging Khazar state and may well have become Turkish-speaking by this time – indeed, their Hun ethnicity is in doubt. Alternatively, the Khazars themselves have been described as originally Huns who had undergone Turkicisation. Either way, the Huns seem to have melted back into the steppe whence they came.

The barefaced duplicity of the Romans' dealings – both the Eastern and the Western Empires – with the Huns even by their own accounts makes astonishing reading. Rarely in the past has there been such a record of lies, plots, betrayals, broken promises, arrogance and vacillation (as is depressingly familiar in today's politics). It must have tried Attila's patience over and over again. Small wonder that this steppe nomad chief had nothing but contempt for the corrupt Romans. One is left almost admiring Attila's restraint.

---

* The use of 'Hun' as a pejorative term for the Germans in the First World War is usually attributed to Winston Churchill, but in fact was first used by the Kaiser in 1900 as a *positive* term for the Germans, as the quotation at the beginning of this chapter shows. It was Kipling who then used it in a poem at the outbreak of the war:

> For all we have and are,
> For all our children's fate,
> Stand up and take the war,
> The Hun is at the gate!

Both are quoted in Kelly 2008: 221 and 225. One is also reminded of Denis Healey's nickname for Margaret Thatcher, 'Attila the Hen'.

Walling off the barbarians

From the Great Wall of China in the east to Hadrian's Wall in the west, states have attempted quite literally to wall off the outsider. It tends to be the Huns. Often – indeed, usually – the 'barbarian' is nothing more than the wall builders' perceptions, such as in the propaganda behind East Germany's construction of the Berlin Wall, and China's Great Wall is as much about Chinese self-perception as any perceived barbarian threat. The tradition is an ancient one, with several examples known in Mesopotamia and the Levant dating back to the second and first millennia BC. In Crimea, the Bosporan kingdom constructed a long land wall across the eastern end of the Crimean peninsula against the Scythians to their west (Figure 4.30). The tradition shows no signs of abating, as the Iron Curtain in recent history demonstrates, not to mention the current 'Palestine Wall' or the proposed (but since shelved) wall along the USA's southern border with Mexico. Attitudes behind such constructions also remain remarkably the same.

The Roman Empire erected some of the most elaborate frontier defences of the ancient world against the peoples beyond their borders. In the main, these were not linear walls in the Chinese sense, but combined barricades, roads and interconnected systems of forts, such as the *limes* systems along the German and Syrian (and to a lesser extent the North African) frontiers. Hadrian's Wall, as well as the later Antonine Wall further north, was the exception rather than the rule in the Roman world. Such walls were more characteristic against the nomads of the wide open steppe lands of Central Asia. Such a fourth-century AD (or earlier) wall comprising rammed earth has been traced for some sixty kilometres across northern Afghanistan, for example,[45] and later frontier walls between Bactria and Sogdia, as well as the vast circuit walls that enclosed entire Central Asian oases at Merv, Balkh and Bukhara to keep the nomad at bay and protect outlying settlements, have also been recorded.[46]

The largest and most elaborate of such Central Asian defensive systems is the 'Great Wall of Gorgan' across north-eastern Iran, built by the Sasanian Empire in the late fifth or early sixth century as a direct response to the threat from the Hephthalites. The sheer scale of the Gorgan Wall and its associated works is staggering. It stretches eastward from the Caspian Sea across the Turkmen steppe for at least 195 kilometres, ending in the Kopet Dagh Mountains forming the present border of Iran with Turkmenistan. Associated is another wall, the Wall of Tammisha, stretching south from the south-eastern corner of the Caspian for eleven kilometres and ending in the Alborz Mountains, part of the same system. The Tammisha wall even extended into the sea for a short distance, as probably did the Gorgan Wall. The Gorgan Wall, built of brick, also had over thirty frontier forts behind it as well as several much larger campaign bases in the hinterland, each on average approximately ten times larger than the wall forts. Each

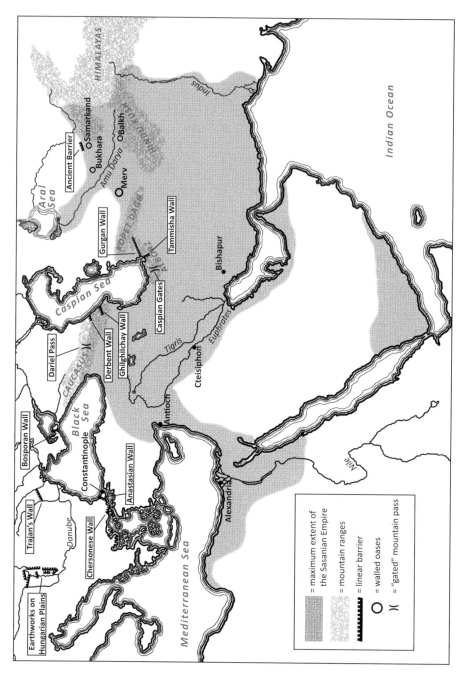

Map 7.2 Antique defensive systems against the nomads (locations are approximate and walls not to scale) (adapted from Sauer et al. 2013)

campaign fort housed approximately ten thousand soldiers (although little is to be seen of the forts today). It has been estimated that the total garrison for the entire wall was at least thirty thousand.

The walls and their associated fortifications were only a part of the complex. Alongside were several thousand kilns for baking the estimated hundred million or more bricks used in the construction, as well as an associated dam and canal system for the brick-making and presumably a road system for building and servicing the wall. The wall also required an ambitious irrigation system for the agriculture to support the garrison. In addition, the site of Dasht-i Qal'a in the hinterland was also investigated, the site of a city founded at about the same time as the wall. This presumably supported both the building of the wall and the maintenance of both the wall and its garrison. Altogether, the Gorgan Wall must have required the direct and indirect participation of a population of many tens of thousands and a military budget that even by modern standards must have been colossal. The archaeologists who investigated this emphasise the Gorgan Wall as 'the core part of the largest and most elaborate frontier system ever built in the ancient and medieval Near East . . . amongst the most ambitious and sophisticated frontier walls ever built world-wide'[47] (Figure 7.5, Map 7.2).

As if the sheer scale of the Gorgan Wall were not enough, it was only a part of an even larger Sasanian imperial defensive scheme against the Huns. The Hun invasions through the Caucasus Mountains in the 390s emphasised that it was not only the wide open steppe that was vulnerable: the seemingly impenetrable barrier of the Caucasus was also permeable. Hence, Sasanian Persia embarked upon a further programme of wall building to stop up the few open gates through the Caucasus. The most ambitious were the fortifications at Derbent (or Darband: the name means 'closed gate' in Persian) between the eastern end of the Caucasus and the Caspian Sea in Daghestan, just north of the present Azerbaijan–Russian border. Although not as long as the Gorgan, it comprised a fort and associated masonry linear wall that also extended into the sea: as with the Gorgan Wall at the opposite end of the Caspian, even the possibility of Huns wading around the wall was not left to chance. A secondary earthworks wall further south, the Ghilghilchai Wall, also blocked the gap between the mountains and sea.

Further west the main pass through the Caucasus was the Darial Gorge in Georgia, site of the nineteenth-century 'Georgian Military Highway' and still the main route between Georgia and Russia. The Georgian name 'Darial' is derived from the Persian *Dar-i Alan* or 'Gate of the Alans', the Sarmatian invaders before the Huns.* This too was closed by a wall and

---

* The present descendants of the Alans, the Ossetians, are still in the region, and were the reason behind the short war between Georgia and Russia in 2008. The latter-day Alans and their Russian allies, however, penetrated the Caucasus through a tunnel west of the

Figure 7.5 *Aerial view of the Gurgan Wall and one of its forts (Fort 09) in north-eastern Iran (Drone photo by Davit Naskidashvili and the Joint Project of the Iranian Heritage, Handcraft and Tourism Organization and the University of Edinburgh, courtesy of Eberhard Sauer)*

associated fortifications by the Sasanians, although with a gap of only a hundred metres or so the scale does not compare with that of Gorgan or even Derbent (Figure 7.6).[48] At the western end of the Caucasus, the gap between the mountains and the Black Sea is reported also to have been closed by fortifications, although less is known of these. Smaller in scale though these mountain defences were, in the context of an overall imperial strategy that included the Gorgan Wall the scale is colossal – a measure not only of the very real and sinister danger that the Huns represented to the Sasanians, but of the vast co-ordinated resources that the Empire could command in defence. Indeed, the archaeologist who led the investigations, Eberhard Sauer, aptly sums this up as follows:

> It was no coincidence that the Western Roman Empire was annihilated in the
> later 5th century, whilst the Sasanian Empire was not just able to maintain

---

Darial gorge, the only road communication between North and South Ossetia. To show solidarity, the conductor Valery Gergiev, an ethnic Ossetian musician (but Moscow-born), took the Mariinsky Orchestra to South Ossetia at the time of the invasion to perform Shostakovich's *Leningrad Symphony*, composed and first performed during the German siege of Leningrad. Ambiguous messages all round for all.

Figure 7.6 *Fortifications at the Dariali Gorge forming the present border between Georgia and Russia*

most of its territories, but even able to expand further in the 6th and early 7th centuries.[49]

Although the Western Roman Empire fell, the Eastern Roman Empire survived – and once again it was the long land walls that contributed to its survival. The massive Theodosian walls of Constantinople, completed in 413, were a direct response to the threat from the Huns and are one of the greatest defensive works of the ancient world. Less well-known are the even longer land walls built a short time later in the fifth century as an outer defensive work against the Huns. These were the Anastasian Walls stretching for fifty-six kilometres across Thrace from the Black Sea to the Sea of Marmara (Figure 7.7).[50] Although not as elaborate as the Theodosian Walls and not as long-lasting – it fell into disuse after the seventh century – the Anastasian Wall was strongly built of worked masonry blocks standing several metres high and must have represented a huge outlay of manpower, money and resources. Most of all, these – and there are more in Bulgaria and Romania – and the Sasanian defences represent a vast chain of fortifications stretching from central Europe to Central Asia whose sole aim was simply to wall off the Huns.[*] These defences speak far more than the

---

[*] The Gorgan Wall, the Darial Wall and the Anastasian Wall have all been investigated in recent years by archaeologists from the Universities of Edinburgh, Durham and Newcastle, all three universities close to Hadrian's Wall.

Figure 7.7 *Part of the Anastasian Wall across Thrace*

ancient sources do of the real threat that these steppe nomads represented
to the greatest military powers of antiquity, and the real horror with which
they were viewed by their citizens.

Legacy of the Huns

The ferocity of Attila is undoubted. But he also had admirable quali-
ties. Attila was on the whole a man of honour; he kept his word but at
the same time was a shrewd negotiator; he was able to understand his
enemies' weaknesses and bide his time; he was able to bind the Hun
tribes to his will; his modest lifestyle impressed Priscus. At the same time
it would be a mistake to overstate Attila's talents. He was in the end
no military genius, nor had he any long-term strategy of building and
consolidating an empire beyond immediate punishment and plunder.
And while he was usually in the right – his aggression was almost invariably in response to Roman duplicity and broken agreements – it would
be a great mistake to cast Attila as some sort of righter of wrongs, a
champion of noble steppe nomads against Roman decadence, a Hun
Braveheart. The pendulum has swung both ways. 'Hun' has entered our
language as the very epitome of savagery, and the very name Attila as
that of the ultimate barbarian. The Huns' name was adopted by British

propaganda to demonise the Germans in the First World War. Their reputation was further embellished in the 1954 Hollywood movie *Sign of the Pagan* starring Jack Palance as a ferocious Attila and the very converse of American values ('proto-communists on horseback' as Christopher Kelly remarked).[51] An Italian movie a year earlier, *Attila the Scourge of God*, starred Anthony Quinn as a more thoughtful but equally savage Attila (where the then-unknown teenage actress Sophia Loren first appeared). Recently, there has been a tendency to view the Huns as much-maligned, as steppe heroes, and Attila as a kind of Robin Hood. The 2001 television movie *Attila the Hun* is a part of this pendulum swing, with the image of Attila owing more to Mel Gibson's *Braveheart* than either the Jack Palance or Anthony Quinn versions.* Both views are, of course, extreme, the first a reflection of contemporary observers, the latter of modern-day politically correct even-handedness. Verdi's *Attila* is surprisingly mature in this respect, lying somewhere in between, with its protagonist even interpreted as a tragic hero in some productions.

In assessing the history of the Huns in Eurasia, David Christian writes:

> In the second century BCE, the formation of a great pastoralist empire in the eastern steppes started a new migratory pulse that was felt in the Inner Eurasian steppes for more than half a millennium. The rise and fall of the Xiongnu empire affected the whole of Inner Eurasia. Indirectly, it also shaped the destiny of agricultural empires from China to Rome.[52]

This is perhaps overstating the case, but in essence it is true. Peter Heather further argues that migrations define the history of first millennium AD Europe, leading ultimately to its birth and the collapse of the Roman frontier policy as a direct result of 'the knock-on effect of Hunnic invasion'.[53]

Peter Golden, on the other hand, writes that

> the Xiongnu collapse had sent the first wave of nomads westward. Europe's first encounter with Central Asian nomads left a lasting memory and a legend far out of proportion to its actual impact. The Huns became symbols of the unbridled barbarian. Despite their ferocious reputations, the Huns, east and west, were never a threat to the existence of China or the Roman Empire.[54]

Relations between the Xiongnu and the Chinese – or those later between the Huns and the Romans – were never simplistic aggressive barbarian versus passive civilisations, but went both ways: in many instances, not only were the 'barbarians' justified in their aggression, but they offered a better life (at least for the sedentary peasant).[55]

---

* Indeed, the cover image on the DVD of the 2001 movie appears deliberately to be copying that of *Braveheart*. The 2013 horror film *Attila*, in which US soldiers inadvertently awaken the mummified Attila when searching for his treasure, need not detain us here.

A reappraisal of the Huns by Hyun Jin Kim has made efforts to reverse the traditional negative image. Far from the Huns' leaving no trace or legacy in Europe, the birth of the post-Roman Germanic states of early medieval Europe are viewed as evolving from the empire of Attila. The firm state foundations put into place by the Huns meant that they 'certainly did not disappear as a people [after the collapse of Attila's empire]'.[56] The author points out that the Hun state was a more organised and structured entity than is generally recognised, not a mere steppe confederation, and more organised than the Germanic kingdoms. The simultaneous invasion of both the Sasanian and Roman Empires, and taking just ten years to conquer an area stretching from the Volga to Hungary in the late fourth century, could only mean a highly organised and centralised state mechanism. Such a vast spread and huge military machine must mean nothing less. On the basis of loose ideas of kingship, tribute systems, royal succession and feudal loyalties, the author concludes that 'the political culture of early medieval Europe was in essence a Hunnic-derived version of the common Central Eurasian political *koine* fused together with the residues of Roman political institutions'.[57]

Such views offer a needed balance. The structure and organisation – and, indeed, material remains – of the Xiongnu in the east certainly suggests something more than the mere ravening horde of European tradition: even if the Huns were not descended from the Xiongnu they must at least have been influenced by them. The Hephthalite Huns of Central Asia and the Indo-Afghan borderlands, it is true, left an abiding legacy in the late Gandharan works of Buddhist art, some architecture both north and south of the Hindu Kush, and perhaps some of the later institutions and traditions of the Rajputs of India. But Kim is making claims for a positive reappraisal of the Huns of Europe rather than of the Hephthalites and Xiongnu further east. As with some of the current views of Attila as a kind of earlier Robin Hood or William Wallace, the author risks taking such claims too far in a retrospective neo-Hunnish nationalism. In the statement that the term 'Hun' was not an ethnic designation but a term of 'steppe ideology',[58] most steppe peoples from Europe to the Far East are re-interpreted under the overall designation 'Hunnic': not only Hun-related groups such as the Chionites and Hephthalites, but the Avars, the Xianbei and Northern Wei in China, the Oghur and Onoghur Turks, Bulgars and the Khazars are described as 'Hunnic', speaking a Hun language. Even the Sarmatians and Goths are described as Hun-influenced (which to a certain extent they doubtless were). For example, the 'Huns [are] now called Bulgars' or Odoacer 'Hunno-Germanic', or 'The various Oghurs . . . and the Bulgars . . . are likely to have been either the same people [as the Huns] or at least members of the same, related political entity'. Steppe peoples go from being 'related' to becoming 'likely to be the same' to being 'certainly' the same. They then become 'Kutrigur Huns', 'Bulgar Huns' and

'Germanic Huns'. In a circular argument, the Franks and other Germanic peoples go from being 'reminiscent' of Hunnish institutions to 'having maybe been influenced' and 'possibly influenced' and then to 'probably influenced', and eventually to 'certainly influenced' and thence to being 'fundamental' to the development of Europe. A Hunnic element – or at least influence – is recognised in the character of Childeric and the beginnings of Merovingian France, and it is even argued that Childeric was a puppet governor set up in Gaul by Attila. 'Hunnish' objects in Childeric's tomb are cited as evidence for this (objects which, as noted in Chapter 6, were at least steppe-influenced if not Hunnic). The Ostrogoths and Lombards who eventually replaced Roman rule in Italy are viewed as political units formed out of the Hun 'empire'. Hence, 'the Huns . . . presented a real, viable alternative to Roman hegemony of the peoples of Europe'.[59]

There were doubtless Hun influences in the emerging states of Medieval Europe at the end of antiquity. Kim's work offers a balance, a swing away from both the traditional Romano-centric and Mediterranean-biased views of the period, as well as more recent Germano-centric views. But there can be little doubt that the Hun invasions – and the earlier Germanic ones – were marked above all by violence. Bryan Ward-Perkins, in guarding against a recent tendency to minimise the violence of these invasions in order to invent a perceived smooth tradition into the Middle Ages, regards the period quite bluntly as 'the end of civilization'; in a similar caveat, Simon James guarded against the 'pacification of the past'.[60]

The Hun invasion hastened the collapse of the Roman Empire in the West, but Peter Heather emphasises that it was going to collapse even without the Huns: 'empires, unlike diamonds, do not last forever'.[61] For all the Huns' ferocity there were practically no long-lasting effects. The successors of the Roman Empire and the revived empire under Charlemagne were mainly Romano-German in character. Medieval and later Europe at least did not acknowledge any Hun legacy. Frederick Barbarossa's chaplain stated specifically that 'Romans and Germans are of one seed . . . Romans and Germans as if one populace'.[62] 'Barbaric' ancestry was readily acknowledged by Merovingian, Carolingian, Hohenstaufen and Habsburg monarchies through mutual Germanic inheritance, but not from the Huns, the steppe nature of Childeric's tomb objects notwithstanding. The Habsburgs in particular, who of all European monarchies made a point of combining the Germanic and Roman past in a concept of a 'universal pan-European empire', numbered Charlemagne, Julius Caesar and Nero as their ancestors as well as the Germanic and Roman legacy broadly. But they also numbered over a hundred Christian saints, the Trojan heroes and even the Old Testament Jewish kings as their ancestors in efforts to include every possible 'European' lineage in their own.[63] Jews were acceptable, Habsburg official discrimination notwithstanding, but there is no mention of Attila or any of the Huns. When they are mentioned, it is only as a byword for all that is savage and alien to the idea of Europe and its civilisation.

Unlike other nomad nations – or indeed the Xiongnu of the eastern steppe – the Huns in Europe seem to have left practically nothing in the way of material remains: a few burials and little art apart from a few doubtful attributions – nothing comparable to the animal style of the Scythians and other groups. Odessa Museum contains the treasure from a rich fifth-century 'Hun' warrior grave, consisting of a sword and scabbard and gold horse and warrior trappings.[64] A distinctive polychrome style of ornamentation and semi-precious stone inlays on jewellery, belt buckles and other trappings from southern Ukraine are ascribed to the 'Hunnish period',[65] but these are presumably locally manufactured for the Huns, rather than actual Hun workmanship. There is nothing like the decorated belt buckles and other art that characterised the Xiongnu. The grave of a rich Hun prince has been found at Pannonhalma in Hungary, but overall efforts to pin material remains to the Huns are still elusive apart from occasional characteristic steppe-style bronze cauldrons found in some graves, recalling Xiongnu practice;[66] even the hundred or so other 'Hun' burials that are known remain largely inconclusive in their identity. And, in Europe at least, there are no later sedentary remains or linguistic survivals in place names or tribal names – they disappear into nowhere as thoroughly as they arrived from nowhere.* When we look back, the legacy of the Huns appears negligible, except perhaps as the last nail in the coffin of an already dying Western Roman Empire, truly the 'end of civilisation' as Bryan Ward-Perkins' subtitle implies. In Asia at least they left some architectural traces: Nogolka in Buryatia, some Buddhist monasteries in Afghanistan. But in Europe there is little else: a great Germanic epic perhaps – not to mention Wagner's formidable opera cycle – and their name in the English language as yet another pejorative term. The massive barriers against them erected by the great powers right across the ancient world stand as mute testimony that the passage of the Huns through history was marked above all by violence.

Europe had received a shock to be sure, but of the language, ethnicity, institutions, religion and culture of the Huns hardly a trace survived and their 'achievements . . . were not adequate to their power and prosperity', in the words of Gibbon. [67] Or 'The Empire of this predecessor of Jenghiz Khan crumbled as rapidly as that of his follower eight hundred years later, leaving nothing to mark its existence but ruins, and a lasting memory of terror in popular imagination', in the words of Henri Pirenne.[68]

---

* The name 'Hungary' does not incorporate 'Hun', as many believe, including many Hungarians themselves, among whom Attila is a popular boy's name. 'Hungary' derives from the Turk tribal name 'Onoghur'.

Indeed, to this day there is still doubt as to who exactly the Huns were: Indo-European, Turk, Scythian, Xiongnu, or a people unrelated to any? They are the ultimate ephemeral steppe nation, despite how large they loomed.

Negative though the Hun legacy may appear, Nicola Di Cosmo and Michael Maas nonetheless make the point that 'their appearance in Europe in the fifth century . . . [inaugurates] a millennium in which the steppes became a permanent element in western affairs'.[69] That millennium and beyond thus forms the remainder of this book.

CHAPTER 8

DESCENDANTS OF THE SHE-WOLF
The Emergence of Turkish-speaking Peoples

> The incursion from the Steppe of yet another pillaging mounted horde – the
> Ottoman Turks, quickly converted to Islam and engaged in holy war against
> Christendom.
> – J. H. Parry[1]

It has become conventional – or at least convenient – to think of the
Turkish capture of Constantinople as an Asiatic conquest: the last of the
barbarian invasions. The image of the Ottoman capture of Constantinople
in 1453 as simply a barbaric horde from the Central Asian steppe no longer
holds true, but is not quite dead: from Henri Pirenne's 1939 reference
to them in their capture as 'primitive uncivilized Barbarians',[2] through
Parry's 1963 reference quoted above, to Felipe Fernández-Armesto's reference in 2000 to the Turks as having 'arrived on horseback from the steppes
of Asia' before the walls of Constantinople.[3] The Ottomans did not arrive
from the steppe, they were no mere pillaging horde, they had been Muslim
for generations, and the idea of simple Muslim–Christian confrontation
was a myth before and would be again.

The original Turkish homeland was in Asia, of course, but Constantinople
was conquered by the Turks from the *west* not from the east: the Ottomans
became a European power before they became a Middle Eastern one
and remained a European power throughout, ruling up to 20 per cent of
mainland Europe from a European power base. Indeed, not only did the
Ottomans conquer Constantinople from Europe, but the Middle East and
even most of Anatolia itself was conquered from Europe. The Ottoman
Empire is often regarded as the last of the great empires of the Near and
Middle East, the successor of the Seljuk Empire, the Arab empires of the
Abbasids and Umayyads and ultimately of the Persian Empire of antiquity.
Again, this is only partially true. In a sense, the Ottoman conquest of the
Near East – even of the Muslim holy places of Mecca and Medina – and its
subsequent eastern empire was as much a *European* conquest as the Roman
empire in the east had been. True, the Ottomans at least practised a Near
Eastern religion. But so too, in the end, did the Romans.

And far from being uncivilised nomads who galloped up to the walls
of Constantinople fresh from the steppe, the Turks had nearly a thousand

years of some of the great sedentary civilisations of Asia behind them: the Seljuk, Ghaznavid and Karakhanid states and even before Islam the resurgence of the Sogdians and Buddhist cultures of Central Asia under the patronage of the Western Turk Empire. The Islamic Turkish Empires are not a part of this story. But their emergence on the steppe and the threshold of world history is.[4]

What is a 'Turk'?

At first, the term 'Turk' might appear straightforward: millions identify with the term, and it has conjured up definite images for many centuries. But Doğan Kuban captures the term's elusiveness:

> In the history of Eurasia, a Turk can be a Pecheneg, a Cuman, an Oghuz or Guz, a Yakut, a Turcoman, a Kalmuk (or Kalmyk), a Seljuk, a Karakhanid, a Ghaznevid, a Kazakh, a Karakoyunlu, an Akkoyunlu, an Özbek, a Kirghiz, a Uighur, an Ottoman, a Kashgai, a Mamluk – or even something else in the vast nomenclature of tribal or dynastic appellations. He can also be Baburshah, the founder of the so-called Mughal Dynasty, with his autobiography written in Turkic, or, more distantly a Wei emperor, or a Hsiung-nu chieftain within the confines of the Great Wall, a Hunnic warrior (perhaps with the name Attila), a pagan Bulgarian king besieging Constantinople . . . even a member of the first royal family of Arpads of Hungary.[5]

'Turks' are more elusive than many other peoples discussed here. For the early Islamic historians it had as little ethnic meaning as the earlier 'Scythian' or 'Hun' did for the western historians: a generic term for steppe peoples.[6] To some extent the term 'Turk' can be compared to 'Roman', which came to mean far more than a citizen of that city and ended up being applied to many different peoples (even to Turks).[*] Or 'German', which encompassed Goths, Franks, Burgundians, Saxons, Austrians as well as other peoples, past and present. 'Turks' are even more complex. Kuban further expresses this elusiveness when introducing a book entitled *The Turkic Speaking Peoples*: 'This is not a history of a nation or a race. It is a supranational history developed as a symbiotic process of great complexity.'[7]

Although the Turks are mainly associated nowadays with the country that bears their name – modern Turkey – it is important to remember that the Turkish conquest of Constantinople in 1453 marked the culmination of a long march westwards by the Turks that had already been in

---

[*] During the Ottoman–Portuguese wars in the Indian Ocean in the sixteenth century, both the Indians and the Portuguese referred to the Turks as 'Romans': *Rumi* or *Rumes*.

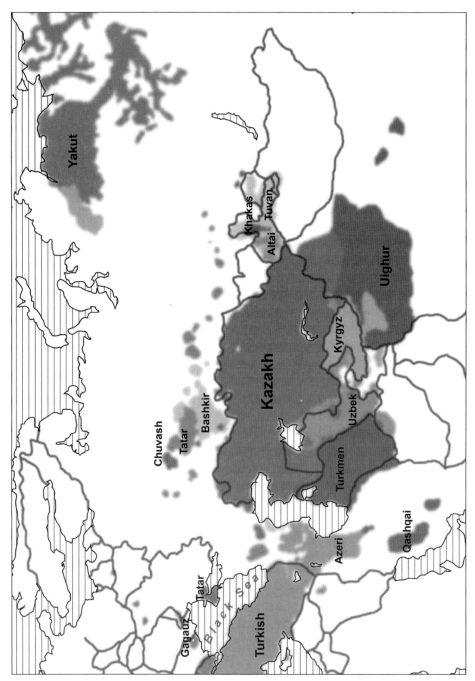

Map 8.1 Turk-related languages

progress a thousand years or more by then. In origin a Far Eastern people whose original homeland was the borderlands of Mongolia and southern Siberia, their language bears no relation (apart from loan words) to the Indo-European and Semitic languages that currently surround Turkey, but belongs to the Altaic group.

Before the twentieth century the term 'Turk' could be a pejorative term, even among Turks themselves, a term of contempt for an Anatolian peasant: citizens of the Ottoman Empire referred to themselves as 'Osmanlis', and it was only Ataturk's revolution that made the term respectable. In the eighteenth century, Edward Gibbon could define the Turks as 'the mass of voluntary and vanquished subjects who, under the name of Turks, are united by the common ties of religion, language, and manners'.[8] Gibbon – and his contemporaries – often used 'Turk' interchangeably with 'Muslim', but as his definition implies, it also encompassed Greeks, Armenians, Arabs, Bulgarians and many others. This was still at a time when the Ottoman Empire was near its peak, but with its collapse 'Turk' came to mean little more than a citizen of the Republic of Turkey.

Another collapse changed its meaning again, when the Soviet Union collapsed in 1990 revealing what had hitherto been largely subsumed: the existence of a swathe of Turkish* speaking peoples stretching from the Balkans to China. From one country before that date whose official language was Turkish,[9] there are now six whose languages are closely related: Kyrgyzstan, Kazakhstan, Uzbekistan, Turkmenistan, Azerbaijan and Turkey itself.[†] In addition, there are some seven or more countries where speakers of Turkish-related languages form significant minorities: China, Russia, Afghanistan, Iran, Cyprus, Moldova, Bulgaria and Ukraine (one might now almost include Germany): Uighur in China, Tatar in Russia and Ukraine, Gagauz in Moldova, Turkmen and Uzbek in Afghanistan, and Azeri, Turkmen and Qashqai in Iran. Some estimates are as high as one third of the population of Iran being native Turk speakers. In Russia, Tatar, Chuvash, Bashkir, Nogay, Yakut, Tuvan and other minority languages are described as 'Turkic'. Other countries with 'indigenous' (as opposed to recent immigrant) Turkish speaking minorities include Tajikistan, Georgia, Iraq, Greece, Serbia, Kosovo and Albania. In addition, most countries in western Europe as well as North America

---

* 'Turkish' strictly speaking only applies to language spoken today in the Republic of Turkey; the Turkish spoken outside Turkey is conventionally called 'Turkic' or (more correctly) *Türk*. The term 'Turk' used adjectivally is preferred here.
† A fact quick to be used to advantage by Turkish businessmen, who were among the first following the collapse of the Soviet Union to beat a path to the former republics and bring Western technology and business enterprise to form economic ties based upon mutual language. Today Turkish business remains dominant in those countries.

Figure 8.1 *A modern mosque built entirely in the Ottoman imperial style at Verkhnyaya Pishma, a Tatar area outside Ekaterinburg in the Urals. This is closely modelled on the vizirial mosques of the sixteenth century built by the great Ottoman architect Sinan, such as the Hadım Ibrahim Paşa Mosque in Istanbul, of which this is a virtually exact copy. Even the marble is imported from Turkey*

and Australia have significant immigrant Turkish communities. This huge spread was brought together in 2005 by a major exhibition at the Royal Academy in London entitled *Turks. A Journey of a Thousand Years*. The exhibition and the accompanying catalogue highlighted for the first time to a general British audience the diversity of a people and culture that many had associated solely with Turkey. A similarly lavish publication brought out soon after, *The Turkic Speaking Peoples. 2,000 Years of Art and Culture from Inner Asia to the Balkans*, broadened the sweep even further and doubled the time span encompassed by the Royal Academy exhibition (Map 8.1; Figures 8.1 and 8.2).[10]

Probably the nearest one can arrive at defining 'Turk' is simply one of self-identity. Throughout Turk history there has been an awareness of being a 'Turk', a common feeling of 'Turkishness' and defining oneself and one's community as 'Turk'. This is true, of course, of many peoples, but with Turks it was perhaps stronger than others. As far back as AD 443, the Northern Wei Emperor Tuoba Dao of China sent an expedition to discover the ancestral cave of the Turk peoples: despite increasing Sinicisation, Tuoba Dao still felt sufficiently aware of his Turk roots (discussed below).[11] The first time that the Turkish language was written was in the eighth century in a series of inscriptions along the Orkhon River

Figure 8.2 *Uighur Turks in a street scene in Kashgar. Note the bilingual sign in Chinese and Uighur Turkish, the only country in the world where Turkish is still written in the Arabic script*

in Mongolia, and these texts convey a sense of 'Turkishness' with such phrases as 'the Turks and all the common people' and repeated appeals to 'O Turkish people'.[12] Nizam al-Mulk, the eleventh-century Persian Prime Minister to two Seljuk sultans, describes Alptegin, founder of the first major Turkish Islamic dynasty, the Ghaznavid, as 'a Turk, prudent, skilful, popular', and Alp Arslan, the founder of the Seljuk Empire, is quoted as saying 'Today God has favoured the Turks'. In writing of these dynasties Nizam al-Mulk's text is littered with the Seljuk rulers' strong sense of Turkishness, referring to the *ummat al-turk* or 'Turkish nation', the political expediency of an Iranian prime minister pandering to a Turkish dynasty notwithstanding.[13] The early Seljuk rulers in Central Asia would often be described as 'leader of all the Turks' in strong contrast to traditional Islamic titulature, where a ruler would usually be 'leader of the faithful' or 'lord of the four quarters' or 'sultan of east and west' and not ethnically defined (unlike Christian European rulers: 'King of the Franks', 'Tsar of all the Russias' and so forth). The seventeenth-century Ottoman traveller, Evliya Çelebi, describes his 'saintly' ancestor, the twelfth-century Central Asian mystic Ahmad Yassavi, as a 'Turk of the Turks'.[14]

Perhaps the best definition of what it is to be a Turk was given by Gurbugha, a Turkish commander in Anatolia addressing Frankish envoys from the First Crusade when he asked: 'Are your lords ready to become Turks? . . . If so, they may stay here. We will give you cities and horses, you will become horsemen like us, and we will extend our friendship to you.'[15] In other words, merely a self definition: anybody could 'become Turk'.

So, a term to proud of, a term of contempt; a speaker of a language irrelevant of political boundaries, a member of an empire regardless of language; an ethnicity, an identity, an idea. The term 'Turk' has many meanings or none, and has changed as perceptions of changed: transitory, as so many definitions are.

Huns, wolves, caves and princesses

Early Turk history has been reconstructed from a combination of literary, linguistic and archaeological sources.[16] Some Classical sources of the first century AD refer to a group of people known as the *Turcae* dwelling on the southern Russian steppe north of the Sea of Azov. These have been viewed by some as the first references to Turks. However, there has been no consensus on this, with no firm evidence of Turks appearing in the region until the sixth century.[17] The earliest mentions of a people definitely identified as Turks are in Chinese sources at the end of the third century BC, where they are referred to as the *Tujue*, Chinese for 'Turk', in relation to the Xiongnu, although equating these with the people we now know as Turks might be too glib.[18] The Tujue were a tribe located somewhere to the north of the Xiongnu, beyond Mongolia.

Many in both Turkey and Hungary believe they are descended from the Huns, fallaciously for both peoples: hence 'Attila' is a not uncommon boys' name in both countries. Turks in modern times have also claimed descent – again fallaciously – from Scythians, Hittites and Sumerians, the latter from an early twentieth-century misunderstanding of the nature of the Sumerian language. Hence, when Ataturk made the adoption of surnames compulsory, many Turks adopted Sumerian surnames such as 'Akurgal' and 'Sümer'.

When attempting to analyse the complex Xiongnu–Turk connections from the Chinese sources, it is important to remember above all that the Chinese probably lumped all 'barbarians' under the one label anyway, regardless of ethnic origin, much all non-Europeans used to be lumped together as 'Indians'. It must also be remembered that the tendency to group different peoples together almost solely on linguistic grounds is a very recent one, and such criteria may not have even occurred to the Chinese, nor seemed very relevant (and may still be largely irrelevant, as the term 'Anglo-Saxon' applying to peoples as diverse as British, Australians and Americans indicate, or the even more fallacious misappropriation of the term 'Caucasian'). Most of all, our very tendency to look for ethnic inter-connections and origins might in itself be fallacious, as not only are there many entirely unrelated groups in the Mongol/North Chinese/ Siberian region, there would have been more in antiquity.

The sources preserve several traditions relating to Turk origins. According to these, the original homeland of the Turks was the sacred Ötükän Forest (or in some versions the Ötükän was a sacred mountain, usually, but not always, associated with a forest) where there were several related Turk tribes, such as the 'White-clothed Turks', the 'Yellow-head Turks', the 'Skiing Turks' and the 'Ox-hoofed Turks'. The latter are further described as a northern people in a land of extreme cold, all indications suggesting an origin in the forest belt (a location also corroborated by an independent Tibetan source). Chinese sources also refer to 'black' and 'yellow' Turk tribes, and early Turk inscriptions refer further to 'Blue Turks'.

Traditions related in the Chinese sources also preserve several legendary versions of Turk origins. According to one, the Turks were originally a separate clan of the Xiongnu confederation who fought and fell out with the Xiongnu king. The Tujue were defeated, their chief killed and the young prince captured, mutilated and abandoned to die. The prince was adopted by a blue-grey she-wolf and raised in a cavern. Out of the resulting union were ten boys who became ancestors of the Turk race. The Turks eventually emerged from the cavern to become blacksmiths for the *Rouran*, a later steppe confederacy (probably related to the Avars, discussed in the next chapter) who succeeded the Xiongnu. Another version also has reference to a cavern as the original home, but the liaison was with the daughter of a lake spirit, with the resultant offspring the ancestors. A different tradition relates how a Xiongnu king had two daughters too beautiful to be married to mere mortals. He accordingly built a tower for them in an uninhabited forest far to the north and asked heaven to provide husbands. One day a wolf came and howled at the foot of the tower day and night, excavating a cave as a dwelling. The younger (and more beautiful) princess realised that this was her intended, so climbed down and lived in the cave with the wolf. The offspring became the ancestors of the Turks.

A number of suggestive factors emerge from these legends. The ancestral cavern occurs in several versions and seems to be peculiar to the Turks – the traditional story surrounding the founder of the Turki Shahi dynasty of the eastern Hindu Kush in the ninth century, for example, relates how he hid in a cavern and then appeared as a miraculous being. The ancestral caverns are presumed to be indirect references to iron-ore mines – and one recalls the tradition where the Turks were originally iron-workers for the Rouran. In later history the Turks were certainly proficient in weaponry – one of the reasons for their success in warfare – and references to 'iron' (Turkish *demir*) are common in Turkish names, such as Demirji and Demirel; more distantly Teimur (Tamerlane) and Mongol Temujin (the name of Genghis Khan) are cognate.

The supposed ancestral cave was discovered in antiquity by an expedition sent by Tuoba Dao of the Northern Wei Dynasty. This was the cave of Gaxian, in a forest in a ravine in the remote Xingangling Mountains in the far north-east of present-day Inner Mongolia. It is a large natural cave with a Chinese inscription which records how reports of the ancestral cavern had reached the Emperor Tuoba Dao in 443, so he sent an expedition to investigate. The inscription describes the cave, the ancestral origins of the Northern Wei kings in a sacred cave, and their migration southwards to become the Tuoba tribe of Turks and thence into China. It further records how local people at the cave were still worshipping the Tuoba ancestors and their mythic descent from an ancestral bear within the cave at the time of the expedition. It was investigated by Chinese archaeologists in modern times.[19]

The ancestral totemic wolf occurs in many ancient origin stories, often among people unrelated, although most can be traced back to steppe traditions (and werewolf myths are probably also related to the same totemic wolf traditions). That relating to the Romans is well known, as is the Indian version famously related by Rudyard Kipling (from which the wolf totem was adopted by the Boy Scout movement). It also occurs widely among Eurasian steppe peoples, such as the Xiongnu and the Wusun on the western borderlands of China – even Ghenghis Khan, according to the Mongol *Secret History*, was descended from a blue-grey wolf, and an alternative derivation of his name *Temuchin* means 'wolf'.[20] The Luwians, a Bronze Age pre-Hittite Indo-European people of Anatolia, have similar wolfish origins, and wolfish myths were also associated with Hun origins according to some ancient authorities. The flags of the armies of the Western Turk Empire were adorned with a golden wolf's head.[21] Modern Turkish far-right political movements use the wolf as a symbol – the Turkish right-wing movement of the seventies, for example, called themselves the 'Grey Wolves'. None of these different people sharing wolfish origins is necessarily connected: the fact the Luwians, the Romans and the Turks all in the end were associated with Anatolia is coincidence.*

The apparent 'colour-coding' of Turk tribes ('White', 'yellow', 'blue', 'black' Turks, etc.) is a long and venerable tradition, and recurs in later

---

* The Luwian is from the Indo-European root word *lupu* = 'wolf' – cf. 'lupus', 'lupine', etc. – and Lycia/Lukoi in western Anatolia is from the same root, as are such 'wolf places' as Lycopolis in Egypt and the Lyceum in Athens. Drompp (2018) also discusses the wolfish origins of such people, suspecting a common origin (for the myth, not the people). Ustinova (2002) has a very thorough summary of Indo-European wolfish and werewolf associations and foundation myths from Hittite references and Scythian burial customs right across to ancient Rome and ancient Irish and Icelandic mythologies, all of which are traced back to Zoroastrian Avestan sources. She makes no mention, however, of the Turks. See also Baldick 2000: 23–4.

historical Turkish tribes such as the *Karakhanids* ('Black Khans'), the *Ak Koyonlu* and *Kara Koyonlu* ('White-sheep' and 'Black-sheep' Turkmen), the *Kizil Bash* ('Red Head'), and so forth. Historical sources also refer to many other tribal groupings and confederations such as the Türgesh, Qarluks, Kirghiz, Uighurs and many more, which are all 'Turk' broadly, much as Goths, Prussians, Bavarians, Saxons, for example, are all loosely 'German'.

The references to forest homelands, as well as to 'White-clothed', 'Skiing' and 'Ox-hoofed' Turks, suggest a northern, sub-arctic origin of forest dwellers, presumably in the Siberian forest belt (Figure 1.11). An analysis of modern Turkish vocabulary too reveals words relating to the fauna, flora and other features relating to a northern forest zone, confirming this hypothesis. 'In short, Türk origins are complex, multiple and in all likelihood involved significant groupings of non-Turks as well.'[22]

In the first millennium BC, therefore, the Turks were probably a nomadic group in the area to the north of the Great Wall who, along with other loosely related tribes, would occasionally raid into the more settled areas of China. Then, from about the second century BC, we see various movements of people from this area as a result of the Han Chinese efforts at pacifying the region and evicting the nomadic tribes from their borders. The construction of the Great Wall – together with related Chinese military campaigns – resulted in a massive disruption of steppe peoples whose ramifications were felt ultimately right across Eurasia (Chapter 7). The Turks were one of the groups that were displaced by these activities, and many Turk tribes moved away from their original homelands in the wake of the Xiongnu migrations, with some groups moving into China.

Turks and Buddhism; the Northern Wei of China

Before the emergence of the Turks as a major steppe power, an eastern Turk tribe, the Tabgach (or Tabgaj; Chinese Tuoba), had entered northern China. This occurred in the fourth century AD after their diaspora from the mythical cavern as a part of the Xianbei confederation, a loose alliance of steppe tribes who emerged after the collapse of the Xiongnu (and probably incorporated some Xiongnu). The Tuoba Turks emerged as the leaders of the confederation and founded the Northern Wei Dynasty in 386 centred on Pingcheng, modern Datong, which they made their capital in 398. Approximately 20 per cent of the Northern Wei elite were Turks.[23]

The Northern Wei rulers were enthusiastic supporters of Buddhism – the first Chinese dynasty to be so – and Emperor Tuoba Dao was the first to elevate Buddhism to an official state level since the time of the Kushans of Afghanistan in the second century AD. In particular, the Tuoba kings

Figure 8.3 *The Yungang caves outside Datong, the Northern Wei capital, where the Tuoba emperors of the Dynasty first introduced giganticism into Buddhist art*

embraced the peculiarly Mahayana element in Buddhism where the secular ruler is invested with the authority of the Buddha. This element took spectacular form in the Buddhist caves constructed throughout the fifth century by the Northern Wei at Yungang outside Datong (Figure 8.3), as well as at the Longmen caves near their later capital of Loyang, where each Tuoba king erected a giant statue of Buddha representing the Buddhist authority invested in himself: each giant Buddha statue, in effect, represented both Buddha and the emperor. This was the first time that giganticism – colossal Buddha statues – had been introduced into Buddhist art.[24]

Pingcheng remained the Northern Wei capital throughout the fifth century, but the court became progressively more Sinicised as they distanced themselves from their tribal origins. As part of this process the Emperor Xiaowen moved the capital in 494 to the old Chinese capital of Luoyang; the Xianbei and Tuoba languages and dress were outlawed and the Tuoba adopted Chinese names. The Xianbei military revolted in 524 and the Northern Wei Dynasty collapsed in 534. There was some revival with the East and West Wei Dynasties later on, but without a Turk element.

René Grousset compares the various steppe invasions of China after the 'Classical' period of the Han Dynasty (206 BC–AD 220) to the 'barbarian' invasions of the Roman Empire at the end of antiquity. These invasions, the Xiongnu, Xianbei, Tuoba, were steppe tribes who eventually established states within the boundaries of the former Chinese Han Empire, just as the Germanic tribes did in the former Roman Empire. A rump China was left in Loyang as the ancient capital of Changan was occupied by the tribes, just as a rump 'Rome' remained in Constantinople after Rome fell to the Goths. The Tuoba Turks brought about a revival of Chinese civilisation under the Northern Wei, and Grousset compares this to the European revival under the Franks and the eventual 'Carolingian renaissance', with the adoption of Buddhism by Emperor Tuoba Dao compared to the adoption of Christianity by Clovis.[25]

The comparison, while appropriate, is an uneasy one: like all historical parallels, there are no neat fits and it breaks down upon analysis. Nonetheless, we can draw important lessons from the history of the Northern Wei. Already we have seen the transformation of a Turk group from steppe nomad to sedentary power, from the conqueror of an empire to its reviver. The decision by Tuoba Dao to combine secular and religious authority in the person of the ruler and translate this into massive, visible architectural statements was to have its counterpart later when Western Turk emperors endowed giant Buddha statues at Bamiyan – or later still when each Ottoman sultan would endow a royal mosque to express their own secular and religious authority. Never mind the comparison between the Northern Wei and the Merovingians, it is their comparison with the Seljuk conquest of Iran and the Ottoman of Constantinople that form the more relevant analogy here: the Tuoba/Northern Wei symbiosis was a 'dress rehearsal' for much that was to characterise later Turk history. We thus leave the earliest history of the Turks as a Far Eastern people on the threshold of world history.

The first Eurasian Empire (Map 8.2)

The history of the Northern Wei reveals how the Turks, barely removed from their forest origins, had already impacted upon one of history's major ancient civilisations. Their subsequent spread westwards affected the history of the remainder of the Eurasian land mass. The Turk migrations from their homelands were never any conscious tribal decision to 'go west' but were just one – albeit one of the more important – of the many groups of people swept up in this perpetual *Volkswänderung*. Subsequent Turkish polities such as the Ottoman or the Timurid states are therefore frequently characterised as somehow 'nomadic'.[26] But it is a cardinal mistake to overstate the nomadic nature of Turkish dynasties and states, just as it would be a mistake to characterise the Arab caliphate as nomadic because of its Bedouin background, or the early English and Russian states as nomadic because of their Viking background. Turkish movements throughout were as much symbiosis and assimilation as conquests, so were equally characterised by sedentary

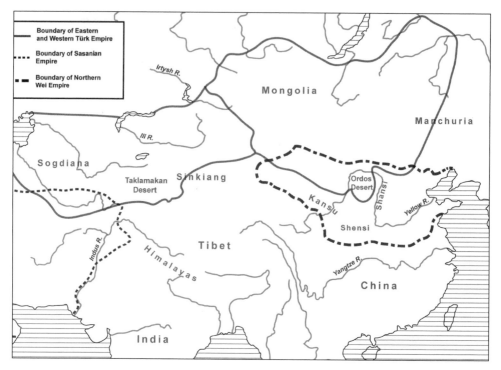

Map 8.2 *The Northern Wei and the First Turk Empire*

civilisations. This symbiosis was to continue as they moved westwards.

Early Turk history has been reconstructed mainly from Chinese sources, supplemented by the Turk runic inscriptions on the Orkhon River in Mongolia and the occasional Byzantine source. These are often contradictory and their interpretation – particularly of the Chinese sources – is frequently disputed, so the modern accounts vary in detail and dates. But the following represents a broad consensus.[27]

The collapse of the Xiongnu at the end of the first century AD resulted in various tribal movements and dissolving and re-forming alliances, with no particular group filling the vacuum. Eventually a new confederation emerged in the fourth century dominated by the Rouran tribes. The Turks were described in Chinese accounts of the Rouran as a group of iron-workers in the Altai Mountains subject to the Rouran. The confederation was seriously weakened first of all by a major defeat inflicted upon them by the Northern Wei in the mid-fifth century, with a final defeat by a Turk revolt in 552 led by Bumin, who destroyed their power and inherited their title of *Khagan*,* first used as the title of the Rouran ruler, who

---

* I have counted at least six different spellings of this title; I have opted for the commonest. The people who originally coined the title were presumably illiterate and spoke in different dialects, so all spellings would be correct.

Figure 8.4 *The early Turk grave of Uibatsky Chaatas in Khakasia*

belonged to a Turk ruling clan known as the Ashina who dominated much of subsequent Turk pre-Islamic history. By 555 the remaining Rouran were forced to flee westwards eventually entering Europe, where they are known as the Avars (Chapter 8). As a consequence, the Turks filled the vacuum in the steppes, emerging as the First Turk Empire (or Khaganate) covering a vast area stretching from the borders of Manchuria to the Amu Darya (the exact extent is uncertain). One of the reasons for their success was the metal armour worn by their elite cavalry known as 'wolves', thus recalling both their traditional skills and their mythic origins. The Turks had arrived on the threshold of world history – and had created the very first Eurasian empire.[28]

Bumin (or T'u-men, a non-Turk name),[29] was the only khagan to rule over a united empire, for on his death he was succeeded by his two sons Muhan (553–72),* who ruled the eastern half of the empire and Ishtemi (553–?) who ruled the western half. The eastern empire comprised mainly Mongolia, but Muhan soon incorporated most of Manchuria. Ishtemi, the khagan of the Western Turks, is known from Byzantine sources and was one of the rulers who overthrew the Hephthalites of Central Asia, in alliance with Khusrau I Anurshirvan of Iran. By about 555 his empire probably extended as far as the Aral Sea and possibly even as far as the Don.[30]

Ishtemi also sent several diplomatic missions to Constantinople, the first contact of the Turks with the city with which they were eventually to be identified above all others. The very first Turk we know about to enter Constantinople was the envoy Aksel in 563, but the main mission was led

---

* Or Muqan or Mughan, who might have been Bumin's brother, not son.

in about 568 by a Sogdian, Maniakh, to the Emperor Justin II. Maniakh was to propose an alliance between the Byzantine and Turk Empires to outflank Sasanian Iran, their previous alliance having lapsed, as well as to pursue the Avars (descendants of the Rouran), at that time raiding Byzantine territory in the Balkans. Justin responded with a diplomatic mission led by Zemarkhos to the Turks in 569 and several more exchanges were made until 576 when the good relations collapsed with a Turk raid on Byzantine possessions in the Crimea.

In the Byzantine accounts of these momentous first contacts between Turk and Roman, the Turk ruler is called 'Silziboulos', which is otherwise unknown in Turk and Chinese sources. He may be a relatively minor Turk provincial ruler, which seems unlikely, or it may be just another name for Ishtemi. Be that as it may, Ishtemi was succeeded as Emperor of the Western Turks by his son Tardu, who ruled until 603.

Meanwhile the khagan of the Eastern Turks, Muhan's successor Taspar (572–81), was converted to Buddhism by a Chinese monk. Buddhism then spread among the Turks in both eastern and western branches, although it faced some resistance from native cults. There was also increasing Chinese cultural influence in the eastern half, to some extent similar to the Sinicisation of the Turks under the Northern Wei. On the whole, however, both Khaganates were marked by religious tolerance, and Zoroastrianism, Christianity and Manichaeism also flourished under the Turk rulers, as well as the indigenous heaven worship of the steppe. The khagans were regarded as semi-divine whose blood must not be shed, even if they were to be executed, a practice that the Ottoman continued centuries later (strangulation by silk cord being the convenient way of sidestepping this inconvenient rule).

The Eastern Turks were instrumental in bringing about the end of the Sui Dynasty of China and establishing the Tang in the early seventh century. Indeed, the Tang themselves were of mixed Chinese and Xiongnu descent and included Turks in their administration (and it is notable that the Tang were almost unique in Chinese dynasties in not building any part of the Great Wall system). However, there was increasing conflict between the Western and Eastern arms of the Turk Empire in the early seventh century, and the eastern branch collapsed with the death of its Khagan Illig (619–30). Much of it was absorbed into the Tang Empire and many Turks settled in the Chinese borderlands after this collapse. The Western Turk Empire absorbed much of the Central Asian territories and increased at the Eastern expense.

Indeed, the Western Turk Empire was expanding rapidly, particularly with the defeat of the Hephthalites. Despite this defeat enabled by an alliance with Sasanian Persia, by 616/7 a Turk army penetrated deep into Iran as far as Rayy, just south of Tehran. In 619 the most powerful of the Western Turk khagans succeeded to the throne, Tong Yabgu Khagan. Under Tong Yabgu the empire reached its greatest extent, incorporating the Tarim Basin, Ferghana, Bactria, and parts of Afghanistan and northern Pakistan, with Tong Yabgu himself advancing as far as the Indus in 625. This resulted in a shift of gravity for the empire, with large numbers of Turk tribes migrating west and increasingly dominating Central Asia. A new alliance was entered between the Turks and the Byzantine Empire under Emperor Heraclius against the Sasanian Emperor Khusrau II Parviz, but Tong Yabgu was killed in a revolt of the Qarluks (another Turk tribe) in 630. He was succeeded briefly by Yipi Duolu Khagan but the empire slowly disintegrated, and the last Khagan of the Western Turks was killed in battle against the Chinese in 659.

With the collapse of both arms of the First Turk Khaganate there followed a period of fragmentation. The Turk tribes were re-united by Elterish Kutlugh (682–92), an adventurer who set out initially with just seventeen men, and established the Second Turk Khaganate. Between 697 and 691 it expanded into Mongolia and the empire soon came to be centred on the Orkhon River. For the first time contemporary Turk sources survive recording these events in the form of rock inscriptions in Turk runes on the Orkhon River (Figure 8.5). Elterish was succeeded by his brother, Kapghan Khagan (691–716), who consolidated the Second Khaganate and entered into a rapprochement with China. His rule is regarded as the height of the Second Turk Empire. Two more brothers succeeded Kapghan: Költegin and Bilgä Khagan (716–34), who ruled together. Under them the Second Khaganate reached its greatest extent, but it collapsed quickly on the death of Bilgä, with the last khagan killed in 745. The Second Turk Empire had lasted barely sixty years.

The period of the collapse corresponds to the expansion of the first Arab caliphate under the Umayyads into Central Asia, and this doubtless was a contributory cause. But it would be a mistake to overemphasise this. Nomadic empires were rarely more than loose tribal confederations on a large scale, which by their nature are always subject to fragmentation: there was rarely the highly centralised rule that characterise the great sedentary empires of antiquity. Hence, it is likely that the Turk Empire would have collapsed even without the Umayyad Caliphate. It would also be a mistake to overemphasise the 'Turk' nature of the empire (although this was without doubt its predominant characteristic). Nomadic states and confederations usually took the name of the dominant tribe or ethnicity – in this case the Turks – but this does not mean that the confederation comprised solely those people: it would comprise many often very disparate tribes and peoples, both nomadic and sedentary, Huns and Mongols as well as Sogdians and Chinese.

At first sight the Turk Empire – in its various manifestations, First and Second, East and West – might appear yet another ephemeral steppe 'empire' like the Huns in the west, leaving little in the way of material remains. This is not to say that it was merely a barbaric horde.

There are the Orkhon inscriptions (Figure 8.5), the earliest indigenous documents from the steppe, and many graves probably marking the burial of nomads much as the kurgans of an earlier era (Figure 8.4). More important, many of the Turk princes were cultured patrons of the arts and many subject peoples, such as the Sogdians in Central Asia, flourished under the Turk rulers. The Sogdians – an indigenous Central Asia people speaking an Iranian-related language, ancestors of the Tajiks – dominated much of the trade and commerce of the Turk Empire, their influence extending deep into China and west as far as the Black Sea.* Their main centres were Varkhsha near Bukhara, Afrasiab at Samarkand and Panjikent in Tajikistan, all of which

Figure 8.5 *Early Turk inscription at Toyukuk on the Orkhon River in Mongolia (photo courtesy Christoph Baumer)*

* The name of the port of Sudak in eastern Crimea is believed to have derived from 'Sugda': Baumer 2014: 178.

Figure 8.6 *A Sogdian feasting scene from Panjikent, Tajikistan, now in the Hermitage*

Figure 8.7 *A continuous frieze of Sogdian combat scenes (in three parts, top to bottom) from Varakhsha, now in the Hermitage*

had palaces and elite residences richly decorated in paintings (Figures 8.6 and 8.7).

But it was further south in the Hindu Kush of Afghanistan that the Turk Empire had the greatest effect. Deborah Klimburg-Salter has drawn attention to the fact that the first three centuries of Islam saw a sudden and massive increase in Buddhist art and architecture in eastern Afghanistan and that the Buddhist centres of Bamiyan, Kabul and Ghazni were part of a complex Buddhist communications network between the seventh and

Figure 8.8 *The Turk dynastic centre of Bamiyan*

tenth centuries, which she attributes to the power of the Turk Kaganate.[31] This has been confirmed by excavations of extensive Buddhist religious complexes in Kabul, which remained active probably as one of the main centres of Buddhism in Afghanistan at least until the ninth century. The most famous Buddhist monuments in Afghanistan, however, are the colossal Buddhas of Bamiyan and their associated cave and monastery complexes (Figure 8.8), dating from the period of the First Turk Empire. During this time the entire Bamiyan region was a part of a vast 'sacred landscape' comprising Buddhist complexes and an extensive fortification system. It is suggested that the reason behind such scale was that Bamiyan was a dynastic centre for the Turk kaghans, a tradition of Turk dynasticism and giganticism that began with the Tuoba of the Northern Wei at Yungang.[32]

After the collapse of the Kaghanate the western parts of Inner Eurasia were increasingly dominated by disparate Turk tribal groups, with new minor confederations emerging such as the Qarluks. There was a general dispersion of Turk tribes westwards, such as the Pechenegs to the Black Sea steppe and the Oghuz Turks (or Ghuzz in the Arab sources) to the Aral Sea region. The Oghuz, originally from Mongolia, were probably a confederation rather than a single tribe, and were to figure largely in the rise of the Seljuks. Many of the cities such as Panjikent were probably still ruled by Turk elites over indigenous Sogdian populations, although there is no evidence of tensions, and further south in the remoter valleys of the Hindu Kush petty Turk princes continued to rule their small fiefdoms. But on the broader steppes outside such enclaves, Turk tribes increasingly formed the majority, albeit nomadic, population. The period of the Turk Empires was thus one of ethnic change marking the disappearance of Scythians and other related Indo-European speakers as the dominant groups on the steppe and the advent of the Turkish groups which still characterises most of Central Asia to this day.

Revival under the Uighurs

At about the time of the second Turk collapse a new state emerged on the eastern steppe under the Uighur Turks and rapidly expanded to much of Mongolia. The Uighur Empire lasted from 744 to 840, ruled from their capital at Karabalghasun on the Orkhon River. The Uighurs regarded themselves as continuing the Turk Khaganate rather than replacing it, and its founder Khagan Kutlugh Bilgä Köl belonged to the same Ashina clan as the earlier Turk Khagans: effectively it was a Third Turk Empire. Kutlugh died in 747 and was succeeded by his son Bilgä Khagan (747–59). Under him the Khaganate underwent considerable expansion and consolidation. It reached its height under Bilgä's son Tängri Khagan (659–79), although the power behind the throne was Tängri's brother Bögü Khan, son of Bilgä and a Chinese princess. Tängri and Bögü also converted to Manichaeism, and Bögü was accordingly awarded the title *Zahan-i Mani* ('Emanation of Mani').

The Uighur state declined in the ninth century, leading to the eventual Uighur defeat by the Kirghiz in 840 and subsequent dispersion. This dispersion resulted in Uighur tribes migrating westwards to Xinjiang, establishing a second Uighur kingdom in about 860 with its capital at Khocho, modern Karakhoja in the Turfan oasis. Manichaeism continued to flourish under the Uighurs, becoming the main religion of Xinjiang after the ninth century, surviving down to the thirteenth. In addition to Manichaeism, Nestorianism and Buddhism flourished. As well as its vibrant and varied religious life, the arts were extensively patronised; painting and music especially featured highly, with the paintings leaving their mark in the rich cave and temple paintings which are a feature of Xinjiang's heritage today. The Uighurs also adopted the Sogdian form of the Aramaic script and passed it onto the Mongols, who still use it.* In 1209 the last ruler voluntarily submitted to Genghis Khan.

---

* Within China only: in Mongolia and the Mongol regions of Russia the Cyrillic script has replaced it.

From slaves to conquerors

The establishment of the Abbasid Caliphate in 750, with the consequent move of the capital from Damascus to the new city of Baghdad, turned Islam's back on the West. This move also internationalised Islam. Hitherto, Islam was associated almost entirely with – or at least dominated by – Arabs. But the Abbasid 'Revolution' originated in the eastern Iranian world and incorporated many non-Arab elements. More importantly, Islam was increasingly adopted by native non-Arab populations. This would have immense ramifications for the Middle East and for Islam generally. It was to be a reinvigorated Islam in the hands of a people from Inner Asia who had no common cultural experience with the Arabs who were to transform the Arabs, the Middle East, Islam and eventually much of Europe and the Mediterranean, when the Turks emerged from Inner Asia.

The first Turks to enter the Middle East were slaves, mainly those captured in slave raids on the steppe by the Samanid dynasty who ruled Bukhara (a native Central Asian Iranian dynasty who had converted to Islam). The Turkish slave trade rapidly became a major commercial enterprise between the Central Asian Muslim kingdoms and the Arab Caliphate during the ninth and tenth centuries. Turkish slaves then began entering the Middle East in greater numbers. In this context it is essential to understand that under Islam, slaves enjoyed considerable legal rights and privileges, and were rarely 'slaves' as the term was later understood in European contexts, such as those transported to the Americas. The fighting quality of these Turkish slaves soon became apparent and more and more of these Turkish slaves were – upon conversion to Islam – incorporated into Muslim armies as mercenary slave units. But their fighting skills were too good and soon the inevitable was to happen: the Turks became the masters, eventually to dominate the Middle East until the fall of the Ottoman Empire at the end of the First World War.

This first happened at the centre of the Caliphate in Baghdad. From the early ninth century the Caliphs, mistrustful of their mainly Arab army increasingly dominated by powerful family factions, began to surround themselves with private bodyguards of Turkish slaves (known as *ghulams* and later as *mamluks*). These Turkish slaves, by not belonging to any of the various families vying for influence at the court, could be relied upon to owe allegiance solely to the Caliph himself, and hence became a powerful praetorian guard. By the middle of the ninth century, clashes in Baghdad between the Arab population and the increasingly powerful Turkish soldiers prompted al-Muʿtasim to move the capital itself further upstream on the Tigris to the new city of Samarra. The power of the Turkish ghulams, however, continued to increase until they became the main power in the Caliphate: Caliph al-Muttawakil was assassinated by his Turkish guard in

861, and thereafter a rapid succession of Caliphs were made and unmade by the Turkish soldiers more or less at whim. The Caliphate effectively became a puppet of the Turkish slaves, one of the main contributory causes to the decline of the Abbasids. The Islamic world was beginning to become a Turkish one; the Turks, in becoming enslaved by the Arabs, had become their masters; in converting to Islam they had become its champions.

Prosperity, power and civilisation: the lure of Islam

The Arabs defeated a Chinese army on the Talas River west of the Tien Shan Mountains in 751. While Arab arms would never penetrate further east than this, despite the victory, it did mark the beginnings of the Islamisation of the Inner Asian steppe and the gradual retreat of the other religions. Zoroastrianism, Manichaeism and Nestorian Christianity were to eventually disappear altogether in Inner Asia. Buddhism remains only among the Mongols and related groups (albeit due to separate Buddhist proselytisation from Tibet after the fourteenth century: modern Mongolian Tantric Buddhism is substantially different from the Mahayana Buddhism of the early Turks). The indigenous steppe religions of heaven worship and various forms of shamanism retreated largely to the Siberian forest belt (although elements remain in some aspects of Central Asian Islam, particularly the Sufi movements, and there was a brief resurgence of paganism in the twelfth century with the Qara Khitai or Western Liao: Chapter 11).

It must be emphasised, first, that this process of Islamisation was spread over a long time,[33] with the ancient religions of Inner Asia still probably the majority religions until the tenth century or even later. And second, the nature of this conversion was largely peaceful and persuasive. Christian propaganda has for centuries misrepresented Islam as 'spread by the sword'. It is not in dispute that this occurred (and occurred in most religions, including Christianity), but by far the greatest extensions of Islam were peaceful. By the end of the ninth century large numbers of both Qarluk and Oghuz converted: conversions seem to have been mainly pacific through contact with Muslim merchants and settlers in the Turk lands. An important part was also played by the various Sufi brotherhoods in Central Asia (from Arabic *suf*, 'wool', referring to the garment they wore) which represented a more mystic side of Islam. The Turks were probably more attracted to the Sufis because of the resemblance to their own native shamans – indeed, many of the Central Asian Sufi movements probably incorporated elements of shamanism. The more mystical nature of Sufism was also closer to Buddhism, previously the main established religion in the Turkish lands of Central Asia – again, many of the early Sufi movements incorporated elements of Buddhism. The situation was probably similar

Figure 8.9 *A Qarluk gravestone at their capital of Balasaghun in Kyrgyzstan*

to that of the Germanic tribes on the borders of the Roman Empire in late antiquity: a major religion practised by a great power represented for the Turkish tribes the lure of prosperity, civilisation and power.

The centre of the Qarluk confederacy in the ninth and tenth centuries was Balasaghun on the Talas River (Figure 8.9). With the defeat of the Uighur Khaganate further east in 840 at the hands of the Kirghiz, the Qarluk chief seized the supreme Turk title and proclaimed himself Khagan. The population was mixed Turk and Sogdian, and religion would have been mixed as well: in addition to Islam and Manichaeism, there was a Christian minority (we read of a large church at Balasaghun that was later converted to a mosque). Within the Qarluk confederacy, a new clan was soon to emerge uppermost: the Karakhanids.

The rise of the Karakhanid state is perhaps an appropriate place to end this survey of the arrival of the Turks into Inner Asia, for the Karakhanids mark a new beginning in Turk history. The Karakhanids were the first of the specifically Islamic Turkish states: one reads of '200,000 Turkish tents' converting to Islam under Sultan Satuq Bughra Khan in 955. It also marks the first time that Turkish was written in the Arabic script, which it continued to use until its replacement in Turkey itself with the Latin script by Ataturk and Cyrillic in the Turkophone countries of the Soviet Union.* Subsequent Turk history is that of the great Turkish Islamic dynasties: the Ghaznavids, the Seljuks, the Ottomans and numerous minor dynasties which belong more to mainstream Middle Eastern and Islamic history than to Eurasian steppe.[34]

Before that, however, following the break-up of the Turk Empire various Turk tribes continued to migrate westwards, eventually into eastern

---

* Although most of these countries have adopted the Latin script since independence; Turkish is still written using the Arabic script in the original Karakhanid heartland in Xinjiang: see Figure 8.2.

Europe. These will be the subject of the following chapters. The collapse of the Turk Empire brought about the end of the beginning of the Turks in world history, but already their achievement was impressive. The wealth of the 'neo-Gandharan' artistic revival in the Hindu Kush, the Sogdian cities north of the Oxus and the spread of Buddhism and Manichaeism east of the Pamirs are testimony to their already significant legacy. But their effect on the subsequent history of Inner Asia was, if anything, even more significant. In the words of Denis Sinor:

> The Türks achieved and maintained for a period, long by Inner Asian standards, the political unification of a stretch of land that reached from the confines of China to the borders of Byzantium. They intervened with lasting effect in the destinies of China, Iran and Byzantium; they conveyed knowledge between the Greek, Iranian, Indian and Chinese worlds. In the Western world, for centuries, their name was used as a common denomination of barbarians, irrespective of their language, whereas for the peoples of Inner Asia the name Türk became, and has remained, the hallmark of the unity of peoples sharing a common language.[35]

Even this achievement was simply a curtain raiser for greater things to come.

CHAPTER 9

EUROPEAN NATIONS FROM THE STEPPE
Nomads and Early Medieval Europe

One of the few things that can be certain about Europe's pre-historic peoples is that they all came from somewhere else.
– Norman Davies[1]

Davies is, of course, referring to prehistory, but the process of new states in Europe being formed by peoples who came from 'somewhere else' continued until well into the historic periods of the first and even second millennia AD. Angles, Scots, Lombards, Normans, Finns, Serbs, Croats, Hungarians, Bulgarians, Turks and others came from places other than the countries or regions which today bear their names, and migrations define the history of the first millennium AD of Europe.[2] In this chapter it is difficult to avoid simply presenting a list of peoples who came from 'somewhere else', and Patrick Geary has cautioned that 'the reality is that neither the written evidence nor the archaeological data are adequate to resolve the most fundamental questions about the magnitude and impact of these putative population movements'.[3] Nevertheless, peoples who came into Europe from the steppe – mainly in the early Middle Ages – provide us with perhaps a different perspective on one of the most important processes in European history: the emergence of the nation state. In the ensuing account – not always in exact chronological order – it is difficult to follow the confusing succession of names of peoples, both familiar and unfamiliar, who seemingly pursued each other across the steppe with a rapidity with which is difficult to keep up, either to disappear into the silence of history whence they came or emerge as modern European nations. Apart from the arrival of Finn-related groups into Scandinavia, the movements of Huns, Avars, Bulgarians, Magyars, Turks, Pechenegs, Cumans and other related groups from the steppe are very confusing, often difficult to separate and controversial both chronologically and archaeologically. The reader, therefore, must forgive the occasional over-simplification.[4]

The idea of the nation state is generally regarded as originating in nineteenth-century European movements of nationalism, itself arising out of some of the earlier movements of the enlightenment and romanticism (although such labels have since been questioned). It is defined as a state where the great majority of its citizens share the same ethnicity and cultural values within matching political boundaries. The idea received added impetus after the First World War when the principle of 'the right to national self-determination' was the prime definition of the right to statehood. In recent times the ideal of the nation state has been both questioned, with the move towards supranational unions such as the European Union, and reinforced with the fragmentation of Yugoslavia, for example, into smaller ethnically and culturally defined units. However, many see the roots of the nation state in early medieval Europe, when states were beginning to be defined in national terms. This was a result of the immense movements of peoples in western Europe at the end of antiquity who began to settle and form kingdoms that were defined by the dominant groups: a kingdom of the Franks, for example, or kingdoms of the Angles, Lombards or Danes. Peoples newly arriving from the east were also among the first to create nationally defined states, such as kingdoms of the Bulgars or Magyars. In some ways the incipient idea of a nation state might have been stronger with the nomadic groups from the steppe, who were bound more closely by tribal loyalties.

Throughout history, different Asiatic groups of people have arrived in Europe via the steppe and (to a lesser extent) the forest belt. Some came as conquerors, others simply as herders; some eventually disappearing in history leaving little trace, others remaining and forming the basis of European nations to this day. A complete history of these is beyond the scope of this book. But we will explore how some of these 'Asiatic' groups entered Europe, eventually to merge into some overall 'idea' of Europe. In giving an account of these movements, mainly just their early history up until the time they became 'European' will be covered. In the process, some later literary, linguistic and intellectual movements will also be briefly mentioned to understand how steppe origins moulded later self perceptions and identities. Both the earlier and the later movements illustrate just how much Europe's identity is also 'Asiatic' – or at least how ambiguous both the perceived divide and identities are.

The modern European countries whose peoples originated beyond – sometimes far beyond – the conventional boundaries of Europe are: Finland, Estonia, Hungary, Bulgaria, Turkey and Malta.* There is also a veritable patchwork of originally 'non-European' minorities scattered throughout (mainly eastern) Europe: remnant Tatars from Lithuania to Crimea and even a Tatar republic in Russia, Turkish Christian Gagauz in Moldova, and a scattering of Bashkirs, Karaim, Szekekys, Kalmyks and others, not to mention Roma and Jews throughout. Most of these minorities are

---

* Malta, being a part of the Phoenician and Mediterranean world, lies outside the scope of the present study.

recognised as distinct ethnicities to a greater or lesser extent, many even organised into autonomous regions in larger states. Of the nation states, the European identity of Finland, Estonia, Hungary and Bulgaria is not in doubt; only that of Turkey is generally regarded as ambiguous (not least in connection with its application to join the European Union).

The most momentous of these movements – the Mongol invasions – forms the subject of separate chapters, but their eruption upon the European scene remains very firmly within the context of the themes explored here. Much the same can be said of perhaps the most successful of all the steppe peoples – the Turks – explored in the last chapter. However, those Turk tribes who entered Europe from the steppe, such as the Bulgars, Pechenegs and Cumans, are explored here, and the Khazars in the next chapter, but it is important to remember that there is considerable overlap between this chapter and those examining the Huns, Khazars, Turks and Mongols.[5]

Finns, Karelians, Estonians and epic identities

The Finns and related groups were one of the earliest to enter Europe from the east – probably from the forest belt rather than the steppe – but among the last to form nation states. In the past, the non-Indo-European steppe groups were lumped together under the general term 'Finnish' – indeed, Henri Pirenne referred to the Magyar migration into Europe at the end of the ninth century as 'the last wave of that Finnish inundation' that included the Huns, the Avars and even Turks and Mongols.[6] Although connected linguistically (albeit very distantly, and certainly disputed in the case of the Huns and Avars), these must be viewed as distinct groups – as distinct, say, as Slavic- and Romance-speaking groups. Finnish belongs to a Baltic language group that also includes Karelian, Estonian and Livonian. Baltic in turn belongs within a broader 'Finnic' group that embraces Saami in the far north and various middle and upper Volga groups that include the Mordvin, Mari, Cheremis and Permian languages. The Mordvin have been identified with the 'Androphagi' of Herodotus Book IV, which he locates beyond the Scythians to the north.[7] For all of these languages, linguists have postulated a 'Finno-Ugric' language root further back, from which Hungarian and other languages branched, with an even older 'Uralic' branch that includes Samoyed in Siberia.[8]

An original 'Uralic homeland' for the Finno-Ugrians (it would be a mistake to view them as a single 'people') has been postulated in the forest belt of the upper Volga-Kama rivers area of eastern European Russia, although more recent studies have placed this homeland further east just across the Urals in north-western Siberia.[9] Although Siberian forest peoples might be viewed as outside the present study of the steppe, 'The steppe-dwellers were the principal catalysts for change in the medieval

Figure 9.1 *Petroglyph of a hunter on skis at Belomorsk in Karelia, near the White Sea*

history of the forest zone', as Peter Golden emphasises.[10] Sometime in the third or second millennium BC there was a gradual migration ('demographic drift' might be a more appropriate term) of peoples speaking Finnish-related languages towards the Baltic when the various languages gradually separated. An Ugrian sub-group of Uralic remained in the Kama-Urals region, elements of which later became the Hungarian language. Another group in the middle Volga, the Chuvash, are linguistically related to Oghur-Turk, but their language is heavily influenced by Finno-Ugrian. Yet another group eventually became the Mordvins and Mari of the upper Volga-Kama, and another moved further south in the Urals to become the Onoghur, ultimate ancestors of the Hungarians. Ugrian-speaking groups later moved southwards into the steppe area and Altaic elements moved into north-western Siberia merging with remnant Ugrian groups. Out of this constant interplay between steppe and forest zones and Ugrian and Altaic languages emerged peoples who were later to figure largely in European history, such as the Bulgarians and Hungarians.[11]

By the late second millennium Finno-Ugrian language speakers had spread around the eastern end of the Baltic and northern Scandinavia, covering roughly the area of modern Finland, Karelia and Estonia as well as neighbouring parts of Russia, Sweden and Norway. They left their mark in large numbers of petroglyphs throughout the forests (Figure 9.1), as well as a series of extraordinary stone 'labyrinths' in and around the White

Figure 9.2 *Prehistoric Finno-Ugrian labyrinth on Bolshoy Zayatsky Island, part of the Solovetsky Archipelago in the White Sea*

Sea. Particularly fine examples are preserved on Bolshoi Zayatsky Island, part of the Solovetsky Archipelago (Figure 9.2).* The petroglyphs depict hunting and animal scenes, with hunters on skis wielding bows and pursuing animals. The labyrinths have been interpreted as some form of cult centres, but their exact nature is not fully understood.[12] Any relationship with the postulated Finno-Ugrian megalithic structures on Lake Vera in the Urals (discussed in Chapter 2) must remain speculative. The break-up of the original Finno-Ugrian groups into separate languages was probably completed by the early first millennium BC.

The later history of the Finns and Estonians was mainly subsumed by the greater powers surrounding them, Sweden to the west, Russia to the east and Germany to the south. It was not until the nineteenth century that national movements began to assert themselves. A part of this movement involved a search into Finno-Ugrian folk and linguistic roots, largely as an assertion of an identity that was distinct from either Swedish or Russian. Nineteenth-century philologists had developed the theory of the Ural-Altaic language group as a conscious answer to the Indo-Europeanists. This presented the idea of a single culture spreading

---

* The plans of these labyrinths are identical to those depicted on Bronze Age petroglyphs in Kazakhstan. See Bonora et al. 2009: 43.

from Finland to Manchuria. It is notable that the theory was subscribed to by Finnish explorers such as Matthias Castrén in the mid-nineteenth century and Carl Gustaf Mannerheim in the early twentieth: Inner Asian exploration was viewed as much as a rediscovery of their own roots as exploring other peoples' cultures. Matthias Castrén was a philologist who led an expedition into the Altai in an effort to identify the roots of the Finno-Ugrian language there in 1845–8. A large-scale expedition into the Altai in the early twentieth century financed by the Finnish state and led by I. R. Aspelin disproved Castrén's theory, but such expeditions were a manifestation nonetheless of emerging Finnish nationalism. Another Finnish philologist, Kai Donner, was closer to the source when he led several expeditions between 1911 and 1914 among the Samoyed and Khanti tribes of Siberia, recording both their language and their customs as part of a search for Finnish roots. The greatest Finnish explorer of Inner Asia was Carl Gustav Mannerheim, often also referred to as the 'father of modern Finland'. Mannerheim led a major expedition through Central Asia, Mongolia and China in 1906–9 on behalf of the Russian Imperial Army, but later became a Finnish nationalist supporting the independence of Finland from Russia. He eventually became president of Finland in 1944 at the age of 77.[13]

As well as searching the furthest parts of Asia for their roots, the Finns and Estonians also searched the folklore in their own forests for the same reasons of identity. The result was one of the great works of European epic literature, as well as some of the greatest works of European music. In the middle years of the nineteenth century, Elias Lönnrot (1802–84), a district health officer in north-eastern Finland who had also accompanied Matthias Castrén on one of his linguistic expeditions, deliberately set out to collect scattered oral traditions in Karelia. Lönnrot assembled them all together to create a national epic: the *Kalevala*, the exploits of the great creator-hero Väinämöinen (Figure 9.3). The *Kalevala* came to be viewed as a part of this broader Eurasian culture and not just Karelian. Lönnrot aimed to provide Finland with national sagas, similar to those

Figure 9.3 *Statue of Väinämöinen, the Finnish creator-hero of the* Kalevala*, in the gardens of 'Mon Repos' outside Vyborg/Viipuri in Karelia*

of Iceland, which was regarded as a model, in order to forge a national identity. He became a national figure and the *Kalevala* has remained the Finnish national epic and part of Finnish national identity.[14]

The *Kalevala* is actually an arrangement, knitted together by Lönnrot from all the different fragments into a cohesive and narrative form, much as musicians might assemble elements from folk origins to produce a cohesive orchestral whole. In other words, it is an artificially created epic. Folk traditions also achieved prominence in other European countries. The *Kalevala* (and the 'epic' of *Ossian* in Scotland which, until later disproven, was hugely influential) was part of a broader movement that came out of the Romantic period, when French, German, Hungarian, Polish and Romanian folk traditions and poetry were collected to create new national consciousnesses. At the same time as Lönnrot was collecting oral literature in Karelia, his almost exact contemporary Friedrich Kreutzwald (1803–82), a village school teacher and doctor, was creating a national epic for Estonia, the *Kalevipoeg* or *Kalevide*. Like the *Kalevala* it recounts the exploits of a hero, Soini, collected together in some nineteen thousand verses and foretelling the future greatness of the Estonian nation.[15] In this way the *Kalevala*, *Kalevide* and parallel European compilations are similar to earlier compilations, such as the national Kyrgyz epic *Manas* or Rustaveli's Georgian epic *The Knight in the Panther Skin* in the twelfth century, or Firdausi's Persian epic *The Book of Kings* in the tenth century – or Homer's *Iliad* and *Odyssey* for that matter. All have had a huge impact on national consciousness.

The *Kalevala* became a rallying point for Finnish nationalism throughout the later nineteenth century and its attempts to free itself from Russian domination. It had a particular impact on Finland's greatest composer, Jean Sibelius, who based no fewer than twelve works on the *Kalevala*. Most notable is his *Lemminkäinen Suite*, regarded as one of his most nationalistic works. Independence from Russia was achieved in 1917. The *Kalevala* is now established as Finland's national epic, with 28 February – the date of Lönnrot's original preface – now officially 'Kalevala Day'.

The influence of Finnish nationalism, however, even affected Russia itself. An artist who subscribed to the 'Finno-Ugrian' ideal was Kandinsky, who became conscious of his Tungus ancestry and many of his early paintings reflected the Ural-Altaic tribal themes.[16] Even Stravinsky was conscious of Karelian roots, having been born in 1882 in Kaarasti, part of the then Finnish-speaking province of Ingria (now modern Oranienbaum outside St Petersburg), and much of his music is drawn from folk roots, Karelian as well as Scythian and Russian. The eastern half of Karelia, including its capital of Viipuri (now Vyborg), was annexed to Russia at the end of the Second World War, the Finnish and Karelian population largely expelled and replaced by Russians, and the region 'Russianised' generally. However, in the post-Soviet Republic of Karelia, a part of the

Russian Federation, a Karelian identity is now encouraged among the Russian population: the *Kalevala* is taught in the schools and statues of Vainamoïnen are in public squares and parks throughout as an encouragement of a distinctive *Karelian*-Russian identity.

The Avars and European knighthood (Map 9.1)

> A mixed group of steppe warriors and their families in flight adopts a prestigious name, victoriously moves across thousands of miles and founds an empire, and can consider itself a people. When, after a quarter of a millennium, its identity and institutions lose their motivating force, this people disappears, apparently without leaving a trace. This is the history of the Avars in a nutshell.[17]

Thus Walter Pohl sums up Avar history. But Pohl's words come right at the end of his magisterial six-hundred-page account demonstrating that Avar history is more than 'a nutshell', and his book has almost single-handedly elevated the Avars to their rightful place in mainstream European history.

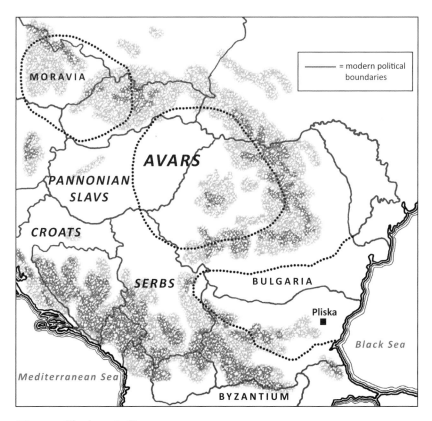

Map 9.1 The Avars in Europe

The Avars are first mentioned in 463 by Priscus as another new nomad group appearing on the steppe, distinct from the Huns.[18] As with the Huns, their exact identity is not known. They are likely to have been the descendants of the Rouran of Chinese sources, the steppe confederation that replaced the Xiongnu. The Chinese defeated the Rouran in 460, resulting in the emergence of the Turks (Chapter 8), former subjects of the Rouran, and displacing Rouran power on the steppe. The subsequent rapid rise and equally rapid collapse of the Turk Empire resulted in a huge disruption of different peoples that was felt from Siberia through to Europe: the classic 'knock-on' effect of movement across the steppe. The Rouran, now bitter enemies of the Turks, were a part of this movement, eventually entering European history as the Avars.

The Avars had reached Alan territory in the Pontic steppe by 557–8, and an Avar envoy visited Justinian in Constantinople (where the Avars' plaited pigtails created a sensation). At first there was some confusion as to exactly who these new arrivals were, and many sources lumped all steppe tribes (including Bulgars and Magyars) together as 'Scythians', 'Huns' or 'Goths', part of the stock prejudice against barbarians, nomads and the 'other' generally. Synesius of Cyrene, for example, writes that 'There are no new barbarians; the old Scythians are always thinking up new names to deceive the Romans'[19] and the *Chronicon Paschale* refers to the Avar khagan as 'the God-abhorred Chagan'.[20] Theophylact Simocatta caricatures the Avar khagan in a way that almost anticipates a Tom and Jerry cartoon when describing the khagan's reaction to an ambassador from Constantinople: 'boiling blood whipped up great passion in the Chagan, his whole face grew crimson with anger, while his eyes gleamed golden-bright with the flame of wrath and . . . his eyebrows shot up and almost threatened to fly off his forehead.'[21] In a long (and confusing) excursus in Book Seven, Theophylact even casts doubt on whether the European Avars were really 'Avars', suggesting that they were unrelated to the 'true' (and braver) Avars/Rouran of the steppe, but were a separate tribe called 'Var and Chunni' (or 'Varchunnitae' according to Menander: Var Huns or Avar Huns) and had simply hijacked the name: 'pseudo-Avars'.[22] As with all steppe names, ethnyms were flexible and could change; a Hun one day might be a Goth the next: one must not pin too much ethnic or cultural identity to the multiplicity of steppe tribal names, and historians are right to be cautious.[23] Even a people as well-known and -defined (in English) as the Germans are also known as the Deutsche, the Nemtsy, the Allemands and the Saksalaiset (not to mention Goths, Vandals, Franks, Suevi, Maromanni, Lombards and many others in the past – and they have even been called 'Huns' in modern times).

During the course of the later sixth century the Avars subjugated the other tribes north of the Black Sea. The first khagan (a title also used by the Turks) of the Avars that we learn of, Bayan, emerged in 562 (in fact Bayan is the only khagan's name to have survived, a name that also occurs among people as disparate as the Bulgars and the Mongols).[24] In the 560s they began their first raids against the Franks, and by 568 they had subjugated the Middle Danube and created a sizeable kingdom – Walter Pohl refers to it as an 'empire' – in the heart of Europe. By the 570s they had become enough of a threat that Emperor Justin II discussed the possibility of an encircling alliance against them with the Turk Empire to the east of the Avars, but Justin's successor, Tiberius, restored peace with the Avars in 574 and broke off negotiations with the Turks.[*]

With Constantinople distracted in the later sixth century with its increasingly bitter series of wars against Iran, the western defences were neglected and the Avars, with their Slav allies, advanced into south-eastern Europe as far as the Peloponnese. They lay siege to Thessalonika in 586, but in turn were threatened on their eastern front by the Turks in Crimea. The Avars were thus one of the many players caught up between Byzantium, Persia, the Slavs and the Turks in this 'last great war of antiquity'.[25]

Between 592 and 602 the Avars raided further west, into Dalmatia, Istria and Bavaria, resulting in the Lombards retreating over the Alps into Italy. In 626 the Avar 'empire' with their Slav allies entered into an alliance with Sasanian Persia, encamping before the walls of Constantinople with a vast army that also included Gepid and Bulgar allies while the Persians camped on the Asian side of the Bosphorus. It was only the Byzantine fleet which prevented the Persians from crossing in any sizeable number to join forces with the Avars, and the siege was lifted. This siege, when Constantinople came within a hair's-breadth of capture, was part of a larger war that has been described – perhaps overstated – as 'the greatest war in the history of the world' marking the end of antiquity. Although only marginal to this history, it did have a ripple effect right across Eurasia, bringing about more long-term changes than any other war in history.[26]

By the seventh century, the Avar kingdom was in any case beginning to weaken. In the mid-seventh century an uprising by the Wends, a western Slav group, threw off Avar domination, while further east the same period sees the rise of the Bulgars and the Khazars, both serious challengers to the Avars for steppe supremacy. However, in 663–4 their former enemies, the Lombards, requested Avar aid in their own wars in Italy. The Avars responded, becoming a serious threat to western Europe. Raids continued into Bavaria and Italy (reaching as far as Verona in 788) in the eighth century, but the rise of Charlemagne in the late eighth century checked

---

[*] Dimitri Obolensky (1971: 224–5) speculates that, if Byzantium had taken better advantage of the relations with the early Turk empire in the sixth century, 'it is arguable that the political and cultural influence of Byzantium would have spread, like that of the Russian Empire in more recent times, through the steppes of Central Asia to Manchuria and the Pacific'.

Avar western expansion. This culminated in a series of campaigns in the 790s against the Avars launched by Charlemagne and led by Pepin, his son, 'the greatest of all wars he [Charlemagne] waged, except for that against the Saxons' according to Einhard, his near-contemporary biographer.[27] In about 805 the Bulgar Khan Krum destroyed what was left of the eastern part of the Avar Khaganate (see below). The kingdom was formally abolished in 822, thus ending a quarter of a millennium's domination of parts of Europe by a people originally from the borders of China.

Some Avars were incorporated into Krum's army as distinct units; otherwise the remaining groups were gradually absorbed into the Slav population. In 805–6 some Avar tribes were still recorded in Greece, descendants from the first incursion two centuries before. They had, however, lost all connection with the khagan and had presumably become Slavicised. As late as the early tenth century Avars were still recorded as distinct people on parts of the middle Danube, but thereafter they effectively disappear from history (apart from some possible remnants in the Caucasus).

As with the Huns before them there is virtually no evidence of the Avar language: few names survive, and only a few runic inscriptions of which interpretations vary. The little evidence there is suggests that it was Altaic: Mongol or Turk – probably the former, as they fled from the rise of the Turk Empire. The archaeological evidence suggests that until about 600 they were totally nomadic, and afterwards semi-sedentary. The little historical evidence that we have suggests that their religion belonged to the broad realm of Inner Asian shamanism, worshipping heaven – 'Tängri' – as did the early Mongols; there is also ample evidence of horse burials, in line with steppe traditions. With few exceptions they resisted Christianity, despite some proselytisation.[28] The Avars thus seem to be yet another steppe people who appeared with a bang and left with a whimper.

Yet traces of them are significant, and their legacy profound. Some two thousand Avar sites have been excavated and an astonishing thirty thousand Avar graves.[29] Many 'Avar' graves, however, should more correctly be termed 'Avar-period' as they contained grave goods characteristic of other cultures, such as Merovingian and Byzantine (which equally does not necessarily exclude them being Avar). Many can be more positively identified with the Avars, such as warrior graves containing weapons and horse burials. Characteristic too were the re-curved composite bow of the steppe, tri-lobed arrowheads, fragments of armour, leaf-shaped lance heads, horse trappings and belt buckles in the animal style. The latter in particular, depicting combat scenes, fantastic beasts and – most typically – griffins appear connected to the characteristic Xiongnu belt plaques discussed in Chapter 6. Several presumed 'royal' burials of Avar khagans have been uncovered at Nagyszentmiklós (modern Sânnicolau Mare in Romania), Kunbábony in Hungary, Vrap in Albania and elsewhere that included rich treasures, such as gold vessels, weapons and animal style art.[30]

Their legacy was also significant as a catalyst for change. The Avars introduced new methods of cavalry warfare to Byzantium that ultimately revolutionised European warfare until the introduction of gunpowder. The most significant was the introduction of the stirrup, but they were also responsible for the European adoption of cavalry pikes, of long mail cavalry kaftans that reached to the knees and the curved sabre.[31] This general apparel of the mounted Avar armed warrior, regarded by contemporaries as a particularly fearsome and impressive sight, is emphasised by Pohl as a 'decisive element in the development of European knighthood', anticipating much of the medieval knightly imagery. The Avars also used classic steppe battle tactics such as the circular charge with Parthian shots and feigned retreats, and were the first steppe army to fight in planned formations, tactics that were adopted into European warfare.[32]

But perhaps more significant was the fact that their core territory corresponded roughly to the area of what later became Hungary. Although the Hungarians were a later arrival and ethnically distinct from the Avars, these horse-riding nomads from the northern borderlands of China were nonetheless one of the main formative elements of a major European state – not only of Hungary, but Peter Heather in his account of the formative migration period of European history, adds that 'Moravia, Bohemia and, to an extent, Poland, can all be seen as successor states to the Avar Empire destroyed by Charlemagne just before the year 800', while Walter Pohl concludes his account of Avar history with 'The Avar Empire should be acknowledged as a relevant part of European history'.[33]

The Bulgars and the beginning of statehood in Russia (Map 9.2)

For centuries, Russia has looked back to Kievan Rus as the first state in Russian (now Ukrainian) territory, founded by Prince Oleg in 882 with the establishment of Kiev as the capital. But the first state to be established on the territory later corresponding to Russia was probably that of the Khazars of the southern steppes in the early seventh century (Chapter 10). There was also the Bulgar state of the middle Volga area later in the seventh century. Of course, this is not meant to diminish the importance of the Kievan origins of the Russian state (avoiding the contentious issue of what constitutes a 'state', over which much ink could be – and has been – spilt, and the origin dates of all three 'states' remain controversial). The Russian national sentiment that is tied so strongly to Kievan Rus is associated with the adoption of Orthodox Christianity by Prince Vladimir in 988. While it would be a mistake to view religious matters in Russia simply as some sort of historic race as to 'which one got there first', Judaism and Islam were the first monotheistic religions to be established on Russian soil, not Christianity, with the adoption of Judaism by the

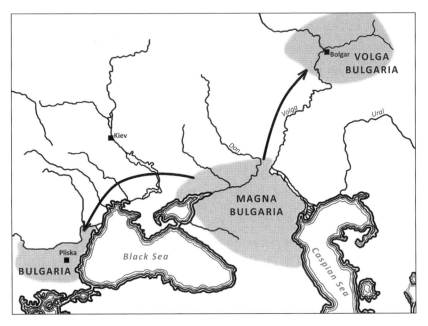

Map 9.2 *The Bulgar migrations*

Khazars in about 740 and Islam by the Volga Bulgars in 922 – and the Bulgar Khan wrote to Vladimir in 986 urging him to follow suit.[34] Islam and the descendants of the Bulgars have been a permanent part of the middle Volga ever since: Islam, in other words, has a longer continuous history in Russia than Christianity and the Russian state itself does.[35] This is not meant to nit-pick, nor to downplay the strength of sentiment surrounding either Russian national consciousness or Russian Orthodoxy. It is merely meant to emphasise that a traditional view of Russian history solely in terms of Slavs and Orthodoxy is by no means the full picture, but just part of a broader, more complex whole.

The Oghur Turks, ancestors of the Bulgars, first appear in the fifth century in the Kazakh and Siberian steppe; a remnant Oghur group, the Chuvash, still exist on the upper Volga (forming the Republic of Chuvashia) as the only surviving Oghur language. The Oghur were on the whole less warlike than many of the other Inner Asian groups and had a more agricultural emphasis. Then, in about 463, Sabir tribes (from whom the name 'Siberia' derives) invaded the Oghur lands, sending them south-westwards to the Pontic steppe, gradually filling the vacuum left behind by the earlier Hun movements further west.[36]

The Pontic steppe at this time was what one historian describes as 'a kaleidoscope of successive populations', and another as 'a kaleidiscope of dissolving and reforming tribal unions'.[37] The Bulgars were a sub-tribe of the broader Oghur nation, 'a kind of Turk' according to Mas'udi,[38] themselves just one fragment of the kaleidoscope at the time that included other Turk groups as well as older groups such as the Huns and newly arriving ones such as the Onoghur (proto-Hungarians, discussed below). The name *Bulgar/Bulghar* probably means 'mixed ones', implying a 'tribal union', and may have incorporated remnants of the Huns. This is important: at this point the name had little ethnic meaning, and would have included other tribes as well as Huns, Sarmatians and perhaps even Slavs from eastern Europe and Wusun from western China.[39] But the Bulgars were the first of these tribes to develop political institutions and consequently emerged as a dominant group with a distinct identity over the course of the following centuries.

In about 670 a coalition of Magyars and Khazars defeated the Bulgars, forcing some of them to move westwards to the lower Danube, where they would form the core of the later Bulgarian state. Others moved northwards to the middle Volga around Kazan, where they formed a separate Bulgar kingdom.[40] Ninth-century Byzantine sources refer to the remaining Bulgar tribes in the steppes between the Sea of Azov and the Kuban River as vassals of the 'Avar Khagan'. After a revolt led by Kubrat against the Avars in the ninth century, they established the first Bulgar state on the southern Russian-Ukrainian steppe: 'Magna Bulgaria'. Kubrat, assuming the title of Khagan, was baptised and formed ties with Byzantium, although he maintained the independence of the Bulgarian state. A number of rich burials in southern Ukraine have been associated with the Bulgars, with a particularly rich one at Pereshchepnye near Poltava tentatively identified with Kubrat himself (the treasure included a gold ring with Kubrat's monogram).[41] After Kubrat's death, however, the unity of the Bulgar tribes began to fragment, partly because of the loose nature inherent in most steppe tribal formations but also due to renewed pressure from the Khazars. Nevertheless, it was a crucial period in the history of the Bulgars: a first Bulgarian state that foreshadowed the creation of the later Bulgarian Empire. Even though these original Bulgars were Turks, Magna Bulgaria is an important part of Bulgarian national identity today, with Kubrat regarded as a national founder figure.

In the meantime, as a part of the 'dissolving and reforming' process, a separate group of Bulgars had migrated northwards to the area of the middle Volga in the seventh century. At the beginning of the tenth century they were still vassals of the Khazars, but soon broke away and, already possessing developed political institutions, were able to establish a nascent state. Many were Muslims, and the rulers actively courted Islam, if only to tread a neutral line between Khazar Judaism on the one hand and Byzantine Christianity on the other. Many of their practices, however, were still closer to their steppe origins: the Arab envoy Ibn Fadlan, who travelled to the Bulgars on behalf of the Caliph in 921–2, describes the burial customs of their chiefs, which were close to ancient Scythian practice (indeed, Ibn Fadlan calls the Bulgars *Saqaliba*: 'Saka' or 'Scythians').[42]

Figure 9.4 *The excavated remains of the Friday Mosque at Bilyar*

The Bulgar state operated from three main cities in the mid-Volga region, Suwar, Bilyar and Bolgar, the latter the main capital not far from later Kazan (itself the capital of a later steppe kingdom: Chapter 10), but during the summers most of the houses were abandoned for tents. However, it would be a mistake to view the Bulgar state as merely an ephemeral steppe agglomeration: Ibn Rusta in the tenth century describes them as a settled agricultural and urban people rather than nomadic, in contrast to the Khazars.[43] The cities too were as large as, or larger than, most cities in western Europe in the tenth century. Bilyar had an area of seven hundred hectares. This was small compared to Constantinople's sixteen hundred hectares during the same period, but compares favourably with Baghdad's 750 hectares, and easily exceeds other European cities: Paris at 439 hectares, Vladimir at 160 or Kiev at 150. Bilyar in the tenth century was a purpose-built capital surrounded by eleven kilometres of walls.[44] The remains of its Friday Mosque and a baths have been excavated (Figure 9.4). Many of the buildings in both Bilyar and Bolgar were built of stone, unlike in the rest of Russia where wood was virtually the sole material. Parts of the twelfth-century Bulgar fortress at Elabuga overlooking the Kama River still stand (Figure 9.5).[45] Trade was well-developed and the Bulgar state had strong links with Abbasid Baghdad via the Khazar Empire, the conduit of the fur trade to Baghdad in exchange for silver. This trade stretched right across northern Europe and even deep into the Arctic Circle during the tenth century: a hoard of Abbasid and Samanid coins, for example, was found near Bodø inside the Arctic Circle in Norway (Figure 9.6).[46]

Figure 9.5 *A reconstructed corner tower of the excavated Bulgar fortress overlooking the Kama River at Elabuga*

Volga Bulgaria was thus a part of a trade network that embraced Khazaria, Russia, the forest belt, the Baltic, Scandinavia, Khwarazm, the Abbasid Middle East and Iran, and the Byzantine Empire. This wealth was reflected in its capital. Al-Andalusi described the city of Bolgar in the eleventh century as 'a great city, all built of pine. Its walls are of oak. Round about it there are an infinite number of peoples.' He also describes skiing in Volga Bulgaria.[47] Today Bilyar and especially Bolgar still have remains of mosques, monumental mausolea and other buildings (Figures 9.4, 9.7 and 9.8)* and excavations have confirmed widespread trade links and wealth.[48]

Figure 9.6 *Abbasid and Samanid silver coins in the Bodø Museum in Norway*

---

* Although most of the standing remains at Bolgar date from the thirteenth–fourteenth centuries, the period of the Golden Horde and the successor Khanate of Kazan – see Chapter 12.

Figure 9.7 Mausoleum and minaret at Bolgar

Figure 9.8 Probable mausoleum at Bolgar, known locally as a 'court house'

In 981 Vladimir I of Rus invaded the Bulgar territory, but in 986 the Bulgars sent envoys to Vladimir urging him to embrace Islam. Thus was an encounter between two peoples from opposite ends of Eurasia who eventually established major European empires, the one Vikings from Scandinavia, the other Turks from Siberia, both eventually becoming Slav in identity. Nowadays both Russians and Bulgarians share a common Slav heritage, but in the formative period there was no such common ground and the relationship was often confrontational. Both competed for domination over the trade in fur and silver and control over the Finno-Ugric peoples of the forest, and in 1107 there was a major but unsuccessful Bulgar raid on Suzdal. By the later twelfth and into the thirteenth century the Bulgars were experiencing increasing attacks from the Rus, mainly for control of the lucrative trade of furs and other luxury commodities with the forest people. There was also increasing Slav colonisation of the northern areas. In 1221 the Rus constructed the kremlin of Nizhni Novgorod at the mouth of the Oka where it enters the Volga in order to control this trade and confront the Bulgars.

However, 1236 saw the eruption of a new people from the east onto the scene, the Mongols, forcing the Bulgars to seek an alliance with the Russians. The Bulgars appreciated the threat long before the Russians did and exhorted an alliance for mutual protection. Their warnings to the Rus went unheeded, and the Bulgar state of the middle Volga was annihilated by the Mongols in 1236–7. However, of all the Bulgar groups, it was those of the middle Volga who retained their language and Turk identity down to the present, with the Mongol conquerors themselves being Turkised. The modern Republic of Tatarstan in the Russian Federation is formed out of the remnants of the original Bulgars and the Qipchak Turks who arrived with the Mongols. Florin Curta concludes his overview: 'Far from being a steppe empire (a phrase often employed as a synonym for an ephemeral polity), Volga Bulgharia is in fact the name of one of the most remarkably stable, prosperous and long-lasting polities in Eastern Europe.'[49] In Tatarstan Attila is regarded as the 'direct ancestor' of Kubrat, Khan of the Bulgars, and the Bulgars in turn are regarded as the 'ancestors' of the Tatars with both regarded as the ancestors of the modern people of Tatarstan, celebrated in 1996 by an exhibition of the so-called 'Treasure of Khan Kubrat' on loan from the Hermitage.[50]

The formation of the Bulgarian Empire

Bulgars had migrated further west long before the establishment of either the Volga or the Kuban kingdoms sometime after the late sixth century (dates in the sources vary).[51] As early as 631–2 a Bulgar group raided Bavaria, but were slaughtered. Another Bulgar group led by Alzeco crossed into Italy in 663 where they eventually settled. Then, in about 679 or a little earlier, yet another group of Bulgars led by Asparukh (one of Kubrat's five sons) migrated to the Balkans and founded the Danubian Bulgar Khanate. In the eighth century the Khanate probably consisted of just a Bulgar-Turk elite over a mainly Slav and indigenous Thracian population. The Bulgars represented a third overlay after the Slavs themselves, who had only migrated into the Balkans at much the same time as – or a little earlier than – the Bulgars. The tribal leaders retained their ethnic Turk identity, but Slavic was becoming the lingua franca and gradually the elite became more Slavicised. Some Turk elements, such as the titles 'khan' and 'khagan' and the military ethos of the steppe nomad, however, were maintained. Other titles were also soon adopted. Asparukh's successor, Khagan Tervel, was awarded the title 'Caesar' in 705 by the Emperor Justinian II as a reward for Bulgar aid in regaining his throne after his exile in Crimea, despite Tervel remaining a pagan.[52] The title Caesar, in its Bulgarian form of 'Tsar', soon became the main title of the Bulgarian monarchs, now more familiarly associated with the Russian emperors who adopted it from them.

The remainder of the eighth century was one of increasingly deteriorating relations with Constantinople. In 803 Khan Krum defeated the Avars and the Khanate became the Bulgarian Empire, 'one of the great militarist powers of Europe' in the opinion of Steven Runciman.[53] Much of this was at the expense of the Byzantine Empire, which Khan Krum fought and defeated in 811, killing Emperor Nicephorus I and turning his skull into a drinking cup in time-honoured steppe fashion. He embellished and enlarged the new Bulgarian capital of Pliska, thus establishing Bulgaria as one of the first nation states of Europe. Steven Runciman sums this up as follows:

> Krum had remade Bulgaria. His first achievement, of uniting the Pannonian with the Balkan Bulgars, had given both of them new life . . . And then he had embarked on a career of spectacular, terrible triumph. He had slain two Emperors in battle and caused the fall of a third. Of the great Imperial fortresses on the frontier he had captured and destroyed four and caused the inhabitants of the two others to flee in terror. He had even seriously threatened the Imperial capital and repeatedly he had beaten the best Imperial armies. Bulgaria, the dying state of half a century before, was now the greatest military power in Eastern Europe . . . Barbarian though he was, with his ostentation and craft and cruelty, his concubines, his human sacrifices and his cup that was an Emperor's head, the Sublime Khan Krum was a very great statesman; and his greatness lies, not in being the conqueror of Emperors, but in being the founder of the splendid Bulgarian aristocracy.[54]

At first they maintained their Turk language and religion (the worship of the steppe sky god Tangra, also worshipped by the Mongols before their adoption of Buddhism). The conversion to Orthodox Christianity by Byzantium in 864 by Khan Boris (the first to adopt a Slavic name) was probably a means of enforcing unity on a mixed population. With the full establishment of Christianity by Symeon (893–927), the Danube Bulgars became increasingly Slavicised: a Slavic language (Old Bulgarian) was adopted as the state language, the title Tsar replaced the Turkish Khan, the capital was moved from Pliska to Preslav, and eventually the Bulgars were to lose all traces of their Turk identity.[55]

Steppe events still continued to affect the history of south-eastern Europe. Relations between Bulgaria and Byzantium were never easy. In 895 Tsar Symeon invaded Byzantine Thrace in response to Byzantine punitive measures against Bulgarian trade. Symeon had timed his campaign well, as Byzantium at that time was distracted by wars with the Arabs on their eastern borders. Emperor Leo VI therefore sent envoys to the Magyars, who by then occupied the area of Bessarabia, to attack Bulgaria in its rear. The Magyars accordingly invaded the Bulgarian Empire, occupying Dobruja and advancing as far as Preslav. Symeon was forced to sue for peace with Byzantium. In 896 he turned on the Magyars, forcing them back across the Danube. Imitating Leo's policy, Symeon then sent envoys to the Pechenegs occupying the steppe to the east of Magyar territory to in turn attack the Magyars in their rear. The Pechenegs accordingly invaded Bessarabia and drove the Magyars across the Carpathian Mountains to Pannonia, which they occupied. The eventual result was the foundation of the Hungarian state.[56]

Alone of virtually all Turk-speaking peoples, the Bulgars in the Balkans allowed their original Turk language and character to be subsumed by the language of the conquered peoples, the Slavs. This is in stark contrast to the Turks who entered Anatolia, where Turkish not only became the dominant language but in most cases replaced the existing indigenous ones.[*] There are several reasons for the loss. To begin with, the Bulgar migrations might not have been of large numbers, but were little more than an elite ruling a majority Slav and Thracian population. More importantly, it was the efforts of the Bulgar elite themselves to preserve their distinct steppe identity against the Slavs that ironically contributed to their eventual Slavicisation (as late as the tenth century Byzantine officials would still occasionally refer to the Bulgarians contemptuously as 'Scythians').[57] This happened when the Bulgar khans turned to the Slavs for support in establishing an autocratic sedentary style of monarchy,

---

[*] The various Turkish-speaking dynasties who ruled India, from the Mamluks to the Mughals, also now leave few linguistic traces, but these were ruling elites rather than mass tribal movements. The main indigenous languages to survive in Turkey today are Laz and (related) Georgian on the Black Sea and in the north-east, Kurdish in the south-east and Greek in Istanbul.

rather than to the Bulgar noble families who wanted to maintain their own collective power under a Khan appointed by themselves: the traditional steppe form of consensual government. This led inevitably to a more central role for the Slav nobility in government and the sidelining of the Bulgar elite.

It must also be remembered that when the Turks entered Anatolia they already had the powerful unifying force of the Islamic religion behind them. The Bulgars entered the Balkans as pagans, and rarely has a pagan steppe society withstood the attraction of one of the mainstream established religions: Buddhism (Mongols), Judaism (Khazars), Christianity (Bulgars, Russians) or Islam (Turks, Tatars). The Huns, Avars and Kara Khitai are virtually the only exceptions. The Bulgars, moreover, were illiterate, and in order to rule over a sedentary population access to written records is essential, in contrast to the literate Turks who entered Anatolia. The only people in the Balkans who wielded this essential tool were the Greek Christians. When literacy did eventually arrive it was the Glagolitic alphabet, soon replaced by the simpler Cyrillic alphabet developed from the Greek specifically for the Slavic languages to disseminate the Christian religion by the monks Cyril and Methodius: no writing system existed for the Turkish language in the west, which inevitably lost out.

Steven Runciman concludes his magisterial account of the First Bulgarian Empire as follows:

> Though clouds pass at times over the face of Bulgaria, she may well be content with her history. The First Empire has left her memories rich in glory. It is a splendid procession that stretches backward into the far-off darkness, past Samuel and his passionate Court beside the high mountain-lakes of Macedonia; past Symeon on his golden throne, his silken raiment weighed down with studded pearls; past Boris, issuing from his aureoled palace with angels to escort him; past Krum, with bowing rows of concubines, crying 'Sdravitsa' to his boyars as he drank from an Emperor's skull; past Tervel, riding in to Constantinople by the side of a slit-nosed Emperor; past Asperuch and, his brothers, and his father, King Kubrat, and past the princes of the Huns, back through dim ages to that wild marriage from which her race was born, the marriage of the wandering Scythian witches to the demons of the sands of Turkestan.[58]

From Siberia to Holy Roman Empire: the formation of Hungary
(Map 9.3)

The Great Hungarian Plain has been characterised as a 'holding-ground – a place where many stayed and from which others moved on' and 'the steppe axis' as 'one of the formative structures underlying European development'.[59] Few peoples demonstrate this more than the Hungarians, the

Map 9.3 *The Magyar migrations*

last of those to arrive, who stayed to make it their homeland and one of the centres of European culture.

The proto-Hungarians were originally a Siberian forest people belonging to the Ugrian language group known as the Onoghur.[60] The names 'Hungarian' and 'Magyar' are both derived from 'Onoghur'; the name is also related to 'Oghur' as well as, ultimately, to 'Utrughur', 'Ugrian', 'Uighur' and other '-*ghur*'-suffix ethnonyms of other Turko-Ugrian-related groups.[61] There is no link between 'Hungarian' and 'Hun' as is often assumed.* The first recorded use of the term 'Ugrian' was in the seventh century by Jordanes, who mentions them as the 'Yugra' of Siberia. As late as the eleventh century the *Novgorod Chronicle* still referred to Siberia as 'Yugorskaia Zemlitsa', with a special trade association, the 'Yugorshshina', set up in Novgorod in the fourteenth century specifically for trade with

---

* For example by Davies (1996: 217–18), who mistakenly writes that Hungary is named after the Huns. Not to mention by many Hungarians themselves, for whom 'Attila' has become a popular name. As far back as the fifteenth century, King Matthias Corvinus of Hungary was calling himself a 'second Attila' and proposing an alliance with Mehmet the Conqueror on the grounds of shared ethnicity: see Almond 2009: 142.

Figure 9.9 *Bashkirs in traditional costume celebrating their national day on 26 June in the main square of Ufa, capital of Bashkortostan*

Siberia.[62] The Onoghur or proto-Hungarians/Magyars probably left the original Finno-Ugrian homeland in the middle of the first millennium BC and migrated to the Tobol–Ishim Rivers in western Siberia. Initially they were just one of many tribes and nations in the region of western Siberia and the Kazakh steppe, including the Sabir and the Turk Oghurs, and their early movements are uncertain. The Onoghur may have been disrupted by the establishment of the Turk Empire, along with the Oghur (and to some extent being absorbed by them), leaving the homeland and moving further west in the great migrations of the middle and later decades of the fifth century. They eventually came to the region of the North Caucasus and Pontic steppe. The large number of Turk loan words in Hungarian suggests close contact in the past: for example the Hungarian tribal name of *Tarján* derived from the Bashkir-Mongolian title *tarkhan*.[63]

By the fifth century the ancestors of the Hungarians were located in the south Urals area, and were deflected further southwards towards the Donets-Dniester-Bug area by the arrival of the Turks in the sixth–seventh centuries. According to another theory, the Onoghur migrated to the area of Bashkiria in the western foothills of the Urals, forming a 'Magna Hungaria' state alongside that of Volga Bulgaria, until their further migrations southwards in the latter half of the eighth century, although many aspects of the date and trajectory remain uncertain. Those who remained behind formed the nucleus of the present Bashkirs of the region (and the Republic of Bashkortostan today: Figures 9.9 and 9.10); indeed, Islamic sources throughout the Middle Ages refer to the Hungarians of Europe as *Basjirt* or *Bashghird*. The great Khazar fortress of Sarkel on the Don was constructed in the mid-ninth century partly as defence against the southward-migrating Magyar tribes from Bashkiria (Figure 10.1). Another possible Inner Asian remnant group are the Madjars, a small isolated minority in Kazakhstan.[64]

The Onoghur/Magyar first appear as a distinct group on the Pontic steppe in the late eighth and early ninth centuries as semi-nomadic cattle breeders. Pecheneg attacks from further east in 889 drove Magyar horsemen westwards. In 894 the Magyars defeated the Danube Bulgars, and in the same year the Pechenegs were pursued across the Volga by the Oghuz Turks. In 895 a Pecheneg and Bulgar coalition defeated the Magyars of the Pontic steppe and drove them into the Carpathian basin where, under their leader Arpad, they filled the vacuum left by the collapse of the Avar state. The Pechenegs then occupied the Pontic steppe from the Don to the lower Danube (discussed further below).[65]

The Magyars formed an alliance with with the kingdom of Moravia in its wars against the Bulgars and Franks, eventually settling in Pannonia (roughly corresponding to modern Hungary). In 906 their infant state was further consolidated when they changed sides and joined the Franks in the destruction of Moravia. The descendants of Arpad continued as chiefs to rule the evolving Magyar state, or Hungary as it is now better known.[*] Ibn Rusta describes the Magyars in the tenth century as nomads occupying a vast area from south-eastern Europe to the Black Sea. Their religion is described as fire worship. The Magyars raided the Slavic lands, capturing large numbers of slaves whom they sold at the big Byzantine slave market at Kerch in eastern Crimea. Although there is evidence of the baptism of some Magyar chiefs visiting Constantinople in the tenth century, a new era began when Hungary's first Christian, first king and first saint, King Stephen (István), adopted Christianity and was crowned in the year 1000 with a crown that had been sent by Pope Sylvester II (Figure 9.11).[†] This ensured that – unlike neighbouring Bulgaria – Hungary looked west to Rome and Catholicism rather than east to Byzantium and Orthodoxy. It also marked the beginning of one of Europe's oldest nation states.[66]

The incoming Magyars probably absorbed the earlier Avars, who may have been linguistically and ethnically related, albeit distantly so, but at least closer in language and spirit than the indigenous Indo-European speakers and sedentary cultures. This process of absorption might also explain the total cultural and linguistic extinction of the Huns in the same general area: although they were probably even more distant from the

---

[*] In fact the name for Hungary in modern Arabic and Persian is *Majaristan* and in Hungary itself *Magyarország*.

[†] Or sent by Constantinople, according to Pohl 2018b: 192, and inscribed tactlessly to *Krales Tourkias*, 'King of the Turks'.

Figure 9.10 *Statue of Salawat Yulayul, eighteenth-century Bashkir national hero, in Ufa*

Figure 9.11 *Statue of Stephen (István), Hungary's first Christian king and patron saint, overlooking the Danube in Budapest*

Magyars, it would nonetheless still be easier for the Huns to be subsumed by the Avars and Magyars than by the indigenous Indo-European speakers.

The establishment of Hungary had another unexpected but profound effect that changed subsequent European history: it drove a wedge between the northern and southern Slavs, who then remained forever separated. Up until then the Slavs formed a continuous, if not united, ethnic group across the eastern marches of Europe from the White Sea to the Adriatic. If the Slavs had ever united[67] they could have become the most formidable power in Europe in the Middle Ages – and perhaps an irresistible threat to Constantinople, as great as or greater than the threat that the Turks later became. The existence of Hungary – not only non-Slav but also non-Orthodox – meant that this would now never happen.

The later history of Hungary – first as a principality, then as one of the important kingdoms of medieval Europe, its role that of a frontier state between the wars of the Ottoman Empire with the Christian powers – is hardly a part of the present history. In the seventeenth century its western part was annexed by the Habsburgs, followed by its eastern Ottoman half after 1718. It thus entered the huge shadow that the Roman Empire still cast over Europe, becoming a core part of the Holy Roman Empire. But although it was at the Empire's heart (and Budapest vied with Vienna to become the grandest city not just of the Empire but of all Europe), it was the Hungarians' search for a separate non-German identity that contributed to the demise of the Empire. Hence, the title of Holy Roman Empire was abolished after 1806 but Hungarian insistence on equal status with Austria led to the renaming of Europe's last nominal link with the ancient Roman Empire as the Empire of Austria-Hungary in 1867.

Hungarians and Bulgarians form an interesting contrast. Both originated far off in the borderlands of Siberia. In these homelands, ancestors of both were linguistically related, albeit distantly. Both left behind remnant populations in their homelands, both of which now form republics within the Russian Federation: Tatarstan in the case of the Bulgarians, Bashkortostan in the case of the Hungarians (although present ethnic links must be viewed as, at best, tenuous). Both eventually moved into adjacent parts of south-eastern Europe that were occupied by Slav populations, themselves also recent arrivals into those areas. But whereas the Bulgarians lost their language and their original Turk identity to the 'indigenous' Slavs, the Hungarians retained their Inner Eurasian language and imposed it upon the population they conquered. Today, regardless of the original identities of the region – which include Celtic, Dacian, Pannonian, Roman, Avar, Slav, Vlach and much else – both now have separate linguistic, ethnic and religious identities: the one Altaic/Hungarian/Catholic, the other Slavic/Bulgarian/Orthodox. And despite Inner Eurasian steppe origins, both absorbed the European imperial tradition sharing the ancient Roman legacy: the one the Austro-Hungarian Empire, heir of the Holy

Roman, the other the First and Second Bulgarian Empires identifying with the Byzantine continuation of the Roman Empire.

As with the Finns of the same period far to the north, the re-assertion of a distinct Hungarian identity in the nineteenth century also took the form of a search for Asiatic roots. Again as with the Finns, much of this was in the field of linguistics. In the field of Central Asian exploration and studies generally, Hungarian scholarship has traditionally been at the forefront. Sandor Csoma de Koros in the early nineteenth century, for example, travelled through Central Asia and into Tibet, compiling the first Tibetan–English dictionary.[*] Later in the century Arminius Vámbéry, also a specialist in Oriental languages, who compiled a Turkish–German dictionary, undertook a journey in disguise to Khiva, Bukhara and Samarkand in the 1860s, the first European to perform such a journey.[68] Probably the greatest of all explorer-archaeologists of Inner Asia was the Hungarian Marc Aurel Stein. Born in Budapest in 1862, Stein became a British subject and undertook numerous surveying and archaeological expeditions in the late nineteenth and first half of the twentieth century through north-western India, the Himalayas, western China, Iran and Syria, becoming one of the pioneers of aerial archaeology in the latter. He died in Kabul in 1942.[69] In the twentieth century the Hungarian tradition in Oriental studies continued. The philologist and historian János Harmatta was one of the editors of the multi-volume UNESCO *History of Civilizations in Central Asia*, and the émigré Islamic art historian at London University, Géza Fehévári, was appointed Hungary's first post-Communist ambassador to Kuwait. The University of Budapest remains a major centre for oriental and Inner Asian studies: in 2017, for example, it hosted a European Research Council-funded international conference on 'Hunnic Peoples in Central and South Asia: Sources of their Origin and History'.[70]

Polovtsian dances

The movement of one group of peoples from the steppe usually results in a vacuum, and the departure of the Bulgars and Magyars resulted in the formation of new confederations dominated by tribal elites.[71] The first to emerge were the Pechenegs (or Patzinaks in Byzantine sources, which also occasionally referred to them anachronistically as Scyths and Sarmatians). Like so many peoples of the Eurasian steppe, we first hear of the Pechenegs from the Chinese, in this case from the Sui annals of the seventh century. Tibetan sources also mention them in the eighth

---

[*] Celebrated by a plaque erected in the 1960s on the former premises of the British Institute of Persian Studies in Tehran by a group of Hungarian émigrés.

century.[72] They were a Turk tribe like most of the steppe peoples by this time, and their homeland seems to have been the Aral–Syr Darya steppe. Then, pressure from incoming Oghuz Turk tribes – part of whom later formed the Seljuk nation – forced them to migrate to the Volga-Urals area in the late eighth–early ninth centuries. Here, pressure in turn from the Khazars forced a second migration in about 889 southwards to the Pontic steppe. The Pechenegs, in alliance with Tsar Symeon of Bulgaria, in turn drove the Magyars into central Europe, thence they migrated further to the Don-Donets steppe, where they remained until the mid-eleventh century – from China to Europe, a classic example of the steppe 'knock-on' effect. However, while their migration is reasonably well-attested in the historical sources, the archaeological evidence remains elusive: 'There is, in other words, no direct archaeological correlate of the migration of the Pechenegs', as Florin Curta cautions.[73] Their movement is also a classic example of the perennial problem of pinning steppe people named in historical sources to the material evidence on the ground.

In southern Ukraine the Pechenegs formed a loose tribal confederation. There was no Pecheneg 'state' as such, and it doubtless incorporated other steppe tribes in the region, both Turk and non-Turk. They also became a useful pool of auxiliaries which surrounding states could dip – or at least buy – into. Hence, by the tenth centuries Kievan Rus was hiring Pecheneg mercenaries. However, mercenaries can be as much a threat as an asset, and in the early eleventh century a series of walls, the so-called 'snake walls', were built by Kiev running south and east of the capital to control the movement of the Pechenegs. These walls were earthworks up to four metres high, topped by a wooden palisade and fronted by a ditch twelve metres wide, extending for a hundred kilometres or more, although there has been little investigation.[74] Here were renewed efforts in 'walling off the barbarian', that the Sasanians used in the sixth century.

By the eleventh century the Byzantines, Poles and Hungarians were also hiring Pecheneg mercenaries – the Hungarians now the pursuer instead of the pursued. In the 950s, according to Arab sources, the Byzantines recruited a combined army of Pechenegs, Bulgars, Russians and Armenians in a campaign against the Muslims of Syria, probably the first time that warriors from the steppe had penetrated that far in the Near East since the Cimmerian raids of the eighth century BC.[75] Byzantine policies were also directed at proselytisation, but their efforts were largely unsuccessful and the Pechenegs remained pagan apart from a few small (and doubtful) groups.* And like

---

* There is some suggestion in the sources of Zoroastrian elements in their religion, implying either earlier contact with Iranian groups in Central Asia or even the survival of Scythian beliefs, but the evidence is slim; Golden 1990b: 275. Traces of Zoroastrianism have been discerned among many of the steppe people, which is unsurprising given their probable Central/Inner Asian origins; Zhivkov 2015: 19–20.

any mercenary force, the Pechenegs could just as easily turn against their employers: hence, in the eleventh century there were devastating Pecheneg raids on Byzantine territory. The court at Constantinople, however, was by then well enough experienced with steppe affairs to know that the best way to fight fire was with fire. Early in the twelfth century, therefore, the Byzantines formed an alliance with a rival steppe group, the Cumans, and the combined forces inflicted a decisive defeat on the Pechenegs. In the ensuing general massacre, men, women and children were killed by the victorious Byzantines and survivors sold into slavery (ample evidence that while so much of the eruption of steppe nomads was characterised by violence, they by no means held the monopoly). After this they disappear as a distinct unit, merging with the other peoples of the steppe.

The Cumans are known under three distinct names in our sources: Qipchak in Muslim sources, Polovtsi to the Russians, and Cumans to the Byzantines (although there is some suggestion that the Qipchak and Cumans/Polovtsi were initially distinct).[76] Like other steppe people at this time they were Turk – Qipchak is their indigenous name – and, again like so many others, were first disrupted and deflected westwards with the collapse of the Turk Khaganate. Their original homeland was probably the Irtysh-Tobol forest zone, and they entered the Dnieper region in the mid-eleventh century. The Cumans ranged over a very wide area on the steppe, from Kazakhstan and the Urals in the east to the Dniester-Dnieper basin in the west. Their leaders were known as *khans*, and while remaining a loose agglomeration of tribes without political institutions, they brought some unity to the steppe. By 1070 they vied with the Pechenegs as the main tribal group on the western steppe. From the twelfth century onwards, Russian expansion onto the steppe was increasingly at Cuman expense, forcing many to seek employment in the Georgian kingdom (King David the Builder employed some forty thousand Cuman auxiliaries).[77] Their steppe supremacy was eventually brought to an end by an even greater steppe force when the Mongols defeated them in the thirteenth century. After the Mongol invasions some Cumans fled westwards into Hungary, where many in the northern mountains still count themselves as their descendants.[78] The remaining Cumans were eventually incorporated into the Golden Horde (whose 'official' name was in fact the Qipchak Khanate), but elements probably survived in the Cossacks of later history: in the constant 'kaleidiscope of dissolving and reforming tribal unions'[79] that has characterised the steppe throughout, they simply merged with the newcomers. Today, the very distinctive stone figures which marked their burials are a feature of museums throughout the region (Figure 6.41). Florin Curta singles the Cumans out as follows:

> Of all groups of 'nomads' considered in this chapter, the Cumans had the greatest influence on the history not only of Eastern Europe, but of the medi-

eval world in general. They gave a king to Hungary (Ladislas IV 'the Cuman'), an emperor (tsar) to Bulgaria (George Terter, 1280–1292), and one of the most famous sultans to the Mamluk dynasty (Baybars, 1260–1277).[80]

And again as with many other steppe people, the allure of the Cumans has been an irresistible draw in a search for identity. The eleventh-century campaign of the Kievan Prince Igor Sviatislav against the Polovtsi (as the Russians knew them) figures highly in the Russian popular imagination as one of their nation-forming myths. It is recorded in the twelfth-century epic *Lay of Igor's Army*, similar for Russian sentiment as the *Chanson de Roland* is for the French. Alexander Borodin's opera based upon this, *Prince Igor*, first performed in 1890, remains one of the most popular in the Russian repertoire, and the 'Polovtsian Dances' taken from the opera is a familiar piece in the orchestral repertoire. Borodin's *Prince Igor* is essentially a celebration of the Russian steppe roots, where the Polovtsi are portrayed sympathetically as a part of Russian heritage. And the similarity with the *Chanson de Roland* goes further: both are based upon similarly distorted – and ultimately insignificant – events: Igor actually fought alongside the Polovtsi against fellow Russian contenders (recalling to mind similar myths about El Cid and the Moors) and his son ended up marrying the daughter of the Polovtsian khan. There is even some suggestion that the *Lay of Igor's Army* is a nineteenth-century fake.[81]

* * *

Hyun Jin Kim views many of the emerging new kingdoms of Europe at the beginning of the Middle Ages as derived from steppe institutions that came in with the various nomad invasions of late antiquity: 'the political and cultural traditions of Inner Asia brought to Europe by Central Asian immigrants, the Huns and the Alans, were just as fundamental to the formation of western Europe as the rich legacy left behind by the Roman Empire. The political and cultural landscape of early medieval Europe was shaped by the fusion of Roman and Inner Asian influences.' Kim even views such states as France, Denmark, Moravia, Poland and Bohemia as born of this fusion, which is perhaps over-interpreting the steppe inheritance.[82] Similar, albeit less extreme, sentiments are expressed by Peter Heather.[83] The steppe origins of Bulgaria and Hungary at least are beyond doubt. The influence of the steppe on Russia and Russian identity is reviewed in later chapters. But the role of the steppe peoples in the formation of national identities is crucial. In the long evolution of the idea of the nation state, from their beginnings in late-antique Europe to their emergence in the nineteenth century, we must look east as well as west.

CHAPTER 10

THE ATLANTIS OF THE STEPPE
The Khazar Empire and its Legacy

> For in the lands of Gog and Magog, who are a Hunnish race and call them-
> selves Gari [Khazars], there is one tribe, a very belligerent one . . . and all of
> them profess the Jewish faith
> – Druthmar of Aquitaine, 864[1]

> Beyond the Caspian Sea is a large region called Khazar, a grim, forbidding
> place full of herd animals, honey and Jews.
> – Muqaddasī, 985–90[2]

The existence of a Judaic empire on the eastern fringes of Europe in the Middle Ages passes almost unnoticed in much of mainstream European history; its existence even comes as a surprise to many Jews. The title of this chapter is adapted from the term coined for the Khazar state by the controversial historian Lev Gumilev, who died in 1992.[3] Gumilev was one of the pioneers in Russia of Inner Asian history. He was an associate of the archaeologist Mikhail Artamonov, who excavated Sarkel, a major centre of the Khazar state, but Gumilev has himself been accused of anti-Semitism. He is also regarded, wrongly or rightly, as one of the fathers of the controversial movement in Russia known as 'Neo-Eurasianism' (explored more in Chapter 13). His life certainly reflects much of Russia's tempestuous twentieth-century history. He was the son of the poet Anna Akhmatova, herself conscious of Tatar roots ('Akhmat' is the Russian version of Ahmad), and spent much of his life in gulags until Stalin's death. As we shall see, Khazar studies are a can of worms for many Russians, Jews and others. Gumilev's Atlantis of the steppe is indeed the ultimate archaeological hot potato.

Both the name and the person who coined it therefore in many ways reflect some of the controversies and ambiguities surrounding perceptions of the Khazars. Despite the Khazars being regarded as 'one of the greatest colossi of medieval Eurasia' by Peter Golden,[4] knowledge of them and their empire has largely sunk without trace in the popular imagination in Europe. Indeed, its main excavated site, Sarkel, has quite literally sunk underneath the vast artificial inland sea constructed in late 1940s between the Volga and Don Rivers, one of Stalin's most grandiose landscape-changing projects (Figure 10.1). Even without the inland sea, it

Figure 10.1 *New excavations overlooking the flooded site of Sarkel*

must be admitted that the material remains of the Khazars are unsubstantial: they have left fewer visible traces on the landscape or archaeological record than many of the other steppe nations reviewed here, and the lack of archaeological excavation (not to mention excavations that remain unpublished) has been highlighted as one of the problems of Khazar studies.[5] Although they are sunk beneath an inland sea their name survives ironically in the largest inland sea in the world, the 'Sea of the Khazars' or Caspian Sea, from which the name derives.[6] The very location of their main capital of Itil on the Volga delta was unknown until a few years ago (indeed, its identification is still questioned). The fact that the Khazars adopted Judaism has contributed to the ambivalence with which they have been viewed, not least in the anti-Semitic climate of the last years of Stalinism when the excavations of Khazar Sarkel were carried out.

Origin of the Khazars: Cossack or Caesar?

The Khazar Empire covered the region of the southern Russian steppe north of the Caucasus between the Black and Caspian Seas between the seventh and tenth centuries (Map 10.1). Initially centred in Daghestan to the west of the Caspian, at its greatest extent it incorporated Crimea and stretched westwards as far as the Dnieper and north-eastwards as far as the southern Urals. The Khazar state lasted three hundred years, one of

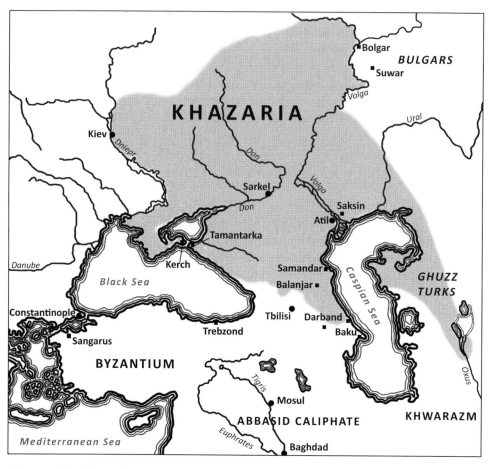

Map 10.1 *The Khazar Empire*

the longest-lasting of the steppe states. It was known for religious tolerance and for its formidable professional army.

Their origins are uncertain.[7] The Khazars were a Turk tribe, part of the great Turk migrations of the fifth and sixth centuries that moved west-wards from the northern Chinese borderlands after the Xiongnu collapse at the end of the first century. The name *Khazar* or *Qazar* derives from the Turk root *qaz*, 'to roam'. It is also at the root of the name *Kazakh* or *Qazaq* and ultimately Cossack. Interestingly, some post-independence Kazakh nationalists have tried to trace the ancestry of the Kazakh Turks to the Khazars.[8] An alternative derivation has been postulated from the Persian and Arabic *qaysar*, 'Caesar'.[9] They first appear in western sources as one of the many tribes that that made up the Hun confederation of the first half of the fifth century. This has led some to regard the Khazars as a revival of the Hun 'empire'.[10] While the Khazars doubtless incorporated remnants of the Huns, their Turk origins and identity are not seriously in doubt. At this time they still seem to have been semi-nomadic, like most of the Turk tribes, living in the felt-covered round tents or yurts that still characterise many of the steppe nomads today.

With the collapse of the Hun supremacy the Khazars formed a part – at least nominally – of the vast but amorphous Western Turk Empire in the sixth century. But the Western Turk Empire was centred further to the east, and was in any case too loose a confederation and too polyglot for strong central rule. The Khazars, therefore, ruled virtually independently, especially after about 630 when the Khazar rulers even assumed the Turk royal title of Khagan; the first rulers, who belonged to the Ashina royal clan of the Turks, might have been related to Tong Yabgu Khagan, the greatest of the Western Turk rulers.[11] In these early days it would be a mistake to think of the Khazars as a distinct 'people'. The Khazars were more an amalgam of different tribes, dominated by a Turk elite but also incorporating different Oghur, Bulgar, Hun, Iranian, Finno-Ugric and Slav peoples.

At this time the Khazars formed a powerful third force between the opposing powers that dominated the stage, the Byzantine Empire in the West and the Sasanian Empire in the East. They were powerful enough for the Sasanian emperor Khusrau Anushirvan in the latter sixth century to rank them diplomatically equal to the Byzantine and Chinese Empires. In the early seventh century both Byzantium and Persia courted the Khazars in their increasingly costly wars against each other. In 626, for example, the Emperor Heraclius negotiated with the Khazars to come to the aid of his embattled empire brought almost to its knees by the war with Persia, betrothing his daughter Eudocia to the Khagan in order to cement the alliance.

After Constantinople lost its Near Eastern possessions to the new power of the Muslim Arabs under the Umayyad Caliphate there were some Umayyad efforts at expansion into Khazar territory through the Caucasian passes, but despite destruction of the Khazar capital of Balanjar on one occasion, there were no long-term gains. The greatly reduced power of Byzantium enabled the Khazar state to expand further into the Empire's northern marches. A coalition of Khazars and Magyars defeated the Bulgars in about 670, enabling the Khazars to expand further through-out the Pontic steppe and into Crimea. As a consequence the Magyars moved into former Bulgar territory between the Dnieper and the lower Danube, where they were made the defenders of the western marches of the Khazar state. The Magyars and Khazars maintained close relations through the eighth and ninth centuries.[12]

With much of their former empire lost, Byzantine relations with the growing Khazar state tended to be diplomatic: they did not have the strength to challenge either the Caliphate or the Khaganate. The deeply unpopular Emperor Justinian II ('Rhinotmetus'), after losing his throne (and his nose) in 695, sought exile in Khazar territory at Chersonesus in Crimea. He was able to regain his throne in 705 with the support of a Khazar-backed coup (and a silver nose). Constantine V in 732 saw the Khazar alliance as so important that he married a Khazar princess – the first such foreign diplomatic marriage by an emperor in Byzantine history – with his half-Khazar son eventually being known as Emperor Leo IV 'the Khazar'. Byzantine diplomatic efforts continued to court the Khazars well into the ninth century: the Khazar stronghold of Sarkel on the Don, for example, was constructed in 840–1 with Byzantine money, expertise and possibly even labour. In return, the Khazars ceded Chersonesus and adjacent parts of Crimea to Constantinople. There is little counterpart in Byzantine history for such a close relationship with a distant power – one, moreover, that was non-Christian.[13]

After 750 the Caliphate had moved to Baghdad under the Abbasid dynasty and incursions against the Khazars through the Caucasus ceased. The Western Turk Empire also collapsed in the eighth century, making Khazar independence real rather than nominal. With the power of Byzantium reduced considerably, the Khazar Khaganate became a major buffer against Muslim incursions into eastern Europe via the steppes, but the Abbasids generally sought accommodation rather than expansion.[14]

Conversion to Judaism

The Khazars had thus become a powerful buffer between the Muslim Caliphate and Christian Byzantium, with both sides vying for influence. This resulted in the Khazars playing both off against each other and in about 740 choosing a middle way: Khagan Bulan took the almost unprecedented step of converting to Judaism.* There were several reasons for this. Surrounded as Khazaria was by two of the great monotheistic powers, it appeared that monotheism was a major tool in consolidation of a powerful monolithic state: both the Roman Emperor in Constantinople and the Caliph in Baghdad wielded enormous power. However, since both the Emperor and the Caliph combined secular and religious leadership, adopting either Christianity or Islam would inevitably mean submission to one or the other power. Judaism, with no great Caesaro-Papist-Caliphal figure to command obeisance, offered a credible third way. Other conversions in Inner Eurasia had also set a precedent for the Khazars: the conversion

---

* The only previous instance of state conversion to Judaism by a Gentile people was the conversion by the Yemeni prince Dhu Raydan and his Himyarite tribe in the fourth century AD.

of the Uighur Turks to Manichaeism in the seventh century, for example, or the Islamisation of the Volga Bulgars.[15]

In addition, there was probably a Judaic lobby at the Khazar court in the eighth century. This would have come from two directions. From the sixth century there was intermittent persecution of Jews by the Byzantines, resulting in them fleeing the Empire. Many sought protection in the various Muslim courts, particularly Cordoba and Baghdad (Islam had little tradition of Jewish persecution), but many too found refuge with the Khazars. Many other Jews would also have found their way to Khazaria from the area of the former Persian Empire after its collapse from the Arab invasions. The Persian Empire had had a large Jewish minority, descendants of those who had originally been exiled by Nebuchadnezzar and had dispersed throughout the Persian Empire. Particularly strong pockets of Judaism remained in Central Asia, Azerbaijan and Daghestan, where there was a prominent Jewish community, all areas that came under Khazar influence. The Jews of Azerbaijan were presumably remnants of the heavily Judaicised state of Adiabene, a Parthian client kingdom. By 837/8 the Khazar state was issuing imitation Abbasid dirhems but with a variation of the standard Islamic confession of faith: 'There is no god but God and Moses is his messenger.'[16]

Of course, to describe the Khazar Empire as a 'Jewish state' on the modern Israeli or even ancient Judaean model is to overstate the evidence.* Even the above account of the Judaisation of the Khazars is based almost solely on modern speculation: in fact there is no evidence for why the Khazar elite converted, or how many did (and much remains controversial). In the tenth century the Arab historian Mas'udi describes all the Khazars as Jewish, who converted at the time of Harun al-Rashid, their numbers swollen by Jews fleeing Byzantine persecution, particularly under Romanus I who enforced Jewish conversion to Christianity. The Khazar army, however, Mas'udi describes as being mainly Muslim, including the commander-in-chief (and one recalls that Seljuk, the eponymous founder of the Seljuk dynasty, was originally a Khazar commander). He also recounts how the Khazar capital of Itil had seven judges: two each for Jews, Muslims and Christians, and one for pagans (Vikings and Slavs). Ibn Rusta, also in the tenth century, describes the dual leadership of the Khazars as comprising the Khagan, with largely symbolic powers, and a grand vizier with executive powers who was also the army commander (and presumably Jewish), a system that was usual in the Turk steppe empires that probably goes back to the Xiongnu. The Khazar elite he describes as all Jewish and semi-nomadic, taking to the pastures in the

---

* 'Judaic' is probably a more appropriate term than 'Jewish', which is often used to describe the Khazar state, as 'Jewish' implies ethnicity whereas 'Judaic' relates solely to religion.

summer. The Muslims in Khazaria, however, were wholly urban. The two greatest kings were Bulan, who adopted Judaism in the first place in the eighth century, and Ubadiah in the ninth century. It would be a mistake, however, to imagine the Khazar conversion to be either sudden or universal. Conversion was gradual and took place in stages. State Judaism was never enforced: the Khazars were noted for their tolerance of other religions, and large communities of Christians, Muslims and even pagans were widely tolerated by the rulers and coexisted in the kingdom.[17]

Peter Golden notes that all steppe conversions were to one of the 'universal' religions: Judaism (the Khazars), Christianity (the Russians), Manichaeism (the Uighurs), Islam (the Turks, Tatars) or Buddhism (the Mongols). 'Eurasian nomads . . . did not create any of the great world religions'[18] (although Zoroastrianism might be viewed as an exception here).

A route paved with silver

In 965, an Arab traveller in western Europe, Ibn Ya'qūb, records his astonishment in finding Samanid silver dirhems of 913 and 914 from Bukhara in circulation in the markets of Mainz. He even encountered Arab traders as far north as Schleswig, and also reported hoards of dirhems minted in Baghdad, Cairo, Damascus, Isfahan and Tashkent coming into Sweden.[19] Such coin hoards have been found as far north as Bodø inside the Arctic Circle in Norway (Figure 9.6).[20]

The reason was the flourishing Arctic and sub-Arctic trade in luxury goods between the late eighth and the tenth centuries with Abbasid Baghdad. Between one hundred and two hundred million silver dirhems were exported to Russia and the Baltic, all of which passed through the Khazar and Volga Bulgar states, eventually to find their way into western Europe. The trade brought furs, amber, feathers, walrus ivory, whale bone, honey, wax and slaves to Baghdad in exchange for Abbasid silver. The Caliphate at the time was at the height of its power, and Baghdad was one of the wealthiest cities of the world, made wealthy by the huge trade that poured into it, mainly from the Indian Ocean: Baghdad lay at the centre of – and largely controlled – a world trade system. The Abbasid economy as a consequence was extremely strong. The early Abbasid gold dinars were of exceptionally high quality, usually 96–8 per cent pure, and both these and its silver dirhems were depended upon for their purity, accuracy and weight. Large numbers were in circulation, and this led to low inflation and low interest rates. For example, interest was usually 20 per cent in wealthy western European towns, but as low as 4 per cent in the Near East.[21]

This trade was made possible by the stability of the Khazar Khaganate, as well as that of the Volga Bulgar state to its north, controlling the routes between Baghdad and the northern sources of luxury goods that the Caliphate demanded. It was to have enormous consequences. In a now famous thesis, *Mohammed and Charlemagne* published in the 1920s, Henri Pirenne related the rise and fall of the 'Carolingian renaissance', viewed as the 'scaffolding of the Middle Ages', directly to the Abbasid Caliphate in Baghdad.[22] It was the flow of Abbasid silver dirhems pouring into Russia and Scandinavia and eventually into western Europe that underpinned the Carolingian renaissance. After the ninth century the Abbasid state began to decline, leading to the drying up of the flow of silver to the north-west.[23] The eventual collapse of the Abbasids contributed to a general collapse: the Khazar state in southern Russia, the collapse of the Carolingian renaissance, and economic recession in Europe. There was a revival of the trade in silver after about 900, mainly from the Samanid lands of Central Asia. This was too late to save the Carolingian dynasty, but it did enable the Khazar Empire to continue into the eleventh and twelfth centuries. In examining the archaeological evidence to test Pirenne's thesis, Richard Hodges and David Whitehouse concluded that 'without Mohammed, Charlemagne would indeed have been inconceivable'.[24]

The trade established by the 'Pax Khazarica' (or 'Pax Nomadica' as Nicola Di Cosmo refers to such steppe empires more generally)[25] also drew a Nordic people into the heart of western Eurasia when the Vikings followed the great Russian river systems southwards to the Caspian and Black Seas. This movement was to culminate at the end of the ninth century with the foundation of the state that would eventually replace the Khazars, the Kievan Rus state, by the Vikings. In providing the stability that made possible its own wealth as well as the wealth of western Europe, the Khazars were also unwittingly sowing the seeds for its decline.

The Khazar Khaganate remained a powerful force in Central Asian and south-eastern European power politics for several centuries, particularly in maintaining the balance between Christian Byzantium, the Muslim states of Iran and Central Asia, and the various pagan tribes and states of Russia. Indeed, in the tenth century the Jewish envoy from far-off Umayyad Andalusia, Hasday Ibn Shaprut, even attempted to make formal contacts with the Khazar state.[26] The decline began in the 950s and 970s with the decline of Abbasid Baghdad and the consequent drying up of the supply of Muslim silver to the north, exacerbated in the middle of the eleventh century by the adoption of Byzantine Christianity by Vladimir of the infant Russian state. Byzantium naturally turned more to Orthodox Kievan Rus as an ally against the nomadic tribes of the southern Russian steppe at the expense of the Judaic Khazars. The Khazars in turn came under more and more pressure from these nomadic states, especially the Oghuz Turks to the east (out of whom the Seljuks were soon to emerge), as well as the Pechenegs, who inflicted a defeat on the Khazars in the tenth century, becoming reduced in both power and size.

The Khazar capital of Itil on the Volga delta was sacked in 965 by the Rus in a river-borne operation. In about 985 the commander of the Khazar army, Seljuk, the son of a high-ranking Oghuz official at the Khazar court and eponymous founder of a new dynasty, led a revolt with his Oghuz followers and escaped with a small group of a hundred followers eastwards to Jand on the lower Syr Darya river just east of the Aral Sea. There is some suggestion that Seljuk's family were – at least at first – Jewish: his sons were Mika'il, Isra'il and Musa (Michael, Israel and Moses), names which, while not unknown as Muslim names, are at least suggestive. The Khazar connection is questioned by some authorities, but there otherwise seems no reason to invent it in the traditional histories of Seljuk origins, so it is probably true, even if Seljuk himself was not Jewish.[27]

In 1036 the rump Khazar state was defeated by a combined Byzantine and Kievan attack. At the end of the eleventh century the Pechenegs in turn were driven out by the Cumans and the remaining Khazars were eventually absorbed into the Golden Horde in the middle of the thirteenth century.

The cities of Khazaria

The Khazars ruled from a number of cities. The first capital was Balanjar in Daghestan, but after it was destroyed by an Arab army in the eighth century it was moved to the more defensible site of Samandar a short distance to the north (The location of both is still uncertain.)[28] The main Khazar city, however, seemed (at least according to the sources) to have been at Itil or Atil in the Volga delta south of Astrakhan (which itself became a Tatar capital in the Middle Ages; in fact 'Itil' was the medieval name for the Volga River). Another important centre was the fortress of Sarkel on the Don. The construction of Sarkel with Byzantine aid in the early ninth century was possibly a part of joint Byzantine–Khazar effort to construct a line of fortifications between the Volga and the Don to defend Byzantium against raids from the north.[29] The name *sar-kel* means 'white fortress', perhaps because of the limestone used in its construction. Its Russian name, Belaya Vezha, means the same. As well as a major fortification, Sarkel was a major commercial centre with a polyglot population. Massive rescue excavations were carried out there in the 1930s and 1940s by Mikhail Artamonov (who became the Director of the Hermitage), the largest excavations ever undertaken in the Soviet period. This was in advance of its flooding by the Tsimlyansk Reservoir, a vast 'inland sea' that forms a part of the Volga–Don Canal system. Pottery kilns, industrial areas, trading areas and residential quarters were traced, and trade objects from all over Russia as well as the Byzantine and Abbasid Empires were recovered. The site has since been submerged under the reservoir, although excavations have recently been carried out at the site of a possible large residence overlooking the site (Figures 10.1 and 10.2).

The main Khazar city of Itil has only recently been located at Samosdelka on the Volga delta, below the later Tatar capital (and subsequent Russian city) of Astrakhan. Less is known about this city, therefore – indeed, the identification of Samosdelka with Itil is still questioned – but ongoing excavations at the site will provide more information.[30] However, what is lacking in material remains at Itil is compensated by more historical sources. Ibn Fadlan visited Itil in the

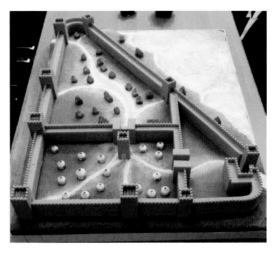

Figure 10.2 *Model of the fortress of Sarkel in Astrakhan University*

tenth century and describes it and the Khazars in detail. The Khazars themselves he describes as 'all Jews', but large numbers of both Muslims and Christians lived under them. The Muslims in Itil had their own quarter and lived under their own laws. Ibn Fadlan recorded an incident of how on one occasion when a synagogue was destroyed, the Khazar Khagan ordered the minaret of the main Itil mosque to be destroyed as a punishment, but with the remark that if it was not for the fact that all synagogues in Muslim lands would be burnt in retaliation, he would have had the whole mosque destroyed. Mas'udi describes Itil as a mixed population of Muslims, Christians, Jews and pagans, and the *Hudūd al-ʿĀlam* mentions seven different self-governing creeds ruled by their own governors.[31] Khazar religious tolerance was guided by pragmatism.

Another important Khazar centre that is reasonably well-documented is Tamatarkha, Russian Tmutarakan, on the Taman Peninsula overlooking the Black Sea. This was built on the site of the ancient Greek colony of Hermonassa. It functioned in the Middle Ages mainly as a commercial city, probably the main port servicing the Khazar Empire and its outlet to the Byzantine Empire. Sources refer to it as having a mixed population of Greeks, Armenians, Russians, Jews, Ossetians, Lezgians, Georgians and Circassians in common with the polyglot nature of the Khazar state, but with a Jewish majority. This is borne out by the very large number of Jewish gravestones that have been recovered from the site (Figures 10.3 and 10.4). Indeed, Tamatarkha might have been a centre of Judaism, as envoys of Prince Vladimir I of Kiev visited 'our lord David, the Khazar prince' there in 985–6 to consult on religious matters. In the end, Vladimir chose Byzantine Orthodoxy, instead of Khazar Judaism. Thus, the subsequent religion of Russia, which might well have been Jewish,

Figure 10.3 *Khazar Jewish gravestones in the Hermonassa Museum*

Figure 10.4 *Khazar warrior relief from Hermonassa*

came to be Christian. 'What is still not adequately appreciated is the extent to which the earliest Rus' state was oriented towards the Khazars and Baghdad rather than towards Byzantium and the Christian world', as David Christian emphasises.[32]

Other Khazar groups reasserted their control in Crimea, which had been under intermittent Khazar rule since the beginning, combining with older Jewish communities in Crimea since before the rise of the Khazars. The Crimean Jews, the Karaim, although now only a tiny minority, are the only Jewish community left that still speak the Khazar language, a dialect of Turkish although the language is almost extinct (Figure 10.5).[33] There was even a form of 'Neo-Khazar' state under Jewish princes on the eastern shores of the Straits of Kerch who ruled under the Genoese in the fifteenth century and later under the Crimean Tatars. Other enclaves survived in the mountainous regions of the Caucasus and southern Crimea, such as the fortress of Chufut Kale (which means 'Jewish fortress') near the Crimean Tatar capital of Bahchyserai (Figure 10.6). The Jewish identity of the Karaim religion is disputed by many orthodox Jews.

Figure 10.5 *The nineteenth-century Karaim* kenassa *or meeting house in Yevpatoria in Crimea*

Figure 10.6 *A seventeenth- or eighteenth-century Karaim* kenassa *at Chufut Kale ('Jewish Castle') in Crimea*

In the campaign of Prince Vytautas of Lithuania in 1397–8 against Toqtamish Khan of the Golden Horde, Karaim Jewish communities were transported from Crimea and settled in Lithuania between Vilnius and Minsk, and the Lithuanian Karaim still speak the Qipchak dialect of Turkish.[34]

Cans of worms and the Khazar legacy

In 1883 the French orientalist and scholar Ernst Renan was the first to propose the theory that east European Jews were descended from the Khazars.[35] But it was the prominent Hungarian-British novelist Arthur Koestler, the son of Jewish parents, who gave the idea more publicity. Koestler argued, in a famously controversial book, *The Thirteenth Tribe* published in 1976, that European Jews were descended from the Khazars rather than the Jewish diaspora from Palestine. From the time of its decline, groups of Khazars began to migrate westwards from the increasing instability of the steppes into eastern and central Europe. After the thirteenth century Jews emerge as an important element in Poland. It has been estimated that 20 per cent of the population of the Poland-Lithuania Commonwealth in 1520 were Jewish.[36] These descendants of the Khazars, argued Koestler, become the ancestors of the Jewish communities there of modern times. It is these Jews who are known as the 'Ashkenaz', a name which means 'Scythian', people from the steppes, such as the Khazars. Hence, the Ashkenazi Jews of Europe, North America and Israel, argued Koestler, are descendants of Khazar Turks.

Whether the suggestion that the majority of European Jews at the time of the Second World War were of Turk origin rather than 'Semitic' might have prevented the Nazi genocide we will now never know (although one suspects that Koestler's argument would not have cut much ice with the SS). But the implication that the original Ashkenazi homeland was the Russian steppe rather than Palestine is certainly a controversial one among Jewish communities – and Zionism – today. An 'International Khazar Colloquium' held in Jerusalem in 1999 and subsequently published as *The World of the Khazars* in 2007 claimed to bring together the current state of knowledge of the Khazars and all related issues.[37] The claim is probably justified: it is certainly an admirable overview of most aspects of Khazar studies. However, Koestler's suggestion that the Jews of eastern Europe are descendants of the Khazars was largely sidestepped, apart from the occasional reference to Koestler's 'populist' book, even though many other contemporary issues are discussed. One Khazar scholar, Boris Zhivkov, even claims that 'the Khazars have disappeared completely and left no ethnic group or nation which could be identified with them'.[38] However, an Israeli scholar, A. N. Poliak, views eastern European Jewry as originating in the Khazars, with the Yiddish language stemming from Crimean Gothic, with an analysis of Yiddish confirming a Khazar component. There is also the provocative, albeit controversial, suggestion by Omeljian Pritsak that the common Jewish surname 'Cohen' derives from Khazar shamans who adopted Judaism but retained their priestly status.[39] Regardless of whether the ancestors of the Ashkenazim were Turks, a mitochondrial DNA study has shown that 'the great majority of Ashkenazi maternal lineages were not brought from the Levant, as commonly supposed, nor recruited in the Caucasus, as sometimes suggested, but assimilated within Europe'.[40]

Of course, the ancestors of a 'Turk' can also be European, as noted in Chapter 8; 'Khazars' might be Turk, Sarmatian, Slav or one of many other ethnicities, as noted above; DNA studies are still in their infancy and do not necessarily provide glib answers (at least in the admittedly ignorant opinion of the present author); and 'Jewishness' is probably largely a question of self-identity. What is more important here is how the Khazar legacy and the 'Koestler thesis' has been perceived and the effects that it has, and here we enter more controversial – and occasionally dangerous – territory.

Peter Golden comments upon the ambivalence of Khazar studies in Russia: the reluctance to recognise a steppe legacy compounded with that of a Judaic one.[41] At one time the 'Khazar yoke' was even denounced as worse for Russia than the so-called 'Tatar yoke'. Viktor Shnirelman, for example, warns of how modern extreme Russian nationalism has exploited a 'Khazar yoke' as a 'Jewish occupation regime' of the early Slav lands, seeing it as a part of the perennial 'Jewish plot' for world supremacy. Shnirelman continues, 'To put it briefly, the Russian Orthodox nationalists associate Khazaria's image with a spiritual enslaving of Rus' and a struggle against Christian statehood. This is treated as an aspect of a general permanent struggle of Judaism against Christianity.'[42] It assumes a direct connection between the Khazar state and the Bolshevik Revolution, viewed by extremists as created and dominated by Jews, and that Russia was run by ethnic non-Russians from 1917 to 1953: Kalmyks (such as Lenin), Jews (Trotsky), Georgians (Stalin, Beria) and so forth.

The identification of the Khazars with the Turks – hence 'Tatars' – has also been seized upon by extremists in Russia to combine stock images of the 'terrible Turk' with anti-Jewish prejudice: part of an ongoing 'Jewish plot' since medieval times to dominate Russia, a 'Khazar yoke' before the 'Tatar yoke'. Taking advantage of the paucity of sources for the Khazars, a mixed bag of extremists – Neo-Eurasianists, Russian Orthodox nationalists, Neo-pagans and anti-Semites – have interpreted the Khazar state as a 'Jewish plot' created to kill off the infant Kievan state still-born, an attempt at the 'Khazar enslavement of the Slavs'. The 'Khazar yoke' has in turn been linked to twentieth-century Communism because of the rule over Slavs by foreigners: Lenin was a Kalmyk, Stalin a Georgian, and many leading Bolsheviks were Jewish. It has even been discovered that the Khazars used a term that could be translated as 'comrade', thus establishing a direct link between the eighth and the twentieth centuries, a universal 'Jewish plot' for 'world domination', with the Russian people central to the struggle against Jewish enslavement; the Ashkenazi Jews are viewed as the direct descendants of the Khazars and the 1917 Bolshevik Revolution a direct result of the Khazars.[43]

Such farragos of nonsense should, of course, be treated with the contempt they deserve. But such polemics are also dangerous, and twentieth-century European history has unfortunately taught us that extremists cannot simply be ignored. Doubtless Arthur Koestler never intended that his theory would unleash such extremist views. It does, at least, demonstrate to us the power that an obscure medieval steppe empire can still exert from beyond the grave. We ignore it at our peril.

Perhaps it is better to end with a positive view of the Khazars taken by Orthodox Christians. In Orthodox Greece at Christmas time, children do not receive their presents from Santa Claus bringing them from the North Pole, but from St Basil who brings them from Khazaria.[44]

CHAPTER 11

THE 'MEN FROM HELL'

Setting the West Ablaze:
The Mongols in Europe

[In the year 1224], for our sins, unknown tribes came, whom no one exactly knows, who they are, nor whence they came out, nor what their language is, nor what race they are, nor what their faith is; but they call them the men from hell.
– *Chronicle of Novgorod 1076–1471*

There are shades of barbarism in twentieth-century Europe which would once have amazed the most barbarous of barbarians. At a time when the instruments of constructive change had outstripped anything previously known, Europeans acquiesced in a string of conflicts which destroyed more human beings than all past convulsions put together. The two World Wars of 1914–18 and 1939–45, in particular, were destructive beyond measure.
– Norman Davies 1996[1]

Both quotations above represent near-contemporary accounts of events in living memory so horrific as to be barely comprehensible. The first, from the twelfth-century Russian *Chronicle of Novgorod*, refers to the initial raid upon Russia by a people known as the 'Tartars', which was thought to derive from the Greek *tartarus*, 'hell'. So savage was their onslaught that medieval Europe thought of the Mongols as not really human: a punishment by God for mankind's sins, a visitation from Hell itself. Hence, they were known incorrectly as 'Tartars' ever since Louis IX of France punned on their name in the thirteenth century (as reported by Matthew Paris),[2] and their name has been used since for anything from the ill-defined geographical designation of Tartary to a French uncooked steak and a term of semi-endearing admonition given by mothers to their naughty children.* The correct term was actually *Tatar*, and they were just one of many contingents in the Mongol army. The Tatars were initially the most powerful of the Mongol tribes before the rise of Genghis Khan – indeed, they were the hereditary enemies of Genghis's own tribe. After his rise, Genghis Khan virtually annihilated the Tatars, and it is an irony that

---

* As in 'you little tartar'. Steak tartare is from the French form of Tartar; 'tart', either as a noun (as in prostitute) or an adjective (as in a sharp taste), and its related words are of unknown origin according to the *Oxford English Dictionary*.

out of all tribes it is the Tatar name that stuck, to be eventually applied to the Mongols[3] – in much the same way that the term 'Frank' (from French) is applied to all Europeans by many Middle Eastern peoples. It is a further irony that the present-day Tatars of Tatarstan in Russia are more likely descended from the Bulgars than from the Mongols. But men from Hell indeed the Tatars seemed, and it was the term 'Tartar' which stuck.

The second quotation has been taken almost at random from the many contemporary histories of the twentieth century, an 'age of catastrophe' according to one of its most prominent historians. Both offer a contrasting view of violence – and a different perspective.

An 'Age of Catastrophe'

Now, well into the twenty-first century, one can attempt a more dispassionate view of the twentieth. Accordingly, the turn of the millennium inspired many retrospectives: books, television programmes and a whole range of articles, both specialist and popular, good and bad, all offering new interpretations of the century just finished.

Histories of and commentaries on the twentieth century routinely describe it as the most violent and destructive in history – Norman Davies' remarks above are typical. Few historians would deny this. A long ago as 1974, A. J. P. Taylor in his own twentieth-century history, *From Sarajevo to Potsdam*, succinctly entitled his chapter headings 'Pre-war', 'War', 'Post-war', 'Pre-war', 'War', 'Post-war'. Eric Hobsbawm prefaces his twentieth-century history *The Age of Extremes* with twelve views by prominent people, with Isaiah Berlin's 'the most terrible century in Western history' or William Golding's 'the most violent century in human history' being fairly typical. Hobsbawm's subtitle, 'The Age of Catastrophe', for the period 1914–45, is also echoed by the titles of other books on the twentieth century, such as *The War of the World: History's Age of Hatred* by Niall Ferguson or *Dark Continent: Europe's Twentieth Century* by Mark Mazower, to take two examples more or less at random. Even a work as sober and objective as the 1960 edition of the *New Cambridge Modern History* entitled its twentieth-century volume *The Era of Violence* – with emphasis on the definite article, as if, while history was littered with many 'eras of violence', the twentieth century was the definitive one. J. M. Roberts, in *A History of Europe*, describes the First World War as 'the bloodiest, most intensely fought and greatest in geographical extent to have occurred [up] to that time' and the Second as 'the bloodiest war in history'.[4]

In fact, what historians are writing merely reflects the twentieth century as being the most recently remembered and recorded in history. Other more dimly remembered centuries were as catastrophic and as full of cataclysmic upheavals: the Thirty Years' War, for example, or the Mongol invasions, or the 'barbarian' invasions at the end of antiquity, or the interminable rounds of inter-Hellenistic wars that characterised the third century BC, from which few statistics survive. Even centuries closer to our own rivalled it in carnage: approximately *seventy million* people in the Americas, for example, died as a direct or indirect result of the Spanish conquest between about 1500 and 1550, with 24 million in Mexico alone between 1500 and 1600;[5] the Taiping Rebellion in the 1850s and 1860s accounted for 40 million dead; more people in Europe died in 1918–19 from Spanish Flu than in the entire Great War;[*] more Americans died in its Civil War than in all subsequent wars that America has fought put together, including both World Wars, Korea, Vietnam, Afghanistan and Iraq. But in any case, history is not a league table of body counts.

Both the twenty-first century and a European standpoint, therefore, can distort perspective. It might even be argued that the twentieth century was one of the least destructive in history. For unlike similar eras of violence, twentieth-century wars were not followed by a dark age or general collapse, such as in Europe after the invasions at the end of antiquity. On the contrary: the late twentieth century was characterised by unprecedented wealth and an astonishing upsurge in creativity, research and advances in virtually every branch of human endeavour, with the two defeated nations, Germany and Japan, leading the way. The end of the twentieth century was dominated by issues of over-abundance: over-population, over-production, over-consumption (with its consequent global warming and environmental threats). In other words, out of the twentieth-century wars and destruction there emerged unprecedented prosperity, a golden age. One suspects that when memories fade, the twentieth century will be viewed in a somewhat different light by future historians.

The difference between the horrors of twentieth-century wars and those of the more distant past is not that the former were more devastating, but merely that they are more documented. The soldiers in the trenches in the First World War were not more anti-war than the foot soldiers of Rome; the only difference is that the former had a voice. Probably the most destructive era in history, one that puts even the twentieth century's 'era of violence' into the pale, was that of the Mongol invasions in the thirteenth century.

---

[*] Probably more than in the Black Death – it is estimated that the Spanish Flu epidemic claimed between 40 and 100 million lives worldwide, a sober perspective on the pandemic current when these words were written (2020).

Dress rehearsal: the Western Liao

The armies of Genghis Khan were not the first Mongols to penetrate west. Leaving aside speculations as to the possible Mongol identity of the Huns or Avars, immediately prior to the Mongol invasions another Mongol-related group created a steppe empire. Mongol tribes known as the Qidan or Khitan first appear in Chinese records as steppe pastoralists during the Northern Wei period (386–534). In 901, one of the Qidan chiefs, Yelu Abaoji, began uniting the Mongol tribes and extending their conquests in a manner that very much anticipated Genghis Khan some centuries later (and at least serves to emphasise that Genghis Khan was not the isolated phenomenon that history gives the impression). Yelu Abaoji established a state in northern China in 916 that was known to the Chinese as the Liao. The Liao destroyed the Later Tang Dynasty in 936, and by the late tenth century had established an empire that stretched across northern China and the steppe region from the Sea of Japan to Central Asia. Its main capital was Shanjing in Inner Mongolia, north of Chifeng, but the Liao also used subsidiary capitals at Datong and built a vast new 'Upper Capital' at Shijing. This was in the form of an immense rectangle, with an inner and outer city surrounded by rammed earth walls fourteen kilometres in perimeter that still stand up to ten metres high.[6]

The Liao Empire declined in the early twelfth century through a series of revolts and uprisings. This culminated in its total collapse in 1125, prompted by a revolt led by the Jurchens, a Tungus tribe distantly related to the Mongols. The Jurchens then assumed the Chinese dynastic name of Jin. Elements of the Khitan tribes fled westwards and settled in Semirechye (the region south of Lake Balkhash). At first, Khitan assistance had been requested by the Muslim Qarakhanid dynasty of Bukhara in their wars, but the Khitan remained and re-established themselves in the area as a new power that eventually subjected the Qarakhanids. This re-established western Mongol Qidan state was known to the Chinese as the Western Liao and known in the Muslim sources as the Qara Khitai (from which medieval Europe derived the name 'Cathay'). Their chief, Yeh-lü Ta-shi, made Balasaghun (east of modern Bishkek in Kyrgyzstan, also a Qarakhanid capital) his capital (Figure 8.9). From there he expanded his empire, largely at the expense of the Qarakhanids, occupying the Qarakhanid capital of Kashgar.

In 1141 the Qara Khitai even defeated the Seljuks under Sultan Sanjar in a battle to the north of Samarkand, and both Samarkand and Bukhara were absorbed into the Qara Khitai Empire. Stories of such a spectacular Seljuk defeat filtered westwards to the Seljuks' other enemies, the Crusader states in the Near East, prompting speculation based upon the legends of Prester John, the mythical Christian Emperor of the East who was supposedly to join the Christian powers to wipe out Islam. But the Qara Khitai were pagan and Buddhist, not Christian, and their defeat of the Seljuks did not signify any further western movement of the Qara Khitai. They remained an important power centred on Semirechye, but the paganism of the Qara Khitai rulers – not to mention their harsh tax extortions – caused bitter resentment among their Muslim subjects leading to increased unrest. This coincided with the rise of a new Muslim Central Asian power in the twelfth century, the Khwarazm Shahs centred on the lower Oxus region, who inflicted a defeat on the Qara Khitai at Taraz on the banks of Talas River in 1208. The same year, on the banks of another river, the Irtysh in Mongolia, two other Mongol tribes, the Naiman and the Merkit, were also defeated by a third Mongol power which was soon to absorb all Mongol tribes into the largest alliance in their history.

Elements of the Khitan survived further west in Europe for several centuries following the collapse of their state. Some were recorded as living among the Crimean Tatars, and their presence has even been detected as far west as Moldavia and Hungary in the thirteenth and fourteenth century. They were recorded among the Bashkirs of the middle Volga and as a tribal sub-unit of the Kalmyks to the west of the Volga as late as the seventeenth century.[7]

From 'just and resolute butcher' to 'Buddhist holy man'

The quotation from the *Chronicle of Novgorod* opening the beginning of this chapter refers to the first Mongol raid into Europe in 1222 by Sübedei, a general of Genghis Khan. The ensuing Mongol invasions are well enough known, so only need outlining here.[8] The Mongols themselves were only one of a group of related tribes in the Mongol steppe. To the north were the Naimans and to the south the Tatars, long-time bitter enemies of the Mongols. To the west were the Karaits, to the south of Lake Baikal were Merkits and to the north-east were the Oirats, ancestors of the Kalmyks. Up until the thirteenth century they had been on the fringes of history, but suddenly they entered centre stage. This was brought about by the genius of Genghis Khan, who, with a combination of shrewd strategy and extraordinary vigour, was able to unite the various, often warring, Mongol-related tribes. Genghis Khan was then able to build up a powerful steppe empire dominating the region north of the Great Wall.

The main power in Central Asia at the time was the kingdom of the Khwarazm Shahs centred on the lower Oxus. Genghis Khan's initial conquests were mainly directed towards the east, but in 1218 the Khwarazm Shahi governor of Otrar (in present-day southern Kazakhstan) had a caravan of some 450 merchants from Mongolia sent by Genghis Khan slaughtered, despite their being Muslim, and their goods confiscated. Genghis Khan sent three ambassadors to demand restitution, but the

Figure 11.1 *Idealised equestrian statue of Genghis Khan in the Inner Mongolian Museum in Hohhot*

Khwarazm Shah summarily executed the main ambassador and publicly humiliated the other two by shaving off their beards.

Such a meaningless provocation, probably prompted by nothing more than sheer arrogance and ignorance, has since baffled historians. But as a consequence, in about 1220 Genghis Khan turned his war machine westwards. Thus it was that the act of arrogance of a king unleashed the greatest holocaust that Central Asia, Western Asia and eastern Europe have ever experienced. The ensuing destruction and genocide were such that had never before – nor since – been experienced. Whole cites, whole populations, whole landscapes were simply wiped out. The great historic cities of Central Asia were especially selected for the Mongols' seemingly insatiable thirst for destruction: these cities – some of the wealthiest and most populous in the east – were reduced to dust. Many remain dust today. At Nishapur, Genghis Khan vowed to destroy the city so completely that in future only sheep would graze where the city once stood. He was as good as his word. Urgench, Bokhara, Samarkand, Balkh and Herat received similar fates, many never to recover.

Some historians have questioned the extent of Mongol ferocity and destructiveness, suggesting that such accounts are largely rhetoric and hyperbole.[9] However, the weight of contemporary evidence is strong and supported by the archaeology. Of the great cities sacked by the Mongols, only Bukhara and Urgench were rebuilt on the same site: Balkh,

Otrar and Nishapur were ruined for ever (despite some minor rebuilding at Balkh). At Merv the old city lay abandoned and a smaller new town (Abdullah Khan Kala) was founded two centuries later several kilometres to the south of the remains of the old. Samarkand was rebuilt outside the old walls while the ancient city remained as it is today, a desolate waste.

The Mongols' phenomenal success might appear baffling. After all, when compared to the great sedentary civilisations of China and the Islamic world which had centuries of hugely developed and sophisticated methods of warfare behind them, the Mongols were an undeveloped nation. David Morgan rightly remarks that 'There was no reason to suppose that armies which had defeated the best that China and the Islamic world could throw against them would meet their match in Europe'.[10] Hugh Kennedy makes the point that for all the undoubted military genius of Sübedei, Genghis Khan's main general, his main weapon was still sheer, unadulterated terror.[11] Another reason for their success was the militaristic nature that the steppe imposed upon nomad powers reviewed in Chapter 1, where in theory – and largely in practice – virtually the entire male adult population would be soldiers – and much of the female as well in support roles. But the idea that these invaders were not quite human echoes earlier descriptions of the Huns, and so extraordinarily savage was their onslaught that many felt that resistance was futile. This is illustrated by an incident in eastern Iran recounted by the historian Ibn al-Athir at the time of the events described. He writes:

> I have heard that one of them [a Mongol horseman] took a man captive but did not have a weapon to kill him with, so he said to his prisoner, 'Lay your head on the ground and do not move,' and he did so and the [Mongol] went and fetched his sword and killed him. Another man told me the following story: 'I was going with seventeen others along a road and we met a Mongol horseman who ordered us to tie up each others' arms. My companions began to do as he said but I said to them, "He is only one man, why don't we kill him and escape?" but he replied, "We are afraid." I then said, "This man intends to kill you immediately so let's kill him and perhaps God will save us." But I swear by God that not one of them dared to do this so I took a knife and slew him and we fled and escaped.' There were many such events.[12]

Whether or not the anecdote is true, it shows how the sinister reputation of the Mongols spread. It also highlights a phenomenon known from other war situations, the passivity and hopelessness which can overcome people when faced with an enemy they believe to be stronger, leading to a meek acceptance of their fate. These attitudes provide some insight into the secrets of Mongol success. Indeed, Ibn al-Athir writes of the Mongol invasions as 'a tremendous disaster such as had never happened before . . . It may well be that the world from now until its end . . . will not experience the like of it again.'[13]

Sergei Bodrov's movie *Mongol*, released in 2008, tells the story of the young Genghis Khan – and portrays as a hero one who was probably the greatest mass killer in history. Mere body counts, or course, do not bear comparison given an era of far smaller populations than our own, but contemporary accounts nonetheless make horrifying reading. Figures of 1,600,000 are given for those slaughtered at Herat and 1,747,00 at Nishapur – Juzjani puts the figure for Herat even higher at 2,400,000. Ibn al-Athir (who died in 1234), for example, writes that for some years he had been averse from mentioning the events, deeming them so horrible that he shrank from recording 'the greatest catastrophe and the most dire calamity' that had ever overtaken the world, but puts the number of those killed at Merv at 900,000. Juvani (1226–83) puts the figure higher at over 1,300,000 when he writes that a delegation 'passed thirteen days and nights in counting the people slain [in Merv] . . . taking into account only those that were plain to see and leaving aside those that had been killed in holes and cavities and in the villages and deserts'. At Nishapur, where a grandson of Genghis Khan died in the siege, all buildings were demolished, trees cut down, crops and canals destroyed, and not even the cats and dogs were left alive. Another contemporary historian refrains from giving casualty numbers for Herat, but more effectively gives the numbers of survivors – and then lists their names: less than a score.[14]

Elsewhere, Genghis Khan gave serious consideration to wiping out the entire peasant population of China so as to give the land over to grazing.* He refrained: not through clemency, but because he was persuaded of the superior merits of letting them live for tax extortion instead. According to Juzjani, Güyük gave serious consideration to either annihilating or castrating the entire Muslim population of China, Turkistan and Tangut.[15] Even without such genocide, the population of China dropped from an estimated 100 million before the Mongol invasion to 60 million by 1393.[16] Genghis Khan actually did wipe out the entire population of the Tangut Kingdom – probably the most successful case of total genocide ever recorded. Destruction in Europe, even on a massive scale such as that which happened in the Second World War, although horrific, was at least recoverable: Europe bounced back in spectacular fashion, the victims of the holocaust achieved statehood, Germany outstripped most other countries. Such destruction in Iran and Central Asia was not recoverable. For the agricultural system upon which these cities depended (mainly the delicate irrigation systems) was extremely fragile, taking many generations to build

---

* Genghis Khan's proposals were anticipated nearly a thousand years before when Shih Le, a Xiongnu leader who founded the short-lived Later Chou Dynasty (319–53), proposed clearing all of northern China of people so as to turn it into grazing land for his horses: Christian 2008: 234.

up. Many of the figures cited above have been questioned by some historians, and perhaps rightly so. But the figures themselves are not as important as the sheer horror at the scale of destruction that was felt by contemporaries, which the figures reflect. Destruction from which it would take many centuries to recover. In many cases, this never happened.[17]

Even taking exaggeration into account (and the figures would be for the city regions, not necessarily just the cities themselves) the death tolls are almost beyond belief. There is in any case probably little exaggeration: the historians cited were not mere annalists given to hyperbole and invention, but some of the great historians of the Middle Ages. In fact the higher numbers were often cited by the Mongols themselves: Hülegü, for example, pointed out in a letter to Louis IX of France that the figure for those killed in the capture of Baghdad was 2 million, not the 200,000 originally reported.[18] Other invasions of the Near East, such as the earlier Seljuk or the later Timurid invasions, were not described with such horror and disbelief as the Mongol invasions were. Many of the historians were even employed by the Mongol rulers themselves so their figures would hardly be mere court flattery; we have every reason to believe the true scale of the devastation, even if we might doubt the statistics.

The Mongol era, however, was never quite as simple – or merely brutal – as that. Like Hobsbawm's 'age of extremes' it was more complex, with huge contrasts, and it is important to contrast the initial destruction with what came after. There was, on the one hand, the unprecedented slaughter. But on the other hand there was also brilliance, creativity and stability – even Juzjani described Genghis Khan as 'a just and resolute butcher', and it is important to remember that both Genghis Khan and other Mongol military leaders devoted more to administration and long-term planning than many other great conquerors, such as Alexander of Macedon. After the initial blood-letting there was growth once more in some areas at least, for Genghis Khan and his successors created the largest land empire in history, unifying most of the Eurasian land mass under one rule. It brought about stability, trade, travel and, on the whole, wise rule, in the end stimulating new upsurges in creativity in Yuan China at one end of the empire and Ilkhanid Iran at the other end (although this might have been despite the Mongols rather than because of them, and more due to the innate ability of the Chinese and Iranians to triumph against adversity). The Mongol invasions haunted the Chinese – indeed, it was the dynasty immediately following the collapse of the Mongol Yuan Dynasty, the Ming, which was largely responsible for the construction of the Great Wall as we know it, and not the first Emperor of China as often claimed: perhaps the greatest example in history of locking the stable door after the horse had bolted. More important, a major achievement of the Mongols was the unification of China, disunited under many states since the collapse of the Tang, and China has remained united ever since down to the present day in roughly the same form that was created by the Mongol Yuan dynasty.*

The legacy in the subsequent art of Persia was huge, and the effect on the development and growth of Russia was fundamental (this will be examined in the last chapter). Mongol stability gave rise to the world's first era of overland travel. Marco Polo is the best-known in the West; less known is Rabban Sauma, a monk from Peking who travelled overland as far as the court of Edward I of England (and left an account of his travels, an abridged version of which survives). Others equally now eclipsed by Marco Polo were: Friar John of Hungary, the envoy of Bela IV on two journeys in 1234–5 and again in 1237; Andrew of Longjumeau, the envoy of Louis IX in 1253–5; John of Marignollo, the papal envoy to China in the 1330s and 1340s; the Franciscan Friar Odoric of Pordenone 1320s; John of Montecorvino, the papal missionary; and there were others.[19] In some ways our comparison with the events of twentieth-century Europe is a valid one, of unusual destruction followed by unusual growth (although I would in no way advocate war as a blueprint for growth).

On the other hand, much of the region that bore the brunt of the conquests, Central Asia, did not recover, and the Mongol achievement has been seriously questioned. Nicola Di Cosmo, for example, questions the extent of the overland trade during the Pax Mongolica, maintaining that it has been overstated and not as structured as is usually thought. It did in any case come to an end with the overthrow of the Yuan in 1368. David Morgan wryly questions the popular use of the term *Pax Mongolica* by comparing it to the term *Pax Romana* from which it was coined, quoting Tacitus' famous remark: 'they make a desolation, and call it peace.'[20]

It must be emphasised too that the Central Asian cities before the Mongol conquest were no backwater. Quite the contrary: they were among the greatest intellectual centres of the Islamic world (if not *the* world), home to some of the greatest minds to have enriched civilisation. The roll-call is too extensive to list here, but mention can be made of the polymath scientist al-Biruni (973–1048) from Khwarazm, the Persian epic poet Firdawsi (c. 934–1020) from Tus, the polymath and scientist Ibn Sina (Avicenna, 980–1037) from Bukhara, the mathematician and poet Omar Khayyam (1048–1131) from Nishapur and the astronomer Nasruddin Tusi (1201–74) from Tus, to give some small measure of the incalculable loss of this world of Central Asia. Frederick Starr entitled his history of this golden age *Lost Enlightenment* with good reason.[21]

---

* Many in the West often view China as a perennial, almost eternal civilisation in contrast to those of Europe. This is myth: China has been subject to at least as much disunity, losses in continuity, foreign invasions, divisions into separate countries and rule by outsiders as Europe has been.

Figure 11.2 *Genghis Khan brand vodka at a restaurant in Bautou in Inner Mongolia*

Following the full independence of Mongolia after the collapse of the Soviet Union, Genghis Khan has been elevated into the Mongolian national hero and father-figure, a symbol of the newly emergent nation's identity (Figure 11.1). Genghis Khan is now everywhere in Ulan Bator, from great statues to the brand name of a vodka (Figure 11.2). But that is not the only way he is now depicted. At the supposed tomb of Genghis Khan near Dongsheng in Chinese Inner Mongolia, a vast cult centre has appeared in recent years surrounding the tomb itself, built only in 1954 (Figure 11.3). This has expanded to an architectural complex covering many square miles with a brand new monumental avenue, probably modelled after the Tang royal mausoleums at Qianling outside Xian. In fact it almost certainly does not represent the burial site of Genghis Khan, who probably lies at an unknown site in eastern Mongolia, but that is not the point. What is so extraordinary is how Genghis Khan has been re-invented in several different ways. First, as a *Chinese* national hero: on the official information at the site the Mongols themselves are referred to as a 'Chinese minority' and Genghis Khan as the 'founder of the Chinese Yuan Dynasty'. The vast, great 'Chinese Yuan Empire' stretching all the way to the lands of the Golden Horde and into Europe is labelled on a map in his tomb as the 'Yuan Empire': a Chinese Empire, not Mongol. And

Figure 11.3 *The purported tomb of and shrine to Genghis Khan on the Ordos steppe in China*

second – and even more extraordinarily – Genghis Khan has become a
Tibetan Buddhist holy man: his tomb and cult centre is officially described
as the place where 'this holy man is worshipped'. Perhaps Genghis Khan's
epitaph had been pronounced nearly a millennium before him by the
fourth-century Christian apologist Lactantius, who wrote:

> If you cut the throat of one man, you are treated as contagiously evil, and no
> one thinks it right for you to be admitted into a god's house here on earth;
> but the man who has slain his tens of thousands, soaking the fields in gore and
> fouling rivers, is let into heaven, not just into temples.[22]

The invasion of Europe (Map 11.1)

Sübedei raided the southern Russian steppe in 1221 and defeated a combined force of Alans, Lezgians and Cumans. In a seeming repetition of
the Khwarazm Shah's provocation, the prince of Kiev, who had formed
an alliance with the Cumans, had ten Mongol ambassadors executed.
Their first engagement with a Mongol detachment was victorious, but
then a combined force of Russians and Cumans was wiped out in May
1222. However, the Mongols did not press their advantage and returned
north of the Caspian at the end of 1222. In 1235 the Great Khan Ögedei,
Genghis Khan's successor, convened a *quriltai* or council for the conquest

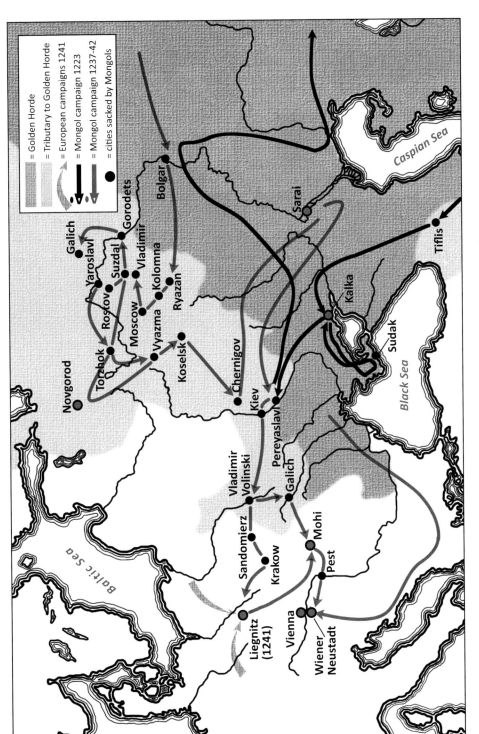

Map 11.1 *The Mongol invasions*

Legend:
- = Golden Horde
- = Tributary to Golden Horde
- = European campaigns 1241
- = Mongol campaign 1223
- = Mongol campaign 1237–42
- = cities sacked by Mongols

Caspian Sea

Tiflis

Sarai

Kalka

Black Sea

Sudak

Bolgar

Galich
Gorodets
Yaroslavl
Suzdal
Vladimir
Rostov
Moscow
Kolomna
Vyazma
Ryazan
Koselsk
Chernigov
Torzhok
Novgorod
Kiev
Pereyaslavl
Galich
Vladimir Volinski
Sandomierz
Krakow
Mohi
Pest
Vienna
Wiener Neustadt
Liegnitz (1241)

Baltic Sea

of Europe. According to Juvayni, at this quriltai all European states were regarded as 'rebels' against the divinely ordained Mongol supreme rule, regardless of whether they had heard of the Mongols or not.[23] All the great warlords assembled to launch the invasion: Batu, Genghis Khan's favourite grandson, was to take command. Two future Great Khans, Güyük and Möngke, were also to take part in the campaign. Most important, Genghis's great general, Sübedei, was also present. Ironically, it was the presence of so many of the Mongols' main leaders in the invasion of Europe that was to lead to the invasions' ultimate limitations, despite success in the field.

The first Russian city to be taken by the Mongols was Riazan. It was destroyed and the population slaughtered as part of a deliberate policy of terror. The invasion of Russia was made easier by the Russian states being divided among themselves, a fact of which Mongol intelligence was fully aware and took fullest advantage. Hence, between 1237 and 1240 it was possible to pick off Kolyma, Moscow, Suzdal and Vladimir one by one. After Vladimir the army was divided and Batu captured Dmitrov and Tver while Sübedei went on and captured Yuriev, Rostov and Yaroslavl. Batu marched on Novgorod but turned back as the spring turned the countryside to marshland, making it impossible for the Mongol horsemen to manoeuvre. Novgorod remained the only major Russian city that never submitted to the Mongols.

Meanwhile, Möngke continued to campaign in the south against the Cumans, Circassians and Alans. Prisoners were sold into slavery to the Ayyubids of Egypt, to become slave units – Mamluks – in the Ayyubid army (one of them, Aybak, founded the Mamluk Bahri dynasty of Egypt). This made the Mamluks bitter enemies of the Mongols, an enmity that was eventually to culminate in the Battle of 'Ain Jalut in 1260 when the Mamluks defeated the Mongols – one of the rare instances of a Mongol defeat.

The Russian campaign was resumed in 1240, when Pereslavl, Chernigov and Kiev were destroyed, putting all of Russia with the exception of Novgorod under Mongol rule. In 1241 the Mongol army split into two, Batu leading the main group into Hungary while Baidar and Kadan led a smaller group that devastated Poland. Lublin and Zawichost were sacked and the Polish capital, Cracow, destroyed. Nothing, it seemed, could stop the Mongol onslaught and Europe at last woke up to the threat and was stirred into response. King Wenceslas of Bohemia and King Henry of Silesia sent armies, and further contingents from Moravia and elsewhere in Poland were sent. Teutonic Knights from Germany and even a contingent of Knights Templars and Hospitallers from France were sent: the cream of Europe's armed forces answered the call to confront the threat. This vast army met the much smaller Mongol force at the Battle of Liegnitz on 9 April 1241. The Mongols wiped it out.

Silesia and Moravia were so depopulated afterwards that they had to be eventually resettled by German immigrants. In the south, under Batu, King Bela IV of Hungary was defeated and he and his family fled to Croatia. Batu advanced to the Danube, destroying Pest. In Hungary, however, the Mongols for the first time made an effort to consolidate their European conquests, and eastern Hungary was made into a Mongol state. Coins were minted and farmers were encouraged to return to their lands: a Mongol European state was in the making.

Rumours spread of the armies of Gog and Magog, of the Antichrist – indeed, many thought the Mongols were only half human, a visitation on humanity as a punishment for their sins. In the winter of 1241 the Mongols raided over the frozen Danube and sacked Gran and Buda. Austria was ravaged as far as Wiener Neustadt to the south of Vienna. The Mediterranean was reached when Kadan entered Croatia, sacking Zagreb and advancing down the Dalmatian coast towards Ragusa (Dubrovnik). When the Mongols reached the Adriatic in 1241, Emperor Frederic II, ever the pragmatist, regarded the Mongols not so much as a threat as a potential ally in his struggle against the Pope (although nothing came of it).[24] Nothing appeared to be able to halt the advancing holocaust, and there is every reason to believe that the Mongols would overrun western Europe and advance as far as the Atlantic as thoroughly as they had overrun the east and advanced to the Pacific.

But western Europe received an unexpected reprieve. In December 1241, news reached the Mongol armies in Europe of the death of the Great Khan Ögedei. Ironically, it was the presence of so many senior Mongol commanders in Europe that was to spell the ultimate failure of the campaign to reach the limits of western Europe, despite unbroken military success. For it was these commanders above all who were required to return to Mongolia to take part in the grand council to be held to decide upon Ögedei's successor. With so many contenders and lobbies, no senior Mongol could afford to be left out of the machinations. Hungary was evacuated and King Bela was able to return to his devastated country and eventually to rebuild it.

The Mongols withdrew from Poland, Austria and Hungary, but remained in the Russian steppe, always a great attraction because of its rich grasslands to feed the immense herds upon which the Mongol military machine depended. But this vast empire was simply too big to manage, and it soon broke into separate khanates for administrative reasons, all ruled by different grandsons of Genghis Khan. Kubilai Khan ruled in China, Chaghatai in Central Asia, Hülagü in Iran and Western Asia, and Batu in Russia. While all were nominally subordinate to the Great Khan in Mongolia, they soon inevitably separated. Batu's domain in Russia became known as the Golden Horde, with its capital at Sarai on the Volga north of Astrakhan.

Prester John and the Crusades

There is no doubt that the death of the Great Khan Ögedei in Mongolia on 11 December 1241, resulting in the withdrawal of Batu and other senior Mongols from Europe, saved Europe from the greatest military threat in its history. But already Europe and much of the world had reason to look to Karakorum. Not only senior army commanders travelled all the way across Eurasia to attend the quriltai in Karakorum to elect a successor to Ögedei; envoys from other countries also came. These included monarchs, such as the Emperor of Trebizond, the Armenian King of Cilicia and the Sultan of the Seljuk state in Anatolia, but Pope Innocent IV also sent an envoy, John of Plano Carpini. Of course, it made sound diplomatic sense for European powers to recognise Möngke, the new Great Khan who succeeded Ögedei, but there were other motives for the Christian powers as well. For another mission, that of Friar William of Rubruck, was solely religious when he travelled to Möngke's court to ask for permission to evangelise. Europe was aware of a Christian presence at the Mongol court and some of the Mongol elite had for several centuries been Nestorian Christian. While Möngke himself was a Shamanist, the Nestorians were an important lobby. The presence of Christians within the high echelons of the Mongol court was one of the sources of the European rumours of the powerful Asiatic Christian kingdom of Prester John. Prester John was supposedly vaguely located in 'the Indies', which at the time was a very imprecise term that included eastern Africa (hence Christian Ethiopia) as well as much else of Asia. According to a forged letter to the Pope from Prester John, he daily entertained thirty thousand at a table made of emeralds, twelve archbishops seated on his right and twenty bishops on his left.[25]

Indeed, in the Mongol invasion of Western Asia, Christians were often spared the general massacres, with some of the Mongol campaigns even carried out with Christian allies, such as the Georgians and Armenians. Möngke's own mother was a Nestorian, although she made a point of endowing a madrasa in Bukhara to demonstrate official Mongol religious even-handedness (doubtless lost on the Muslim survivors). It is doubtful that the Nestorian lobby under Möngke urged the Mongols to make war on the Muslims as Gumilev and others claimed,[26] as the Nestorians had no quarrel with the Muslims. Friar William was granted permission by Möngke to preach among the Mongols, but his extreme evangelical preaching did not go down well: Möngke advised that he modify his preaching and recommended that he emphasise the more gentle side of the Christian message if he wished for converts. (A Mongol ruler lecturing a Christian evangeliser on gentleness is one of history's more amusing ironies.)

Another visitor to Möngke's court was Hethoum, king of the Cilician kingdom of Armenia. Hethoum tried to persuade Möngke that his cousin

Hülagü's invasion of the Near East and the establishment of Ilkhanid Iran should be cast as a Crusade. The idea was not as ridiculous as it might sound: Hülagü's wife was, after all, a devout Christian, and Hülagü's Christian Georgian allies had helped in the sack of Baghdad. Many Christians of the Near East actually rejoiced at Hülagü's coming, believing him to be Prester John. Both King Hethoum of Cilicia and Count Bohemond of Antioch, son-in-law of Hethoum and ruler of one of the more powerful Crusader principalities, actually joined Hülagü after the fall of Aleppo with Armenian and Crusader contingents. The alliance of the Ilkhans and Christians for a joint Crusade was Hethoum's idea, although Armenian sources exaggerate the Armenian role and their influence on the Ilkhans. The joint Mongol-Armenian-Crusader army then proceeded to attack Damascus. At the news of Möngke's death in 1259, however, Hülagü returned to Mongolia. Then, on 1 March 1260, Damascus surrendered to the Mongols, and Ked-Buka (Hülagü's deputy, left behind as commander-in-chief), Bohemond and Hethoum entered Damascus and rode in triumph along the Street Called Straight: the local Muslim population were forced to bow down to the crosses borne by Bohemond and Hethoum.[27]

Meanwhile, Berke had succeeded his brother Batu as Khan of the Golden Horde and went on the offensive in 1259. Poland was laid waste and Pope Alexander IV proclaimed a Crusade against the Mongols. This occurred at exactly the same time as the Christians of the Near East were urging a Crusade with the Mongols. This led Pope Alexander to excommunicate Bohemond in 1260. The one real power in eastern Europe who might well have tipped the balance either way was King Bela IV of Hungary, but having been once bitten, Bela wisely stayed neutral.

In the Near East, after Bohemond's excommunication (the Pope could not excommunicate Hethoum, who, being Armenian, was outside the Roman church), the various Crusader powers were divided. Some saw the Mongols as the only hope for eastern Christendom, but others viewed them as a greater threat and sought an alliance with the Mamluks of Egypt as the only hope of defeating the Mongols. Matters came to a head at the Battle of 'Ain Jalut – the Springs of Goliath – in Galilee on 3 September 1260. Sultan Qutuz of Egypt led a Mamluk force against Ked-Buka and his Mongols and defeated them – a rare time that Mongols had been defeated in open battle.* It is arguable whether the victory of 'Ain Jalut saved Islam in the Near East, but it certainly destroyed the myth of Mongol invincibility, and Mongol advances henceforth would never be the same. It also spelt the end of the Crusades: henceforth there would be

---

* The only previous time was the Battle of Parwan north of Kabul in 1221 by Jalaluddin Mankobirti and his Khwarazmian forces.

no alliances against the rising power of Mamluk Egypt, which, in the end, was to drive the Crusaders out.

Among the Mongols of the Golden Horde, however, there was a fundamental change. Berke, Khan of the Golden Horde, in his struggle against the Christian powers of Europe, converted to Islam. The Mamluks henceforth saw their fellow-believers in Russia as potential friends rather than enemies, and in 1262 Sultan Baybars proposed an alliance against the still-pagan Mongol Ilkhanid empire of Persia under Hülagü. Berke agreed, not so much for religious reasons (it is doubtful whether his conversion was ever more than superficial) but for reasons of family rivalry. Hence, Baybars went on the offensive against the Crusader states and Berke against Hülagü and the Ilkhans. Accordingly, in 1264 Hülagü sent an ambassador to Pope Urban IV with proposals for a joint Crusade. The proposals were turned down by Urban, and Hülagü died before his ambassador's return. Hülagü was succeeded in 1265 by Abaka, and both rival Mongol powers faced each other across the Kura River in the Caucasus. However, Berke also died, and his successor Möngke-Teimur called for a reconciliation, with both khans recognising Kubilai in Mongolia as Great Khan with ultimate jurisdiction over both branches of the Mongol Empire.

This still left the Mongols' old enemy, the Mamluks of Egypt, and Abaka sent an envoy to Europe with renewed calls for a Crusade. Pope Clement IV, however, insisted upon Abaka's baptism before he would even discuss a Crusade, while King Louis IX of France was more interested in the conquest of Tunis than of Jerusalem, which was of greater strategic interest to France. Abaka's proposal received a more favourable reception from Prince Edward of England (son of Henry III, the future Edward I). Edward came to the Holy Land in 1268 accompanied by Tebaldo Visconti, Archbishop of Liege (soon to be Pope Gregory X), and envoys were sent to Abaka to discuss an alliance. Abaka, however, was distracted at that time by a war on his eastern front against a rival Mongol ruler, which allowed Baybars to pick off the Crusader possessions one by one. Prince Edward returned empty-handed.

The Council of Lyons of 1271 was convened by the new Pope, Gregory X, to launch a Crusade. The Council was to be the most ambitious since Pope Urban's call at the Council of Clermont which launched the First Crusade. The kings of France, England, Scotland, Norway, Sweden, Hungary, Sicily, Bohemia, Castile, Navarre, Aragon and Armenia were invited. None attended except King James of Aragon and the (by now a completely empty title) 'Emperor' Baldwin II of Constantinople (evicted from the city in 1261). But on the completion of his eastern campaign Abaka sent sixteen ambassadors from Iran to discuss a Mongol alliance. Nothing came of the discussions.

Abaka Khan died in 1282, but in 1287 Arghun, the new Mongol

ruler of Iran, sent one last envoy, the remarkable Nestorian priest from Peking, Rabban Sauma, who travelled to the court of Edward I of England (probably at Bordeaux), as well as to those of the Byzantine Emperor, the Pope and the French king.* His terms were generous: in return for alliance with the greatest power of the East in a Crusade, the Christians would have the holy places returned to them. Rabban Sauma held an audience with Pope Nicholas IV (who had succeeded Gregory) in 1288; as a consequence Nicholas sent John of Montecorvino on a mission to China the following year. Arghun's envoy, however, received only a lukewarm and non-committal response: by then the rulers of Europe were more concerned with domestic affairs – Edward, especially, with Wales and Scotland despite his earlier Holy Land venture – and the light had gone out of the Crusading spirit. Nothing came of the proposals.

Meanwhile, in 1285 the Golden Horde attempted another invasion of the west, imitating Sübedei's tactics, but it was largely unsuccessful, despite widespread plundering of Poland. Instead, the Mongols turned to consolidation, the Golden Horde in Russia and the Ilkhanids in Iran. Both were to have major consequences for their adoptive countries. The revival of Ilkhanid Iran is not a part of the present history, but Russia under the Golden Horde will be reviewed in the next chapter.

Xanadu to the Volga

The sheer size of the empire founded by Genghis Khan and his successors can be illustrated by two of its former capitals at opposite ends of Eurasia, both founded by grandsons of the great conqueror.† One was Shangdu in Inner Mongolia, the 'Upper Capital' founded by Kublai Khan, better known (in literature at least) as Xanadu. The other was Sarai-Batu, capital of the Golden Horde, founded by Batu Khan on the lower Volga River in southern Russia.

In 1816 Samuel Taylor Coleridge penned one of English literature's best-loved (albeit never finished) poems – and conjured up one of literature's most evocative images in his 'stately pleasure-dome[d]' city of Xanadu. Since then, Xanadu has become a byword for all that is remote, fabulous and exotic. The reality is quite different from Coleridge's stately pleasure-domes – but is, if anything, even more unforgettable. Situated

---

* In travelling all the way from Peking to western Europe, Rabban Sauma was one of the great travellers of the Middle Age – a Chinese counterpart to Marco Polo. He wrote an account of his travels, translated and published by Budge 2014. See also Rossabi 1992.
† This was brought home forcibly to me when, during the course of 2008, I found myself visiting both capitals.

near the small town of Zhenglian in the immensity of Inner Mongolia's grassy steppe – the 'twice five miles of fertile ground' – is a vast but empty walled enclosure, Coleridge's 'walls and towers . . . girdled round': all that remains of Emperor Kublai Khan's summer capital of Shangdu. The square city is laid out according to standard Chinese planning principles of an outer city, an imperial city and a palace city, and these divisions are still clearly visible. Street and building plans can be traced, as well as the main city gateways. The city walls were built of beaten earth, but the palace buildings were of brick and some stone. On hills in the distance are the remains of beacon towers used for communicating with Peking. The whole city was built in just four years, completed in 1256. Archaeologists from Hohhot have uncovered the ground plans of some of the buildings in the palace city, as well as glazed tiles, marble building fragments and numerous stone and metal objects – all that remains of Coleridge's pleasure-domes where Kublai Khan received Marco Polo (Figures 11.4 and 11.5).[28]

Batu's domain in Russia became known as the Golden Horde, with its capital at Sarai founded soon after 1242. Today, the site of Sarai is occupied by the small village of Selitrennoye, north of Astrakhan overlooking the east bank of the River Volga (in fact the Akhtuba River, one of the minor branches of the Volga in the broad river valley). It was a large city covering about ten square kilometres with a well-laid-out network of streets, markets, artisans' quarters and palatial complexes, as well as mosques and churches reflecting the Mongol's tolerant (or at least disinterested) attitude to religion. The city was sacked by Tamerlane in 1395. Although there was some recovery afterwards, it slowly declined, particularly after the establishment of a rival Tatar Khanate at Astrakhan in 1466, when much of the population moved downstream. Many of the buildings were stripped to build Astrakhan, and Sarai lay abandoned. As late as the nineteenth century travellers observed some brick mausoleums and other unidentified walls still standing, but now even these have disappeared. Today, the site stretches for some kilometres north of Selitrennoye along the river bluff, consisting of low eroded mounds littered with potsherds and building rubble; there is no longer even a single wall standing (Figures 11.6 and 11.7).

Although many thousands of miles apart, the sites are in many ways very similar. They are both surrounded by extensive grasslands, crucial for the location of any Mongol capital for the vast herds of horses upon which Mongol military success depended – indeed, horses are still grazed at both sites. Both were originally extensive bustling cities with large building complexes, and both are now even more devoid of buildings than Merv or Karakhoto or the other cities wiped out by the Mongols. And while neither offers much to see now, it is this feature that is perhaps their most appealing: sheer nothingness surrounded by emptiness where

Figure 11.4 *The excavated remains of part of the inner palace at Xanadu*

Figure 11.5 *The outer ramparts of Xanadu*

Figure 11.6 *The site of Sarai Batu on the Volga at Selitrennoye*

Figure 11.7 *Excavated remains at Sarai Batu*

great bustling cities stood has a haunting quality, demonstrating more effectively than anything else the transitory nature of the great steppe empires.

* * *

Shocking though the defeats at Leignitz and Wiener Neustadt were, Europe had experienced little more than a scare and a reprieve, not to be compared with the genocidal holocaust that swept through Central and Western Asia. But the Mongols did inflict two horrors on Europe that were more devastating than the weapons of the hordes themselves. The first was the Chinese invention of gunpowder, brought by the Mongols. It had reached the Middle East by the 1360s but its first use in western Europe is surprisingly earlier, with the first definite record of firearms in 1326, where its potential for warfare was quickly realised.[29]

The second, however, was even more devastating: the Black Death. Although the Mongols hardly used gunpowder as an offensive weapon, the Black Death was just that. In perhaps the world's first recorded instance of germ warfare, during a Tatar siege of the Genoese port of Caffa (modern Feodosia: Figure 11.8) in Crimea in 1347, the Tatars catapulted decapitated heads that were infected with the Black Death into the walled city.[30] The defendants managed to hold out against the Tatars, but not against the

Figure 11.8 *The ruined Genoese walls of Caffa, modern Feodosiya in Crimea, over which a besieging Tatar army catapulted decapitated heads infected with the Black Death*

infection. Two months later, according to one story, Genoese ships from Caffa put in at Messina in Sicily with its sailors dying at the oars. The Black Death was unleashed on Europe, soon to wipe out (according to some estimates) up to two thirds of its population.[31]

CHAPTER 12

GOLDEN HORDES
The Tatar Khanates of Russia

Scratch a Russian and you will find a Tatar.
– Attributed to Napoleon[1]

What is the legacy of what were arguably the most destructive invasions in history? At first glance the Mongol legacy appears to be wholly one of destruction, having no long-term effect. However, one can make a clear distinction between the impact of the initial invasions, which were without doubt of a nature almost without parallel, and the recovery that came after. For there was recovery and even resurgence, much of it, moreover, under Mongol rule. Some of this has already been referred to in passing in the last chapter, in relation to Ilkhanid Iran and Yuan China. But what of the legacy in the West?

The Mongol invasions fundamentally changed the course of European history in many ways, albeit often indirectly. At the end of his chapter appropriately entitled 'The Mongol Whirlwind', Peter Golden concludes:

> The Mongol Empire marked the greatest incursion of the steppe peoples into settled society. It brought the steppe, the forest zone, and many of the neighbouring states (China, Iran, Medieval Rus') into a vast world realm, the largest, contiguous, land empire in human history. It profoundly influenced global history, putting into place international networks of communications, the beginnings of an early 'world system' in the period 1250–1350, the precursor of the modern world.[2]

In examining the legacy of the Mongol invasions in this and the next chapter, mainly in Russia, many of the conventional ideas of what it is to be 'European' and where Europe's boundaries lie are questioned. But before that it is necessary to take a last glance at the steppe empire that succeeded the Mongol – and penetrated Europe, albeit briefly – and unwittingly gave one of Europe's greatest civilisations a last-minute reprieve.

Under the shadow of Genghis Khan: the house of Tamerlane

The decline of the Mongol Empire in the Inner Asian heartland created a vacuum of conflicting rival groups and families, all fighting to succeed the Mongols. It was Teimur – Tamerlane – at the end of the fourteenth century who filled this vacuum. Although he traced his descent (albeit tenuously) back to Genghis Khan on the maternal side, Tamerlane was a Chaghatai Turk born in about 1336 in the region of Chaghanian south of Samarkand with its capital at Kish (present Shahr-i Sabz). During the course of the 1370s Tamerlane was able to unite the various factions in the region and raid Iran and Afghanistan. With success the raids soon became more far-reaching, becoming full-scale campaigns of conquest to establish a new Eurasian Empire.[3]

Tamerlane's invasions seemed like the Mongol devastations all over again. Central and Western Asia, barely reviving, saw its rebuilt cities and resettled populations destroyed once more, and even cities that had escaped the earlier holocaust were destroyed. Baghdad at one end of Asia was captured in 1393, and Delhi at the other end, which even the Mongols did not reach, five years later. Tamerlane even advanced as far as Moscow but turned back, campaigning down the Volga in pursuit of Khan Toqtamish, a former protégé of his who had become khan of the Golden Horde, sacking the capital of Sarai in 1395, forcing Toqtamish to flee. The year 1402 sees one of Tamerlane's greatest victories at the Battle of Ankara against the Ottoman Turks when Sultan Bayazit was killed (incidentally giving the dying Byzantine Empire an eleventh-hour reprieve from the Ottomans for a further fifty years). At first, Tamerlane stood in awe of the memory of the Mongol Empire and hesitated to challenge even the shadow of Mongol power that survived in Inner Asia. He never claimed the supreme title of 'Khan', for example, or even 'Sultan', but remained content with the modest 'Amir' throughout, even though he built almost as great an empire as his predecessor. But after a victory against a Mongol force, Tamerlane stood unchallenged, no longer under Genghis Khan's daunting shadow. How great an empire Tamerlane might have created can only be guessed at. His death at Otrar in 1405 interrupted his most ambitious campaign to date: the conquest of China (birthplace of his wife, Bibi Khanum, whom his great mosque in Samarkand commemorates).

Tamerlane's destruction was never quite as wholesale as that of the Mongols. Horrific though it was, Mongol destruction nearly always had a purpose (usually extortion, admittedly). With Tamerlane, on the other hand, one senses barbarity that was more gratuitous: the pyramids of decapitated heads were as much to satiate sheer cruelty as to punish. But Tamerlane was as great a builder as he was a destroyer. He instigated a resurgence of the arts and architecture, and his dynasty remained as rulers until the nineteenth century. His capital of Samarkand remains one of

Figure 12.1 *The Gur-i Amir, the tomb of Tamerlane in Samarkand*

the great monumental cities of Asia, and a visible legacy of the dynasty's founder (Figure 12.1).

Although the personality of Tamerlane himself is marked – indeed, marred – as much by acts of barbarity as by building, in the dynasty he created he left behind one of the most talented families in Asia's history. His son, Shah Rukh, moved the capital in the early fifteenth century to Herat, establishing one of the most brilliant schools of Persian painting – as well as other arts and sciences – in Iranian and Central Asian history. Today, gems of Timurid architecture can still be found not only in the great cities of the Timurid Empire – Samarkand, Bukhara, Herat and Mashhad – but in the remote countryside as well, such as at Khargird in Iran or the vast Shrine of Ahmad Yassavi in the remote steppe at Turkestan in Kazakhstan, perhaps the most spectacular building of Tamerlane's era of giganticism (Figure 12.2). These monuments, often to be found in mere villages, are masterpieces that sometimes exceed those of Samarkand. This perhaps more than anything is a true mark of Timurid greatness: a great rural as well as an urban civilisation.

But Samarkand, for all its glories, was just a one-generation capital, for Tamerlane's son and successor Shah Rukh moved the capital to Herat. Samarkand was left in the hands of Shah Rukh's son, Ulugh Beg. In addition to being an enlightened and tolerant governor, Ulugh Beg was a great scholar and astronomer, whose star charts became the standard work

Figure 12.2 *The shrine of Ahmad Yassavi at Turkestan in Kazakhstan*

of reference in Europe until the sixteenth century as well as in the lands of Islam. After Ulugh Beg's murder in 1449, Samarkand declined, eventually being taken over by the Uzbeks under Shaybani Khan after 1500. But it was not the last of the house of Timur: indeed its greatest days were yet to come. The Timurid court continued to flourish in Herat under the successors of Shah Rukh. In particular, under Husain-i Baiqara in the latter half of the fifteenth century Herat witnessed a golden age, the age of the great poets Shir 'Ali Nawa'i and Jami and the painter Behzad and his school.

The revival of the house of Timur came from the Ferghana Valley in the heartland of Central Asia with the rise of a new conqueror in the early sixteenth century, Babur, a descendant of Tamerlane. Babur is one of the most extraordinary rulers in history – if only because of the memoirs he left behind, among the more remarkable ever written. His conquest of India and establishment of the Mughal dynasty was probably the greatest legacy of the Timurid dynasty. The dynasty is mis-named because of the Mongol, or Mughal, element in the army. The Mughal Empire of India is only marginal to this history. But the first Mughal Emperors – Babur, Humayun, Akbar, Jahangir, Shah Jahan and Aurangzeb – were variously mighty conquerors, brilliant generals, wise rulers, talented writers, poets, painters and builders, true successors to Tamerlane's extraordinary house. The house finally came to an end with the exile of Emperor Bahadur Shah II by the British to Burma after 1857. The era of Tamerlane and his successors was a gigantic era:

gigantic personalities, gigantic achievements, gigantic buildings. From Samarkand, Bukhara and Herat to Agra, Delhi and Lahore, the Timurid legacy is one of the world's more extraordinary.

A people of Europe?

The main history of the Mongols in English, by David Morgan, opens with the statement that 'The Mongols are not very obviously a "people of Europe"', in reference to the series *Peoples of Europe*, of which the book forms a part. Morgan justifies its inclusion, however, because of the huge effect that the Mongols had upon European history (although in the revised version of the book he concedes that if it were to be published now for the first time, a 'people of Asia' might be deemed more appropriate).[4] This is true to an extent, but in fact some Mongols at least *are* a 'people of Europe' – and have been for some eight centuries. Of course, the argument only goes so far: Mongolia itself is in no way 'European'. But there are Mongols who are. Just as Finns, Bulgarians and Hungarians, people whose origins lie similarly beyond the boundaries of Europe, are unhesitatingly considered to be 'of Europe', so too are a number of Mongol communities. For it is not often appreciated that the Mongol invasions were more than just a brief, albeit destructive, 'whirlwind' in Europe: they came, they conquered and they stayed.

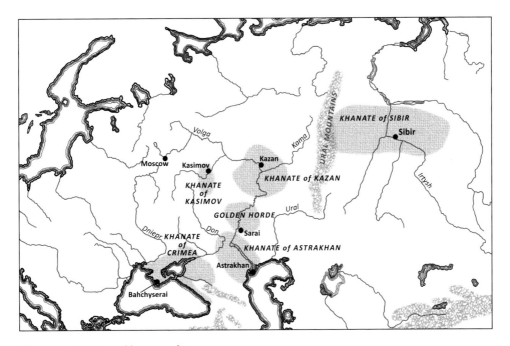

Map 12.1 *The Tatar khanates of Europe*

The first Mongol state in Russia* was that of the Golden Horde established by Batu, Genghis Khan's grandson, with its capital at Sarai on the lower Volga soon after 1227. The term 'Golden Horde' is of uncertain origin and does not appear until the seventeenth century. The fifteenth-century Russian traveller Afanasy Nikitin, on his journey from Tver to India, refers to the Tatar Khanate in 1487 simply as 'the Orda'.[5] Marco Polo refers to the Golden Horde as the 'Lord of the West' as opposed to the 'Lord of the East', which was the Ilkhanate of Iran.[6] Its official name was the Ulus Jochi or Qipchak Khanate after the Qipchak steppe and the large number of Qipchak Turks – perhaps outnumbering the incoming Mongols – already in the area. This led to the gradual Turkification of the Mongols in the west. Many of the soldiers under Batu's command in the invasion of Russia were Turkish auxiliaries from Central Asia. On entering Russia, Batu incorporated more Turks into his army from Europe, both the Turk Cumans/Qipchaks of southern Russia and the Turk Bulgars of the upper Volga. This resulted in Turkish soon becoming the main – and eventually the only – language of the Golden Horde.

As early as the 1280s Turkish replaced Mongolian as the language on coins.[7] Mongol or Turk, the European name that stuck to them was Tatar, a people related to the Mongols, for reasons given in the previous chapter. Hence, it is as Tatars that all descendants of the Horde are universally now known in Russia, both by the Russians and now by the Tatars themselves, the term applying not only to the incoming Mongols but also to the earlier Cumans and Bulgars.[†]

Berke, the fourth ruler of the Golden Horde, was the first to convert to Islam, although only later under Özbeg, the ninth Khan (1313–41), did the Golden Horde became officially Muslim.[8] In fact, adoption of the religion of the conquered was a characteristic of the Mongol dynasties, just as the Ilkhanids in Iran also adopted Islam and the Yuan in China adopted Buddhism (and most of Mongolia today is Tibetan Buddhist). One wonders, however, how different the history of Russia might have been had the Golden Horde adopted Christianity, just as the Russians had under Prince Vladimir in the tenth century (or indeed as many Mongolians did in their homeland). Doubtless there would have been less hesitation in accepting them as 'of Europe'.

For the first century and a half or so after its establishment the Golden Horde was by far the main power in Russia, demanding heavy tribute from the Russian states. Indeed, it extended deep into central Europe

---

* 'Russia' used anachronistically here (but as a convenient shorthand), as the Russian state did not exist then, and did not extend as far as the Volga until the fifteenth century.
† 'In China the Mongols remained Mongols, but frequently ceased to be nomads. In the Golden Horde they remained nomads, but ceased to be Mongols', as Khazanov (1985: 250) observed.

Figure 12.3 *A fourteenth-century Golden Horde bath house at Orheiul-Vechi in Moldova, probably the westernmost architectural remains of the Golden Horde*

beyond the Danube, establishing permanent administrative centres whose remains still survive (Figure 12.3). In Russia and Poland there were complex and constantly shifting balances of alliances and warfare between Poles, Teutonic Knights, pagan Lithuanians and the Golden Horde. The Lithuanians were driven eastwards by the Teutonic Knights in crusading zeal. They formed an alliance with David of Galicia against the Mongols which was at first successful. Alexander Nevsky viewed the Lithuanians and Swedes as a greater threat to Russia than the Tatars, so negotiated a deal with them in order to concentrate on the others. Indeed, he formed a blood brotherhood tie with Sartak, the son of Batu Khan, in 1240 and in the ensuing alliance Alexander Nevsky was able to defeat the Teutonic Knights with the aid of Mongol contingents in his army.[9] The relationship worked both ways: Russian mercenaries recruited by the Golden Horde, for example, were used as guard units in Mongol Yuan China in the mid-fourteenth century.[10]

By the latter half of the fourteenth century, however, the princes of Moscow began to unite the various other Russian states and, under their leadership, Russia was beginning to retaliate against the Horde. With it united under Dmitri, the son of Ivan II, Tatar raiders were defeated in front of Riazan in 1365 and in 1367 they were driven back from Nizhny Novgorod. In 1374 a Tatar force of some fifteen hundred was slaughtered at Nizhny Novgorod. It was not all plain sailing, however, and there were some reverses: a Russian force was routed in 1377 and in 1378 the Tatars fired Nizhny Novgorod. This culminated in the Battle of Kulikovo on 8 September 1380 when a Russian force, estimated between 140,000 and 400,000, defeated a Tatar army, but only forty thousand Russians survived.[11]

Victories, therefore, were often pyrrhic, there were notable reverses, and a modified form of tribute to the Tatars remained in force. There was also collusion as well as conflict: there were even Tatars fighting alongside Prince Dmitri at Kulikovo, and the ensuing centuries would see more and more assimilation of the Tatars into the Russian mainstream.[12] But Russian advances remained real nonetheless, for what counted more than military victory was psychological: the myth of Tatar invincibility had been removed. No longer were they men from hell but men of flesh and blood just like the Russians themselves. This factor was worth even all the dead of Kulikovo: the removal of the Tatar threat was now at least conceivable.

Poland-Lithuania and the Horde versus Muscovy and Crimea

There was some revival of the Golden Horde after Kulikova under Khan Toqtamish, but it declined after the sack of Sarai by Tamerlane in 1395. In 1438 it divided into two: the Great Horde remaining at Sarai, and a separate Khanate at Kazan on the middle Volga (Figures 12.4 and 12.5). Further divisions were created a few years later in the time of Ivan III with the establishment of the Khanates of Astrakhan and Crimea in 1441, the latter founded by Edigei Khan with its first capital at Stari Krim and allied with Moscow against the Golden Horde (Figures 12.6–12.9). The new Crimean Khanate was put on a firm footing by Mengli Girai, who founded a dynasty and allied himself with the rising power of the Ottomans. Both Astrakhan and Crimea lay claim to the legacy of the Golden Horde. The Girai dynasty of Crimea had the stronger claim, as the founder of the dynasty (as opposed to the state, founded by Edigei) was Hajji Toktamish Girai, a grandson of the last Khan of the Golden Horde and a descendant of Batu. Hence, the Girais always claimed historical suzerainty over the Russian principalities. However, the Astrakhan Khans claimed to be the continuation of the Golden Horde, occupying much the same territory, in rivalry to the Crimean Khans.

The year 1447 saw the creation of another Khanate from an entirely unexpected quarter: Ivan III created the Khanate of Kasimov from Muscovite territory to the south-east of Moscow. This was partly to reward those Tatars who joined Moscow and partly as a buffer against Kazan to the east. Remains in Kasimov today include the Shah-Ali Tekkiye, dated 1555, a mosque and minaret dated 1457, and many inscribed Muslim graves.[13] The end of the fifteenth century thus sees five Mongol states in Russia: the original Golden Horde – or Great Horde – at its old capital of Sarai, the Kazan Khanate upstream on the Volga, the Astrakhan Khanate only just downstream from Sarai, the Crimean Khanate and the Kasimov Khanate (Map 11.2).

There were other Mongol Khanates further east, such as those of the Nogays and Sibirs. The Nogay Khanate ruled mainly east of the Urals, as did the Khanate of Sibir north-east of the Urals around Tobolsk (both rulers also descended from Genghis Khan). However, although centred around the Sea of Azov, groups of Nogay Tatars did roam the Kuban steppe in the south of European Russia from the sixteenth century onwards, coming successively under Russian, Ottoman, Crimean and Kalmyk claims to hegemony in the region. By the late eighteenth century they numbered about seventy thousand 'households' (tents) and were often confused with the Kalmyks; many of the present-day inhabitants of Astrakhan are probably descendants of the Nogay.[14]

The late fourteenth century also saw the rise of Poland-Lithuania under the Jagellionian dynasty, which formed an alliance with the Tatars. Jogaila, the founder of the dynasty, had formed an alliance with Khan Mamai of the Golden Horde for a joint attack on Muscovy, but following Mamai's defeat at Kulikovo nothing came of the plan. Jogaila's successor Vytautas (Witold) 'the Great' of Lithuania (1392–1430) renewed the Tatar alliance with Khan Toqtamish, who now ruled the Golden Horde after Mamai's defeat. Vytautas gave refuge to Toqtamish when he was forced to flee the invasion of Tamerlane (Toqtamish later died in Siberia). In the Battle of Tannenberg on 15 July 1410 between Vytautas and the Teutonic Knights, the Lithuanians were aided by a Tatar unit commanded by Jalal ad-Din, the son of Toqtamish. The alliance resulted in complete victory over the Knights, who never again threatened Lithuania.[15]

Between 1454 and 1475 the Ottomans made Moldavia a vassal and annexed the Genoese colonies of the Black Sea, recognising the Crimean Khan Mengli Girai as a vassal in 1475. Caffa (modern Feodosiya) was made the seat of the Ottoman Sanjak of Crimea. Formerly, Poland-Lithuania had enjoyed cordial relations with the Genoese colonies, an informal 'Catholic alliance' across the steppe that encouraged trade between the Baltic and Black Seas. With their loss, Poland-Lithuania was confronted with a new hostile power to the south in the form of Crimea and the Ottomans, in addition to a hostile Muscovy to its east. It also questioned much of the balances of power elsewhere in Europe: both Poland and Astrakhan, hostile to both the Ottoman Empire and Muscovy, even sent a delegations to the Turks' most vigorous opponent in Europe, the Republic of Venice, in 1476 to propose alliances, but nothing came of the discussions.[16]

In 1477 the Astrakhan Tatars formed an alliance with the Lithuanians for a planned joint attack on Moscow. In 1480 Ivan III abrogated the

Figure 12.4 *The Kremlin at Kazan built by Russia after its conquest, dominated by the new twenty-first-century mosque supposedly referencing the original Tatar mosque*

Figure 12.5 *The first mosque in Kazan since the conquest, built 1787 after Catherine the Great legalised the building of mosques in Russia*

Figure 12.6 *The Kremlin at Astrakhan built by Russia after its conquest*

Figure 12.7 *Nothing remains of Tatar Astrakhan, but the Persian caravanserai built by the Russians in the eighteenth century is a reminder of its eastern links*

Figure 12.8 *Numerous modern mosques are in the Tatar quarter of Astrakhan (left), the design more closely following that of Russian churches (right) than Middle Eastern models*

tributary status to the Golden Horde and proposed an alliance with Crimea against both Poland-Lithuania and Astrakhan. This was formed in deliberate opposition to the alliance between Astrakhan and Poland-Lithuania. As a consequence there emerged two opposing axes in the late fifteenth century on the steppe that cut completely across the ethnic, linguistic and religious divide: a Muscovy/Crimea alliance versus a Poland-Lithuania/Astrakhan alliance.

As if this were not confusing enough, Genoa in the meantime entered into secret negotiations with both King Casimir Jagellion of Poland and Khan Mengli Girai of Crimea in the 1480s for a return of the Genoese ports in the Black Sea and support against the Ottomans, although Casimir had already signed a treaty with the Ottomans. Lacking support from the in-fighting Italian states and other Mediterranean powers, however, Genoese designs for the return of the Black Sea possessions collapsed. Mengli Girai too, while favouring the Genoese and resenting his khanate's tributary status under the Ottomans, was pragmatic enough to recognise its greater power, joining them in a raid on Ruthenia.[17] Poland, however, still managed to hang on to its southern territories until 1672 when the Ottomans advanced further into south-eastern Europe, capturing the

Figure 12.9 *A madrasa at the first Crimean Tatar capital at Stari Krim*

Polish fortress town of Kamyanets-Podolski and establishing the Ottoman province of Podolia. A Turkish minaret still stands over the converted Polish cathedral in Kamyanets-Podolski today (Figure 12.10) (although it reverted to the Catholics when the Ottomans retreated in 1699).

The Tatar khanates, in other words, had become another European power in the constant shifting of alliances and balances of power across eastern Europe. Crimea, furthermore, despite resentment at its inferior status, was strengthened by its alliance with the Ottomans. Ironically, therefore, it was the might of the Ottoman Empire coming to the support of Crimea that led, first, to the decline of Astrakhan, and second, indirectly to the eventual rise of Muscovy. The Turkish historian Halil Inalcik rightly views this Ottoman–Crimean co-operation in the period from 1492 to 1532 as 'a period crucial for the rise of the Muscovite power, which is understandably ignored in Russian historiography'.[18] The rivalry between

Figure 12.10 *The Catholic cathedral at the former Polish city of Kamyanets-Podolski in Ukraine, still with its minaret from when it was converted to a mosque under the Ottomans*

the Ottomans and the Poles over the Ukrainian steppe would also lead later to the rise of the Ukrainian Cossack state.

A result of the alliance between Astrakhan and Poland-Lithuania was the establishment of Tatar communities in the territory of the latter in the fifteenth century. Ghillebert de Lannoy describes Tatar settlements in Lithuania as early as 1414. Although the Lithuanian Tatars lost their language after the fifteenth century, they proudly maintained their religion and identity. There were even Polish Tatars fighting on the side of King Jan Sobieski's relief of the Siege of Vienna in 1683, fighting against the Crimean Tatar allies of the Ottomans.[19] Tatars remain a distinct, albeit heavily Polonised, minority in Poland, Lithuania and Belarus today, where they are known as the Lipka.[*]

In 1492, Ivan III was able to invade Lithuania with his ally, Mengli Girai of Crimea. In 1500 a Crimean raiding party of just a thousand seized five thousand Lithuanians and the following year fifty thousand Lithuanians were captured. Indeed, after West Africa, eastern Europe was the largest source of slaves in the world: a Tatar raid on Austria in 1567, for example, captured ninety thousand slaves, a trade in human trafficking that had the tacit support of Muscovy (even though Russians were often

---

[*] The Hollywood actor Charles Bronson was an ethnic Lipka.

the victims).[20] One recalls that the most famous – and most powerful – of Ottoman Sultanas, Roxelana the wife of Sultan Süleyman, was a former Ruthenian or Ukrainian slave.

Moscow, for all its rise to pre-eminence, still remained surprisingly Tatar in character (and nominally at least a Golden Horde vassal). Up until 1480 Muscovite coins still carried inscriptions in Arabic. As late as 1531 Vasili III of Moscow was still paying tribute to the successors of the Golden Horde: Crimea, Kazan and Astrakhan. Between 1512 and 1551, however, Crimea, which had destroyed the power of the Great Horde in 1502, gradually extended hegemony over Kazan and Astrakhan. Out of the competing patchwork of Russian principalities and Tatar khanates that had existed up to now, therefore, the balance of power in Russia was resolving on just Crimea and Muscovy. The old alliance between the two would inevitably lead to confrontation. Because of rivalry with Poland over Moldavia, the Ottoman Sultans Selim I and Süleyman I (1512–66) continued to maintain good relations with Muscovy until Khan Sahib Girai of Crimea (1532–51) convinced the Ottomans of the greater threat.[21]

Europe's last Mongol state

The collapse of Kazan and Astrakhan left Crimea the sole surviving state descended from the Mongols in Europe. In its isolated peninsula, the Crimean Khanate ruled from its capital at Stari Krim, and after the late sixteenth century at Bahchyserai, was able to mount devastating raids into Russia (Figures 12.11 and 12.12). In about 1565 an allied army of Crimea and the Ottoman Empire invaded Russia to try to liberate and re-establish the Khanate of Astrakhan, which was besieged in 1569 under Kasim Paşa. It was Ottoman distraction further west with the war against Spain, culminating in 1571 with Lepanto, that probably meant that Astrakhan – and ultimately Kazan – remained Russian. At its height the Crimean Khanate was able to raise an army of 120,000. In 1571 Crimea under Khan Daulet Girai was even able to sack its former ally, Moscow, reportedly killing 800,000 and taking 130,000 off into captivity to be sold in the slave markets of Caffa. The Crimeans returned in 1573 but were driven off. In the last half of the sixteenth century Crimean-Ottoman policy was aimed at limiting Russian expansion southwards along the Volga. To this end a Don–Volga canal project was proposed by Süleiman's prime minister, Sököllü Mehmet Paşa, along with a grand strategy to establish a string of Turkish–Tatar buffer principalities along the steppes as far as the Caspian. By the 1580s the policy had failed, and Astrakhan was unable to be retaken due to heavy Russian fortifications (Figure 12.6). However, Astrakhan remained a cosmopolitan city with a large Tatar population, as well as Russian,

Figure 12.11 *The eighteenth-century Tatar palace of Bahchyserai in Crimea*

Figure 12.12 *The Tatar mosque in the palace of Bahchyserai*

Armenian, Persian, Indian and even Chinese communities (Figures 12.7 and 12.8).[22]

The seventeenth century sees the emergence of new steppe groups on the southern steppes. These were the Cossacks. To call them a 'people' in the strict ethnic sense is perhaps incorrect. The Cossacks comprised mainly Russians – usually renegades, escaped serfs or criminals – but they also included Turks, Tatars and remnant Polovtsi. The name Cossack is of Turk origin, the same root as the name Kazakh, both deriving from the Turk *qazak* meaning 'roam'. And although of the Russian Orthodox faith – indeed, fiercely so – they emerged

Figure 12.13 *The former capital of the Don Cossacks at Starocherkassk on the southern Russian steppe*

with a distinct identity that was quite separate from the Russian and often resisting Russian attempts at rule. By the seventeenth century there emerged two groups, the Zaporozhian Cossacks on the Dnieper and the Don Cossacks with their capital at Starocherkassk (Figure 12.13). In 1648 the Zaporozhian Cossacks in the Ukraine formed an alliance with the Crimean Tatars in a revolt against Polish attempts to impose Roman Catholicism. The Cossacks were aided for a while by a Tatar army from Crimea. Then in about 1650 the leader of the Dnieper Cossacks approached Khan Islam Girai III (1644–54) with the proposal to establish a Cossack vassal state in the Ukraine under the Ottomans, similar in status to those of Ottoman Moldavia and Transylvania. The proposal was passed on to Constantinople, but was rejected due to Ottoman preoccupation with the war in Crete (1645–69).[23]

Campaigns deep into Europe continued in the seventeenth century: the Crimeans raided Moscow as late as 1570, Cracow in 1648 and the outskirts of Vienna in 1683.[24] In the 1686–9 Balkan war, Crimea came to the aid of its Ottoman ally and fought against Austria. The absence of Crimean forces on the Black Sea, however, allowed Russia to capture the great fortress of Ak-Kerman overlooking the mouth of the Dniester (Figure 1.12). Furthermore, an agreement that Russia made with Poland in 1647 had ended their rivalry and created a common front against the

Crimean Tatars. But ultimately, it was the Ottomans' preoccupation with the Mediterranean and south-eastern Europe that led it on a number of occasions to turn its back upon Crimea and the Russian steppe. This was one of the major factors ensuring that it would be the Russians who eventually dominated the southern steppe, not the Tatars.

The Crimean Khanate can thus be seen as a wholly European state participating in European politics – and at over three and a half centuries an unusually long-lived one. However, in the end it remained essentially what its original parent state (the Golden Horde) had been: a steppe society. There were few towns and little attempt to create any economy beyond booty and slaves – foreign conquest was viewed solely in these terms rather than as any attempt to extend the state's border and establish a permanent empire.

With the establishment of Russia as a major power in the eighteenth century by Peter the Great, this sole remnant of Batu Khan's once-powerful Golden Horde became increasingly insignificant. By the time the last Crimean Khan, Shagin Girai, came to power in 1779 after a long series of khans being deposed as rapidly as they ascended the throne, he was little more than a Russian puppet. In 1783 Khan Shagin finally made the Khanate over to Catherine the Great, who immediately annexed it to Russia. Thus ended over half a millennium when Mongol-Tatar states were European powers – and hence Khan Shagin was the last descendant of Genghis Khan to rule a European kingdom.[25]

The last migration

The Mongol invasions were probably the most important – and certainly the most devastating – episode in the later history of the movement of steppe peoples into Europe. However, it must be emphasised that they – like the Turks before them – are very much a part of a continuous history, and not a distinct episode, a part of constant movement across the Eurasian steppe. This ongoing fluidity of Europe's open gateway is effectively demonstrated by the last major tribal movement into Europe, that of the Kalmyks.[26]

In the seventeenth century a group of nomadic Mongols migrated from Jungaria in western China into Central Asia. This was caused by their traditional grazing lands becoming encroached upon by both Kazakhs and rival Mongol tribes. Known to themselves as Oirats or Jungar, they are better known in the West under the Russian name of Kalmyks. Initially practising Shamanism, in the course of the seventeenth century the Kalmyks converted to Tibetan Buddhism. This was in line with most other Mongol tribes, as well as many Siberians such as the Buryats and Tuvans, although elements of Shamanism remained. The Buddhist conversion provides

Figure 12.14 *Kalmyk Buddhist temple at Rechnoye on the lower Volga, built in 1818 to commemorate the victory over Napoleon*

another possible motivation for their migration: according to the Kalmyk tradition, the Buddha Maitreya (the future Buddha) would appear from the north.[27] In the 1620s pressure from Chinese expansion into grazing areas forced the Torgut Mongols, a branch of the Oirats, to leave Jungaria led by their khan Khô Örlökh with 200,00–250,000 of his tribe. They eventually arrived into the area of the lower Volga and Don in southern Russia, in turn displacing the Nogay Tatars who were forced to leave the Don in the 1650s for Crimea.

The Kalmyks were thence caught up in the interplay between Russia and Crimea, particularly after the annexation of Ukraine by Russia in 1654 and the subsequent Russian expansion to the Black Sea. The first agreement between the Russians and Khô Örlökh was drawn up in 1655. This set the pattern for subsequent agreements whereby Russia offered protection against the Tatars and other enemies in return for military allegiance by the Kalmyks. By 1690 the Kalmyk ruler, Ayuki, had been invested as khan by the Dalai Lama. This was shortly afterwards recognised by Russia as an acknowledgement of the Kalmyks as the most powerful military force in southern Russia, although they remained in close contact with Jungaria and Tibet. The Kalmyks became a noted fighting force, contributing important contingents to Peter the Great's campaigns against the Swedes, Turks and Persians. There was a historic meeting between Peter and Ayuki at Saratov in 1722 to cement the alliance. Ayuki grew wealthy as a result.

The Russian authorities paid subsidies to the Kalmyk leaders both for stability on the steppe and for a ready supply of horses. However, incoming Russian settlers increasingly encroached upon Kalmyk grazing lands, impoverishing many of the nomads and forcing them off the land. As a result, many Kalmyks were forced to settle in shanty towns on the outskirts of the new Russian towns as a poor underclass. Many Kalmyk children were even offered for sale, effectively becoming slaves. There were also Russian missionary efforts aimed at converting the Kalmyks to Orthodoxy, as well as a leadership crisis following the death of Ayuki Khan in 1724. Inevitably tensions built up between Russians and Kalmyks.

Aggressive Russian colonisation in the 1760s forced more and more Kalmyks away from good pasture land, resulting in even further destitution and antagonism. In 1770, therefore, the Kalmyk leader who had emerged following leadership disputes after Ayuki Khan's death, Ubashi Khan, proposed to return to China with his people. The following year some 300,000 Kalmyks with 10 million head of sheep and cattle embarked upon a mass migration to the east. This was viewed as an act of treason by Russia, but efforts to halt the exodus were mainly unsuccessful, although some were persuaded to remain. Fighting also broke out with the Kazakhs en route, who captured and sold many into slavery. Many more died from cold and exposure, and by the time they re-entered Chinese territory their numbers were depleted by almost two thirds.

However, about fifty thousand Kalmyks did stay behind and some also managed to find their way back. Although their leaders lost many of their former privileges, their quality as a fighting force continued to be recognised. Kalmyks formed three regiments in the Russian army that fought all the way to Paris, spearheading the victorious Russian entry into that city in 1814. The Kalmyks were commanded by a Kalmyk cavalry officer, Serenjab Tyumen, the head of Khosheut tribe of Kalmyks; in 1818, Tyumen, being thankful to Buddha for victory over Napoleon, sponsored the construction of a Buddhist temple at Rechnoye on the west bank of the lower Volga – probably the only Buddhist temple in the world built in commemoration of Napoleon's defeat (Figure 12.14).[28]

Russian relations with the Kalmyks were not always antagonistic, and there were many cases of mutual co-operation and cross-marriages – Lenin, notably, was part-Kalmyk. The doctors at the Moravian colony of Sarepta on the Volga in the nineteenth century practised acupuncture and 'Tibetan medicine', practices that they could only have adopted from the Kalmyks.[29] Their travels and travails, however, were still not over: in 1943 the entire Soviet Kalmyk nation was deported to Siberia because of Stalin's suspicions of Kalmyk complicity in the German invasion, where they remained for thirteen years until allowed back in the Krushchev era.

Today the distinct Kalmyk identity and history are recognised in the form of the Republic of Kalmykia within the Russian Federation, even though, with a population of less than 300,000, it is one of the smallest in the Federation. Unsuspected by most Europeans, Europe includes a Tibetan Buddhist state with a Mongolian population: its capital Elista, in the middle of the steppe between Astrakhan and Rostov-on-Don, is adorned with Tibetan temples and photographs of the Dalai Lama (Figures 12.15–12.19).

Figure 12.15 *A Kalmyk Buddhist monastery outside Elista*

Figure 12.16 *The main Buddhist temple in Elista, capital of the Republic of Kalmykia*

Figure 12.17 *In Elista today, images of the Dalai Lama compete with those of Buddha, Genghis Khan and Lenin; the Kalmyk steppe stretches in the distance*

Figure 12.18 *Lenin, the part-Kalmyk atheist, overlooking the central Buddhist pagoda in Elista*

Figure 12.19 *A people of Europe: Mongols at prayer, rest and play in Elista*

CHAPTER 13

A MODERN STEPPE EMPIRE
Russian Identity and the Steppe

Russia is not in Europe alone, but also in Asia, because a Russian is not only
European, but also Asian.
– Dostoevsky[1]

What a people! They are Scythians! What resoluteness! The barbarians!
– Attributed to Napoleon[2]

In the middle of a busy street in the centre of modern Novosibirsk stands
a small chapel that in its way is one of the more significant churches in
Russia: the Chapel of St Nicholas built during the First World War to
mark the exact geographical centre of Russia (in fact demolished by the
Bolsheviks but rebuilt in the 1990s: Figure 13.1). In many ways this structure encapsulates Russia's ambivalence: its centre is in Asia, some fourteen
hundred kilometres east of the Urals, 3,400 east of Moscow; Novosibirsk
(or Novonikolaevsk as it was then called after Nicholas II) is on about
the same longitude as Lucknow. As Michael Khodarkovsky points out, the
Russian double-headed eagle faces east as well as west.[3]

Russia east or west?

The influence of Kievan Rus upon the development of the Russian state
has been downplayed in some studies, which have argued that it has
been exaggerated in order to establish Russia's European (as opposed to
Asiatic) credentials. Edgar Knobloch,[4] for example, makes a case for the
equal if not greater nomadic and Asiatic influences on the development
of Russia, arguing that Russia is as much Asiatic as European. Even the
Kievan Rus state and society, it is argued, was organised essentially along
nomadic lines, effectively a continuation of the Sarmatian, Hun and
Khazar states that had existed in the same area before, and its claims of
connections with Byzantium overrated. The nomadic steppe title 'khagan'
had been adopted by European steppe societies: a Varangian chief on the
upper Volga adopted the title in the mid-ninth century, for example, and
even Yaroslav the Wise of Kiev, who died in 1054, incorporated it into
his titles.[5]

Knobloch views the concept of 'Holy Russia' or 'Mother Russia' as 'far more the mystical concept of Mother Earth derived from nomadic ideology rather than a political concept of Fatherland'[6] (and Stalin's promotion of the Mother Russia cult is discussed in Chapter 5). Prince Vladimir's adoption of Christianity in the tenth century was purely circumstantial, and he might just as easily have opted for Islam (or even Khazar Judaism, as noted in Chapter 10), as Kiev oscillated between Byzantium and Baghdad. The reign of Sviatoslav from 964 to 973 consolidated the Kievan state. Sviatoslav extended his rule across the steppe, defeating the Khazars. In doing so he adopted the techniques and warfare of the steppe nomad: in other words, Kievan Rus was at first simply another steppe

Figure 13.1 *The Chapel of St Nicholas in Novosibirsk, marking the geographical centre of the Russian Empire*

nomad state, albeit with a Scandinavian element. Sviatoslav never decisively defeated the Pechenegs and was killed by them in 963, and his skull was made into a cup in steppe tradition.[7]

Kiev's successor, Muscovy, adopted and continued many Mongol systems, institutions and even state ceremonials and titles. Knobloch further argues that Russian serfdom is unrelated to the European medieval system, but rooted in the essentially nomadic steppe relationship between the chief and people whom he 'owned'.[8] The Soviet-Leninist system might be viewed as rooted, on the one hand, in the Byzantine Caesaro-Papist legacy and, on the other, in the steppe nomad tradition of chieftain rule and centralised chain of command. Geoffrey Hosking emphasises the paradox of how the perennial theme of the client–patron relationship in Russian history was ironically reinforced by the very efforts to change it, such as those by Peter the Great or the Bolsheviks. Both Peter and Lenin, in drawing upon this relationship to bring about change, simply ended up reinforcing the status quo.[9]

Such interpretations of Russian history are perhaps controversial. But there can be no doubt that the effect of the steppe legacy upon Russia is fundamental. Michael Khodarkovsky estimates that the money poured just into Crimea in the first half of the seventeenth century alone – both directly in the form of tribute and indirectly in the form of redeemed slaves – cost Russia the equivalent of twelve hundred small towns. 'That Russia was under-urbanized in comparison to its Western European neighbors is an undisputed fact, but that this shortage of urban centers may, in no small degree, be related to the nature of Russia's southern frontier is poorly understood.'[10]

The late nineteenth and early twentieth centuries saw a romantic rediscovery of Russia's Asiatic-steppe roots. Anthropology also showed many 'Russian' folk customs to have originated with the Chuvash, Bashkirs and Tatars rather than the Slavs.[11] Stravinsky's *Rite of Spring* in 1913, a celebration of steppe roots, was a part of this movement, and eastern elements are also recognised in the music of Glinka, Balakirev, Borodin, Rimsky-Korsakov and Mussorgsky. It continued into the middle of the twentieth century with many of the works of Khachaturian and Shostakovich (and the movement was not confined to Russia: composers from Mozart to Szymanowski and Britten have borrowed oriental elements). Many Russian intellectuals and writers – notably Lomonosov, Lermontov, Pushkin and Tolstoy – became attracted to a 'romantic orient' following the Russian campaigns in the Caucasus: Pushkin in particular, with his *Fountain of Bahchyserai* based on the legend of a Tatar prince in Crimea, and his *Imitations of the Koran*, a cycle of nine poems on the life of Muhammad, whose exile resonated with Pushkin's own. Pushkin's fascination with Islam, however, was never more than a temporary flirtation, tempered by later disillusion.

Tolstoy studied at the University of Kazan, one of the foremost centres of oriental studies in Europe, where he was a student of the Perso-Russian orientalist Mirza Kazem-Beg. He accordingly came under the spell of the romantic orient after his service in the Caucasus campaigns, but he also looked beyond the Caucasus to India and China, even corresponding with Gandhi (who in turn was influenced by Tolstoy). Kazan is one of the oldest and most important universities in Russia (Figure 13.2). Its most active faculty was the School of Oriental Studies until 1854 when it moved to St Petersburg. 'Part of an archetypal institution of the Western Enlightenment, Kazan University joined Oriental "other" with Occidental "self" more than any other school in Europe . . . the Kazan school . . . reminded Russians that they could learn from Asians just as they might from other Europeans.'[12]

Figure 13.2 *The University of Kazan*

The Mongol legacy

Russia is heir to a more diverse range of external influences than most: Scandinavian via the Vikings; the Finno-Ugrian cultures of the forest belt; Byzantine, and through that Greek and Roman, via Kievan Rus; Polish-Lithuanian, and through that the Catholic; and Mongol-Tatar. Yet according to national myth, the Mongols left no mark on Russian culture or character: Russian civilisation is viewed as rooted primarily in Byzantine Christianity and only slightly less in Scandinavian and German traditions. In his massive 28-volume *History of Russia from the Earliest Times* by the nineteenth-century historian Sergei Soloviev, for example, the Mongols are passed over in just three pages.[13] If Russians referred at all to their Mongol inheritance, it was in terms of their having stemmed the tide of the Mongol horde and saved western Christendom at heroic self-sacrifice from the 'Tatar yoke'.* The only attribute acknowledged is the old myth of 'oriental despotism': that despotism by its very definition must be oriental, as opposed to occidental notions of freedom. As Ostrowski cautions,

---

* To some extent this finds its echoes in the attitude of many Russians to the Second World War, or 'Great Patriotic War' as it is known in Russia, who view Russia as having single-handedly saved the West from Nazism at huge self sacrifice. The Nazi–Soviet pact is denied, and I was once even assured by an otherwise educated articulate Russian that 'England and the United States only entered the War in 1944'.

'We should be very careful about trying to use it [the term 'despotism'] as a scholarly tool to explain how a particular government functioned, especially governments in Asia'.[14] The Mongol legacy in Russia, in other words, is regarded as minimal.

The effect, however, was fundamental. For through the Mongols came influences from China and the steppe, as well as from the Turkish, Persian and Islamic worlds. After the Mongol invasion Russia would never be the same. The future of Russian greatness was both a response to and a legacy of the Mongols. Up until then Russia was a series of disunited Slavic petty states: Kiev, Moscow, Riazan, Novgorod, and others. There is every reason for assuming that this might have remained so until the modern period, just as the German or Italian states remained separate – there was no inevitability in the emergence of Russia as a unified state. But the Mongol invasions forced the states to unite in self-defence, eventually under the banner of Moscow.

Indeed, to a large extent Muscovite power was a creation of the Golden Horde: the khans required a stable central authority as a client state which could be relied upon to raise auxiliaries for the khan's armies and to collect and deliver taxes and tribute. Moscow fitted the bill, so the Golden Horde deliberately strengthened it against the other Russian cities and appointed its prince as their chief tax collector. At the same time the Pax Mongolica brought Russia, hitherto isolated and off the main international routes, for the first time since the Abbasid silver trade into an international system that spanned Eurasia. The early fourteenth century also sees a substantial increase in stone (as opposed to timber) construction in Russia. This was mainly in churches, but also in fortifications, and this was prompted by the Pax Mongolica. The Mongols, in other words, brought about the emergence of Russia.[15]

The Mongols create a Church

Surprisingly, the one Russian institution that gained most from the Mongols was the Orthodox Church. For the official Mongol policy of religious toleration (or at least disinterest) awarded the Church the status of *tarkhan*, 'a charter of immunity' for priests and church lands.[16] Tarkhan was also a title for a high-ranking commander, and is possibly of Xiongu or Scytho-Sarmatian origin; it also occurs among the Tuoba Northern Wei, the Rouran, the Hephthalites, the Turks, the Orkhon inscriptions, and the Khazars.[*] Priests therefore were exempt from tribute, indented labour

---

[*] It is also the root of the place name Astrakhan; it resurfaces in C. S. Lewis's *The Chronicles of Narnia* as the term he adopted for the knights of his mythical oriental Empire of Calormen, the 'Tarkaans'.

and military service, and the church was allowed to own land not subject to tax. Many Russians accordingly flocked to the clergy to escape military service, and there was a rise in monasticism. Orthodoxy became increasingly Russian in its identity, becoming more distant from its Byzantine roots. The monasteries, not having to pay tribute, became increasingly removed from the secular power which had to pay tribute to the Horde. At the time of the Mongol conquest, much of Russia (perhaps most?) was still pagan; by the end most had become Orthodox. By ensuring that the Church stayed outside and above the rival Russian states, the Mongols ensured its future power – and ultimately the pre-eminence of Moscow. Hence, when the Patriarch moved his headquarters from Kiev to Moscow rather than to other more obvious and more powerful cities such as Suzdal or Vladimir or Novgorod, Moscow's rise was ensured.[17]

Claims have been made – for example by some Ukrainian and other western Slav nationalist historians – that the western Slavs were freedom-loving but that Russians were servile, a Tatar legacy of 'oriental despotism'. Donald Ostrowski dismisses the myth of economic oppression under the 'Tatar yoke' out of hand. On the contrary, Russia did very well under the Mongol economic system. The church in particular became very wealthy. Indeed, the Patriarchate of Moscow was more wealthy than its parent Patriarchate in Constantinople in the late fourteenth century – wealthier even than the Byzantine Emperor himself – and there is evidence for large donations to Constantinople from Russia around that time.[18]

The seclusion of women in Muscovy is often cited as a legacy of the Muslim Tatars. But the high status of nomad women, even under Islam, has been emphasised in Chapter 5: Muscovite female seclusion, therefore, is more likely to have been a Byzantine legacy. In summing up his account of the relationship of Russia with the Mongols, Ostrowski emphasises that

we can speak of Mongol influence on the military and on the civil administration of Muscovy. Military influence in regard to weapons, strategy, and tactics is primary and direct. Administrative influence is secondary but still direct: dual civil and military administration from China and *iqtā* from Islamic countries came through the conduit of the Qipchaq Khanate. We cannot speak of Mongol influence in either a primary or a secondary way, either direct or indirect, on the Muscovite practice of seclusion of elite women, or on theories of despotism or autocracy. No doubt the Mongol invasion of 1237–40 brought death and destruction. But the long-term economic devastation of northern Rus' has been exaggerated. Following the apparent economic stagnation of the second half of the thirteenth century, northern Rus' in general, and northeastern Rus' in particular, displayed vital signs of recovery in the early fourteenth century, followed by a flourishing economy from the mid-fourteenth century on. This economic revival was based primarily on commercial activity, and resulted in the acquisition of wealth not only by the grand princely court and the Church but also by merchants, craftsmen, and artisans.[19]

Muscovy becomes a steppe empire

Thus strengthened, it was an opportune time for Muscovy to begin moving against the Khanates, and matters came to a head with the emergence of a powerful new ruler in Moscow, Ivan IV, 'The Terrible'. Even Ivan, however, could not do entirely without Tatar help, and in 1550 he formed an alliance with the Nogay Khan east of the Urals in order to encircle the Kazan Khanate. Then, in 1552, Ivan IV led an army of a hundred thousand against Kazan. The city fell after immense fighting and its citadel and mosque burnt to the ground. Ivan commemorated the event with the construction of a victory church in Moscow supposedly modelled on the Kazan great mosque: St Basil's Cathedral (Figure 13.3).[*] The fall of Kazan left Astrakhan increasingly isolated, and in 1553 the Khan of Astrakhan requested Ivan to nominate a prince for them. Ivan eventually annexed it in 1556. Of Ivan's conquests, Bernard Pares observes: 'Russia [of Ivan the Terible] already bid fair to be and has since become the largest national unit in Europe; and the oneness of its language, its instincts, its atmosphere, its aroma, is henceforward one of the cardinal factors of European history.'[20]

After Ivan IV's conquests of Kazan and Astrakhan, Tatars[†] formed the third-largest ethnic group in the Russian Empire after the Russians and Ukrainians (and perhaps more numerous than the latter). Russian conquest of the Tatars henceforward had to be as much accommodation as suppression. The creation of the Khanate of Kasimov to the south-east of Moscow by Ivan's predecessor had already demonstrated the benefits of this policy. When Ivan IV invaded Livonia a short time after the capture of Kazan, he appointed a Tatar khan, Shad Ali, as the head of his troops. By the late sixteenth century Tatars were beginning to be admitted to the Russian nobility as rewards for loyalty. Tatar nobles, both converts to Christianity and non-converts, rose to senior court positions in Muscovy – there was (at least at first) no trace of any prejudice against people of Tatar origin. Peter Ordyansky, for example, was at once a Tatar noble and a Russian count, and (later) a Russian Orthodox saint. Thus, there arose the paradox of Russian Christian serfs in the service of Tatar nobles, ensuring that Russia would ultimately be a Eurasian empire rather than a

---

[*] The design of the 'reconstructed' Great Mosque of Kazan after 1996 in the Kazan Kremlin is based partly on contemporary descriptions and partly is an acknowledgement of St Basil's supposed resemblance. See Figure 12.5. In the French occupation of Moscow in 1812, Moscow was viewed as an Asiatic city with 'oriental domes' more akin to Delhi than Paris – indeed, Napoleon thought the churches looked like mosques. See Figes 2002: 155. 'St Basil's Cathedral' – officially the Church of the Intercession – is often viewed by non-Russians as the archetypal Russian church, but in fact is unique and quite unlike the standard form of Russian church (and, needless to say, nothing like a mosque).
[†] With the fall of the khanates I henceforth use the term 'Tatar' rather than 'Mongol' unless where retrospectively referring to the initial conquest and administration.

Figure 13.3 *St Basil's Cathedral in Moscow, built to commemorate the conquest of Kazan and supposedly modelled on the Kazan mosque*

European nation state. Ivan IV, the first Russian to proclaim himself Tsar[*] (in Russian the title is actually *Tsezar*), added *Ulugh Khan*, 'Great Khan', to his titles.[21]

This 'Tatarisation' of Russia amounted to more than simply awarding Russian titles to tame Tatars. Institutions in the emerging Russian state

---

[*] The Ottomans for their part refused to recognise Moscow's title of *Tsar*, 'Caesar', as it was one – *Kaysar* – that the Sultans themselves claimed.

were also adopted from the Tatars. Even by the fourteenth century the civil and military institutions of Muscovy 'were overwhelmingly Mongol in origin'.[22] The Mongols had inherited the Chinese systems of administration from the Qara Khitai, whose system of imperial administration they adopted wholesale, and these in turn were passed on to Russia. The Russian institution of the *zemskii sobor*, first called in 1549, derives from the Mongol *quriltai*. Thus, in his conquest of Kazan, Ivan IV took over not only many of the trappings but even the institutions of the khanate: in effect, Ivan created a 'Moscow Khanate'. Ivan also adopted the Mongol policy of 'collective guilt' where all male relatives and retainers of a guilty man would be executed, a policy even extended to entire communities. Stalin's similar policy was a continuation of this.[23] Ivan was as much a continuer of the Tatar legacy as its destroyer.

The term 'Tatar yoke' first appeared in 1575. Ostrowski argues that the myth of the Tatar yoke was deliberately formulated by the Othodox Church to 'divert the Muscovite ruling class from a pro-Tatar orientation'. As a part of this, the title *Tsar*, which did not appear officially until 1547, and the purported descent of the Monomakh dynasty of the medieval princes of Kiev from Augustus, were all a part of a deliberate policy by the Orthodox Church to 'de-Tatarise' the Moscow monarchy. Ostrowski emphasises that 'Only now, with a better understanding of the evidence, can we historians come out from under the oppressive myth of the Tatar yoke'.[24]

In its later medieval and modern history, Russia on the one side faced aggression from Lithuanians, Poles and Swedes; on the other, from the Mongols. Stalin himself remarked in 1941 that Russia 'was beaten by the Mongol Khans, she was beaten by the Turkish Beys, she was beaten by Swedish feudal lords, she was beaten by Polish-Lithuanian Pans, she was beaten by Japanese barons, she was beaten by all'.[25] Such threats from all sides both defined and determined Russia. But it was the Mongol invasions from the east that have haunted the Russian mind, and the fear of holocaust from the east remained ever-present in the Russian mentality. Rimsky-Korsakov's opera *The Invisible City of Kitezh* illustrates this very graphically when a city's only possible defence against the Mongols is to become invisible. Even the gigantic Amazonian memorial to the Siege of Stalingrad in Volgograd (Figure 5.4) does not face west, the direction of the German invasion, but east. Hence, to prevent it ever happening again, Russia embarked upon eastern conquest. At first, this was against the Khanates of Kazan and Astrakhan in the sixteenth century. Then Russia's very first entry into Siberia in 1581 was a raid led by the Cossack adventurer Yermak, who attacked the Tatar Khanate of Sibir. Thus were the origins of the Russian Empire. Between about 1500 and 1900 Russia expanded by an average of fifty square miles per day.[26] Hence, Bernard Pares emphasises that '[t]he Russian march to the Pacific had begun. It was to be marked by singularly few armed conflicts, rather by the sheer force of flowing, and by 1643, with but little help from the government, Russian colonisation had reached the Pacific'[27] – and beyond, to Alaska and down the coast of California to Fort Ross ('Rossiya'),[28] almost on the outskirts of San Francisco.* Such Russian dread of the East at the same time forced Russia to look to the West for its identity. This culminated in the westernising revolution of Peter the Great. The Russian tradition of extreme centralisation and self-dependence, characteristic of both the Peter the Great and the Soviet eras, was also a manifestation of this.

Many Russian noble coats of arms include symbols such as sabres, arrows, crescents and eight-pointed stars, evidence of Tatar ancestry. It even went further when many Russian noble families invented a Tatar ancestry when the Tatar legacy was still strong between the fifteenth and seventeenth centuries, and there was a revival of Tatar interest in the nineteenth century. The supposed 'crown' of Prince Vladimir Monomakh (1113–25), the first Kievan Russian prince to convert to Christianity and a grandson of the Byzantine Emperor Constantine Monomakh, was venerated as a holy Russian symbol as late as the nineteenth century, but was probably fourteenth-century Tatar in origin.[29]

The legacy left an indelible mark upon Russian ethnicity. Many of the great names of Russian history are Tatar in origin: Turgenev, Rachmaninoff, Kutuzov, Suvorov and Yusupov, to give just some of the best known. Tsar Boris Godunov himself was of Tatar descent. General Yermolov, the Russian conqueror of the Caucasus in the early nineteenth century, while a fierce – indeed, fanatic – Russophile, claimed descent from Genghis Khan. Russia's most famous dancer, Rudolf Nureyev, was a Tatar. Anna Akhmatova's surname was the name of a Tatar ancestor on her maternal side (Akhmat is the Russianised form of Ahmad). The list covers all walks of Russian life: artistic, religious, scientific, literary, military, political and royal. The list is virtually endless.[30]

Eurasia as politics

A minor – albeit increasing – political movement that has roots in the steppe is Eurasianism. To some extent its roots go back to orientalising ideas by George Vernadsky in the 1820s and the idea of a 'historical symbiosis' of Slavs and steppe nomads into a 'Turanian superethnos'.[31] In 1837 the philosopher Pyotr Chaadaev wrote that '[Russian culture was] based

---

* The last Spanish mission in California and Spain's northernmost possession, Mission San Francisco Solano, in Sonoma Valley north of San Francisco, was founded in 1823 specifically to counter the expansion of Russia southwards. See Downey 2013.

wholly on borrowing and imitation . . . And yet, situated between the two great divisions of the world, between East and West, with one elbow leaning on China and the other on Germany, we should have . . . united in our civilisation the past of the whole world.'[32]

Such orientalising movements increased in the late nineteenth and early twentieth century among many prominent Russian intellectuals and artists: the orientalist Sergei Oldenburg, for example; the painter, mystic and activist Nikolai Roerich; the historian and orientalist V. V. Barthold; the painter Vasilii Vereshchagin; the poet Alexander Blok's 'Scythianism'; mystics such as Madame Blavatsky, George Gurdjieff and others. Theosophy, eastern medicine, Buddhism and Indian esoteric philosophy all formed part of the intellectual life, especially in St Petersburg.[33] Vereshchagin, as well as painting India and the Far East, depicted Russian Central Asia in startling realism, although his depictions of the often brutal aspects of Russian expansion got him into trouble with the authorities, requiring him to spend much of his life in exile.[34] Even Stravinsky's 'discovery' of a Scythian past in the *Rite of Spring*, or Tolstoy's tales of the Caucasus and his vaguely orientalist mysticism, were part of a rising swell of interest in Russia's oriental roots. As a formal movement Eurasianism began in 1921 with the publication of a pamphlet, 'Turn to the East'.[35] It was then articulated between the two wars by Russian exiles, mainly by Prince Nikolai Trubetskoi (1890–1938), a member of a prominent noble family (a descendant of one of the Decembrists) and Pyotr Savitskii (1893–1968), a member of the pre-revolutionary foreign ministry.

Essentially, the movement was attempting to rationalise Russia's position between East and West, in both Europe and Asia, by the idea of a 'third continent' that both incorporated Europe and Asia but at the same time was distinct from them and led by Russia: Eurasia. In its way, Eurasianism was not entirely dissimilar to the idea of the USSR: its incorporation of European and Asian peoples led by Russia, its rejection of the West and, under Stalin, its rejection of internationalism ('Communism in one country'). Eurasianism in practice? In fact N. N. Alekseev in the 1920s and 1930s formulated Eurasianisim as a 'party' but without other parties allowed: essentially totalitarian:[36] Bolshevism without Communism?

Eurasianism also drew some elements from the ideas of pan-Slavism proposed in the nineteenth century and its rejection of the 'western yoke', to which the Eurasianists added the Turco-Mongol element to create a 'steppic Russia': Orthodoxy, but with Islam and Buddhism. In the words of Savitskii in 1921:

> Is it possible to find in Russia people who don't have khazar or polovtsi, tatar or bachkir, mordve or tchouve blood? Are there many Russians who are completely devoided [*sic*] of the oriental mind . . . this organic fraternity between the orthodox and the nomad or the Asian, Russia is eventually an orthodoxo-Moslem, orthodoxo-Buddhist country.[37]

Trubetskoi viewed the Mongol Empire as the true foundation of Russia, the first Eurasian state and a natural unit of which Russia is the rightful 'heir to the great legacy of Genghis Khan'.[38] In the heroisation of Genghis Khan, Eurasianism was drawing on the Pan-Turanianism proposed by many Turks, such as Enver Pasha, which was pan-Turk and pan-Finno-Ugrian with the idea of 'Turan' as a common homeland. But Trubetskoi, the Russian noble prince, viewed Eurasianism as a conscious attempt to maintain the integrity of the Russian Empire after its collapse in confrontation with pan-Turanianism.

By the end of the Second World War the person who was often regarded (rightly or wrongly) as the 'father of Eurasianism' was the Russia historian of Inner Asian history, Lev Gumilev (1912–92). Hence, he is commemorated on a postage stamp and by the 'L. N. Gumilev Eurasian National University' in Astana, Kazakhstan, as well as by a public monument in the centre of the main street in the Tatar capital of Kazan, and his apartment in St Petersburg has become a museum.[39] Gumilev was the son of the poet Anna Akhamtova, who herself identified with Tatar roots by the adoption of the Tatar pen-name 'Akhmatova' rather than her maiden Gorenko or married name Gumilev. Although, like Akhmatova, Lev Gumilev fell foul of Stalin and spent many years in prison, the two became estranged and Gumilev made a point of distancing himself from his mother. He viewed the Mongol conquest not as the 'Tatar yoke' but as an alliance of Tatars and Russians. However, he held extreme views on ethno-genesis where 'immigrants' corrupt and poison the native inhabitants, and this extended to the Jews, who are excluded from his idea of Eurasia. Despite being one of Artamonov's team who excavated the Khazar fortress of Sarkel, Gumilev viewed the Khazar period in negative terms (although he himself was accused of secret Jewish and Zionist sympathies).[40]

Two formal Eurasianist parties were launched in Moscow in 2002, but the twenty-first century has seen the rise of a new movement, 'Neo-Eurasianism', which goes further. Western Europe (excluding Great Britain, viewed as 'Atlanticist') is to be adopted into the idea of 'Eurasia' (but dominated by Russia), as is the Arab and Islamic world, in opposition to 'Atlanticism': America, Israel and liberalism. Essentially, it has become an extreme form of nationalism. In 2009, a Kremlin academic and member of the Russian foreign ministry, Igor Panarin, predicted the birth of a powerful 'Eurasian alliance' led by Russia with its capital in St Petersburg within four years. It was not only to be a reconstituted Soviet Union but a reconstituted Russian Empire, to incorporate both former Soviet republics and the Iron Curtain countries of Europe, as well as Alaska.[41]

A 'movement' not unlike Neo-Eurasianism (but not formalised) emerged with the discovery of Arkaim and the 'Country of Towns' reviewed in Chapter 2. Some similarities with ancient Iranian and Indian cultures were noted in the archaeology which, with the general recognition of the associated Yamnaya Culture as the birthplace of the Indo-European languages (Chapter 3), led to the suggestion that the area was the homeland of the Indo-Aryans and birthplace of Zoroaster. Arkaim therefore was promoted in the late 1980s as the 'Aryan homeland', which has turned the area into a dubious pilgrimage centre for new age Aryan supremacists. The period coincided with the new openness – 'glasnost' – of the final years of the Soviet Union. Then, with the collapse of the Union shortly after, many Russians found themselves isolated in former Soviet republics as minorities, especially as the new non-Russian nationalisms asserted themselves. This exacerbated the need for such isolated Russian communities to search for a 'homeland', and Arkaim was seized upon as the mystical origin of the Russians/Slavs/Aryans/white race. The date of the site was even put back several thousand years to make it the oldest civilisation in the world, older than the Egyptian; the circular plan of Arkaim was viewed as a mystic universal symbol (linked to the similarly circular plan of Stonehenge, which also attracts New Age cultists) and a swastika was also discerned in its plan. It has become a major pilgrimage centre for whole range of New Age cultists and extremists, gathering in the summer equinox.* The idea of the primordial homeland, the origins of Indo-European languages, Zoroaster and civilisation itself even fed into calls in the 1990s for a Urals Republic that would lead Russia. 'Arkaim appeared like a blinding meteor in the dark sky of post-Soviet reality, lighting sparks of both doubt and hope in the minds of the inhabitants of Russia. Time will pass and the mirage will disappear', in the words of Viktor Shnirelman. 'One would like to believe that the extravagant ultra-nationalist versions of ancient history be a passing phenomenon and that the Museum Reserve of Arkaim will be allowed a long and peaceful life.' In some ways the opposite of Eurasianism – the Arkaim Aryan supremacists exclude Turks, Tatars and Asians – it is at the same time its first cousin.[42]

The steppe, archaeology and identity in Russia

In 1715 Peter the Great created the *Kunstkammer* or 'Cabinet of Curiosities', as it was the intellectual fashion of the day to collect objects for scientific investigation and amusement.[43] Then, to commemorate the birth of his son in the same year, the Tsar was presented with a spectacular collection of Scythian gold objects from Siberia by Nikita Demidov, a tycoon industrialist from the Urals, the son of a serf who became one of the wealthiest men in Russia. The demand to house this and other discoveries of Scythian

---

* This might explain why, on a long day excursion to Arkaim on 16 June 2011 from Magnitogorsk, we were explicitly denied visiting the site, but confined to the museum.

Figure 13.4 *The Hermitage, St Petersburg, built to house the royal art treasures*

gold in an appropriate setting was one of the reasons for the eventual foundation of the Hermitage Museum. Another find of Scythian gold came from the southern steppe. This was the Litoi Kurgan discovered by Baron Melgunov and added to the Kunstkammer in 1763 (the 'Melgunov Treasure'), causing a sensation when it was displayed in St Petersburg. Catherine the Great's mania for collecting art works prompted her a year later to found the Hermitage Museum, eventually to become one of the greatest single repositories of art treasures in the world (Figure 13.4). The burgeoning collection of Scythian treasures and the interest it aroused was one of the reasons behind her decision, moving those still in the Kunstkammer to the new museum, although all of the gold treasures were not brought together until the construction of the New Hermitage under Nicholas I (1825–55).

Further discoveries, not to mention the massive collecting policies by Catherine the Great and her successors, prompted continued expansion of the Hermitage. Once again Scythian gold played an important part. This was the discovery of the royal Scythian burial at Kul-Oba in Crimea near Kerch in 1830, 'possibly the largest known classical-period body of precious metal items'[44] and among the most spectacular items in the Hermitage. Its transfer to St Petersburg and imperial protection was instrumental in the establishment of the New Hermitage, purpose-built as a Museum in 1852. The Greco-Scythian antiquities were given pride of place in the most unusual gallery in the New Hermitage, the 'Hall of the Cimmerian Bosporus', designed deliberately in a vaguely 'oriental' style.[45]

Interest in the Scythian and nomadic tradition suited the Russian state's purpose. The Graeco-Scythian antiquities and the increasing number of other accidental discoveries – mainly in the southern steppe – prompted the establishment of the Imperial Archaeological Commission by Emperor Alexander II in 1859 to supervise and impose some formal control on archaeological discoveries and sites in Russia. This was one of the first professional archaeological bodies in the world. Members of the Commission immediately began controlled archaeological investigations into the Scythian burials around Kerch in Crimea, subsequently expanding their work around the Black Sea and the Kuban steppe. It also marked the beginning of a close collaboration between the Commission and the Hermitage, with most of the finds going to the latter. Among the Commission's first results was the excavation of the spectacular Scythian gold treasure from Chertomlyk Kurgan near the lower Dnieper. Further major discoveries of Greco-Scythian workmanship were made at the ancient Greek colonies of Panticapaeum (adjacent to the Kul-Oba burials), Phanagoria and Theodosia, as well as another Scythian gold treasure at Solokha. In 1897 the spectacular gold treasure and hitherto unsuspected fourth millennium culture at Maikop on the Kuban steppe was unearthed (Figure 2.5; all discussed in earlier chapters).

Parallel to this was a spate of Russian exploration of Inner Asia in the late nineteenth century. This was often, if not always, with archaeology as their object – but the end result was further enrichment of the Hermitage with dazzling works of art. There were a number of motives prompting this. The earlier discoveries around the Black Sea certainly provided a powerful motivation. But spectacular discoveries of lost civilisations and works of art preserved virtually intact in the dry sands of Chinese inner Asia – mainly the Taklamakan and Gobi Deserts – prompted an international 'race' by the great powers to get there first and enrich their museums back home. The Russians were the first to bring this to international attention in the 1870s.[46] This, we may remember, was a period when archaeology and national collections were very much a part of great power rivalry. The acquisition by the British Museum of the Elgin Marbles, for example, meant that Germany, a latecomer to great power politics, had to acquire its own spectacular work of Classical art, the Pergamon Altar. To some extent this was also a reflection of each great power attempting to seize the Classical legacy for its own legitimacy. Whatever it was, world powers had to have world collections adorning their world capitals, and the British, the French, the Germans, the Japanese and (much later) the Americans all sent missions into Chinese Inner Asia to collect the archaeological wealth there.[47] The Russians – with their national showpiece, the Hermitage – would not be left out.

Figure 13.5 The tomb of Nikolay Przhevalsky in Kyrgyzstan

The Russians also had an advantage over their rivals: much of Inner Asia was already theirs. Hence, its exploration had been a part of imperial policy ever since their expansion into Siberia and the first official mapping and exploration expeditions there from the eighteenth century onwards. Such expeditions soon came under the auspices of the Imperial Geographical Society, established in 1845 by Nicholas I. A pioneer of Inner Asian exploration of China and Tibet was Nikolai Przhvalsky, who carried out four expeditions under their auspices between 1876 and 1888 (Figure 13.5). Others were the Swedish explorer Sven Hedin and the Finnish explorer Carl Gustaf Mannerheim, who operated under imperial Russian sponsorship. The Tien Shan and adjacent areas were explored in 1856–7 and again in 1888 by Piotr Semyon-Tianshansky (Figure 13.6), his surname granted the honorific in recognition. The historian Vasili Barthold was a member of a team that explored the Ili and Chu Valleys in 1893, and Barthold's studies of Central Asia are still major works of reference for historians today. The Russian consul in Kashgar, N. F. Petrovsky, was the first to send fragments of art objects back to St Petersburg in the 1880s, but the greatest discoveries were made by Piotr Kozlov. A protégé of Przhevalsky, Kozlov rediscovered the thirteenth-century Tangut city of Karakhoto in the Gobi Desert while leading an expedition to Tibet in 1907–9 (Figure 13.7). The objects preserved in the dry sands were nothing short of spectacular, and they have a whole gallery in the Hermitage

Figure 13.6 *Monument to Piotr Semyon-Tianshansky in Kyrgyzstan, facing the mountains he explored*

Figure 13.7 *The Kozlov house museum in St Petersburg*

devoted to them. This was followed up by the mission of Sergei Oldenburg, Permanent Secretary of the Academy of Sciences, to Dunhuang in Gansu in 1909 and again in 1914–15.* The Dunhuang Buddhist monastery caves was the scene of one of the greatest discoveries of ancient manuscripts by the Hungarian-British archaeologist Aurel Stein in 1904, but most of the manuscripts had been removed by him and his French rival, Paul Pelliot, by the time of Oldenburg's arrival on the scene. Oldenburg, however, was able to retrieve some manuscripts and other sculptures and paintings, as well as make the first proper photographic and scientific record of the monastery itself.[48]

Activities were interrupted by the Revolution, and the work of the Archaeological Commission was taken over by the newly founded Academy of Sciences. This resumed archaeological investigations throughout the Soviet Union, which further built up the Hermitage's collections. Indeed, after the Revolution subsequent Soviet austerity and international isolation meant that the Hermitage could no longer purchase collections abroad. Hence, apart from confiscations of private collections, archaeological excavations were almost the sole source of new acquisitions. Accordingly, the Hermitage benefited from this policy, with further excavations around the Black Sea of both Greek colonies and Scythian kurgans. There was also increased cultural diversity, ranging from ancient Near Eastern artefacts from the excavations of the former Urartian capital of Karmir Blur in Armenia, and the pre-Islamic Sogdian wall paintings from Panjikent in Tajikistan, to objects from the medieval Khazar capital of Sarkel on the Volga, to name just some. But the most spectacular was once again in the field of Scythian art, with the excavation of the frozen tombs at Pazyryk in Siberia (Figures 1.3 and 4.10–4.14).

This emphasis on archaeology meant that although the Hermitage was – and remains – primarily a museum of European art, latterly most of the directors have been archaeologists or orientalists (usually both). For much of the early twentieth century Oriental Studies in Russia was dominated by the maverick Georgian scholar and archaeologist Nikolai Marr, who excavated the medieval Armenian capital of Ani (in Turkey) and also loomed large in the Hermitage and its policies. The first archaeologist Director of the Hermitage was a student of Marr's, Iosif Orbeli, Director from 1934 to 1951, an Armenian who, at the beginning of the twentieth century, made the first major discoveries of the Urartian civilisation in eastern Turkey. He was succeeded by Mikhail Artamonov, the Director of the excavations of Sarkel and author of the first major study of Scythian

---

* Oldenburg was himself of inner Asian origin, being born in Transbaikal in Siberia. He was later a friend and colleague of Alexander Ulyanov, the brother of Lenin. Oldenburg remained a Bolshevik sympathiser, becoming the first Minister of Education in the Provisional Government.

art, who was then succeeded in 1964 by the Piotrovsky father and son who have dominated the Hermitage ever since. Boris Piotrovsky was the excavator of the Urartian site of Karmir Blur in Armenia. Like Artomonov before him, Piotrovsky also published an important work on Scythian art. He was succeeded in 1992 by his son, Mikhail Piotrovsky, a specialist in South Arabian archaeology where he carried out excavations. Mikhail Piotrovsky oversaw the difficult transition of the museum after the collapse of the Soviet Union and is (at the time of writing) still the Director.

The Hermitage Museum, therefore, possibly the largest museum in the world and certainly one of the greatest showcases of Western art, has had a continual thread of steppe art and oriental archaeology from its very beginning to the present day. But steppe art and archaeology have affected Russia in other ways as well. It is significant that much of the initial archaeological interest in the steppe after Catherine the Great was in the ancient Greek colonies around the Black Sea. This led to the excavation of large numbers of these colonies: Olbia, Berezin, Chersonesus, Panticapaeum, Nymphaeum, Phanagoria, to name just a few – probably the largest number of ancient Greek sites excavated outside Greece itself. For Russians, this emphasis was important. This is because Russian Orthodoxy was founded by and identified with Byzantium – and after Patriarch Nikon's reforms in the 1650s the religious links with the Greek Church were re-asserted. But with Russia isolated in the far northern world before Peter's and Catherine's southward expansions, Greece and Greek culture were very remote and indirect. The expansion southwards into the steppe brought Russia into direct contact with ancient Greek culture: the worlds of Russia and ancient Greece finally overlapped. It led directly to the foundation of new Russian cities around the Black Sea deliberately named after the Greek colonies: Odessa, Kherson, Sevastopol, Simferopol, Theodosia and others. Of course, I do not suggest their archaeological emphasis to be a conscious Russian policy or even a logically thought-out argument on the part of the early archaeologists (and ancient Greece in any case was not the same as Greek Orthodoxy), but a direct line back to the ancient Greeks themselves was nonetheless an added motivation in a Russian Orthodox world.

There is another reason for such interest in these Black Sea colonies. For as well as the Greek they represented the *Classical* past, and Russia after Peter the Great sought to identify with Europe's Classical – mainly Roman – past more than any other country (and in this context most of the Black Sea colonies had Roman-period remains as well as Greek). The Russian monarchs proclaimed themselves Caesars: Tsars, a title they adopted from the Bulgarians; it was the Russians who laid claim to being the 'Third Rome' (on religious grounds, admittedly); it was Peter the Great's new capital of St Petersburg that deliberately set out to identify with a Classical past by the creation of what is arguably the greatest

Neo-Classical city in the world. As a part of Peter's Classicising movement he sought to acquire Classical art – mainly sculpture – for the imperial collections; the Tauride Venus is a notable example, but this was only one part of a consignment over a hundred Classical sculptures imported from Italy.[49]

In this context, one of the people most responsible in the early nineteenth century for the creation of a Russian 'national art style', Aleksei Olenin, deliberately sought to present the archaeological discoveries of the Black Sea region as a direct Russian link back to ancient Greece and Rome.[50] Olenin was working under the direct patronage of Nicholas I, who sought to look to Russia's past for a national identity that was distinct from the westernising tendencies of Peter I and his successors, especially Catherine. The different threads of Russian self-identity came together in an 1836 watercolour by a pupil of Olenin's, Fedor Solntsev, of a meeting of the Kievan Prince Sviatoslav with the Byzantine Emperor John Tzimisces. The overall theme of the painting (in the State Russian Museum in St Petersburg) is, of course, the direct link established by the first Russian to convert to Christianity with the Classical past: although Russian Orthodoxy prevails, Greek and imperial Roman elements are there – along with Scythian.[51]

The Russian obsession with Classicism was revived under Stalin, who suppressed the innovative Constructivist and other styles of the early Revolution in favour of an over-powering Neo-Classical style.[52] When Sevastopol – itself a Greek name – for example, had to be rebuilt after its almost total destruction in the Second World War, Stalin ordered it to be rebuilt in a Neo-Classical style. Similar requirements lay behind the reconstruction of Stalingrad (renamed Volgograd after Stalin's death), with a particular focus on its opulent railway station. Of course, all Europe lays claim to its Roman imperial past to a greater or lesser extent, and museums in Paris, Berlin and London all vied with each other for the greatest Classical *objets d'art*. But Russia's claims were the loudest – and also the weakest, it being the one great power that lay outside the Roman imperial boundaries. And here at last in these southern-steppe archaeological sites the Russian and the Roman Empires overlapped, a direct link with the Classical past.

Such threads – new cities with Classical names, Neo-Classical architecture, archaeological collections of local Classical antiquities – came together with the establishment of the Archaeological Museum in Odessa, capital of 'New Russia' (as the Black Sea territories were officially called), in unabashed imitation of a Greek temple, with a replica of the Lacoön and the serpents standing outside it (Figure 13.8). And as if to drive home the message – no subtleties required – a statue of the city's founder, the Duc du Richelieu, was erected at the top of the 'Potemkin Steps' dressed in a Roman toga. Caspar Meyer emphasises that 'the anticipated national

Figure 13.8 *The Archaeological Museum of Odessa*

collections [in the Hermitage] were made to communicate the civiliz-
ing mission of the Russian nation in the evolving empire by associating
Russian cultural products with the legacies of Greece and Rome, including
northern Black Sea antiquities'.[53] Again, this was never deliberate policy
or articulated justification, but a powerful cultural imperative nonetheless.

The steppe, art and identity in Russia

Scythian art had a further influence in Russia. In the late nineteenth and
early twentieth centuries the Russians 'rediscovered' their Scythian and
other folk and oriental roots, a reaction against the Classicising and westernising by many elements of Russian society, particularly among artists.
This took a variety of forms. Many of the nobility and – in particular – the
wealthy merchant classes began to build their mansions in the traditional
old Russian wooden styles. But rather in the manner of Marie-Antoinette
dressing up as a milkmaid without the reality of getting up at 4 a.m. to
milk the cows, these houses were built on far grander and more elaborate
scale than the peasants' huts on which the style is based (Figures 6.46
and 6.47). Such a 'pseudo-Russian' style could also assume monumental

Figure 13.9 *Red Square in Moscow with the 'neo-Russian' Russia History Museum at the end framed by the GUM trading rows on the right and the Kremlin on the left*

form with several major buildings, mainly in Moscow: for example, the huge 'neo-Byzantinesque' Church of the Saviour begun in 1837 to commemorate the Russian victory over France,* the ornate red brick Russian History Museum begun in 1874 on Red Square and the transformation of Red Square itself with the vast Trading Rows (GUM) of 1889 forming the east side of the square opposite the Kremlin (Figure 13.9). One particular group of artists, known as the 'Wanderers', decided that art had to be taken to the masses and took to travelling throughout Russia to bring art to the ordinary people. Artists began to look to Russian roots for inspiration rather than to movements from western Europe.[54]

Such movements must be viewed against the background of the enormous social upheaval that took place in Russia after the emancipation of the serfs in 1861. This affected all walks of society, and had a huge effect on all the arts. These various movements culminated in the so-called 'Abramtsevo Circle', a colony of artists and designers patronised by the railway tycoon and philanthropist Savva Mamontov on his estate at Abramtsevo outside Moscow in the 1870s (Figure 6.44–645, 13.10 and 13.11).[55] Another notable patron was P. M. Tretyakov, who bought the

---

* Stalin, displaying quite possibly the only instance of good taste in his life, had it blown up in 1931; it was rebuilt after 1997.

Figure 13.10 *Part of the Abramtsevo artists' colony outside Moscow*

paintings and whose collection formed the basis of the Tretyakov Gallery in Moscow. A similar centre for the neo-Russian style was the artist colony at Talashkino near Smolensk, founded by Princess Tenisheva in 1893. These movements deliberately sought to distance themselves from the St Petersburg Academy of Art with its emphasis on court patronage and Neo-Classical and Western forms (although it must be remembered that the artists were products of the Academy, despite distancing themselves from it). It attracted not only painters, but also craftsmen, designers, sculptors, musicians, performers and even historians and archaeologists. It was expressed in new interpretations of theatre and even opera, but most of all in art and design. For inspiration it looked more to Russian roots in the ordinary people and in Russia's past: folk art, icons, distaffs (Figure 6.44), and Slavic, Finno-Ugrian, Scythian and oriental motifs generally. It included elements drawn from the Caucasus, very much the 'romantic orient' to the nineteenth-century Russian mind, but it was also 'the very vastness and flatness of the steppe' that affected so many artists of the late nineteenth-century (the landscape painter Isaak Levitan even used a wide-angle lens to photograph such scenes for his paintings).[56]

These elements were brought together to create a more authentic Russian idiom. In 1870, for example, the painter and prominent member of this group Ilya Repin, in his 'rediscovery' of the Russian peasant, went to live at Shiryaevo on the Volga near Samara. He sees the face of one of

Figure 13.11 *The conscious revival of a traditional Russian style in one of the interiors at Abramtsevo*

Figure 13.12 *Reproduction of Repin's 'The Barge Haulers' at the Repin House Museum at Shiryaevo on the Volga*

the peasants: 'There was something eastern and ancient about it . . . the face of a Scyth.'[57] His work *The Barge Haulers of the Volga* is one of the best-known works of Russian art (Figure 13.12). Other prominent artists included Isaak Levitan, Vassily Surikov, Alexander Golovin, Mikhail Vrubel and Nikolai Roerich, as well as writers such as Nikolai Gogol

Figure 13.13 *The Roerich house museum at Velikiy Uimon in the Altai*

and Ivan Turgenev. Roerich in particular, a member of the Talashkino circle, was to gain a huge following in later years. As well as a painter and designer, Roerich became a prominent explorer and orientalist mystic, travelling in the Altai and Himalayas. Indeed, he recognised the steppe animal style surviving among the tribes of northern Tibet.[58] He still has a cult following in India and America as well as in Russia, where the 'Urals Spiritual-Ethical Centre', a temple in Chelyabinsk named after Roerich to study his teaching, has also been linked to the Arkaim cult (described above).[59] Recent years have witnessed a rediscovery of Roerich in Russia, with a special gallery of his paintings in Novosibirsk and his house at Velikiy Uimon in the Altai rebuilt as a shrine (Figure 13.13); his paintings when they come up at auction sell for astronomical sums.*

From this emerged the 'World of Art' movement under the leadership of the artistic polymath Alexander Benois and the impresario Sergei Diaghilev and their circle in the 1890s.[60] It 'believed . . . Russia should not return to the status of a provincial outpost of Western Europe, nor remain the stronghold of an isolated national tradition'.[61] A dedicated magazine entitled the *World of Art* launched by Diaghilev began to appear

---

* Nicholas Roerich's *Madonna Laboris* sold for an astonishing and record-breaking £7.8 million at auction at Bonhams in London in 2013. https://www.bonhams.com/auctions/20841/lot/63/

after 1898, proclaiming 'art for art's sake'. Of course, the artists were well aware of and influenced by similar movements elsewhere in Europe, such as those of William Morris and the Arts and Crafts movement in Britain, the art nouveau in France (or 'style moderne' as it was known in Russia; Chapter 6) and the avant-garde (of which the Russians were among the leading practitioners). But the reaction against Classicism began earlier in Russia than elsewhere in Europe: new styles of art and innovation emerged here first.[62] It was the richness of the Russian past, not to mention the tumult of the Russian present in the first decades of the twentieth century, that set the Russians apart with the creation of the 'Style Russe', and it comes as no surprise that art nouveau surged in popularity throughout the former Russian Empire. As well as many of the Abramtsevo Circle, the movement attracted many of the more adventurous new artists and practitioners such as Leon Bakst and, most notably, Sergei Diaghilev, who went on to launch the Ballets Russes (many of which featured oriental-style costumes) to worldwide fame, and ultimately the career of Igor Stravinsky.[63]

Stravinsky's momentous *Rite of Spring* in 1913 – the work often regarded as having launched twentieth-century music – was one of the outcomes of this movement. The work was almost as much Nikolai Roerich's costume and stage designs as Stravinsky's composition (not to mention Nijinsky's choreography on the Paris stage). Its first performance in Paris was received with shock, for among scenes of a sexual nature there was a re-enactment of an ancient Scythian sacrifice of a young maiden. While the music itself was drawn from Russian traditional music, the ballet itself was a conscious evocation of Russia's Scythian past. This was a part of a wider movement of 'Scythianism' among Russian intellectuals. A parallel assertion of Scythian roots was by Russia's 'poet laureate of the Revolution', Alexander Blok, in his poem *The Scythian*:

> You're millions, we are hosts – and hosts – and hosts!
> Engage with us and prove our seed!
> We're Scythians and Asians too, from coasts
> That breed squint eyes, bespeaking greed![64]

The illustration to accompany it, by the avant-garde artist Mikhail Larionov, depicted a caricature Russian peasant's face as a mask ripped off to reveal a grinning Scythian face underneath (Figure 13.14).[65] Larionov further in his radical *Rayonist Manifesto*, 'We are against the West, vulgarizing our Oriental forms, and rendering everything valueless.'[66] And in art, Larionov's fellow avant-garde artist and lifelong companion (and eventual wife), Natalia Goncharova, wrote, 'My path leads towards the original source of all the arts, towards the East. The art of my country is incomparably deeper than anything I know in the West',[67] and, 'For me

Figure 13.14 Mikhail Larionov's illustration Skify, *the face of a Scythian underneath a Russian mask, to accompany Blok's poem* The Scythian

Figure 13.15 The triumphal arch in Vladivostok to celebrate Crown Prince Nicholas' visit in 1891 (demolished by the Bolsheviks and rebuilt in the early 2000s)

the East means the creation of new forms, an extending and deepening of the problems of colour.'[68]

Of course, Orientalism was a craze in Western art at the same time,[69] and Russian Orientalism drew from this. But in Russia there was a fundamental difference: the 'Orient' was not only an integral part of Russia but its very centre, as the Chapel of St Nicholas in Siberia cited at the beginning of this chapter demonstrates (Figure 13.1). This was expressed by another 'Nicholas' monument in many ways more symbolic than that chapel, the Triumphal Arch in Vladivostok built in honour of the then Crown Prince Nicholas' visit in 1891 on a grand tour of inspection of the East he was about to rule (Figure 13.15). Hence, Russian art drew much inspiration from the East – and the East came to the Russian far west in the form of a mosque in the style of Samarkand in the centre of St Petersburg as well as a Tibetan Buddhist temple in an art nouveau style on its outskirts (Figures 13.16 and 13.17).[70]

A building where many of these movements came together was the Moscow Art Theatre, opened in 1898 as a venue specifically for new experimental styles. The founders were Konstantin Stanislavsky, who gave his name to a new style of acting, and Vladimir Namirovich-Danchenko, who took on the task of administering the theatre. The building itself is one of the masterpieces in Moscow of the art nouveau style (Figure 13.18) built by Fyodor Schechtel, one of the style's main practitioners whose buildings include the famous Ryabushinsky Mansion. Chekhov's *The Seagull* was

Figure 13.16 *The dome of the St Petersburg Mosque copied from the Gur-i Emir in Samarkand*

Figure 13.17 *The St Petersburg Tibetan Buddhist Temple*

Figure 13.18 *Interior of the Moscow Art Theatre*

one of the first performances there, the beginning of a long association which contributed to both the theatre's and the playwright's success.

The musical legacy of Diaghilev and Stravinsky hardly needs reasserting, with such giants of twentieth-century music as Prokofiev, Shostakovich, Schnittke, Vainberg, and other Soviet era composers drawing upon it. But it was in the Russian art movements of the early twentieth century that we see the greatest legacy of the Abramtsevo and World of Art movements: Kandinsky, Chagall, Bakst, Popova, Goncharova, Larionov, Filonov, Tatlin, Exter, Malevich, Lissitsky and many more who, in turning away from the received wisdom of convention, were able to draw inspiration from the rich world of the Eurasian forest and steppe around them and the art forms that flourished there in perhaps the most astonishing outpouring of innovative art of the early twentieth century.[71] The landscape artist Pavel Kuznetsov painted dreamlike images of the steppe in the 1910s and 1920s, and even Vasilii Kandinsky found inspiration in Russian folk art, despite his paintings appearing completely abstract, as well as a fascination for Islamic and eastern art following a visit to Tunisia.[72] In writing of this Russian 'silver age' John Bowlt sees it as much rooted in 'the territorial enormity of Russia, which, incalculable and formless like the long, still winter, became a tabula rasa for unprecedented investigations into the contrary idioms of expression such as cryptic language, silence, abstract painting, and dissonant music'.[73] Probably the most revolutionary work

Figure 13.19 *Malevich as revolutionary artist: the Malevich room in the Tretyakov with his* Black Square *as the centrepiece*

of art from that age, Kazimir Malevich's iconic *Black Square* of 1915, which even today still provokes controversy (Figure 13.20), might appear as alien to the steppe art reviewed in Chapter 6 as could possibly be. But at the same time might it be viewed as its logical outcome?[74] In the 1930s Malevich returned to folk and steppe themes: the themes of peasants, of reaping and of wide flat landscapes – his 1932 canvas *Red Cavalry* could almost be depicting mounted steppe nomads at full gallop. Malevich's work remains iconic in Russia to this day (Figure 13.20).[75]

Although this extraordinary outburst of creativity came to an end with Soviet stultification, aspects of it continued and even expanded: in music, for example, as we have noted. But Soviet Russia also looked back to its folk and steppe roots: the emphasis on folk traditions seen in rich folk decoration of some of the Moscow Metro stations such as Byelorusskaya, for example (Figure 13.21), or the emphasis on vegetal motifs seen on so many buildings such as those depicted so flamboyantly at the All Union Exhibition Grounds (VDNKh; Figure 13.22), or many of the idealised scenes of life on the steppe (albeit with an agricultural bias) depicted in many a Soviet realist painting.

* * *

In absorbing the Crimean Tatars into Russia in 1783, Catherine issued a decree of religious tolerance of Muslims. Mosques and madrasas were

Figure 13.20 *Malevich as iconic décor: a department store in St Petersburg*

Figure 13.21 *Decorative panel in Byelorusskaya Metro Station in Moscow*

allowed to be opened. In 1788 a Muslim Spiritual Assembly was created to oversee Muslim affairs and education, both religious and secular. This was applied not only to the newly absorbed Crimean Tatars, but throughout Russia, in particular to the former khanates of Kazan and Astrakhan. Today, the descendants of the Mongol 'hordes' – the Tatars – are the second-largest minority in Russia after the Russians themselves, and the Republic of Tatarstan is the second-largest republic in European Russia.* Since its semi-independence from central rule in 1994 it has been viewed as a model towards market rule and multiculturalism.[76] The Tatars serve as an important reminder, first, that a Muslim and originally Asiatic

---

* The term 'Tatar', however, is a fairly loose one, applied not only to the Muslim inhabitants of Tatarstan but to the Muslim populations as a whole speaking a Turk-related dialect throughout Russia, although their self-identification as 'Tatars' is a modern one. See Schamilou 2006.

Figure 13.22 *Vegetal motifs on the Ukraine Pavilion at the All Union Exhibition Grounds in Moscow*

people form a major and integral part within Europe, European tradition and European culture; and second, more importantly, that for centuries the ethnic, religious and cultural domination of eastern Europe as a whole and Russia in particular hung on a knife-edge between Muscovy and an Ottoman-Tatar supremacy: Russia – originally a Viking, not a Slavic, state – might have become either Tatar and Muslim or Slavic and Orthodox. There was no historical inevitability that it became the latter, merely historical circumstance. Perhaps it is still on that knife-edge.

Notes

Introduction

1 Amitai and Biran 2005: 1.
2 Bonner 2019: 96. See also his lecture 'Sasanian Iran: A Personal View' at the Pourdavoud Center for the Study of the Iranian World at the UCLA on 2 December 2020, https://pourdavoud.ucla.edu/video/sasanian-iran-a-personal-view/ (last accessed 2 December 2020) as well as Bonner 2020 (which I had not been able to obtain before going to press).
3 Vogelsang 1992; Potts 2014; Bonner 2020.
4 Barfield 1989; Di Cosmo 2002.
5 E.g. Ball 2009, 2010, 2012, 2016.
6 Koryakova and Epimakhov 2007.
7 Taylor 1948: 11.
8 Pohl 2018a: 198.
9 Schimmelpennink van der Oye 2010: 180.
10 Rietbergen 2006: xvii.
11 Personal observation.
12 Olivier 2020: 108.
13 Ball 2012.
14 Ball 2019b and references.
15 Pohl 2018a: 12.

Chapter 1

1 Translated by Constance Garnett, 1919.
2 Applebaum 1996: xi.
3 Bartlett 2004.
4 Gibbon III 1897: 75; Khodarkovsky 2002: 29–30.
5 See Ponamarenko and Dyck 2007 for comparative studies of the Eurasian and North American grasslands.
6 See the various essays in Bemmann and Schmauder (ed) 2015, especially Kradin 2015; Pohl 2018: 198–209 for a general summary of the steppe, nomadism and related matters. A general overview is given by Cunliffe 2015: Chapter 1 and 454–66.
7 Frachetti 2008: 105.

8 Yang, Shao and Pan 2020: 112–13. See also Frachetti 2008: 92–9, especially Table 6.

9 Kilunovskaya and Semenov 1995.

10 Yang, Shao and Pan 2020: 417. See also Kilunovskaya and Semenov 1995.

11 See the thoughtful essay by Popova 2009.

12 Frachetti 2008: 7.

13 Scott et al. (eds) 2004.

14 See discussions in: Ponamarenko and Dyck 2007; Frachetti 2008: 18–22; Yang, Shao and Pan 2020: 271–3. See also: Bell 2000; Honeychurch 2015.

15 Di Cosmo 1999; Bell 2000.

16 See e.g. Frachetti 2008: 15–18.

17 See Di Cosmo 1999: 3–4.

18 Kohl 2006: 5; Kohl 2007: 18.

19 Heather 2009: 347–8.

20 Cunliffe 2019: 312.

21 Bosworth 2012: 200.

22 Baumer 2012: 35–8.

23 Anthony 2010: Chapter 10; Baumer 2012: 84–92; Cunliffe 2015: 75–80.

24 Koryakova and Epimakhov 2007: 233.

25 Scott et al. (eds) 2004.

26 Barfield 1989: 8 and 2001. See also Di Cosmo 1999.

27 Sulimirsky 1963.

28 E.g. Curta 2020: 102–3.

29 Herodotus IV.14–15. See also Bolton 1962.

30 Golden 2002: 110.

31 Maenchen-Helfen 1973: 52; Golden 2002: 109.

32 Lattimore 1940: 238 ff. See also the discussion by Anthony 2010: 102.

33 Lattimore 1940: 344 ff.

34 See in general Di Cosmo 2002; Yang, Shao and Pan 2020: 465.

35 Lattimore 1940: 411. See also now in general Chaichian 2013.

36 Khazanov 1985: 195. See also: Di Cosmo 1999; Khazanov 2013.

37 Peacock 2010: 83.

38 Ponomarenko and Dyck 2007: 46.

39 Golden 2011: 130. See in general Di Cosmo 1999 and 2002, Khodarkovsky 2002 and Golden 2002 on inner Asian warfare (the latter including an unfortunate typological error in a subtitle on 'The Marital Image of the Eurasian Nomad'.)

40 Lattimore 1940: 173–4; 491–5; Di Cosmo 2002: 249.

41 Ball 1998.

42 Waugh 2010.

43 Ball 2000: 133–9 (old edition); new edition 2016: 150–6.

44 Ball 2008: 80–1.

45 Rezakhani 2010.

46 Pope 2005.

47 Whitfield: 2007; 2020: 15.

48 Hansen 2015.

49 Brosseder 2015: 199, 282.
50 E.g. Di Cosmo and Maas 2018: 2–5. See also the perceptive remarks by Cameron 2018.
51 E.g. Brosseder 2015: 199.
52 Ronan and Needham 1978: Chapter 6.
53 Deeg 2018.
54 Mallory and Mair 2000: 62.
55 I am grateful to Wendy Ball for pointing out this comparison.
56 E.g. Walter 2015: xviii.
57 See Ball 2016: 141–50, for a summary of the evidence.
58 E.g. Whitfield 2007; Walter 2015.
59 The actual title of Kuzmina 2008.
60 Personal observation 2012.
61 The main one being the catalogue, edited by Susan Whitfield in 2004, but the same author also produced *Aurel Stein* in the same year, *Life Along* in 1999 and *Silk, Slaves* in 2018, while in the run up to the exhibition the Library also published Susan Wood's *Silk Road*.
62 Frankopan 2015.
63 Mallory and Mair 2000: 62, 64.
64 Abu-Lughod 1989: 170.
65 Yuan 2014.
66 Personal observation.
67 *Armenia Now*, 20 January 2009.
68 BBC News, Monday 26 April, 2004.
69 *China Daily*, 10 January 2008; Yuan, *New Silk Road*.
70 *China Daily*, 4 February 2009.
71 *The Age*, 27 June 2006.
72 BBC News, Friday, 16 October 1998.
73 Observed at Baku Airport in March 2004.
74 On YouTube.
75 Golden 2011 (2001): 135–6.
76 Heather 2009: 386.

Chapter 2

1 Koryakova and Epimakhov 2007: 316.
2 Immortalised in John Masters' classic 1954 novel, *Bhowani Junction*.
3 Cunliffe 2015 is a rare exception.
4 Koryakova and Epimakhov 2007: 211.
5 Pares 1955: 69.
6 Andrews 1999: 7–35.
7 For Eurasian Bronze Age, see in general: Kohl 2007; Koryakova and Epimakhov 2007; Anthony 2010; Frachetti 2008; Kuzmina 2008; Yang, Shao and Pan 2020.
8 Francfort 2019: 100.
9 Frachetti 2009: 41, and 2008: 8.

10 Frachetti 2008: 125–49, 157–8.

11 Anthony 2010: 164–74, 229–36; 264; 277–82; Kohl 2007: 37–56, 236. A source for much of the Ukrainian investigations of the Tripolye is Menotti and Korvin-Piotrovski 2012. For general summaries, see: Baumer 2012: 78–82; Cunliffe 2015: 80–4; Gannon 2020.

12 Hoddinott 1986: 121.

13 Gimbutas 1971: 50; Rolle 1989: 117–19.

14 Phillips 1965: 30–7; Anthony 2010: 287–99; Kohl 2007: 84–8; Kohl 2009; Baumer 2012: 92–5; Cunliffe 2015: 91–5.

15 Abregov et al. 2007.

16 Information at Adygea National Museum 9 June 2012 and on site visit to Gelendzhik. See also Phillips 1965: 36–7; Trifonov et al. 2019.

17 Burney and Lang 1971: Chapters 3 and 4; Algaze 1989; Anthony 2010: 87–95; Kohl 2007: 84–5.

18 Burney and Lang 1971: 81–2.

19 Akurgal 2001: 4–32.

20 West 2007: 21–2.

21 Chernykh 1995: 143.

22 Kuzmina 2008: 34–8.

23 Grigoriev and Vasina 2019.

24 Piggott 1992: 20–7; Andrews 1999: 7–35; Anthony 2010: Chapter 13.

25 Kuzmina 2008: 34–8.

26 Gryaznov 1969: 46–51; Baumer 2012: 95–7; Anthony 2010: Chapters 10–11; Frachetti 2008: 44–7.

27 Anthony 2010: Chapter 10.

28 Gryaznov 1969: 31–66; Christian 1998: 106; Leontiev, Kapelko and Esin 2006; see also Eremin 2007; Baumer 2012: 137–9.

29 Anthony 2010: Chapter 15; Kohl 2007: 144–52; Koryakova and Epimakhov 2007: 86–98; Kuzmina 2008: 40–9; Anthony 2009; Baumer 2012: 141–9; Cunliffe 2015: 130–8; Yang et al. 2020: 52–9.

30 Frachetti 2008: 139–40, 160.

31 Francfort 2019: 100.

32 Koryakova and Epimakhov 2007: 28–40.

33 Cunliffe 2015: 135.

34 Koryakova and Epimakhov 2007: 94

35 Anthony 2010: 437–41.

36 Kuzmina 2008: 47. See also Koryakova and Epimakhov 2007: 28–32, 114–15.

37 For the main characteristics see Gryaznov 1969: 46–51; Anthony 2010: 448–51; Kohl 2007; Koryakova and Epimakhov 2007: 123–50; Kuzmina 2008: 59–63; Frachetti 2008: 31–72; Yang, Shao and Pan 2020: 59–68.

38 Lyonnet in Allchin, Ball and Hammond 2019: 159–60.

39 Yang, Shao and Pan 2020: 52.

40 Anthony 2010: 410–11; Brown and Anthony 2019: 104–5.

41 Kuzmina 2007.

42 Koryakova and Epimakhov 2007: 123–80.

43 Cong 2019; Liu 2019; Yang, Shao and Pan 2020: 89–103.

44 Kuzmina 2008; Yang, Shao and Pan 2020: 112–25.
45 Kuzmina 2008: 60–3.
46 Anthony 2010: 443–8; Yang, Shao and Pan 2020: 73–88.
47 First named by Francfort 2003; Lyonnet and Dubova (eds) 2020.
48 Kohl 2007: 235. See also Francfort 2019.
49 Kohl 2007: 37–9, 132–3; Frachetti 2008: 51–5; Yang, Shao and Pan 2020: 2–13, 133.
50 Koryakova and Epimakhov 2007: 27–8.
51 Andrews 1999: 7–35; Kohl 2007: 84–5.
52 Christian 2008: 113–15.
53 Koryakova and Epimakhov 2007: 338.
54 Frachetti 2008: 173–6.
55 Anthony 2010: 435–7.

Chapter 3

1 West 2007: 2.
2 Piggott 1992: 49; Anthony 2010: 5.
3 See: Sulimirski 1985: 152; Mallory and Adams 2006: 433–4; Anthony 2010: 92; West 2007: 29–31 and 142–3.
4 Much of this chapter is based on 'one of the grand old men of the Indo-European homeland debate' as Olander (2019: 10) refers to J. P. Mallory, mainly his overview in Mallory 1989; later overviews he gives in Sarianidi 1998 or Mallory and Mair 2000, Mallory and Adams 2006 or Mallory 2019 do not substantially alter this. See also: Lamberg-Karlovsky 2002; West 2007; Anthony 2010; and the various essays in Olsen, Olander and Kristiansen 2019. A more extreme example is Rajaram 1993. The archaeological viewpoint is given in Renfrew 1997, although this has remained controversial, but is followed by Cunliffe 2008.
5 Anthony 2010: 6–11.
6 Olander 2019: 7.
7 Muller 1986.
8 Bernal 1987; Lefkowitz and Rogers (ed) 1996.
9 See Mallory 1989 and Anthony 2010: Chapter 2 for the process of reconstruction.
10 Mallory 1989; Shnirelman 1999.
11 Renfrew 1987; Cunliffe 2008.
12 Gray and Atkinson 2003.
13 Anthony 2010: 59–63.
14 Ibid.: 50–82.
15 The main arguments are given in Mallory 1989: Chapter 6, and Anthony 2010: Chapters 3–5.
16 The initial DNA studies are by Allentoft et al. 2015 and Haak et al. 2015, both published in *Nature* and the results and conclusion published by Kristiansen et al. 2017. See also the essays in Olsen, Olander and Kristiansen 2019.
17 Iversen 2019: 91.

18 Kristiansen et al. 2017: 334.

19 Geary 2018: 136.

20 Richards 2003.

21 Shnirelman 1999; Lamberg-Karlovsky 2002.

22 West 2007: 2. See also Anthony 2010.

23 West 2007: 46.

24 Gimbutas 1971: 161.

25 Ustinova 2002.

26 Armstrong Oma and Melheim 2019: 134–5.

27 Brown and Anthony 2019: 104–5.

28 Mallory and Adams 2006: 431–41; Anthony 2010: 52–8. 134–5; West 2007: 135, 143–4, 152, 157, 184–5, 186–91, 281–3, 376, 379–82.

29 West 2007: 120.

30 Although see Anthony 2010: 31 for the pitfalls of such connections.

31 Rezaie 2020.

32 Yarshater 1983: 347; Mallory and Adams 2006: 408–11, 431–5; West 2007: 166–9.

33 Mallory 1989: 272.

34 Mallory and Adams 2006: 453.

35 Davis-Kimball 2002: 149.

36 Ball et al. 2019.

37 Lamberg-Karlovsky 2002: 74.

38 Barber 1999; Mallory and Mair 2000.

39 Davis-Kimball 2002: 148. See also e.g. Ahuja 1998.

40 Davis-Kimball 2002: Chapters 8 and 9.

41 Abudurasule, Li and Hu 2019. See also in general: Shunying 1994; Abdulreshit 1999.

42 So and Bunker 1995: 21–2.

43 Armstrong Oma and Melheim 2019: 138.

44 Abudurasule, Li and Hu 2019.

45 Renfrew 1987.

46 Cunliffe 2008: vii and 26.

47 Ibid., Chapters 4–5.

48 Ibid.: 111, 127.

49 Ibid.: 112–13.

50 Ibid.: 123, 112.

51 Ibid.: 139.

52 Ibid.: 179.

53 Cunliffe 2015: viii.

54 Richards 2003.

55 Anthony 2010: 75–81.

56 Anthony 2010: 138–47.

57 Yablonsky 2006.

58 Rajaram 1993.

59 Gimbutas 2001. See also Anthony 2006.

60 This figure cited by Devine 2011: 90.

61 Lamberg-Karlovsky 2002: 74–5.

Chapter 4

1 See also Radulescu 2020.
2 Maenchen-Helfen 1973: 23.
3 Phillips 1965: 41–5; Gryaznov 1969: 97–130; Baumer 2012: 151–7; Cunliffe 2019: 76–82; Yang, Shao and Pan 2020: 170–6.
4 Yablonsky 1995; Yablonsky 2006.
5 Bokovenko 1995a: 265–71; Cugunov, Parzinger and Nagler 2010; Baumer 2012: 175–85; Cunliffe 2019: 95–103; Yang, Shao and Pan 2020: 233–43.
6 Gryaznov 1969: 213–19; Bokovenko 1995b.
7 M. A. Castren, quoted in Jettmar 1967: 65.
8 Bokovenko 1995b: 301–2.
9 Eremin 2007.
10 Rudenko 1970; Piotrovsky et al. 1978; Baumer 2012: 186–96; Cunliffe 2019: 184–90.
11 Baumer 2012: 187–8; Cunliffe 2019: 160–7.
12 Anon. 2013; Oleszczak, Borodovskiy et al. 2018.
13 Peterson 2020.
14 Lunde and Stone 2012: 18.
15 Gibbon 1897–1900, III: 72.
16 Vogelsang 1992; Yablonsky 1995: 193; Torday 1997.
17 Olbrycht 2015; Herrmann 1977.
18 Watson 1971: 110–12; Pls 84, 85.
19 Muscarella 1977; Ghirshman 1979.
20 Vogelsang 1992.
21 Tate 1910: 10, 217; Bailey 1978: 2. See also Frye 1984: 193–4.
22 Bailey 1978: 5; Yarshater 1983: 454–7; Ball 2016: 6.
23 Cousens 1929; Lambrick 1973: 113–27; Ball 1989: 120–1; Ball 1997; Callieri 2016; Ball et al. 2019: 265–6, 342–3.
24 So and Bunker 1995: 56, 57–9.
25 Bailey 1978: 5–6; Bailey 1979; Melyukova 1995: 57.
26 Bonora et al. 2009: 43.
27 Stein 1904: 226–50; Baumer 2014: 138–42.
28 Jettmar 2002: 96–104.
29 Senior 2005; Ball et al. 2019: 342–3.
30 Bopearachchi 1999; Ball et al. 2019: 257–8.
31 Payne 1989; Vogelsang 2002: 30.
32 For general accounts of the Scythians in the west, see Phillips 1965, Talbot Rice 1967, Braund 2005, Ivantchik 2018, Cunliffe 2019.
33 Murzin 2005: 33.
34 Bulwer Lytton 2004 (1837): 222.
35 Novozhenov 2018.
36 Gimbutas 1971: 50; Rolle 1989: 117–22; Melyukova 1995: 47–8; Murzin 2005: 36–7; Cunliffe 2019: 22, 129–35.
37 Cunliffe 2015: 230–1; 2019: 150–8.
38 Jettmar 1967: 47. See also: Megaw and Megaw 1989.

39 Vogelsang 1992.
40 Cicero *De Republica* 2, 4, quoted in Obolensky 1971: 25.
41 Boardman 1980.
42 Bäbler 2005; Ivanchik 2005.
43 Rostovtzeff 1928; Olkhovsky 1995: 72.
44 Ustinova 2005.
45 Petrenko 1995: 18. In fact only one Median fire temple is known, that at Tepe Nush-i Jan in western Iran: see Stronach and Roaf 2007.
46 Alekseyev 2005.
47 Rolle 1989: 123–7; Ascherson 1995: 56–8.
48 Rostovtzeff 1928: 147–8; Olkkhovsky 1995.
49 Olkkhovsky 1995: 81.
50 Dvornichenko 1995.
51 Zhivkov 2015: 33–4.
52 Aruz et al. 2000; Yunusova et al. 2007.
53 Davis-Kimball et al. (eds) 1995: Part II.
54 Koryakova and Epimakhov 2007: 11.
55 Moshkova 1995: 187.
56 Christian 2008: 197.
57 Olbrycht 2015.
58 Sulimirski 1963: 282 and 293.
59 Davis-Kimball 2002: 32.
60 Ibn Rusta in Lunde and Stone 2012: 126.
61 The very confusing migrations of tribes into Europe in late antiquity is summarised in Zhivkov 2015: Chapter 1, with many a cautious caveat of both the historical and archaeological evidence.
62 De Busbecq 2001: 136–8.
63 Heather 2009: 152–3.
64 Gumilev 1987 (1970): 375 fn. 24.
65 Sulimirski 1963 gives an excellent summary of the long history of the Sarmatians.
66 Rostovtzeff 1928: 114; Abramova 1995: 182–3; Moshkova 1995: 188. Richard N. Frye dedicated his now classic 1963 account of pre-Islamic Iran, *The Heritage of Persia*, 'To my Iranian friends (Afghans, Baluchis, Kurds, Ossetes, Persians, Tajiks).
67 Damgaard et al. 2018.
68 This is a Sarmatian legacy rather than Hunnish as Kim 2013: 153 claims.
69 Sulimirski 1963: 295–6; Ascherson 1995: 238–40; Yatsenko 2010.

Chapter 5

 1 De Clavijo 1840.
 2 There has been a spate of books on or relating to the Amazons and the idea of the warrior woman. The main ones are: Blok 1995; Salmonson 1991; Davis-Kimball 2002; Mainon and Ursini 2006; Kästner, Langner and Rabe 2007; Stuller 2010; Mayor 2014; Man 2018.

3 Herodotus IV.110–17.
4 Boardman 1993: 105.
5 Blok 1995: 21–37.
6 Boardman 1993; 102, 105, 109, etc.; Kästner, Langner and Rabe 2007; Vout 2018: 25–6.
7 Vout 2018: 32. See also Blok 1995: 384–94 for a discussion of the Amazonomachy themes.
8 Herodotus IV.28–30. See also Bolton 1962: 105–14.
9 Salmonson 1991: 7; Mayor 2014: 371–2.
10 Bäbler 2005; Ivanchik 2005.
11 See Blok 1995: Chapter 1 for an exhaustive study of ancient and modern interpretations of the Greek Amazon myths.
12 Blok 1995: 39.
13 Gimbutas 1971: 18.
14 Gimbutas 1989, 2001; Baring and Cashford 1991: 52–82; Goodison and Morris: 1998.
15 Anthony 1995; Tringham and Conkey 1998; Anthony 2010: 214; Balter 2005: 320–4 for Gimbutas and the Mother Goddess cult.
16 Anthony 2010: 343.
17 Vidal 2014.
18 Ibn Fadlan in Lunde and Stone 2012: 50.
19 Anthony 2010: 329.
20 So and Bunker 1995: 27, 36, 44–6.
21 Golden 2011: 24.
22 Melyukova 1995: 46.
23 Shelekhan 2020: 137, 159–62.
24 Davis-Kimball 2002: 46–9; Chapter 5.
25 Yang, Shao and Pan 2020: 303.
26 Yablonsky 1995: 202–7, 218, 337.
27 Anthony 2010: 91.
28 Davis-Kimball 2002: Chapter 4.
29 Marco Polo 1871, II: 463–5; Golden 2011: 85.
30 Ostrowski 1998: Chapter 3.
31 Broadbridge 2018; De Nicola 2018.
32 Curta 2019: 89.
33 Cited in Golden 2011: 125, 131.
34 Pohl 2018a: 368–9.
35 For much of this section I am indebted to Hunt 2010.
36 A point emphasised by Tetley 2009: 14–15.
37 Hunt 2010: 4, 38–9, 196–7.
38 See in general Necipoğlu 2005.
39 Warner 1985.
40 Now in the British Library: Record number 2192, Shelfmark Add. 15268.
41 Mandeville n.d.: 130 and Chapter L.
42 Dixon 2002: 40–1.
43 Ibid.: 15, 59, 165, 177.
44 Ibid.: 65, 66, 69, 76, 82–3, 148, 153.

45 Ibid.: 118, 167.
46 Warner 2013: 71–2.
47 Runciman 1954: 139–43.
48 Günther 2003.
49 Ibid.: 77, 92.
50 Warner 2013: xxi.
51 Mainon and Ursini 2006: viii, xii, xiv, 15, 45–7, 50–9, etc. Mainon and Ursini give a comprehensive survey up until the publication of their book in 2006; the trend shows no sign of stopping since. See also Stuller 2010 for the cinematic super-heroines and their twentieth and twenty-first centuries cultural background.
52 Described as 'the pornography of violence' by one academic commentator (Winkler 2004: 101), a description that might be appropriate to a greater or lesser extent for many of the films cited here. See also Renger and Solomon (eds) 2013.
53 See also Mainon and Ursini 2006: 65.
54 Davis-Kimball 2002; Mayor 2014; Man 2018.
55 Salmonson 1991.
56 E.g. Man 2018: 106–21.
57 Man 2018: 269–73.

Chapter 6

1 Jacobsen 1995: 1.
2 Rolle 1989: 32–4; Cunliffe 2019: 305.
3 Honeychurch, Wright and Amartuvshin 2009; Houle 2009; Fitzhugh 2009b; Liu Wensuo 2014.
4 There are numerous books on Scythian art, e.g. Rostovtzeff 1929, Jettmar 1967, Rolle 1989, Jacobsen 1995, Korolkova 2006, Meyer 2013.
5 Jacobsen 1995: 1–2.
6 Baldick 2000: 16–17.
7 Meyer 2013: 127.
8 Rostovtzeff 1929.
9 So and Bunker 1995: 13.
10 Jettmar 1967: 35–6.
11 Jacobsen 1995: 69.
12 Jacobsen 1995: Fig. 123; So and Bunker 1995: 65, 129–30; Yablonsky 1995: 219 Figures 60, 61, 82; Watson 1971: 107–9 Pl. 69 and 1995: 71–2; Ponamarenko and Dyck 2007: 118; Cunliffe 2019: 284–5; Yang, Shao and Pan 2020: 267–71, 283–4 and 329, see especially Figures 4.20: 7, 8 and 5.4: 1.
13 O'Sullivan and Hommel 2020. See also Watson 1971: Pls 69–74.
14 E. g., Frachetti 2008: 136–8, especially Figure 38.
15 Shunying 1994: 52, Pl. 107; Li n.d.: Pl. 25; So and Bunker 1995: 56, Figure 20 and 64, Figure 28; Boardman 2010: Pl. 2.20; Yang, Shao and Pan 2020: 417–20; Wu En 2003: 192.
16 O'Sullivan and Hommel 2020: 66.

17 Watson 1971: 112–14; Pls 88–92.

18 Ball 2010: Pl. 20.

19 Shunying 1994: 47, Pls 83–8; So and Bunker 1995; Yue Feng 1999: 159, Pl. 0410; 163, Pl. 0419; 318, Pl. 0883; Wu En 2003; Boardman 2010; Brosseder 2011; Yang, Shao and Pan 2020: 400–1, 421–3, 440–2, 526–9.

20 Mepisashvili and Tsintsadze 1977: 39; Soltes (ed.) 199: 109, 194–5.

21 Kessler 1993: 47; Shunying 1994: 59, Pls 143, 145; Li, undated: Pls 13, 14; Yue Feng 1999: 160, Pl. 0411; 163, Pls 0419, 0420, 0421; Wu En 2003.

22 Rostovtzeff 1928: Chapter 5; Rolle 1989: 58–9, 66–8, 77–81, Pls 7, 11, 12 and 22; Jacobsen 1995: Figures 78–91.

23 Anthony 2010: 91.

24 Bokovenko 1995a: 281 Figure 35; Shelekhan 2020: 142–3.

25 So and Bunker 1995: 96–7; Yang, Shao and Pan 2020: 304, 323–4, 358–9, 365–6.

26 Petrenko 1995.

27 Rolle 1989: Pls 14–18; Jacobsen 1995: Figures 11–14.

28 Rolle 1989: Pl. 13; Jacobsen 1995: Figures 34–5.

29 Although lack of proof that it was male is not proof that its 'real identity' was female, as Davis-Kimball (2002: Chapter 6) claims.

30 Reeder 1999: 226–32; Jacobsen 1995: Figure 102.

31 An example of an Ottoman royal ceremonial gorytus is on display in the Topkapi Museum in Istanbul, and recent ones made out of leather are displayed in the National Museum in Chişinau.

32 Reeder 1999: 251–3; Jacobsen 1995: Figures 103–10.

33 Yang, Shao and Pan 2020: 177–96.

34 Shelekhan 2020: 46–8, Figures 2.11, 2.12.

35 Reeder 1999: 256–61.

36 Yang, Shao and Pan 2020: 189–91.

37 Kessler 1993: Figure 25; Baumer 2014: 4.

38 Aruz et al. (eds) 2000.

39 Soltes (ed.) 1999: 166; Chqonia 2008.

40 Francfort 2012; see also: Olbrycht 2015; Peterson 2020.

41 Jettmar 2002: 100–1, Figures 26.1–26.14.

42 Boardman 2010: 85.

43 Jacobsen 1995: 77–8.

44 Leontev, Kapelko and Esin 2006.

45 Francfort 2019: 99.

46 E.g. Frachetti 2008: 139, Figure 40.

47 Phillips 1965: 43–5.

48 Frachetti 2008: 52–3, Fig. 7; Yang, Shao and Pan 2020: 87–9, Figure 2.28: 1–3; 208–15.

49 Frachetti 2008: 52–3.

50 Watson 1971: 105–7; Pls 37, 38, 83; Kessler 1993: 36, 39–40, 44 Figure 15; So and Bunker 1995: 34 Pl. 4; 100–2; Watson 1995: 70–1.

51 Baumer 2012: 152.

52 Volkov 1995; Yang, Shao and Pan 2020: Chapter 3.1, 137–69, Figures 3.2: 5 and 3.5: 2, 3 and especially 3.15; 177–96.

53 Volkov 1995; Allard and Diimaajav 2005; Fitzhugh 2009a; Baumer 2012: 156–63.
54 Fitzhugh 2009b.
55 Anthony 2010: 338–9; Baumer 2012: 79.
56 Sevin 2000; Sagona 2006: 68–71.
57 Bowlt, Misler and Petrova 2013: 214–19.
58 Bokovenko 1995a: 265–71; Cugunov, Parzinger and Nagler 2010; Baumer 2012: 175–85; Cunliffe 2019: 95–103; Yang, Shao and Pan 2020: 233–43.
59 Süleymanova 2006: 219 Figure 2; Andreeva 2018: Chapter 4.
60 Shapakovsky and Nicolle 2013: 35.
61 Talbot Rice 1967: 178–97.
62 Jettmar 1967: 44–7; Megaw and Megaw 1989; Cunliffe 2015: 230–1; 2019: 150–8; 306–9.
63 Sulimirski 1985: 173, 192–3; Crawford and Ulmschneider 2020.
64 See the various essays in Nimura et al. 2020, especially Wells; O'Sullivan and Hommel 2020; Cunliffe 2019: 160–7.
65 Talbot Rice 1967: 178–97.
66 Lasko 1965.
67 Thomas 1965.
68 Bunker and Farkas 1970: 167–74. See also Nimura et al. 2020.
69 Fern, Dickinson and Webster 2019.
70 Jettmar 1967: 198–200; Bunker 1970: 167–74.
71 Pohl 2018a: 234, 336–9, 337, 347–8. Avar belt buckles also depicted on the covers of Pohl 2018 and Di Cosmo and Maas 2018.
72 Bunker 1970: 13.
73 Wilson 1965.
74 Talbot Rice 1967: 187, Figure 67; Chaykovskiy et al. 1993: 60–1; Melyukova 1995: 57; Andreeva 2018: Chapter 4.
75 Rostovtzeff 1929: 106; Talbot Rice 1967: 178–97.
76 Pevsner 1936 (2005).
77 Jettmar 1967: 39; Greenhalgh 2000: 36–53; Odom 2010, especially p. 59.
78 Talbot Rice 1965: 149.
79 Talbot Rice 1967: 178–97; Chaykovskiy et al. 1993: 66; Petrova and Marcadé 2005: 118; Bowlt, Misler and Petrova 2013: 20–1; Iliukhina 2013.
80 Bowlt 2008: 140.
81 Ibid.: 129.

Chapter 7

1 Addressing troops at Bremerhaven about to depart to China for the Boxer Rebellion. Quoted by Kelly 2008: 221.
2 Golden 2011 (2001): 135–6.
3 Ponamorenko and Dyck 2007: 140.
4 Ward-Perkins 2005.
5 Golden 2006: 83 and 2011: 34–5.
6 Ammianus Marcellinus 31. 2 (Loeb ed.). Quoted in Kelly 2008.
7 Gibbon 1897–1900, III: 84.

8 Ward-Perkins 2005: 59.
9 For the Balkan origin of vampire myths, see Barford 2001: 190.
10 Kelly 2008: 155.
11 Heather 2009: 227–8.
12 Ptolemy's reference to the 'Chions' north of the Black Sea might be a reference to the Huns, but this seems too early.
13 Golden 2011: 33.
14 Kessler 1993: 37–44; Yang, Shao and Pan 2020: 352–72.
15 Kessler 1993: Figure 25.
16 Kessler 1993: 37–44; Baumer 2014: 4–18; Yang, Shao and Pan 2020: 373–479.
17 Ibid.: 44–65.
18 Barfield 2001. See also Khodarkovsky 2002: 9 in reference to later Tatar confederations.
19 Barfield 1989: 57.
20 Ibid.: 45–9, 51–9; 77–8.
21 de la Vaissière 2012, 2015; Christian 2008: 203, 227; Golden 2011: 31–3; Brosseder 2018.
22 de la Vaissière 2012.
23 Brosseder 2018: 187.
24 Golden 2002: 153; Kelly 2008: 157.
25 Christian 2008: 225.
26 Baldick 2000: 22–8.
27 Gibbon 1897–1900, III: 416.
28 Heather 2009: 153–73.
29 On-site information. See also Yang, Shao and Pan 2020: 467–76.
30 Watson 1971: 97–8.
31 Personal observation 2016.
32 Yang, Shao and Pan 2020: 515.
33 Brosseder 2009; Yang, Shao and Pan 2020: 476–502, 530–1.
34 Personal observation 2016.
35 Rezakhani 2017; Baumer 2014: 94–101; Ball et al. 2019a: Chapter 6; Haug 2019: Chapter 2.
36 Cited by Haug 2019: 63.
37 Buryakov et al. 1999.
38 Litvinsky 1996: 176–82; Vogelsang 2002: 186–7.
39 See in general Maenchen-Helfen 1973; Golden 2002; Kelly 2008.
40 Meier 2015.
41 Kim 2013: 73–93.
42 Gibbon 1897–1900: III, 398.
43 Heather 2009: 207.
44 Bede V.9.
45 Ball 2019a: Site 520; Ball et al. 2019: 386–8.
46 Ball 2016: 364–5.
47 Sauer et al. 2013: xiii and following for full descriptions.
48 Sauer et al. 2020.
49 Sauer 2013: 3. I am grateful to Eberhard Sauer for discussions of these defences and for Figure 7.00.

50 Crow 1995.
51 Kelly 2008: 225.
52 Christian 2008: 183.
53 Heather 2009: 173.
54 Golden 2011: 34.
55 Gumilev 1987 (1970): 30.
56 Kim 2013: 136.
57 Ibid.: 136 and148. See also 43–69.
58 Ibid.: 60, 140.
59 Ibid.: 59, 87–8, 132–3, 137. Also 81–3, 130, 136, 143, 149, 150, 151.
60 The subtitle of Ward-Perkins 2005 book; Simon James' term is cited in Sauer 2003: 15
61 Heather 2009: 618.
62 Wheatcroft 1995: 46.
63 Ibid.: 95, 191; Winder 2013: 53–7.
64 Personal observation.
65 Chaykovskiy et al. 1993: 49–51.
66 Brosseder 2018; Pohl 2018a: 105.
67 Gibbon 1897–1900, III: 416
68 Pirenne 1939, 30.
69 Di Cosmo and Maas 2018: 5.

Chapter 8

1 Parry 1963: 6.
2 Pirenne 1939: 495–8. In fact Pirenne wrote those words under house arrest in 1914–18.
3 Fernández-Armesto 2009: 352.
4 Much of this chapter has been adapted from Ball 2012. Since then Baumer 2014: 173–270 and numerous papers by Golden have updated it.
5 Çağatay and Kuban 2006: 14, although Huns and Arpads cannot be considered Turk.
6 Schamiloglu 2006; Golden 2011 (2008–9); Golden 2015.
7 Çağatay and Kuban (eds) 2006 2006: 14.
8 Gibbon Vol VII: 79.
9 Two, counting the unrecognised Turkish Republic of North Cyprus.
10 Roxburgh 2005; Çağatay and Kuban 2006.
11 Kessler 1993: 70.
12 Quoted in Barfield 1989: 146–50.
13 E.g. Nizam al-Mulk 1960: 104, 139, 158–9, 160–1.
14 Peacock 2010: 65; Çelebi 2010: 108.
15 Quoted in Peacock 2010: 60.
16 The following account is mainly drawn from: Sinor 1990; Litvinsky (ed.) 1996; Golden 2011 (2008–9), 2018; Stark 2016. See also: Torday 1997; Baldick 2000: 38–43; Baumer 2014.
17 Golden 2011 (2008–9): 22–3.

18 Hansen 2018: 115.

19 Kessler 1993: 70.

20 Maenchen-Helfen 1973: 8.

21 Golden 2002: 148.

22 Golden 2011 (2008–9): 49 and 37–8; Golden 2018.

23 Kessler 1993; Golden 2011: 35; Baumer 2014: 86–90. There is some dispute as to whether the Tuoba were really Turk. See, however, Sanping Chen 2005, who confirms their Turk language. Tabgach also remained a Turkish name, such as the Karakhanid ruler Tabghach Bughra Khan in 1069' see Tetley 2009: 37.

24 Yi 2018; Ball 2021.

25 Grousset 1970: 60–6.

26 Manz in Amitai and Biran 2005.

27 Golden 2006 and 2011.

28 Sinor 1990: 385–416; Bregel 2003: 14, Map 7; Potts 2014: 149–56; Stark 2016; Golden 2018.

29 Golden 2011: 37.

30 Payne (2016) writes of increasing 'Iranisation' of the Turk elite from their contact with the Sasanians in late antiquity and the formation of a hybrid Turko-Iranian culture: 'Turan'.

31 Klimburg-Salter 2008 and 2010.

32 Ball 2021.

33 As late at the mid-nineteenth century for the majority of Kazakhs, who adopted Islam largely at the encouragement of the Russians: see Fielding 2020: 138–40.

34 Ball 2012.

35 Sinor 1990: 315–16.

Chapter 9

1 Davies 2011: 239.

2 A point emphasised by Heather 2009.

3 Geary 2018: 135.

4 For a masterly if breathtaking overview of the following dance across the steppe, see Golden 2002.

5 Much of the following account has been taken from the various chapters by Golden 1990.

6 Pirenne 1939: 136; see also 83, 494, where Turks are referred to as 'Barbarians of Finnish origin'.

7 Gimbutas 1971: 46–7.

8 Golden 1990a; Anthony 2010: 93–4.

9 Grigoriev and Vasina 2019: 195–6.

10 Golden 1990a: 234.

11 Golden 1990a.

12 Martynov 2012.

13 Figes 2002: 360. See also Gryaznov 1969: 17–18. Mannerheim is celebrated in the CD-ROM *C. G. Mannerheim. Ratsain halki Aasian/Across Asia on*

Horseback produced by the Finnish National Board of Antiquities in 2000.

14 Bosley 1989.
15 Davies 2011: 693–5.
16 Figes 2002: 360.
17 Pohl 2018: 397.
18 As well as Pohl 2018a, I have largely followed Szádeczky-Kardoss 1990, Golden 2011 and Curta 2019: 51–62 in this account.
19 Quoted by Pohl 2018a: 5, and in general 5–11 concerning source bias.
20 *Chronicon Paschale* 1989.
21 Theophylact Simocatta i. 6. 1 (1986: 28).
22 Theophylact vii. 7. 6–vii. 9. 12 (1986: 188–93); Pohl 2018a: 38–46.
23 Zhivkov 2015: Chapter 1; Pohl 2018a.
24 Pohl 2018a: 217; Curta 2019: 72.
25 In the words of Howard-Johnston 2010.
26 Ball 2010: 120–35. See also Howard-Johnston 2010: 45–6.
27 Cited by Curta 2019: 101.
28 Pohl 2018a: 254–62; 270–3.
29 Curta 2019: 29; or sixty thousand according to Pohl 2018a: 4, 14.
30 Stark 2009; Pohl 2018a: 209–15, 234, 236–9, 337, 347–8.
31 Csiky 2015.
32 Pohl 2018a: 209–15.
33 Heather 2009: 561; Pohl 2018: 402.
34 Golden 1990a: 239.
35 Süleymanova 2006. Zhivkov (2015: 159) dates the independence of the Volga Bulgars (from the Khazars) to '950 at the latest'.
36 For early Bulgar history I have largely followed Golden 1990 and Curta 2019. See also now Stepanov 2010 (which I have not been able to consult before going to press).
37 Obolensky 1971: 56; Golden 2011: 258. See also Zhivkov 2015: Chapter 1.
38 Cited in Curta 2019: 144.
39 Golden 2011 (2001): 135–46; Zhivkov 2015: Chapter 1.
40 Róna-Tas 2007: 273.
41 Piotrovsky et al. 1997; Curta 2019: 74–6. Also interpreted as Khazar rather than Bulgar: Curta 2019: 131.
42 Ibn Fadlan in Lunde and Stone 2012: 3.
43 Ibid.: 120–1.
44 Information board in Bilyar Museum. Also Leonid Nedashkovsky, personal communication.
45 Shapakovsky and Nicolle 2013: 39.
46 Personal observation. See also Zhivkov 2015: Chapter 3.
47 Al-Andalusi in Lunde and Stone 2012: 66, 71–2.
48 Shapakovsky and Nicolle 2013: 10–18; Curta 2019: 145–8.
49 Curta 2019: 151.
50 Piotrovsky et al. 1997; Teliashov 1997.
51 Curta 2019: 71–100.
52 Obolensky 1971: 92–3.

53 Runciman 1930: 52.
54 Ibid.: 68–70.
55 Barford 2001: 92–4.
56 Obolensky 1971: 145–7.
57 Ibid.: 159.
58 Runciman 1930: 261.
59 Cunliffe 2008: 43, 171
60 Golden 1990a.
61 Golden 2011 (2001): 136–46; Pohl 2018a: 27–32.
62 Naumov 2006: 5–6, 53.
63 Róna-Tas 2007: 271–2.
64 Ibid.: 272; Geary 2018: 145–6; Curta 2019: Chapter 13.
65 Róna-Tas 2007: 275–6.
66 Barford 2001: 894–6; Ibn Rusta in Lunde and Stone 2012: 122–3. See Zimonyi
    2015 for Islamic sources for early Magyar history.
67 Which was not inconceivable according to Runciman 1930: 150.
68 MacLean 1958: 111–55.
69 Mirsky 1977; Walker 1995.
70 Due to be published by Barkhuis, Eelde, under that title in late 2020; not
    available at the time of going to press.
71 Golden 1990b; Curta 2019: Chapter 10.
72 Although this is questioned: Curta 2019: 158.
73 Curta 2020: 110–11.
74 Heather 2009: 521.
75 Zhivkov 2015: 141.
76 Golden 2011 (2005); Curta 2019: 171.
77 Baumer 2016: 71–2.
78 Schimmelpennink van der Oye 2010: 206.
79 Golden 1990b: 258.
80 Curta 2019: 169–70.
81 Schimmelpennink van der Oye 2010: 16–17. See also Gumilev 1987: 285–7.
82 Kim 2013: 143, 146.
83 Heather 2009: 561.

Chapter 10

1 Quoted in Davies 1996: 236.
2 Muqaddasī in Lunde and Stone 2012: 171.
3 Gumilev's words were actually 'a steppe Atlantis', quoted in Golden 2007a:
   11.
4 Golden et al. 2007: 7.
5 Zhivkov 2015: 172–3.
6 Minorsky, Barthold and Bosworth 1970: 53.
7 Main publications in English on the Khazars are: Golden, Ben-Shammai and
   Róna-Tas 2007; Golden 2011 (2001); Zhivkov 2015; others are given in the
   notes.

8 Golden 2007a: 9.

9 Ibid.: 15; Róna-Tas 2007: 270.

10 Kim 2013.

11 Christian 2008: 283; Golden 2011 (2009): 152.

12 Róna-Tas 2007: 273–4.

13 Howard-Johnson 2007; Zuckerman 2007.

14 Wasserstein 2007.

15 Golden 2007b: 126–8.

16 Golden 2007a: 56; Curta 2019: 142.

17 Ibid.: 8; Masʿudi and Ibn Rusta in Lunde and Stone 2012: 116–17, 132–3; Zhivkov 2015: 56–60.

18 Golden 2007b: 123.

19 Ibn Yaʿqūb in Lunde and Stone 2012: 163. See also Norris 2009: 9–10.

20 Observed in Bodø Museum in January 2011.

21 Ashtor 1976: 85–6 and 148; Hodges and Whitehouse 1983; Noonan 2007; Zhivkov 2015: Chapter 3.

22 Pirenne 1939.

23 Barford 2001: 245; Heather 2009: 466–81.

24 Hodges and Whitehouse 1983: 19.

25 Di Cosmo 1999: 21.

26 O'Shea 2006: 84; Zhivkov 2015: 1–3.

27 Peacock 2010: 20–40.

28 Golden 2011 (2001): 152.

29 Howard-Johnson 2007; Curta 2019: 139.

30 Dmitri Vasiliev, personal communication, 8 September 2009.

31 Minorsky, Barthold and Bosworth 1970: 161–2; Ibn Fadlan and Masʿudi in Lunde and Stone 2012: 55–8, 131.

32 Christian 2008: 335.

33 Johanson 2006.

34 Ibid.; Norris 2009: 22–3.

35 Rossman 2007: 136–7, n. 11; Curta 2019: 128.

36 Hale 1993: 167.

37 Golden, Ben-Shammai and Róna-Tas (eds), 2007.

38 Zhivkov 2015: 102.

39 Golden, Ben-Shammai and Róna-Tas (eds) 2007: 29, 40, 207

40 Costa et al. 2013.

41 Golden 2007a: 27. See also Zhivkov 2015: 213–15.

42 Shnirelman 2007: 361. See also Curta 2019: 128–9.

43 Shnirelman 2007.

44 Davies 1996: 237.

Chapter 11

1 Davies 1996: 897.

2 Morgan 1986: 57.

3 Ibid.: 57–9; Schamiloglu 2006.

4 Roberts 1996: 432.
5 Brotton 2002: 180.
6 Kessler 1993; Biran 2005a; Baumer 2016: 144–51.
7 Sinor 1990: 242.
8 The main work in English is Morgan 1986. See also Chambers 1988;
   De Hartog 1989; Jackson 2005b.
9 Rossabi 2017.
10 Morgan 1986: 1.
11 Kennedy 2002: 144.
12 Quoted in Kennedy 2002: 138.
13 Quoted in Morgan 1986: 17.
14 Boyle 1965; Morgan 1986: 74.
15 Raverty 1881: 1,157–9.
16 Morgan 1986: 83.
17 Ibid.: 80–1.
18 Ibid.: Chapter 9.
19 Yule and Cordier 1915; Morgan 1986: 130–1, 182, 179–80.
20 Di Cosmo in Amitai and Biran 2005: 401–6; Morgan 1986: 83.
21 Starr 2013. See also Frye 1993.
22 Lactantius 1.18.10.
23 Morgan 1986: 181.
24 Gumilev 1987 (1970): 365–6.
25 Boxer 1969: 19–20.
26 Gumilev 1989 (1970): 189.
27 Runciman 1954: 293–314, 427–61.
28 Wang Dafang 2011.
29 Allsen 2018: 274–6.
30 Ascherson 1995: 95–6.
31 Cunliffe 2015: 466–8.

Chapter 12

1 Quoted in Figes 2002: 150.
2 Golden 2011: 90.
3 Manz 1989. See also: Darwin 2007; Starr 2013.
4 His initial justification was made in the 1986 version of the book; his later
   comment was in Chapter 9, 'The Mongol Empire Since 1985'. See Morgan
   2007: 1.
5 Major and Wielhorsky 1857: 5.
6 See Morgan 1986: 142–3; Ostrowski 1998: xiii, 182.
7 Ostrowski 1998: 32.
8 Morgan 1986: 143.
9 Ibid.: 141–5.
10 Gumilev 1987 (1970): 374; Fielding 2020: 173.
11 Pares 1955: Chapter V; Hosking 2001: 79–80.
12 Schimmelpennink van der Oye 2010: 22.

13 Rakhimzyanov 2009.
14 Teissier 2011: 58–9.
15 Norris 2009: 24–5, 39–43.
16 Quirini-Poplawska 2020: 169–71.
17 Ibid.
18 Inalcik 2006: 129. See also Hosking 2001: 160–3 and Norris 2009: 24–5.
19 Norris 2009: 25–6; 66; Svanberg and Westerlund (eds) 2016.
20 Khodarkovsky 2002: 22, 78–81.
21 Ostrowski 1998: 166; Khodarkovsky 2002: 65.
22 Bosworth 1967: 157–9; Allen 1970: 5–6; Ball 2012: 137–8.
23 Faroqhi 2004: 50; Inalcik 2006: Ch 8.
24 Allen 1970: 4.
25 Williams 2001.
26 Golden 2011: 117–20. See also King 2004: 150–4; Tessier 2011: Chapter 4.
27 Information in the Kalmyk National Museum in Elista.
28 Fielding 2020: 201–2.
29 Personal observation at the Sarepta Museum, 3 May 2012. See also O Flynn 2016: 184–225.

Chapter 13

1 Quoted by Terkel in Bowlt, Misler and Petrova 2013: 51.
2 Quoted in Figes 2002: 361.
3 Khodarkovsky 2002: 226.
4 Knobloch 2007.
5 Barford 2001: 103 and 235; Zhivkov 2015: 98–9.
6 Knobloch 2007: 116.
7 Barford 2001: 245–8.
8 Knobloch 2007: 135.
9 Hosking 2001: 198.
10 Khodarkovsky 2002: 223.
11 Figes 2002: 365–6.
12 Schimmelpennink van der Oye 2010: 119, 121.
13 Figes 2002: 367–8.
14 Ostrowski 1998: 88. See also Ball 2010: 23.
15 Ostrowski 1998: Chapter 5; Khodarkovsky 2002: 222; Biran 2004; Golden 2011: 93.
16 Hosking 2001: 57; Golden 2002: 141; Jackson 2005b: 264; Zhivkov 2015: 62; Pohl 2018a: 363–4.
17 Hosking 2001: 57.
18 Ostrowski 1998: Chaper 4 and 5.
19 Ibid.: Chapter 3 and 131.
20 Pares 1955: 144.
21 Ostrowski 1998: 54–5; Hosking 2001: 142; Schimmelpennink van der Oye 2010: 22, 26.
22 Ostrowski 1998: 26, 34–48 and 185–6.

23 Ibid.: 185–6.
24 Ibid.: 244–8.
25 Quoted in Bobrick 1992: 417.
26 Golden 2011: 168.
27 Pares 1955: 134.
28 See Hudson and Bates 2015 for an account of Russian exploration in America and the native Californian collection in St Petersburg's Kunstkamera.
29 Wortman 2010: 32.
30 Figes 2002: 361–3.
31 Schimmelpennink van der Oye 2010: Chapter 4; see akso Figes 2002: Chapters 5 and 6.
32 Quoted in Polonsky 2010: 326.
33 Bowlt 2008: 78.
34 Shilova et al. 2017.
35 Laruelle 2007.
36 Paradowski 2007.
37 Quoted in Laruelle 2007: 33.
38 Wiederkehr 2007: 53–4.
39 Teliashov 1997.
40 Rossman 2007; Zhivkov 2015: 213–15.
41 *Daily Telegraph* article, Thursday 2 April 2009: 20.
42 Shnirelman 1999; Lamberg-Karlovsky 2002: 69.
43 Blom 2002: 69–74.
44 Meyer 2013: 11.
45 Ibid.: 81–3.
46 Dreyer 2008: 64.
47 Hopkirk 1980.
48 See in general: Hopkirk 1980; Fielding 2020: Chapter 6.
49 Meyer 2013: 42–3.
50 Wortman 2010, see especially 21–2.
51 Ibid., 26–8.
52 Hosking 2001: 478.
53 Meyer 2013: 61. See also his discussion (26–37) of the effects of Rostovtzeff's pioneering work on the Greeks and Scythians of the Black Sea in the early twentieth century.
54 Gray 1986; Murrell 1997.
55 Bowlt 2008: 71–3.
56 Ibid.: 205.
57 Figes 2002: 229.
58 Jettmar 1967: 200.
59 Shnirelman 1999: 275–6.
60 Bowlt 2008: 161–99.
61 Gray 1986: 39.
62 Jacobs 1985: 11.
63 Bowlt, Misler and Petrova 2013: 20–1. See in general for this era: Gray 1986; Bowlt 2008; Blakesley 2016.
64 Quoted by Jettmar 1967: 39.

65 The quotation from Blok is taken from Jettmar 1967: 39; the Larionov illustration is in Meyer 2013: 92–3.

66 Quoted by Gray 1986: 138. The art historian of Russian modernism, Camilla Gray, was the daughter of the British art historian Basil Gray, a major twentieth-century authority on Oriental art, and the daughter-in-law of the composer Sergei Prokoviev.

67 Quoted by Burini in Bowlt et al. 2012: 35; see also Bowlt, Misler and Petrova 2013: 19.

68 Quoted in Hughes 1991: 82; Iliukhina 2013: 119.

69 Lemaire 2005.

70 See in general the essays in Bowlt, Misler and Petrova 2013. Crown Prince Nicholas' tour is described on pp. 45–9 by Ol'ga Sosnina; the Buddhist temple is described on pp. 79–80, by Svetlana Romanova.

71 Gray 1986; Hughes 1991: 81–97; Petrova and Marcadé 2005; Bowlt et al. 2012; Bowlt, Misler and Petrova 2013: 200–13; Rodionov et al. 2014.

72 Lemaire 2005: 287–92.

73 Bowlt 2008: 11.

74 Bowlt, Misler and Petrova 2013: 139–47.

75 Svetlyakov 2015: 50–5; Milner et al. 2017: 147–79.

76 Bukharaev 2006.

Bibliography

Abazov, Rafis, 2008. *The Palgrave Concise Historical Atlas of Central Asia*. New York: Palgrave.

Abdulreshit, Abulat (ed.), 1999. *A Grand View of Xinjiang's Cultural Relics and Historic Sites*. Urumqi: Suntime International.

Abramova, Maya P., 1995. 'Sarmatians in the North Caucasus'. In Davis-Kimball et al. (eds): 165–83.

Abregov, Almir et al., 2007. *Adygeya National Museum*. Maikop.

Abudurasule, Yidilisi, Wenying Li and Xingjun Hu, 2019. 'The Xiaohe (Small River) Cemetery and the Xiaohe Culture'. In Betts et al. (eds): 19–51.

Abu-Lughod, Janet L., 1989. *Before European Hegemony. The World System A.D. 1250–1350*. Oxford University Press.

Ahuja, Anjana, 1998. 'Are China's Mummies Our Lost Cousins?' *The Times*, 23 March: 17.

Akurgal, Ekrem, 2001. *The Hattian and Hittite Civilizations*. Ankara: Republic of Turkey Ministry of Culture.

Alekseyev, A. Yu., 2005. 'Scythian Kings and "Royal" Burial-Mounds of the Fifth and Fourth Centuries BC'. In Braund (ed.): 39–55.

Algaze, Guillermo, 1989. 'The Uruk Expansion: Cross-cultural Exchange in Early Mesopotamian Civilization'. *Current Anthropology* 5: 571–608.

Allard, Francis, and Diimaajav, Erdenebaatar, 2005. 'Khirigsuurs, Ritual and Mobility in the Bronze Age of Mongolia'. *Antiquity* 79: 547–63.

Allchin, Raymond, Warwick Ball and Norman Hammond (eds), 2019. *The Archaeology of Afghanistan. From the Earliest Times to the Timurid Period*. Edinburgh University Press.

Allen, W. E. D. (ed.), 1970. *Russian Embassies to the Georgian Kings 1589–1605*. 2 vols. Cambridge University Press.

Allentoft, M., M. Sikora, K. Sjögren, et al., 2015. 'Population Genomics of Bronze Age Eurasia', *Nature* 522: 167–172.

Allsen, Thomas T., 2018. 'The Circulation of Military Technology in the Mongolian Empire'. In Di Cosmo (ed.): 264–93.

Almond, Ian, 2009. *Two Faiths, One Banner: When Muslims Marched with Christians Across Europe's Battlegrounds*. London: I. B. Tauris.

Amitai, Reuven, and Michal Biran, 2005. *Mongols, Turks, and Others. Eurasian Nomads and the Sedentary World*. Leiden: Brill.

Andreeva, Petya, 2018. 'Fantastic Beasts of the Eurasian Steppes: Toward a Revisionist Approach to Animal-Style Art'. *Publicly Accessible Penn Dissertations*. 2963. https://repository.upenn.edu/edissertations/2963

Andrews, Peter Alford, 1999. *Felt Tents and Pavilions. The Nomadic Tradition and Its Interaction with Princely Tentage*. 2 vols. London: Melisende.

Anon., 2013. '"Cleopatra's necklace" found in a Siberian grave'. *Siberian Times*, 1 February. https://siberiantimes.com/culture/others/features/cleopatras-necklace-found-in-a-siberian-grave/ Last accessed 18 August 2014.

Anthony, David W., 1995. 'Nazi and Eco-Feminist Prehistories: Ideology and Empiricism in Indo-European Archaeology'. In Kohl and Fawcett: 82–96.

Anthony, David W., 2006. 'Three Deadly Sins in Steppe Archaeology: Culture, Migration and Aryans'. In Peterson, Popova and Smith (eds): 40–61.

Anthony, David W., 2009. 'The Sintashta Genesis. The Roles of Climate Change, Warfare, and Long-Distance Trade'. In Hanks and Linduff: 47–73.

Anthony, David W., 2010, *The Horse, the Wheel, and Language. How Bronze-Age Riders from the Eurasian Steppes Shaped the Modern World*. Princeton University Press.

Applebaum, Anne, 1996. *Between East and West. Across the Borderlands of Europe*. New York: Pantheon.

Armstrong Oma, Kristin and Lene Melheim, 2019. '"Children of the Light": On Yoga, Body Schemes and Altered States of Consciousness in the Nordic Late Bronze Aga – a link to India?' In Olsen, Olander and Kristiansen (eds): 123–44.

Aruz, Joan, Ann Farkas, Andrei Alekseev and Elena Korolkova (eds), 2000. *The Golden Deer of Eurasia. Scythian and Sarmatian Treasures from the Russian Steppes*. New York: Yale University Press.

Ascherson, Neal, 1995, *Black Sea. The Birthplace of Civilisation and Barbarism*. London: Jonathan Cape.

Ashtor, E., 1976. *A Social and Economic History of the Near East in the Middle Ages*. London: Collins.

Asimov, A. S. and C. E. Bosworth (eds), 1998. *History of Civilizations in Central Asia. Volume IV. The Age of Achievement: A.D. 750 to the End of the Fifteenth Century*. Paris: UNESCO.

Bäbler, Balbina, 2005. 'Bobbies or Boobies? The Scythian Police Force in Classical Athens'. In Braund (ed.): 114–22.

Bailey, H. W., 1978. 'The Orbit of Afghan Studies'. *Afghan Studies* 1: 1–8.

Bailey, H. W., 1979. *Dictionary of Khotan Saka*. Cambridge University Press.

Baldick, Julian, 2000. *Animal and Shaman. Ancient Religions of Central Asia*. London: I. B. Tauris.

Ball, Warwick, 1989. 'The Buddhists of Sind'. *South Asian Studies* 5: 119–31.

Ball, Warwick, 1997. 'Kandahar, the Saka and India'. In Raymond Allchin and Bridget Allchin (eds), *South Asian Archaeology, 1995. Proceedings of the 13th International Conference of the European Association of South Asian Archaeologists*. New Delhi: Oxford & IBH Publishing. Vol 1: 439–50.

Ball, Warwick, 1998. 'Following the Mythical Road'. *Geographical Magazine* 70, 3: 18–23.

Ball, Warwick, 2008. *The Monuments of Afghanistan. History, Archaeology and Architecture*. London: I. B. Tauris.

Ball, Warwick, 2009. *Out of Arabia: Phoenicians, Arabs and the Discovery of Europe*. London: East and West.

Ball, Warwick, 2010. *Towards One World. Ancient Persia and the West*. London: East and West.

Ball, Warwick, 2012. *Sultans of Rome. The Turkish World Expansion*. London: East and West.

Ball, Warwick, 2015. *The Gates of Asia. The Eurasian Steppe and the Limits of Europe*. London: East and West.

Ball, Warwick, 2016. *Rome in the East. The Transformation of an Empire. Second Edition*. London: Routledge.

Ball, Warwick, 2019a. *Archaeological Gazetteer of Afghanistan. Revised Edition*. Oxford University Press.

Ball, Warwick, 2019b. '"Band Wagon and Gravy Train." The Rise and Rise of the Silk Road'. *Afghanistan* 2, 2: 171–94.

Ball, Warwick, 2021. 'Giganticism and Bamiyan. Turk, Iranian and Chinese Traditions of Dynasticism'. In Matthew Canepa (ed.), *Persian Cultures of Power and the Entanglement of the Afro-Eurasian World*. Los Angeles: Getty Foundation.

Ball, Warwick, Olivier Bordeaux, David W. Mac Dowall, Nicholas Sims-Williams and Maurizio Taddei, 2019. 'From the Kushans to the Shahis'. In Allchin, Ball and Hammond (eds): 344–459.

Barber, Elizabeth Wayland, 1999. *The Mummies of Ürümchi. Did Europeans Migrate to China 4,000 Years Ago?* London: Macmillan.

Barfield, Thomas J., 1989. *The Perilous Frontier. Nomad Empires and China 221 BC to AD 1757*. Cambridge, MA: Blackwell.

Barfield, Thomas J., 2001. 'The Shadow Empires: Imperial State Formation along the Chinese–Nomad Frontier'. In S. E. Alcock, T. D. D'Altroy, K. D. Morrison and C. M. Sinopoli (eds), *Empires: Perspectives from Archaeology and History*. New York: 10–41.

Barford, P. M., 2001, *The Early Slavs. Culture and Society in Early Medieval Eastern Europe*. Ithaca: Cornell University Press.

Baring, Anne, and Jules Cashford, 1991. *The Myth of the Goddess. Evolution of an Image*. London: Arkana.

Barthold, W. 1977, *Turkestan Down to the Mongol Invasions*. London: E. J. W. Gibb Memorial Trust.

Bartlett, Rosamund, 2004. *Anton Chekhov. A Life in Letters*. London: Penguin.

Baumer, Christoph, 2012. *The History of Central Asia. Volume One. The Age of the Steppe Warriors*. London: I. B. Tauris.

Baumer, Christoph, 2014. *The History of Central Asia. Volume Two. The Age of the Silk Roads*. London: I. B. Tauris.

Baumer, Christoph, 2016. *The History of Central Asia. Volume Three. The Age of Islam and the Mongols*. London: I. B. Tauris.

Beckwith, Christopher I., 1987. *The Tibetan Empire in Central Asia*. Princeton University Press.

Beckwith, Christopher I., 2011, *Empires of the Silk Road. A History of Central Asia from the Bronze Age to the Present*. Princeton University Press.

Bedrik, A. I. et al., 2002. *Heritage of the Don from Museum Collections of the Rostov Province*. Rostov-on-Don: Omega Print.

Bell, Andrew (ed.), 2000. *The Role of Migration in the History of the Eurasian Steppe. Sedentary Civilization vs. "Barbarian" and Nomad.* Basingstoke: Palgrave Macmillan.

Bemmann, Jan, and Michael Schmauder (eds), 2015. *Complexity of Interaction along the Eurasian Steppe Zone in the First Millennium* CE. Bonn Contributions to Asian Archaeology Volume 7. Bonn: Rheinische Friedrich-Wilhelms-Universität.

Bernal, Martin, 1987. *Black Athena, The Afro-Asiatic Roots of Classical Civilization: The Fabrication of Ancient Greece 1785–1985.* Brunswick: Rutgers University Press.

Bespali, E. et al., 1996. *Treasures of the Warrior Tombs.* Glasgow Museums.

Betts, Alison V. G. et al. (eds), 2019. *The Cultures of Ancient Xinjiang, Western China: Crossroads of the Silk Roads.* Oxford: Archaeopress.

Betts, Alison, 2019. 'Xinjiang in Prehistory'. In Betts et al. (eds): 9–18.

Biran, Michal, 2004. 'The Mongol Transformation: From the Steppe to Eurasian Empire'. *Medieval Encounters* 10, 1–3: 339–61.

Biran, Michal, 2005a. *The Empire of the Qara Khitai in Eurasian History. Between China and the Islamic World.* Cambridge University Press.

Biran, Michal, 2005b. 'True to Their Ways: Why the Qara Khitai Did Not Convert to Islam'. In Amitai and Biran: 175–200.

Bivar, A. D. H., 1983. 'The History of Eastern Iran'. In Yashater (ed.), *The Cambridge History of Iran. Volume 3 (1)*: 181–231.

Blakesley, Rosalind P., 2016. *Russia and the Arts. The Age of Tolstoy and Tchaikovsky.* London: National Portrait Gallery.

Blok, Josine H., 1995. *The Early Amazons. Modern and Ancient Perspectives on a Persistent Myth.* Leiden: Brill.

Blom, Philipp, 2002. *To Have and to Hold. An Intimate History of Collectors and Collecting.* London: Allen Lane.

Boardman, John (ed.), 1993. *The Oxford History of Classical Art.* Oxford University Press.

Boardman, John, 1980. *The Greeks Overseas. Their Early Colonies and Trade.* London: Thames & Hudson.

Boardman, John, 1994. *The Diffusion of Classical Art in Antiquity.* London: Thames & Hudson.

Boardman, John, 2010. *The Relief Plaques of Eastern Eurasia and China. The 'Ordos Bronzes', Peter the Great's Treasure, and Their Kin.* Oxford: Archaeopress.

Bobrick, Benson, 1992. *East of the Sun. The Conquest and Settlement of Siberia.* London: Heinemann.

Bokovenko, Nikolai A., 1995a. 'Tuva During the Scythian Period'. In Davis-Kimball et al. (eds): 265–82.

Bokovenko, Nikolai A., 1995b. 'The Tagar Culture in the Minusinsk Basin'. In Davis-Kimball et al. (eds): 299–314.

Bolton, J. D. P., 1962. *Aristeus of Proconnesus.* Oxford University Press.

Bonner, Michael Jackson, 2019. 'Nomad Riders of the Steppe'. *The Dorchester Review*, Spring/Summer: 92–6.

Bonner, Michael R. Jackson, 2020. *The Last Empire of Iran.* Piscataway, NJ: Gorgias Press.

Bonora, Gian Luca, Niccolò Pianciola and Paolo Sartori, 2009 (eds). *Kazakhstan. Religions and Society in the History of Central Eurasia*. Turin: Umberto Allemandi.

Bopearachchi, Osmund. 1999. 'Afghanistan 1993: le dépôt de Mir Zakah. Le plus grand trésor du monde, son destin et son intérêt'. *Dossiers de l'archéologie*. 248: 36–43.

Bosley, Keith, 1989. 'Introduction to and translation of *The Kalevala*'. Oxford University Press.

Bosworth, Clifford Edmund, 1967. *The Islamic Dynasties. A Chronological and Genealogical Handbook*. Edinburgh University Press.

Bosworth, C. Edmund, 2012. *Eastward Ho! Diplomats, Travellers and Interpreters of the Middle East and Beyond 1600–1940*. London: Melisende.

Bowlt, John E., 2008. *Moscow and St. Petersburg in Russia's Silver Age 1900–1920*. London: Thames & Hudson.

Bowlt, John E., Nicoletta Misler and Evgenia Petrova (eds) 2013. *The Russian Avant-garde. Siberia and the East*. Milano: Skira.

Bowlt, John E., Nina Lobanov-Rostovsky, Nikita Lobanov-Rostovsky and Olga Shaumyan, 2012. *Masterpieces of Russian Stage Design 1880–1930*. 2 vols. London: Antique Collectors' Club.

Boyle, J. A., 1965. 'The Mongol Invasion of Eastern Persia 1220–1223'. *History Today* 13, 9: 614–23.

Boxer, C. R. 1969, *The Portuguese Seaborne Empire 1415–1825*. London: Hutchinson.

Braudel, Fernand. 1987. *Grammaire de Civilisations*. Paris: Flammarion.

Braund, David (ed.), 2005. *Scythians and Greeks. Cultural Interactions in Scythia, Athens and the Early Roman Empire (Sixth Century BC–First Century AD)*. University of Exeter Press.

Bregel, Yuri (2003). *An Historical Atlas of Central Asia*. Leiden: Brill.

Brent, Peter, 1976. *The Mongol Empire. Genghis Khan: His Triumph and His Legacy*. London: Weidenfeld & Nicolson.

Broadbridge, Anne F., 2018. *Women and the Making of the Mongol Empire*. Cambridge University Press.

Brosseder, Ursula, 2009. 'Xiongnu Terrace Tombs and Their Interpretation as Elite Burials', ed. Jan Bemmann, Hermann Parzinger, Ernst Pohl and Damdinsuren Tseveendorzh, *Current Archaeological Research in Mongolia*. Bonn: Rheinische Friedrich-Wilhelms-Universität: 247–80.

Brosseder, Ursula B., 2011. 'Belt Plaques as an Indicator of East–West Relations in the Eurasian Steppe at the Turn of the Millennia'. In Brosseder and Miller (eds): 349–424.

Brosseder, Ursula B., 2015. 'A Study on the Complexity and Dynamics of Interaction and Exchange in Late Iron Age Eurasia'. In Bemmann and Schmauder: 199–332.

Brosseder, Ursula B., 2018. 'Xiongnu and Huns. Archaeological Perspectives on a Centuries-Old Debate about Identity and Migration'. In Di Cosmo and Maas: 176–88.

Brosseder, Ursula B., and Bryan K. Miller (eds), 2011. *Xiongnu Archaeology. Multidisciplinary Perspectives of the First Steppe Empire in Inner Asia*. Bonn: Rheinische Friedrich-Wilhelms-Universität.

Brotton, Jerry, 2002. *The Renaissance Bazaar. From the Silk Road to Michelangelo.* Oxford University Press.

Brown, Dorcas R. and David W. Anthony, 2019. 'Late Bronze Age Midwinter Dog Sacrifices and Warrior Initiations at Krasnosamarskoe, Russia'. In Olsen, Olander and Kristiansen (eds): 97–121.

Browning, Iain, 1979. *Palmyra.* London: Chatto & Windus.

Bryce, Trevor, 1998. *The Kingdom of the Hittites.* Oxford University Press.

Budge, E. A. Wallis, 1928. *The Monks of Kublai Khan, Emperor of China: Medieval Travels from China Through Central Asia to Persia and Beyond.* London. (New edition 2014, with an introduction by David Morgan.)

Bukharaev, Ravil, 2006. *Tatarstan: A 'Can-Do' Culture.* Leiden: Brill.

Bulwer Lytton, Edward, 2004 (1837). *Athens: Its Rise and Fall.* Bicentenary Edition, ed. Oswyn Murray. London: Routledge, 2004.

Bunker, Emma C., Bruce Chatwin and Ann R. Farkas, 1970. *Animal Style Art from East to West.* New York: Intercultural Art Press.

Burney, Charles, and David Marshall Lang, 1971. *The Peoples of the Hills. Ancient Ararat and Caucasus.* London: Weidenfeld & Nicolson.

Bursche, Aleksander, John Hines and Anna Zapolska (eds), 2020. *The Migration Period between the Oder and the Vistula (2 Vols).* Leiden: Brill.

Buryakov, Y. F., K. M. Baipakov, Kh. Tashbaeva and Y. Yakubov, 1999. *The Cities and Routes of the Great Silk Road.* Tashkent: International Institute for Central Asian Studies.

Çağatay, Ergun, and Doğan Kuban, 2006. *The Turkic Speaking Peoples. 2,000 Years of Art and Culture from Inner Asia to the Balkans.* Munich: Prestel.

Callieri, Pierfrancesco, 2016. "SAKAS: IN AFGHANISTAN." *Encyclopædia Iranica*, online edition, available at http://www.iranicaonline.org/articles/sakas-in-afghanistan (last accessed 14 December 2016).

Cameron, Averil, 2018. 'Epilogue'. In Di Cosmo and Maas: 410–30.

Chaichian, Mohammad A., 2013. *Empires and Walls. Globalization, Migration, and Colonial Domination.* Leiden: Brill.

Chambers, James, 1988. *The Devil's Horsemen. The Mongol Invasion of Europe.* London: Cassell.

Chaykovskiy, S. M. et al., 1993. *Golden Warriors of the Ukrainian Steppes.* City of Edinburgh Art Centre.

Chernykh, E. N., 1995. 'Postscript: Russian Archaeology after the Collapse of the USSR – Infrastructural Crisis and the Resurgence of Old and New Nationalities'. In Kohl and Fawcett: 149–75.

Chqonia, Anna, 2008. 'Colchina Goldwork'. In Darejan Kacharava and Guram Kvirkvelia, *Wine, Worship, and Sacrifice. The Golden Graves of Ancient Vani.* New York: Institute for the Study of the Ancient World: 80–95.

Christian, David, 1998. *A History of Russia, Central Asia and Mongolia. Volume I. Inner Eurasia from Prehistory to the Mongol Empire.* Oxford: Blackwell.

Chronicon Paschale 284–628 AD, 1989. Trans. with notes and introd. by Michael and Mary Whitby. Liverpool University Press.

Chuganov, Konstantin et al., 2001. 'The Golden Grave from Arzhan'. *Minerva* 13, 1: 39–42.

Clark, Katerina, 2003. 'Socialist Realism and the Sacralizing of Space'. In Dobrenko and Naiman: 3–18.

Cobbing, Felicity, 2011. Review of *Out of Arabia*. *Palestine Exploration Quarterly* 143, 2: 157–9.

Cong, Dexin, 2019. 'Tianshan as a Bridge: New Studies of Bronze Age Archaeology in the Western Tianshan, Xinjiang, China'. In Betts et al. (eds): 52–63.

Costa, Marta D., Joana B. Pereira1, Maria Pala, Verónica Fernandes et al., 2013. 'A Substantial Prehistoric European Ancestry amongst Ashkenazi Maternal Lineages'. *Nature Communications*, October: 1–10. https://www.researchgate. net/publication/257534539_A_substantial_prehistoric_European_ancestry_ amongst_Ashkenazi_maternal_lineages/link/0deec525884006385100000000/ download (last accessed 16 October 2020).

Cousens, Henry, 1929. *The Antiquities of Sind with Historical Outline*. Calcutta: Archaeological Survey of India.

Crawford, Sally and Katharina Ulmschneider, 2020. 'Refugees, Networks, Politics and East–West Connections in Early Celtic Art; Paul Joacobsthal's "History of a Monster" in context'. In Nimura, Chittock, Hommel and Gosden (eds): 197–207.

Cribb, R., 1991. *Nomads in Archaeology*. Cambridge University Press.

Cristea, Ovidiu and Liviu Pilat (eds), 2020. *From Pax Mongolica to Pax Ottomanica. War, Religion and Trade in the Northwestern Black Sea Region (14th–16th centuries)*. Leiden: Brill.

Crow, J. G., 1995. 'The Long Walls of Thrace'. In C. Mango and G. Dagron, *Constantinople and Its Hinterland*. Aldershot: 100–24.

Csiky, Gergely, 2015. *Avar-Age Polearms and Edged Weapons. Classification, Typology, Chronology and Technology*. Leiden: Brill.

Čugunov, K. V., H. Parzinger and A. Nagler, 2010. *Der skythenzeitliche Fürstenkurgan Aržan 2 in Tuva*. Mainz am Rhein: Philipp von Zabern.

Cunliffe, Barry, 2008. *Europe Between the Oceans. 9000 BC–AD 1000*. New Haven: Yale University Press.

Cunliffe, Barry, 2015. *By Steppe, Desert, and Ocean. The Birth of Eurasia*. Oxford University Press.

Cunliffe, Barry, 2019. *The Scythians. Nomad Warriors of the Steppe*. Oxford University Press.

Curta, Florin, 2019. *Eastern Europe in the Middle Ages (500–1300)*. 2 vols. Leiden: Brill.

Curta, Florin, 2020. 'Migrations in the Archaeology of Eastern and Southeastern Europe in the Early Middle Ages (Some Comments on the Current State of Research)'. In Johannes Preiser-Kapeller, Lucian Reinfandt and Yannis Stouraitis (eds), *Migration Histories of the Medieval Afroeurasian Transition Zone Aspects of Mobility between Africa, Asia and Europe, 300–1500 C.E.* Leiden: Brill: 101–38.

Curtis, John, 2000. *Ancient Persia*. London: British Museum Publications.

Damgaard, P. de B., N., Marchi, S. Rasmussen et al., 2018. '137 Ancient Human Genomes from across the Eurasian Steppes'. *Nature* 557: 369–374. https://doi. org/10.1038/s41586-018-0094-2

Darwin, John, 2007. *After Tamerlane. The Rise & Fall of Global Empires, 1400–2000*. London: Allen Lane.

Davies, Norman, 1996. *Europe. A History.* Oxford University Press.

Davies, Norman, 2007. *Europe East & West.* London: Jonathan Cape.

Davies, Norman, 2011. *Vanished Kingdoms. The History of Half-Forgotten Europe.* London: Allen Lane.

Davis-Kimball, Jeannine, 1998. 'Amazons, Priestesses and Other Women of Status'. *Silk Road Art and Archaeology* 5: 1–50.

Davis-Kimball, Jeannine, 2002. *Warrior Women. An Archaeologist's Search for History's Hidden Heroines.* New York: Warner.

Davis-Kimball, Jeannine, B. Bashilov and L. Yablonsky (eds), 1995. *Nomads of the Eurasian Steppe in the Early Iron Age.* Berkeley: Zinat Press.

Davis-Kimball, Jeannine, et al. (eds), 2000. *Kurgans, Ritual Sites, and Settlements. Eurasian Bronze and Iron Age.* Oxford: BAR.

de Busbecq, Ogier Ghislen, 2001. *Turkish Letters.* London: Eland.

de Clavijo, Ruy Gonzalez, 1840. *Narrative or the Embassy of Ruy Gonzalez de Clavijo to the Court of Timour at Samarcand A. D. 1403–6.* Trans. with notes, a preface and an introduction by Clements R. Markham. London: Hakluyt Society.

de Hartog, Leo, 1989. *Genghis Khan. Conqueror of the World.* London: Tauris Parke.

de la Vaissière, Étienne, 2012. 'Central Asia and the Silk Road'. In S. Johnson (ed.), *Oxford Handbook of Late Antiquity.* Oxford University Press: 142–69.

de la Vaissière, Étienne, 2015. 'Away from the Ötüken: a Geopolitical Approach to the Seventh Century Eastern Türks'. In Bemmann amd Schmauder (eds): 453–61.

De Nicola, Bruno, 2018. *Women in Mongol Iran. The Khatuns, 1206–1335.* Edinburgh University Press.

Deeg, Max, 2018. 'The Spread of Buddhist Culture to China between the Third and Seventh Centuries'. In Di Cosmo and Maas: 220–34.

Delmar Morgan, E., and C. H. Coote (eds), 2009. *Early Voyages and Travels to Russia and Persia by Anthony Jenkinson and Other Englishmen.* 2 vols. Cambridge University Press.

Devine, T. M., 2011. *To the Ends of the Earth. Scotland's Global Diaspora, 1750–2010.* London: Allen Lane.

Di Cosmo, Nicola (ed.), 2018. *Warfare in Inner Asian History (500–1800).* Leiden: Brill.

Di Cosmo, Nicola, 1999. 'State Formation and Periodization in Inner Asian History'. *Journal of World History* 10, 1: 1–40.

Di Cosmo, Nicola, 2002. *Ancient China and its Enemies. The Rise of Nomadic Power in East Asian History.* Cambridge University Press.

Di Cosmo, Nicola, 2018. 'Introduction: Inner Asian Ways of Warfare in Historical Perspective'. In Di Cosmo (ed.): 1–29.

Di Cosmo, Nicola and Michael Maas (eds), 2018. *Empires and Exchanges in Eurasian Late Antiquity. Rome, China, Iran, and the Steppe, ca. 250–270.* Cambridge University Press.

Dixon, Annette (ed.), 2002. *Women Who Ruled. Queens, Goddesses, Amazons in Renaissance and Baroque Art.* London: Merrell.

Dobrenko, Evgeny and Eric Naiman (eds), 2003. *The Landscape of Stalinism. The Art and Ideology of Soviet Space*. Seattle: University of Washington Press.

Downey, Lyn, 2013. *A Short History of Sonoma*. Reno: University of Nevada Press.

Dreyer, Caren, 2008. 'Russian Archaeological Explorations in Chinese Turkestan on the Turn of the 19th Century', *Indo-Asiatische Zeitschrift* 12: 62–71

Drompp, Michael R., 2018. 'Infrastructures of Legitimacy in Inner Asia. The Early Türk Empires'. In Di Cosmo and Maas: 302–16.

Durand-Guédy, David (ed.), 2013. *Turko-Mongol Rulers, Cities and City Life*. Leiden: Brill.

Dvornichenko, Vladimir V., 1995, 'Sauromatians and Sarmatians of the Eurasian Steppes: The Transitional Period from the Bronze Age'. In Davis-Kimball et al. (eds): 101–16.

Eremin, Leonid, 2007. *Along the Path of Mountain Goats. Kazanovka. The Archaeological Excursions to the Khakas National Museum-reserve*. Krasnoyarsk.

Fahr-Becker, Gabriele, 1997. *Art Nouveau*. Köln: Könemann.

Faroqhi, Suraiya, 2004. *The Ottoman Empire and the World Around It*. London: I. B. Tauris.

Fern, Chris, Tania Dickinson and Leslie Webster, 2019. *The Staffordshire Hoard. An Anglo-Saxon Treasure*. London: Society of Antiquaries.

Fernández-Armesto, Felipe, 2000. *Civilizations*. London: Macmillan.

Fernández-Armesto, Felipe, 2009. *1492. The Year Our World Began*. London: Bloomsbury.

Fielding, Nick, 2020. *Travellers in the Great Steppe from the Papal Envoys to the Russian Revolution*. Oxford: Signal Books.

Figes, Orlando, 2002. *Natasha's Dance. A Cultural History of Russia*. London: Allen Lane.

Findley, Carter Vaughn, 2005. *The Turks in World History*. Oxford University Press.

Fitzhugh, William W., 2009a. 'The Mongolian Deer Stone-Khirigsuur Complex: Dating and Organiation of a Late Bronze Age Menagerie'. In Jan Bemmann, Hermann Parzinger, Ernst Pohl and Damdinsuren Tseveendorzh (eds), *Current Archaeological Research in Mongolia*. Bonn: Rheinische Friedrich-Wilhelms-Universität: 183–99.

Fitzhugh, William W., 2009b. 'Pre-Scythian Ceremonialism, Deer Stone Art, and Cultural Intensification on Northern Mongolia'. In Hanks and Linduff: 378–411.

Fitzhugh, William W., Morris Rossabi and William Honeychurch (eds), 2009. *Genghis Khan and the Mongol Empire*. Houston Museum of Natural Science.

Frachetti, Michael D., 2008. *Pastoralist Landscapes and Social Interaction in Bronze Age Eurasia*. University of California Press.

Frachetti, Michael D., 2009. 'Differentiated Landscapes and Non-uniform Complexity among Bronze Age Societies of the Eurasian Steppe'. In Hanks and Linduff: 19–46.

Francfort, Henri-Paul, 2003. 'La civilisation de l'Asie Centrale à l'âge du Bronze et à l'âge du Fer'. In O. Bopearachchi, C. Landes and C. Sachs (eds), *De l'Indus à l'Oxus. Archéologie de l'Asie Centrale. Catalogue de l'exposition*. Lattes: Association IMAGO: 29–60.

Francfort, Henri-Paul, 2005. 'La civilisation de l'Oxus et les Indo-Iraniens et Indo-Aryens'. In *Aryas, Aryens et Iraniens en Asie Centrale*, ed. G. Fussman, J. Kellens, H.-P. Francfort and X. Tremblay. Paris: 253–328.

Francfort, Henri-Paul, 2012. 'Tillya Tepe and Its Connections with the Eurasian Steppes'. In Joan Aruz and Elisabetta Valtz Fino (eds), *Afghanistan. Forging Civilizations along the Silk Road*. New Haven: Yale University Press: 88–101.

Francfort, Henri-Paul, 2019. 'Shifting Exchange Patterns During the Bronze and Iron Ages Between China and The West in Eurasia'. In Betts et al. (eds): 97–112.

Frankopan, Peter, 2015. *The Silk Roads. A New History of the World*. London: Bloomsbury.

Frye, Richard N., 1984. *The History of Ancient Iran*. Munich: Verlag C. H. Beck.

Frye, Richard N., 1993. *The Golden Age of Persia*. London: Weidenfeld & Nicolson.

Gannon, Megan, 2020. 'Megasites of Ukraine'. *Archaeology*, May/June: 33–7.

Gawlikowski, M., 1994. 'Palmyra as a Trading Centre'. *Iraq* 56: 1–26.

Geary, Patrick J., 2018. 'Genetic History and Migration in Western Eurasia, 500–1000'. In Di Cosmo and Maas: 135–50.

Geary, Patrick, 2002. *The Myth of Nations. The Medieval Origins of Europe*. Princeton University Press.

Ghirshman, R. 1979, *Tombe Princière de Ziwiyé et le Début de l'art Animalier Scythe*. Paris: E. J. Brill.

Gibbon, Edward, 1897–1900, *The History of the Decline and Fall of the Roman Empire*. 7 vols, Ed. J. B. Bury. London: Methuen.

Gimbutas, Marija, 1971. *The Slavs*. London: Thames & Hudson.

Gimbutas, Marija, 1989. *The Language of the Goddess*. London: Thames & Hudson.

Gimbutas, Marija, 2001. *The Living Goddesses*. Berkeley: University of California Press.

Golden, Peter B., 1990a. 'The Peoples of the Russian Forest Belt'. In Sinor (ed.): 229–55.

Golden, Peter B., 1990b. 'The Peoples of the South Russian Steppes'. In Sinor (ed.): 256–84.

Golden, Peter B., 2002. 'War and Warfare in the Pre-Činggisid Western Steppes of Eurasia'. In Di Cosmo (ed.): 105–72.

Golden, Peter B., 2006. 'The Turkic Nomads of the Pre-Islamic Eurasian Steppes. Ethnogenesis and the Shaping of the Steppe Imperial Tradition'. In Çağatay and Kuban: 83–103.

Golden, Peter B., 2007a. 'Khazar Studies: Achievements and Perspectives'. In Golden et al.: 7–58.

Golden, Peter B., 2007b. 'The Conversion of the Khazars to Judaism'. In Golden et al.: 123–62.

Golden, Peter B., 2010. *Turks and Khazars. Origins, Institutions, and Interactions in Pre-Mongol Eurasia*. Abingdon: Routledge.

Golden, Peter B., 2011 (2005). 'The Shaping of the Cuman-Qïpčaqs and Their World'. In F. Schmieder and P. Schreiner (ed.), *Il Codice Cumanico e il suo mondo*, Rome: Edizioni di storia e letteratura, 247–77. Reprinted in *Studies on the Peoples and Cultures of the Eurasian Steppes*. Bucharest: Editura Academiei Române: 303–32.

Golden, Peter B., 2011 (2001). 'Nomads of the Western Eurasian Steppes: Oÿurs, Onoÿurs and Khazars'. In H. Roemer et al. (ed.), *Philologiae Turcicae Fundamenta*, III, Union Internationale des Études Orientales et Asiatiques, Berlin: Klaus Schwarz Verlag: 282–302. Reprinted in *Studies on the Peoples and Cultures of the Eurasian Steppes*. Bucharest: Editura Academiei Române: 135–62.

Golden, Peter B., 2011 (2008–9). 'Ethnogenesis in the Tribal Zone: The Shaping of the Turks'. *Archivum Eurasiae Medii Aevi*, 16: 73–112. Reprinted in *Studies on the Peoples and Cultures of the Eurasian Steppes*. Bucharest: Editura Academiei Române: 17–63.

Golden, Peter B., 2011. *Central Asia in World History*. Oxford University Press.

Golden, Peter B., 2015. 'The Turkic World in Mahmud al-Kâshgharî'. In Bemmann amd Schmauder (eds): 503–55.

Golden, Peter B., 2018. 'The Ethnogonic Tales of the Turks'. *The Medieval History Journal* 21, 2: 291–327.

Golden, Peter B., Haggai Ben-Shammai and András Róna-Tas (eds), 2007. *The World of the Khazars. New Perspectives. Selected Papers from the Jerusalem 1999 International Khazar Colloquium*. Leiden: Brill.

Goodison, Lucy and Christine Morris (eds), 1998. *Ancient Goddesses. The Myths and the Evidence*. London: British Museum Press.

Gorbunova, N. G., 1986. *The Culture of Ancient Ferghana VI Century B.C.–VI Century A.D.* Oxford: BAR.

Gray, Camilla, 1986. *The Russian Experiment in Art 1863–1922*. London: Thames & Hudson.

Gray, R., and Q. Atkinson, 2003. 'Language-tree Divergence Times Support the Anatolian Theory of Indo-European Origin'. *Nature* 426: 435–9. https://doi.org/10.1038/nature02029

Greenhalgh, Paul, 2000. 'Alternative Histories'. In Greenhalgh (ed.) *Art Nouveau*. London: 36–53.

Grenet, F. and N. Sims-Williams, 1987. 'The Historical Context of the Soghdian Ancient Letters'. Transitional Periods in Iranian History. *Studia Iranica* 5: 101–22.

Grigoriev, Stanislav and Yulia Vasina, 2019. *The Megaliths of Vera Island in the Southern Urals*. Oxford: Archaeopress.

Grousset, René, 1970. *The Empire of the Steppes: a History of Central Asia*. New Brunswick: Rutgers University Press.

Gryaznov, Mikhail. 1969. *The Ancient Civilization of South Siberia*. Geneva: Nagel.

Gumilev, Lev, 1987. *Searches for an Imaginary Kingdom. The Legend of the Kingdom of Prester John*. Cambridge University Press. (Moscow 1970.)

Günther, Hans, 2003. '"Broad Is My Motherland": The Mother Archetype and Space in Soviet Mass Song'. In Dobrenko and Naiman: 77–95.

Haak, W., I. Lazaridis, N. Patterson et al., 2015. 'Massive Migration from the Steppe Was a Source for Indo-European Languages in Europe'. *Nature* 522: 207–11. https://doi.org/10.1038/nature14317

Hale, John, 1993. *The Civilization of Europe in the Renaissance*. London.

Halecki, Oscar, 1952. *Borderlands of Western Civilization. A History of East Central Europe*. New York: Ronald Press.

Hanks, Bryan K., and Katheryn M. Linduff (eds), 2009. *Social Complexity in Prehistoric Eurasia. Monuments, Metals, and Mobility.* New York: Cambridge University Press.

Hansen, Valerie, 2015. *The Silk Road. A New History.* New York: Oxford University Press.

Hansen, Valerie, 2018. 'The Synthesis of the Tang Dynasty'. In Di Cosmo and Maas: 108–22.

Harmatta, János (ed.), 1994. *History of Civilizations in Central Asia. Volume II. The Development of Sedentary and Nomadic Civilizations: 700 B.C. to A.D. 250.* Paris: UNESCO.

Hartley, Janet M., 2014. *Siberia. A History of the People.* New Haven: Yale University Press.

Haug, Robert, 2019. *The Eastern Frontier. Limits of Empire in Late Antique and Early Medieval Central Asia.* London: I. B. Tauris.

Haywood, A. J., 2010. *Siberia. A Cultural History.* Oxford: Signal.

Heather, Peter, 2009. *Empires and Barbarians. Migration, Development and the Birth of Europe.* London: Macmillan.

Hedin, Sven, 1928. *The Silk Road.* London.

Herrmann, Georgina, 1977. *The Iranian Revival.* London: Phaidon.

Hoddinott, R. F., 1986. 'From the Chalcolithic to the Early Bronze Age in West and North Pontic Lands'. *Anadolu Araştırmaları. Jahrbuch für Kleinasiatische Forschung.* Istanbul: 117–28.

Hodges, Richard and David Whitehouse, 1983. *Mohammed, Charlemagne & the Origins of Europe.* London: Duckworth.

Honeychurch, William, 2015. *Inner Asia and the Spatial Politics of Empire. Archaeology, Mobility, and Culture Contact.* New York: Springer.

Honeychurch, William, Joshua Wright and Chunag Amartuvshin, 2009. 'Re-writing Monumental Landscapes as Inner Asian Political Process'. In Hanks and Linduff: 330–57.

Hopkirk, Peter, 1980. *Foreign Devils on the Silk Road. The Search for the Lost Cities and Treasures of Chinese Central Asia.* London: John Murray.

Hosking, Geoffrey, 2001. *Russia and the Russians from Earliest Times to 2001.* London: Allen Lane.

Houle, Jean-Luc, 2009. 'Socially Integrative Facilities and the Emergence of Societal Complexity on the Mongolian Steppe'. In Hanks and Linduff: 358–77.

Howard-Johnson, James, 2007. 'Byzantine Sources for Khazar History'. In Golden et al: 163–94.

Howard-Johnston, James, 2010. *Witnesses to a World Crisis. Historians and Histories of the Middle East in the Seventh Century.* Oxford University Press.

Hudson, Travis and Craig Bates, 2015. *Treasures from Native California. The Legacy of Russian Exploration.* Walnut Creek, CA: Left Coast Press.

Hughes, Robert, 1991. *The Shock of the New. Art and the Century of Change.* Updated and enlarged edition. London: Thames & Hudson.

Hunt, Margaret R., 2010. *Women in Eighteenth-century Europe.* Harlow: Longman.

Hupchick, Dennis P. and Harold E. Cox, 2001. *The Palgrave Historical Atlas of Eastern Europe.* New York: Palgrave.

Iliukhina, Evgenia, 2013. 'Mikhail Larionov, Natal'ia Goncharova: Turning to the East'. In Bowlt, Misler and Petrova 2013: 118–23.

Inaba, Minoru, 2005. 'The Identity of the Turkish Rulers to the South of the Hindukush from the 7th to the 9th Centuries A.D'. *Zinbun* 38: 1–19.

İnalcık, Halil, 2006. *Turkey and Europe in History*. Istanbul: EREN Yayıncılık.

Isadore of Charax, 1914. *Parthian Stations*. Trans. W. H. Schoff. Philadelphia.

Ivanchik, A. I., 2005. 'Who Were the "Scythian" Archers on Archaic Attic Vases?' In Braund: 100–13.

Ivantchik, Askold, 2018. 'SCYTHIANS'. *Encyclopædia Iranica*, online edition, available at http://www.iranicaonline.org/articles/scythians (last accessed 25 April 2018).

Iversen, Rune, 2019. 'On the Emergence of Corded Ware Societies in Northern Europe'. In Olsen, Olander and Kristiansen (eds): 73–95.

Jackson, Peter, 2005a. *The Mongols and the West, 1221–1410*. London: Longman.

Jackson, Peter, 2005b. 'The Mongols and the Faith of the Conquered'. In Amitai and Biran: 245–90.

Jacobs, Michael, 1985. *The Good and Simple Life. Artist Colonies in Europe and America*. London: Phaidon.

Jacobson, Esther, 1995. *The Art of the Scythians. The Interpenetration of Cultures at the Edge of the Hellenistic World*. Leiden: Brill.

Jettmar, Karl, 1967. *Art of the Steppes. The Eurasian Animal Style*. London: Methuen.

Jettmar, Karl, 2002. *Beyond the Gorges of the Indus. Archaeology before Excavation*. Oxford University Press.

Johanson, Eva Csatö, 2006. 'The Karaims. The Smallest Group of Turkic-Speaking People'. In Çağatay and Kuban: 385–403.

Juliano, Annette L. and Judith A. Lerner, 2001. *Monks and Merchants. Silk Road Treasures from Northwest China. Gansu and Ningxia, 4th–7th Century*. New York: Harry N. Abrams.

Kästner, Ursula, Martin Langner und Britta Rabe, 2007. *Griechen Skythen Amazonen*. Berlin: Pergaminmuseum.

Katsuhiko, Oga and Sumil Gupta, 2000. 'The Far East, Southeast and South Asia: Indo-Pacific Beads from Yayoi Tombs as Indicators of Early Maritime Exchange'. *South Asian Studies* 16: 73–88.

Kelly, Christopher, 2008. *Attila the Hun. Barbarian Terror and the Fall of the Roman Empire*. London: Bodley Head.

Kennedy, Hugh, 2002. *Mongols, Huns & Vikings*. London: Cassell.

Kessler, Adam T. (ed.), 1993. *Empires Beyond the Great Wall. The Heritage of Genghis Khan*. Los Angeles: Natural History Museum.

Khazanov, Anatoly, 1985. *Nomads and the Outside World*. Cambridge University Press.

Khazanov, Anatoly M., 2013. 'The Eurasian Steppe Nomads in World Military History'. In Jürgen Paul (ed.), *Nomad Aristocrats in a World of Empires*. Wiesbaden: Dr Ludwig Reichert Verlag: 187–207.

Khodarkovsky, Michael, 2002. *Russia's Steppe Frontier. The Making of a Colonial Empire, 1500–1800*. Bloomington: Indiana University Press.

Kilunovskaya, Marina and Vladimir Semenov, 1995. *The Land in the Heart of Asia*. St Petersburg: EGO.

Kim, Hyun Jin, 2013. *The Huns, Rome and the Birth of Europe*. Cambridge University Press.

King, Charles, 2004. *The Black Sea. A History*. Oxford University Press.

Klimburg-Salter, Deborah, 2008. 'Buddhist Painting in the Hindu Kush ca. VIth to Xth Centuries'. In Étienne de la Vaissière (ed.), *L'Islamisation de l'Asie Centrale. Processus locaux d'acculturation du VIᵉ au XIᵉ siécle*. Leuven: Peeters: 131–59.

Klimburg-Salter, Deborah, 2010. 'Corridors of Communication Across Afghanistan 7th to 10th Centuries'. In Véra Marigo et al. (eds), *Paysages de centre de l'Afghanistan. Paysages naturels, paysages culturels*. Paris: CERDERAF: 173–86.

Knobloch, Edgar, 2007. *Russia & Asia. Nomadic & Oriental Traditions in Russian History*. Hong Kong: Odyssey.

Koestler, Arthur, 1976. *The Thirteenth Tribe. The Khazar Empire and Its Heritage*. London: Hutchinson.

Kohl, Philip L., 2006. 'The Early Integration of the Eurasian Steppes with the Ancient Near East: Movements and Transformations in the Caucasus and Central Asia'. In Peterson, Popova and Smith: 3–39.

Kohl, Philip L., 2007. *The Making of Bronze Age Eurasia*. Cambridge University Press.

Kohl, Philip L., 2009. 'The Maikop Singularity. The Unequal Accumulation of Wealth on the Bronze Age Eurasian Steppe?' In Hanks and Linduff: 91–103.

Kohl, Philip L., and Clare Fawcett (eds), 2005. *Nationalism, Politics, and the Practice of Archaeology*. Cambridge University Press.

Komroff, Manuel (ed.), 1928. *Contemporaries of Marco Polo*. London: Jonathan Cape.

Korolkova, E. F., 2006. *Vlastiteli Stepei*. St Petersburg: Izdatelstvo Gosudarstvennogo Ermitazha.

Koryakova, Ludmila, and Andrej Epimakhov, 2007. *The Urals and Western Siberia in the Bronze and Iron Ages*. Cambridge University Press.

Kradin, Nikolai N., 2015. 'Nomadic Empires in Inner Asia'. In Bemmann amd Schmauder (eds): 11–48.

Kristiansen, K., M. Allentoft, K. Frei, R. Iversen, N. Johannsen, G. Kroonen and E. Willerslev, 2017. 'Re-theorising Mobility and the Formation of Culture and Language among the Corded Ware Culture in Europe'. *Antiquity*, 91, 356: 334–47.

Kurochkin, G. N., 'Generator kochevykh naradov v Trentralnoi Aziyi I mekhanizm ego funktionirovaniya'. In V. V. Bobrov (ed.). *Paleodemografiya i migrationnye protsesy v Zapadni Sibiri v drevnosti I srednevekovy'e*. Barnaul: Altai State University: 89–92.

Kuz'mina, Elena, 2007. *The Origin of the Indo-Iranians*. Leiden: Brill.

Kuzmina, E. E., ed. J. Mallory, 2008. *The Prehistory of the Silk Road*. Philadelphia: University of Pennsylvania Press.

Kydyev, V. E. et al., 1998. *Ancient Altai Barrows (Kurgans)*. Gorno-Altaisk: Ak Yekek.

Lactantius, 2003. *Divine Institutes*. Trans. with introd. and notes by Anthony Bowen and Peter Garnsey. Liverpool University Press.

Lamb, Harold, 1928. *Genghis Khan. The Emperor of All Men*. London.

Lamberg-Karlovsky, C. C., 2002. 'Archaeology and Language. The Indo-Iranians'. *Current Anthropology* 43, 1: 63–88.

Lambrick, H. T., 1973. *Sind Before the Muslim Conquest*. Hyderabad: Sindhi Adabi Board.

Lang, David Marshall, 1970. *Armenia. Cradle of Civilization*. London: Allen & Unwin.

Laruelle, Marlène, 2007. 'The Orient in Russian Thought at the Turn of the Century'. In Shlapentokh: 9–38.

Lasko, Peter, 1965. 'Prelude to Empire. The Frankish Kingdom from the Merovingians to Pepin'. In David Talbot Rice (ed.), *The Dark Ages. The Making of European Civilization*. London: Thames & Hudson: 197–218.

Lattimore, Owen, 1940. *Inner Asian Frontiers of China*. New York: The American Geographical Society.

Lefkowitz, Mary R., and Guy McLean Rogers (eds), 1996. *Black Athena Revisited*. Chapel Hill: University of North Carolina Press.

Lemaire, Gérard-George, 2005. *The Orient in Western Art*. Köln: Könemann.

Leontev, I. V., V. F. Kapelko and Y. I. Esin, 2006., *Izvayaniya i Steli Okunevskoi Kulturi*. Abakan: Khakas.

Leslie, D. D. and K. H. J. Gardener, 1982. 'Chinese Knowledge of Western Asia During the Han'. *T'oung Pao* 68: 255–308.

Lewis, Archibald R., 1998. *Nomads and Crusaders. A.D. 1000–1368*. Bloomington: Indiana University Press.

Li, Yuchun, n.d. [c. 1997]. *Xinjiang Museum Compilation*. Urumqi: Xinjiang Art & Photography Press.

Linduff, Katheryn M. and Karen Sydney Rubinson (eds), 2008. *Are All Warriors Male? Gender Roles on the Ancient Eurasian Steppe*. (Lanham: Altamira Press,), https://books.google.co.uk/books/about/Are_All_Warriors_Male.html?id=Xd5bAAAAQBAJ&printsec=frontcover&source=kp_read_button&redir_esc=y#v=onepage&q&f=false

Litvinsky, B. A., 1996. 'The Hephthalite Empire'. In Litvinsky (ed.): 135–61

Litvinsky, B.A. (ed.), 1996. *History of civilizations in Central Asia. Volume III. The Crossroads of Civilizations: A.D. 250 t o 750*. Paris: UNESCO.

Liu Wensuo, 2014. 'Archaeological Remains of Sacrificial Rituals in the Eastern Altay Mountains'. In Yu Taishan, Li Jinxiu and Bruce Doar, *Eurasian Studies II*. English Edition. Sydney: Asia Publishing Nexus: 1–28.

Liu, Xinru, 1988. *Ancient India and Ancient China. Trade and Religious Exchanges AD 1–600*. Delhi: Oxford University Press.

Liu, Xinru, 1998. *Silk and Religion. An Exploration of Material Life and the Thought of People, AD 600–1200*. Delhi: Oxford University Press.

Liu, Xuetang, 2019. 'A Report on Archaeological Findings in the Upper Yili Valley'. In Betts et al. (eds): 64–83.

Lönnrot, Elias, 1989. *The Kalevala*. Oxford University Press.

Lovell, Julia, 2006. *The Great Wall. China Against the World 1000 BC–AD 2000*. London: Atlantic Books.

Lunde, Paul and Caroline Stone (trans. and introd.), 2012. *Ibn Fadlān and the Land of Darkness. Arab Travellers in the Far North*. London: Penguin.

Lyonnet, Bertille and Nadezhda A. Dubova (eds), 2020. *The World of the Oxus Civilization*. Abingdon: Routledge.

MacLean, Fitzroy, 1958. *A Person From England and Other Travellers*. London: Jonathan Cape.

Maenchen-Helfen, Otto, 1973. *The World of the Huns: Studies in Their History and Culture*. Berkeley: University of California Press.

Mainon, Dominique, and James Ursini, 2006. *The Modern Amazons. Warrior Women On-Screen*. Pompton Plans, NJ: Limelight Editions.

Major, Richard H. (ed.) and Mikhail M. Wielhorsky (trans.), 1857. 'The Travels of Athanasius Nikitin', *India in the Fifteenth Century*. London: Hakluyt Society.

Mallory, J. P., 1989. *In Search of the Indo-Europeans. Language, Archaeology and Myth*. London: Thames & Hudson.

Mallory, J. P., 1998. 'Afterword'. In Viktor Sarianidi, *Margiana and Protozoroastrianism*. Athens: Kapon Editions.

Mallory, J. P., 2019. 'Proto-Indo-European, Proto-Uralic and Nostratic: A Brief Excursus into the Comparative Study of Proto-languages'. In Olsen, Olander and Kristiansen (eds): 35–58.

Mallory, J. P., and D. Q. Adams, 2006. *The Oxford Introduction to Proto-Indo-European and the Proto-Indo-European World*. Oxford University Press.

Mallory, J. P. and Victor H. Mair, 2000. *The Tarim Mummies. Ancient China and the Mystery of the Earliest Peoples from the West*. London: Thames & Hudson.

Malouf, David, 1978. *An Imaginary Life*. London: Chatto & Windus.

Man, John, 2018. *Searching for the Amazons. The Real Warrior Women of the Ancient World*. London: Bantam Press.

Mandeville, Sir John (n.d.). *The Voiage and Travyle of Syr John Maundeville Knight*. London: Dent.

Manz, Beatrice Forbes, 1989. *The Rise and Rule of Tamerlane*. Cambridge University Press.

Marco Polo, 1871. *The Book of Ser Marco Polo the Venetian, Concerning the Kingdoms and Marvels of the East*. 2 vos. Trans. and ed. Henry Yule and Henri Cordier. London: John Murray.

Marshall, R., 1993. *Storm from the East. From Genghis Khan to Khubilai Khan*. London: Penguin.

Martynov, Aleksandr, 2012. *Archaeological Past of the Solovetsky Islands*. Arkhangelsk.

Mayor, Adrienne, 2014. *The Amazons, Lives & Legends of Warrior Women Across the Ancient World*. Princeton University Press.

Megaw, Ruth and Vincent, 1989. *Celtic Art. From Its Beginnings to the Book of Kells*. London: Thames & Hudson.

Meier, Mischa, 2015. 'Dealing with Non-state Societies: The Failed Assassination Attempt against Attila (449 CE) and Eastern Roman Hunnic Policy'. In Bemmann amd Schmauder (eds): 635–58.

Melyukova, Anna I., 1990. 'The Scythians and Sarmatians'. In Sinor (ed.): 97–117.

Melyukova, Anna I., 1995. 'Scythians of Southeastern Europe'. In Davis-Kimball et al. (eds): 26–58.

Menotti, Francesco and Aleksey G. Korvin-Piotrovskiy (eds)., 2012. *The Tripolye Culture Giant-settlements in Ukraine. Formation, Development and Decline.* Oxford: Oxbow.

Mepisashvili, Rusudan, and Vakhtang Tsintsadze, 1977. *The Arts of Ancient Georgia.* London: Thames & Hudson.

Meyer, Caspar, 2013. *Greco-Scythian Art & the Birth of Eurasia. From Classical Antiquity to Russian Modernity.* Oxford University Press.

Miller, J. Innes, 1969. *The Spice Trade of the Roman Empire 29 BC to AD 641.* Oxford University Press.

Milner, John et al., 2017. *Revolution. Russian Art 1917–1932.* London: Royal Academy of Arts.

Minorsky, V., V. V. Barthold and C. E. Bosworth (eds), 1970. *Hudūd al-ʿĀlam. 'The Regions of the World'. A Persian Geography 372 A.H.–982 A.D.* London: E. J. W. Gibb Memorial.

Mirsky, Jeannette, 1977. *Sir Aurel Stein. Archaeological Explorer.* University of Chicago Press.

Morgan, David, 1986. *The Mongols.* Oxford: Blackwell.

Moshkova, Marina G., 1995. 'Sarmatians. Some Concluding Remarks'. In Davis-Kimball et al. (eds): 186–8.

Muller, Jean-Claude, 1986. 'Early Stages of Language Comparison from Sassetti to Sir William Jones (1786)'. *Kratylos* 31: 1–31.

Murrell, Kathleen Berton, 1997. *Moscow Art Nouveau.* London: Philip Wilson.

Murzin, V. Yu., 2005. 'Key Points in Scythian History'. In Braund (ed.): 33–8.

Muscarella, Oscar White, 1977. '"Ziwiye" and Ziwiye: The Forgery of a Provenience'. *Journal of Field Archaeology* 4, 2: 197–219.

Narain, A. K., 1990. 'Indo-Europeans in Inner Asia'. In Sinor (ed.): 151–76.

Naumov, Igor V., 2006., *The History of Siberia.* Abingdon: Routledge.

Necipoğlu, Gülru, 2005. *The Age of Sinan. Architectural Culture in the Ottoman Empire.* London: Reaktion.

Nedashkovsky, L. F. 2004. *Ukek. The Golden Horde City and Its Periphery.* Oxford: BAR.

Neverov, Oleg and Mikhail Piotrovsky, 1997. *The Hermitage. Essays on the History of the Collection.* St Petersburg: Slavia.

Nimura, Courtney, Helen Chittock, Peter Hommel and Chris Gosden (eds), 2020. *Art in the Eurasian Age. Context, Connections and Scale.* Oxford: Oxbow.

Nizam al-Mulk, 1960. *The Book of Government or Rules for Kings.* Trans. Hubert Darke. London: Routledge & Kegan Paul.

Noonan, Thomas S., 2007. 'The Economy of the Khazar Khaganate'. In Golden et al.: 207–44.

Norman, Geraldine, 1997. *The Hermitage. The Biography of a Great Museum.* London: Jonathan Cape.

Norris, Harry, 2009. *Islam in the Baltic. Europe's Early Muslim Community.* London: I. B. Tauris.

Novozhenov, V. A., 2018. 'Whence the Cimmerians Came? Transcontinental Communications of the Early Nomads in the Lights of the Origin of the Cimmerians'. *Journal of Historical Archaeology & Anthropological Sciences* 3, 1: 1–15.

O Flynn, Thomas S. R., 2016. *The Western Christian Presence in the Russias and Qājār Persia, c.1760–c.1870*. Leiden: Brill.

O'Shea, Stephen, 2006. *Sea of Faith. Islam and Christianity in the Medieval Mediterranean World*. London

O'Sullivan, Rebecca and Peter Hommel, 2020. 'Fantastic Beasts and Where To Find Them: Composite Animals in the Context of Eurasian Early Iron Age Art'. In Nimura, Chittock, Hommel and Gosden (eds): 53–69.

Obolensky, Dimitri, 1971. *The Byzantine Empire. Eastern Europe 500–1453*. London: Weidenfeld & Nicolson.

Odom, Anne, 2010. 'A Revolution in Russian Design: Solntsev and the Decorative Arts'. In Whittaker: 41–59.

Okladnikov, A. P., 1990. 'Inner Asia at the Dawn of History'. In Sinor (ed.): 41–98.

Olander, Thomas, 2019. 'The Indo-European Homeland: Introducing the Problem'. In Olsen, Olander and Kristiansen (eds): 7–34.

Olbrycht, Marek Jan, 2015. 'Arsacid Iran and the Nomads of Central Asia – Ways of Cultural Transfer'. In J. Bemmann and M. Schmauder (eds), *Complexity of Interaction along the Eurasian Steppe Zone in the First Millennium CE*. Bonn: Fgarch Press Uni-Bonn: 333–90.

Oleszczak, Łukasz, Andriey P. Borodovskiy et al., 2018. 'The Origin of Culturally Diversified Individuals Buried in the Early Iron Age Barrow Cemetery at Chultukov Log-1 (Upper Altai) in Light of the Analysis of Stable Oxygen Isotopes'. *Collegium antropologicum* 42, 1: 27–37.

Olivier, Laurent, 2020. 'How Celts Perceived the World: Early Celtic Art and Analogical Thought'. In Nimura, Chittock, Hommel and Gosden (eds): 95–109.

Olkhovsky, Valery S., 1995. 'Scythian Culture in the Crimea'. In Davis-Kimball et al. (eds): 63–81.

Olsen, Birgit Anette, 2019. 'Aspects of Family Structure among the Indo-Europeans'. In Olsen, Olander and Kristiansen (eds): 145–63.

Olsen, Brigit A., Thomas Olander and Kristian Kristiansen (eds), 2019. *Tracing the Indo-Europeans. New Evidence from Archaeology and Historical Linguistics*. Oxford: Oxbow.

Ostrowski, Donald, 1998. *Muscovy and the Mongols. Cross-Cultural Influences on the Steppe Frontier, 1304–1589*. Cambridge University Press.

Pankova, Svetlana and St John Simpson (eds), 2017. *Scythians: Warriors of Ancient Siberia*. London: Thames & Hudson.

Paradowski, Ryszard, 2007. 'Absolutism and Authority in Eurasian Ideology: Karsavin and Alekseev'. In Shlapentokh 2007: 95–108.

Pares, Bernard, 1955. *A History of Russia*. London: Jonathan Cape.

Parry, J. H., 1963. *The Age of Reconnaissance*. London: Weidenfeld & Nicolson.

Payne, John R., 1989. 'Pamir Languages'. In Schmitt, R. (ed.), *Compendium Linguarum Iranicarum*. Wiesbaden: Reichert: 417–44.

Payne, Richard, 2016. 'The Making of Turan: The Fall and Transformation of the Iranian East in Late Antiquity'. *Journal of Late Antiquity* 9, 1: 4–41.

Peacock, A. C. S., 2010. *Early Seljūq History. A New Interpretation*. Abingdon: Routledge.

Periplus of the Erythraean Sea, 1989. Trans. L. Casson, Princeton. Also trans. G. W. B. Huntingford, London 1980, and W. H. Schoff, New York 1912.

Peterson, D. L., L. M. Popova and A. T. Smith (eds), 2006. *Beyond the Steppe and the Sown. Proceedings of the 2002 University of Chicago on Eurasian Archaeology*. Leiden: Brill.

Peterson, Sara, 2020. 'A Glimpse from the Ancient World: What a Gold Necklace from Tillya-Tepe Reveals about Opium in Afghanistan'. *Afghanistan* 3, 2: 135–73.

Petrenko, Vladimir G., 1995. 'Scythian Culture in the North Caucasus'. In Davis-Kimball et al. (eds): 5–22.

Petrova, Yevgenia, and Jean-Claude Marcadé (eds), 2005. *The Avant-Garde Before and After*. St Petersburg: Palace Editions.

Pevsner, Nikolaus, 2005. *Pioneers of Modern Design. From William Morris to Walter Gropius*. 4th edition. Yale University Press.

Phillips, E. D., 1965. *The Royal Hordes. Nomad Peoples of the Steppes*. London: Thames & Hudson.

Piggott, Stuart, 1992. *Wagon, Chariot and Carriage. Symbol and Status in the History of Transport*. London: Thames & Hudson.

Piotrovsky, B. B. et al., 1978. *Frozen Tombs. The Culture and Art of the Ancient Tribes of Siberia*. London: British Museum Publications.

Piotrovsky, Boris, et al., 1997. *The Treasures of Khan Kubrat*. St Petersburg: State Hermitage.

Piotrovsky, Boris, Liudmila Galanina and Nonna Grach, 1987. *Scythian Art*. Leningrad: Aurora.

Piotrovsky, Mikhail (ed.), 1993. *Lost Empire of the Silk Road. Buddhist Art from Khara Khoto (X–XIIIth century)*. Milano: Electa.

Pirenne, Henri, 1939. *A History of Europe. From the invasions to the XVI century*. London: Allen & Unwin.

Pirenne, Henri, 1992 (1927). *Mohammed and Charlemagne*. New York: Barnes & Noble.

Pohl, Walter, 2018a. *The Avars. A Steppe Empire in Central Europe, 567–822*. Ithaca: Cornell University Press.

Pohl, Walter, 2018b. 'Ethnicity and Empire in the Western Eurasian Steppes'. In Di Cosmo and Maas: 189–205.

Polonsky, Rachel, 2010. *Molotov's Magic Lantern. Discovering Russia's Secret History*. London: Faber & Faber.

Ponomarenko, Elena, and Ian Dyck, 2007. *Ancient Nomads of the Eurasian and North American Grasslands*. Samara Museum of History and Regional Studies/ Canadian Museum of Civilization Corporation.

Pope, Hugh, 2005. 'The Silk Road – A Romantic Deception?' *The Globalist*, 24 November. www.theglobalist.com/the-silk-road-a-romantic-deception/ (last accessed 24 February 2019).

Popova, Laura M. S., 2009. 'Blurring the Boundaries. Foragers and Pastoralists in the Volga-Urals Region'. In Hanks and Linduff: 296–320.

Potts, D. T., 2014. *Nomadism in Iran from Antiquity to the Modern Era*. Oxford University Press.

Pseudo-Dionysius of Tel-Mahre, 1996. *Chronicle*. Trans. with notes and introd. by Witold Witakowski. Liverpool University Press.

Ptolemy, 2000, *Geography*. Annotated and trans. by J. Lennart Berggren and Alexander Jones. Princeton University Press.

Quirini-Poplawska, Danuta, 2020. 'Attempts at Forging a Genoese–Polish–Tatar Alliance against the Ottoman Empire in 1480–1484'. In Ovidiu Cristea and Liviu Pilat (eds), *From Pax Mongolica to Pax Ottomanica. War, Religion and Trade in the Northwestern Black Sea Region (14th–16th Centuries)*. Leiden: Brill: 169–91.

Rakhimzyanov, Bulat, 2009. *Kasimovskoe Khanstvo (1445–1552 gg.). Ocherki istorii*. Kazan: Tatarskoe Knizhnoe Izlatelstvo.

Radulescu, Adrian, 2020. *Ovid in Exile*. Las Vegas: Vita Histria.

Rajaram, Navaratna S., 1993. *Aryan Invasion of India. The Myth and the Truth*. New Delhi: Voice of India.

Raschke, M. G., 1978. 'New Studies in Roman Commerce with the East'. *Aufstieg und Niedergang der römischen Welt* II, 9, 2: 604–1,378.

Raverty, H. G., 1881. *Tabakat-i Nasiri: A General History of the Muhammadan Dynasties of Asia*. Calcutta.

Rayfield, Donald, 1976. *The Dream of Lhasa. The Life of Nikolai Przhevalsky (1838–88) Explorer of Central Asia*. London: Elek.

Reeder, Ellen D. (ed.), 1999. *Scythian Gold. Treasures from Ancient Ukraine*. New York: Harry N. Abrams.

Renfrew, Colin, 1987. *Archaeology and Language. The Puzzle of Indo-European Origins*. London: Jonathan Cape.

Renger, Almut-Barbara and Jon Solomon (eds), 2013. *Ancient Worlds in Film and Television. Gender and Politics*. Leiden: Brill.

Rezaie, Iraj, 2020. 'Locating the Ancient Toponym of "Kindāu": The Recognition of an Indo-European God in the Assyrian Inscriptions of the Seventh Century BC'. *Iran* 58, 2: 180–9.

Rezakhani, Khodadad, 2010. 'The Road That Never Was: The Silk Road and Trans-Eurasian Exchange'. *Comparative Studies of South Asia, Africa and the Middle East* 30, 3: 420–33.

Rezakhani, Khodadad, 2017. *ReOrienting the Sasanians. East Iran in Late Antiquity*. Edinburgh University Press.

Richards, M., 2003. 'The Neolithic Invasion of Europe'. *Annual Review of Anthropology* 32: 135–162.

Richards, Martin, 2003. 'The Neolithic Invasion of Europe'. *Annual Review of Anthropology* 32: 135–62.

Rietbergen, Peter, 2006. *Europe. A Cultural History*. London: Routledge.

Roberts, J. M., 1996. *A History of Europe*. Oxford: Helicon.

Rodionov, Dmitrii et al., 2014. *Russian Avant-garde Theatre: War, Revolution & Design*. London: Nick Hearn Books.

Rolle, Renate, 1989. *The World of the Scythian*. Berkeley: University of California Press.

Ronan, C. A. and J. Needham, 1978. *The Shorter Science and Civilisation in China, 1*. Cambridge University Press.

Róna-Tas, András, 2007. 'The Khazars and the Magyars'. In Golden et al.: 269–78.

Rossabi, Morris (ed.), 2017. *How Mongolia Matters: War, Law, and Society*. Leiden: Brill.

Rossabi, Morris, 1992. *Voyager from Xanadu. Rabban Sauma and the first Journey from China to the West*. Tokyo: Kodansha International.

Rossman, Vadim, 2007. 'Anti-Semitism in Eurasian Historiography: The Case of Lev Gumilev'. In Shlapentokh 2007: 121–91.

Rostovtzeff, Michael, 1928. *Greeks and Scythians in South Russia*. Oxford University Press.

Rostovtzeff, Michael, 1929. *The Animal Style in South Russia and China*. Princeton University Press. Reprinted Rome, 2000.

Roxburghe, David J., 2005. *Turks. A Journey of a Thousand Years, 600–1600*. London: Royal Academy.

Rudenko, Sergei I., 1970. *Frozen Tombs of Siberia: The Pazyryk Burials of Iron Age Horsemen*. Berkeley: University of California Press.

Runciman, Steven, 1930. *A History of the First Bulgarian Empire*. London: G. Bell & Sons.

Runciman, Steven, 1954. *A History of the Crusades. Volume III. The Kingdom of Acre and Later Crusades*. Cambridge University Press.

Sagona, Antonio, 2006. *The Heritage of Eastern Turkey from Earliest Settlements to Islam*. South Yarra (Australia): Macmillan.

Salmonson, Jessica Amanda, 1991. *The Encyclopedia of Amazons. Women Warriors From Antiquity to the Modern Era*. New York: Paragon House.

Sarianidi, Victor, 1998. *Bactrian Gold from the Excavations of the Tillya-tepe Necropolis in Northern Afghanistan*. Leningrad: Aurora.

Sauer, Eberhard et al., 2013. *Persia's Imperial Power in Late Antiquity. The Great Wall of Gorgān and Frontier Landscapes of Sasanian Iran*. Oxford: Oxbow.

Sauer, Eberhard W. et al., 2020. 'Interconnected Frontiers: Trans-Caspian Defensive Networks of the Sasanian Empire'. In Adelheid Otto, Michael Herles and Kai Kaniuth (eds), *Proceedings of the 11th International Congress on the Archaeology of the Ancient Near East. Volume 2. Field Reports*. Wiesbaden: Harrassowitz Verlag: 363–72.

Sauer, Eberhard W., Hamid Omrani Rekavandi, Jebrael Nokandeh and Davit Naskidashvili, 2019. 'The Great Walls of the Gorgan Plain Explored via Drone Photography'. In Yousef Moradi (ed.) *Afarin Nameh. Essays on the Archaeology of Iran in Honour of Mehdi Rahbar*. Tehran: The Research Institute of Cultural Heritage and Tourism.

Sauer, Eberhard, 2003. *The Archaeology of Religious Hatred in the Roman and Early Medieval World*. Stroud: The History Press.

Sauer, Eberhard, et al., 2020. *Dariali: The 'Caspian Gates' in the Caucasus from Antiquity to the Age of the Huns and the Middle Ages*. Oxford: Oxbow.

Saunders, J. J., 1971. *The History of the Mongol Conquests*. Philadelphia: University of Pennsylvania Press.

Schafer, Edward, H. 1963. *The Golden Peaches of Samarkand*. Berkeley: University of California Press.

Schamiloglu, Uli, 2006. 'Tatar or Turk? Competing Identities in the Muslim Turkic World during the Late Nineteenth and Early Twentieth Centuries'. In Çağatay and Kuban: 233–43.

Schimmelpennink van der Oye, David, 2010. *Russian Orientalism. Asia in the Russian Mind from Peter the Great to the Emigration*. New Haven: Yale University Press.

Scott, E. M., Andrey Yu. Alekseev and Ganna Zaitseva (eds), 2004. *Impact of the Environment on Human Migration in Eurasia. Proceedings of the NATO Advanced Research Workshop, Held in St Petersburg*. New York: Springer.

Scott, John, 1973. *Behind the Urals. An American Worker in Russia's City of Steel*. Bloomington: Indiana University Press.

Senior, R. C., 2005. 'INDO-SCYTHIAN DYNASTY'. *Encyclopædia Iranica*, online edition, available at http://www.iranicaonline.org/articles/indo-scyth ian-dynasty-1 (last accessed 30 April 2017).

Sevin, Veli, 2000. 'Mystery Stelae'. *Archaeology* 53, 4: 46–51.

Shapakovsky, Viacheslav and David Nicolle, 2013. *Armies of the Volga Bulgars & Khanate of Kazan*. Oxford: Osprey.

Shelekhan, Oleksandr, 2020. *Swords and Daggers of the Scythian Forest-Steppe*. Oxford: BAR.

Shilova, Ekaterina et al., 2017. *Vasilii Vereshchagin*. St Peteresburg: Palace Editions.

Shlapentokh, Dmitry (ed.), 2007. *Russia between East and West. Scholarly Debates on Eurasianism*. Leiden: Brill.

Shnirelman, V. A., 1999. 'Passions about Arkaim: Russian Nationalism, the Aryans, and the Politics of Archaeology'. *Inner Asia* 1, 2: 267–82.

Shnirelman, Victor, 2007. 'The Story of a Euphemism: The Khazars in Russian Nationalist Literature'. In Golden et al.: 353–72.

Shunying, Mu, 1994. *The Ancient Art in Xinjiang, China*. Urumqi: Xinjiang Fine Arts and Photo Publishing House.

Sinor, Denis (ed.), 1990. *The Cambridge History of Early Inner Asia*. Cambridge University Press.

Sinor, Denis, 1990. 'The Hun Period'. In Sinor (ed.): 177–205.

So, Jenny F. and Emma C. Bunker, 1995. *Traders and Raiders on China's Northern Frontier*. Seattle: University of Washington Press.

Solovyov, S. L. (ed.) 2007. *Greeks and Natives in the Cimmerian Bosporus 7th–1st Centuries BC. Proceedings of the International Conference October 2000, Taman, Russia*. Oxford: BAR.

Soltes, Ori Z. (ed.), 1999. *National Treasures of Georgia*. London: Philip Wilson.

Spuler, Berthold, 1969. *The Mongol Period*. Leiden: Brill.

Stark, Sören, 2016. 'Türk Khaganate'. In John M. MacKenzie (ed.), *The Encyclopedia of Empire*. Chichester: Wiley Blackwell: 2,127–42.

Stark, Sören. 2009. 'Central and Inner Asian Parallels to a Find from Kunszentmiklós-Bábony (Kunbábony): Some Thoughts on the Early Avar Headdress'. *Ancient Civilizations from Scythia to Siberia* 15: 287–305.

Starr, Frederick S., 2013. *Lost Enlightenment. Central Asia's Golden Age from the Arab Conquest to Tamerlane*. Princeton University Press.

Stein, M. Aurel, 1904. *Sand-Buried Ruins of Khotan*. London: Hurst & Blackett.

Stein, M. Aurel, 1921. *Serindia*. Oxford University Press.

Stepanov, Tsvetelin, 2010. *The Bulgars and the Steppe Empire in the Early Middle Ages. The Problem of the* Others. Leiden: Brill.

Stronach, D., and M. Roaf, 2007. *Nush-i Jan I. The Major Buildings of the Median Settlement*. Leuven: Peeters.

Stuller, Jennifer K., 2010. *Ink-Stained Amazons and Cinematic Warriors*. London: I. B. Tauris.

Süleymanova, Güzel Valeeva, 2006. 'Tatar Art and Culture at the Crossroad of Civilization'. In Çağatay and Kuban: 214–31.

Sulimirski, T., 1985. 'The Scyths'. In Ilya Gershevitch (ed.), *Cambridge History of Iran*: 149–99.

Sulimirski, T., 1963. 'The Forgotten Sarmatians. A Once Mighty Folk Scattered among the Nations'. In Edward Bacon (ed.), *Vanished Civilizations. Forgotten Peoples of the Ancient World*. London: Thames & Hudson: 279–98.

Svanberg, Ingvar, and David Westerlund (eds), 2016. *Muslim Tatar Minorities in the Baltic Sea Region*. Leiden: Brill.

Svetlyakov, Kirill (ed.), 2015. *The State Tretyakov Gallery at Krymsky Val. A Guide to Russian Art of the 20th Century*. Moscow: Paulson.

Szádeczky-Kardoss, Samuel, 1990. 'The Avars'. In Sinor (ed.): 207–28.

Talbot Rice, David (ed.), 1965. *The Dark Ages. The Making of European Civilization*. London: Thames & Hudson.

Talbot Rice, Tamara, 1965. 'The Crucible of Peoples. Eastern Europe and the rise of the Slavs'. In Talbot Rice (ed.): 139–56.

Talbot Rice, Tamara, 1967. *The Scythians*. London: Thames & Hudson.

Tate, G. P., 1910. *Seistan. A Memoir on the History, Topography, Ruins, and People of the Country*. Calcutta: Superintendent Government Printing.

Taylor, A. J. P., 1948. *The Habsburg Monarchy*. London: Hamish Hamilton.

Teissier, Beatrice, 2011. *Russian Frontiers. Eighteenth-century British Travellers in the Caspian, Caucasus and Central Asia*. Oxford: Signal.

Teliashov, Rakhim, 1997. 'From Great Bulgaria to Tatarstan: Continuity in History'. In Piotrovsky 1997: 41–7.

Tetley, G. E., 2009. *The Ghaznavid and Seljuk Turks. Poetry as a Source for Iranian History*. Abingdon: Routledge.

Theophylact Simocatta, 1986. *The* History *of Theophylact Simocatta. An English Translation with Introduction and Notes by Michael and Mary Whitby*. Oxford: Clarendon Press.

Thomas, Charles, 1965. 'The Coveted Isles. Celtic Britain and the Anglo-Saxons'. In Talbot Rice (ed.): 241–68.

Thompson, E. A., 1996. *The Huns*. Oxford: Blackwell.

Todd, Malcolm, 2001. *Migrants & Invaders. The Movement of Peoples in the Ancient World*. Stroud: The History Press.

Torday, Laszlo, 1997. *Mounted Archers. The Beginnings of Central Asian History*. Durham University Press.

Trifonov, V., N. Shishlina, O. Chernova, V. Sevastyanov, J. van der Plicht and F. Golenishchev, 2019. 'A 5000-year-old Souslik Fur Garment from an Elite Megalithic Tomb in the North Caucasus, Maykop Culture'. *Paléorient* 45,1: 69–80.

Tringham, Ruth, and Margaret Conkey, 1998. 'Rethinking Figurines: A Critical View from Archaeology of Gimbutas, the "Goddess" and Popular Culture"'. In Goodison and Morris (eds): 22–45.

Tsetskhladze, Gocha R. (ed.), 1996. *New Studies on the Black Sea Littoral*. Oxford: Oxbow.

Tsetskhladze, Gocha R. (ed.), 1998. *The Greek Colonisation of the Black Sea Area.* Stuttgart: Franz Steiner Verlag.

Tsetskhladze, Gocha R. (ed.), 2001. *North Pontic Archaeology. Recent Discoveries and Studies.* Leiden: Leiden.

Tuplin, C. J. (ed.), 2004. *Pontus and the Outside World. Studies in Black Sea History, Historiography and Archaeology.* Leiden: Brill.

Ustinova, Y., 2002. 'Lycanthropy in Sarmatian Warrior Societies: The Kobyakovo Torque'. *Ancient East and West* 1, 1: 102–23.

Ustinova, Yulia, 2005. 'Snake-Limbed and Tendril-Limbed Goddesses in the Art and Mythology of the Mediterranean and Black Sea'. In Braund (ed.): 64–79.

Vidal, Jordi, 2014. 'Aryan warriors. The Invented Heroes of the Ancient Near East'. In Borja Antela-Bernárdez and Jordi Vidal (eds), *Central Asia in Antiquity: Interdisciplinary Approaches.* Oxford: Archaeopress: 17–22.

Vogelsang, W. J., 1992. *The Rise & Organisation of the Achaemenid Empire. The Eastern Iranian Evidence.* Leiden: Brill.

Vogelsang, Willem, 2002. *The Afghans.* Oxford: Blackwell.

Volkov, Vitali V., 1995. 'Early Nomads of Mongolia'. In Davis-Kimball et al. (eds): 319–33.

Vout, Caroline, 2018. *Classical Art. A Life History from Antiquity to the Present.* Princeton University Press.

Waldron, Arthur, 1990. *The Great Wall of China. From History to Myth.* Cambridge University Press.

Walker, Annabel, 1995. *Aurel Stein. Pioneer of the Silk Road.* London: John Murray.

Walter, Mariko N., 2015. 'Introduction'. In Mariko N. Walter and James P. Ito-Adler (eds), *The Silk Road: Interwoven History.* Cambridge, MA: Cambridge Institute Press: xiii–xxv.

Wang Dafang, 2011. *Xanadu.* Hohhot.

Ward-Perkins, Bryan, 2005. *The Fall of Rome and the End of Civilization.* Oxford University Press.

Warner, Marina, 1985. *Monuments and Maidens. The Allegory of the Female Form.* London: Weidenfeld & Nicolson.

Warner, Marina, 2013. *Joan of Arc. The Image of Female Heroism. New edition.* Oxford University Press.

Wasserstein, David, 2007. 'The Khazars and the World of Islam'. In Golden et al.: 373–86.

Watson, William, 1971. *Cultural Frontiers in Ancient East Asia.* Edinburgh University Press.

Watson, William, 1995. *The Arts of China to AD 900.* New Haven: Yale University Press.

Waugh Daniel C., 2010. 'Richthofen's "Silk Roads": Toward the Archaeology of a Concept'. Originally pub. in *The Silk Road* 5/1 (2007): 1–10, with a revised version online at http://faculty.washington.edu/dwaugh/publications/waugh richthofen2010.pdf

Wells, Peter S., 2020. 'Eurasian Iron Age interactions: A Perspective on the Sources and Purposes of La Tène Style ('Celtic') Art'. In Nimura, Chittock, Hommel and Gosden (eds): 37–51.

West, M. L., 2007. *Indo-European Poetry and Myth*. Oxford University Press.

Wexler, Peter, 2007. 'Yiddish Evidence for the Khazar component in Ashkenazic Ethnogenisis'. In Golden et al.: 387–98.

Wheatcroft, Andrew, 1995. *The Habsburgs. Embodying Empire*. London: Viking.

Whitehouse, D., 1989. 'Begram Reconsidered'. *Kölner Jahrbuch für Vor- und Frühgeschichte* 22: 151–7.

Whitfield, Susan (ed.), 2020. *The Silk Road*. London: Thames & Hudson.

Whitfield, Susan and Ursula Sims-Williams (eds), 2004. *The Silk Road. Trade, Travel, War and Faith*. London: The British Library.

Whitfield, Susan, 2007. 'Was there a Silk Road?' *Asian Medicine* 3: 201–13.

Whittaker, Cynthia Hyla (ed.), 2020. *Visualizing Russia. Fedore Solntsev and Crafting a National Past*. Leiden: Brill.

Wiederkehr, Stephan, 2007. 'Eurasianism as a Reaction to Pan-Turkism'. In Shlapentokh 2007: 39–59.

Williams, Brian, 2001. *The Crimean Tatars. The Diaspora Experience and the Forging of a Nation*. Leiden: Britll.

Wilson, David M., 1965. 'From the Vigorous North. The Norsemen and their Forerunners'. In Talbot Rice (ed.): 219–40.

Winder, Simon, 2013. *Danubia. A Personal History of Habsburg Europe*. London: Picador.

Winder, Simon, 2019. *Lotharingia. A Personal History of Europe's Lost Country*. London: Picador.

Winkler, Martin M., 2004. '*Gladiator* and the Colosseum: Ambiguities of Spectacle'. In Martin M. Winkler, *Gladiator. Film and History*. Oxford: Blackwell: 87–110.

Witzel, Michael, 2006. 'Rama's Realm: Indocentric Rewritings of Early South Asian Archaeology and History'. In Garrett G. Fagan (ed.), *Archaeological Fantasies*: 203–32.

Wood, Frances, 1995. *Did Marco Polo Go to China?* London: Secker & Warburg.

Wood, Frances, 2003. *The Silk Road. Two Thousand Years in the Heart of Asia*. London: British Library.

Wortman, Richard, 2010. 'The Development of a Russian National Aesthetic'. In Whittaker: 17–39.

Wu En, 2003. 'On the Origin of Bronze Belt Plaques of Ancient Nomads in North China'. *Chinese Archaeology* 3, 1: 186–92.

Yablonsky, Leonid T., 1995. 'Saka Material Culture and Historical Reconstruction'. In Davis-Kimball et al. (eds): 201–39.

Yablonsky, Leonid T., 1995. 'Written Sources and the History of Archaeological Studies of the Saka in Central Asia'. In Davis-Kimball et al. (eds): 194–7.

Yablonsky, Leonid T., 2006. 'General Migration Processes in the Aral Sea Area in the Early Iron Age'. In Peterson, Popova and Smith (eds): 63–85.

Yang, Jianhua, Hiuqiu Shao and Ling Pan, 2020. *The Metal Road of the Eastern Eurasian Steppe. The Formation of the Xiognu Confederation and the Silk Road*. Singapore: Springer.

Yarshater, Ehsan, 1983. 'Iranian Common Beliefs and World-view'. In Ehsan Yarshater (ed.), *The Cambridge History of Iran. Volume 3 (I). The Seleucid, Parthian and Sasanian Periods*. Cambridge University Press: 343–58.

Yatsenko, Sergey A., 2010. 'Marks of the Ancient and Early Medieval Iranian-Speaking Peoples of Iran, Eastern Europe, Transoxiana and South Siberia'. In Joám Evans Pim, Sergey A. Yatsenko and Oliver Perrin (eds), *Traditional Marking Systems. A Preliminary Survey*. London: Dunkling: 133–54.

Yi, Joy Lidu, 2018. *Yungang. Art, History, Archaeology, Liturgy*. London: Routledge.

Yü, Ying-Shih, 1990. 'The Hsiung-nu'. In Sinor (ed.): 118–50.

Yuan, Ma, 2014. *New Silk Road. A Journey Restarts*. Beijing: China Intercontinental Press.

Yule, Henry and Henri Cordier, 1915. *Cathay and the Way Thither. Being a collection of Medieval Notices of China*. 5 volumes. London: Hakluyt Society.

Yunusova, A. B. et al. 2007, *Muzei Arkheologii i Etnografii. Katalog muzeinoii ekspozitsii Tsentra etnologicheskikh issledovanii Ufimskogo naychnogo tsentra RAI*. Ufa: National Museum of Bashkortostan.

Zasetskaya, I. P. et al., 2008. *Sokrovishcha Sarmatov. Katalog Vistavki*. St Petersburg.

Zhivkov, Boris, 2015. *Khazaria in the Ninth and Tenth Centuries*. Leiden: Brill.

Zimonyi, Istvan, 2015. *Muslim Sources on the Magyars in the Second Half of the 9th Century. The Magyar Chapter of the Jayhānī Tradition*. Leiden: Brill.

Zuckerman, Constantine, 2007. 'The Khazars and Byzantium – The First Encounter'. In Golden et al.: 399–432.

Index

Note: page numbers in *italics* indicate figures